GEOFFREY CHAUCER

THE PARDONER'S TALE

Geoffrey Chaucer

THE PARDONER'S TALE

[Edited with Complete text and analysis, also Gathering Information on Background Studies, Study Questions and Critical Essays]

Aditya Nandwani
B.A. English (Hons) , Delhi University;
M.A. (English), IGNOU; Print Journalism (English) YMCA

ANMOL PUBLICATIONS PVT. LTD.
NEW DELHI - 110 002 (INDIA)

ANMOL PUBLICATIONS PVT. LTD.

H.O.: 4374/4B, Ansari Road, Darya Ganj,
New Delhi-110 002 (India)
Ph.: 23278000, 23261597

B.O.: No. 1015, Ist Main Road, BSK IIIrd Stage
IIIrd Phase, IIIrd Block
Bangalore - 560 085 (India)
Visit us at: www.anmolpublications.com

The Pardoner's Tale

First Published, 2009

PRINTED IN INDIA

Printed at Mehra Offset Press, Delhi.

Contents

Preface

Geoffrey Chaucer (c. 1343 – October 25, 1400?) was an English author, poet, philosopher, bureaucrat, courtier and diplomat. Although he wrote many works, he is best remembered for his unfinished frame narrative *The Canterbury Tales*. Sometimes called the father of English literature, Chaucer is credited by some scholars as being the first author to demonstrate the artistic legitimacy of the vernacular English language, rather than French or Latin. Geoffrey Chaucer wrote *The Canterbury Tales*, a collection of stories in a frame story, between 1387 and 1400. It is the story of a group of thirty people who travel as pilgrims to Canterbury (England). The pilgrims, who come from all layers of society, tell stories to each other to kill time while they travel to Canterbury.

If we trust the General Prologue, Chaucer intended that each pilgrim should tell two tales on the way to Canterbury and two tales on the way back. He never finished his enormous project and even the completed tales were not finally revised. Scholars are uncertain about the order of the tales. As the printing press had yet to be invented when Chaucer wrote his works, *The Canterbury Tales* has been passed down in several handwritten manuscripts.

The Pardoner's Tale is one of the *The Canterbury Tales* by Geoffrey Chaucer. The story is in the form of an exemplum: the Pardoner first explains the theme he will address, then he tells the actual story and finally he draws the conclusion he had already mentioned in his introduction.

At the time, a "Pardoner" was a person offering indulgences officially recognized by the Roman Catholic Church. Indulgences were given in exchange for money during corruption in the Middle Ages. The story opens with the host inviting the Pardoner to tell the next tale. The Pardoner's Prologue is a sermon against greed, gluttony and gambling, linking into the main tale. After the tale, the Pardoner invites the other pilgrims to pay him for pardons and sell them relics.

Author

Chapter 1

Biography: Geoffrey Chaucer

Geoffrey Chaucer, English poet. The name Chaucer, a French form of the Latin calcearius, a shoemaker, is found in London and the eastern counties as early as the second half of the 13th century. Some of the London Chaucers lived in Cordwainer Street, in the shoemakers' quarter; several of them, however, were vintners, and among others the poet's father John, and probably also his grandfather Robert. Legal pleadings inform us that in December 1324 John Chaucer was not much over twelve years old, and that he was still unmarried in 1328, the year which used to be considered that of Geoffrey's birth. The poet was probably born from eight to twelve years later, since in 1386, when giving evidence in Sir Richard le Scrope's suit against Sir Robert Grosvenor as to the right to bear certain arms, he was set down as "del age de xl ans et plus, armeez par xxvij ans." At a later date, and probably at the time of the poet's birth, his father lived in Thames Street, and had to wife a certain Agnes, niece of Hamo de Compton, whom we may regard as Geoffrey Chaucer's mother.

In 1357 Geoffrey is found, apparently as a lad, in the service of Elizabeth, countess of Ulster, wife of Lionel, Duke of Clarence, entries in two leaves of her household accounts, accidentally preserved, showing that she paid in April, May and December various small sums for his clothing and expenses. In 1359, as we learn from his deposition in the Scrope suit, Chaucer went to the war in France. At some period of the campaign he was at "Retters," i.e. Rethel, near Reims, and subsequently had the ill luck to be taken prisoner. On the 1st of March 1360 the King [Edward III] contributed £16 to his ransom, and by a year or two later Chaucer must have entered the royal service, since on the 10th of June 1367 Edward granted him a pension of twenty marks for his past and future services. A pension of ten marks had been granted by the king the previous September to a Philippa Chaucer for services to the queen as one of her "domicellae" or "damoiselles," and it seems probable that at this date Chaucer was already married and this Philippa his wife, a conclusion which used to be resisted on the ground of allusions in his early poems to a hopeless love-affair, now reckoned part of his poetical outfit. Philippa is usually said to have been one of two daughters of a Sir Payne Roet, the other being Katherine, who after the death of her first husband, Sir Hugh de Swynford, in 1372, became governess to John of Gaunt's children, and subsequently his mistress and (in 1396) his wife.

It is possible that Philippa was sister to Sir Hugh and sister-in-law to Katherine. In either case the marriage helps to account for the favour subsequently shown to Chaucer by John of Gaunt.

In the grant of his pension Chaucer is called "dilectus vallectus noster," our beloved yeoman; before the end of 1368 he had risen to be one of the king's esquires. In September of the following year John of Gaunt's wife, the duchess Blanche, died at the age of twenty-nine, and Chaucer wrote in her honour The Book of the Duchesse, a poem of 1334 lines in octosyllabic couplets, the first of his undoubtedly genuine works which can be connected with a definite date. In June 1370 he went abroad on the king's service, though on what errand, or whither it took him, is not known. He was back probably some time before Michaelmas, and seems to have remained in England till the 1st of December 1372, when he started, with an advance of 100 marks in his pocket, for Italy, as one of the three commissioners to treat with the Genoese as to an English port where they might have special facilities for trade. The accounts which he delivered on his return on the

23rd of May 1373 show that he had also visited Florence on the king's business, and he probably went also to Padua and there made the acquaintance of Petrarch.

In the second quarter of 1374 Chaucer lived in a whirl of prosperity. On the 23rd of April the king granted him a pitcher of wine daily, subsequently commuted for an annuity of 20 marks. From John of Gaunt, who in August 1372 had granted Philippa Chaucer £10 a year, he himself now received (June 13) a like annuity in reward for his own and his wife's services. On the 8th of June he was appointed Comptroller of the Custom and Subsidy of Wools, Hides and Woodfells and also of the Petty Customs of Wine in the Port of London. A month before this appointment, and probably in anticipation of it, he took (May 10, 1374) a lease for life from the city of London of the dwelling-house above the gate of Aldgate, and here he lived for the next twelve years. His own and his wife's income now amounted to over £60, the equivalent of upwards of £1000 in modern money. In the next two years large windfalls came to him in the form of two wardships of Kentish heirs, one of whom paid him £104, and a grant of £71,4s,6p; the value of some confiscated wool. In December 1376 he was sent abroad on the king's service in the retinue of Sir John Burley; in February 1377 he was sent to Paris and Montreuil in connexion probably with the peace negotiations between England and France, and at the end of April (after a reward of £20 for his good services) he was again despatched to France.

On the accession of Richard II Chaucer was confirmed in his offices and pensions. In January 1378 he seems to have been in France in connexion with a proposed marriage between Richard and the daughter of the French king; and on the 28th of May of the same year he was sent with Sir Edward de Berkeley to the lord of Milan and Sir John Hawkwood to treat for help in the king's wars, returning on the 19th of September. This was his last diplomatic journey, and the close of a period of his life generally considered to have been so unprolific of poetry that little beyond the Clerk's "Tale of Grisilde," one or two other of the stories afterwards included in the Canterbury

Tales, and a few short poems, are attributed to it, though the poet's actual absences from England during the eight years amount to little more than eighteen months.

During the next twelve or fifteen years there is no question that Chaucer was constantly engaged in literary work, though for the first half of them he had no lack of official employment. Abundant favour was shown him by the new king. He was paid £22 as a reward for his later missions in Edward III's reign, and was allowed an annual gratuity of 10 marks in addition to his pay of £10 as comptroller of the customs of wool.

In April 1382 a new comptrollership, that of the petty customs in the Port of London, was given him, and shortly after he was allowed to exercise it by deputy, a similar licence being given him in February 1385, at the instance of the earl of Oxford, as regards the comptrollership of wool.

In October 1385 Chaucer was made a justice of the peace for Kent. In February 1386 we catch a glimpse of his wife Philippa being admitted to the fraternity of Lincoln cathedral in the company of Henry, Earl of Derby (afterwards Henry IV), Sir Thomas de Swynford and other distinguished persons. In August 1386 he was elected one of the two knights of the shire for Kent, and with this dignity, though it was one not much appreciated in those days, his good fortune reached its climax.

In December of the same year he was superseded in both his comptrollerships, almost certainly as a result of the absence of his patron, John of Gaunt, in Spain, and the supremacy of the Duke of Gloucester. In the following year the cessation of Philippa's pension suggests that she died between Midsummer and Michaelmas. In May 1388 Chaucer surrendered to the king his two pensions of 20 marks each, and they were re-granted at his request to one John Scalby. The transaction was unusual and probably points to a pressing need for ready money, nor for the next fourteen months do we know of any source of income possessed by Chaucer beyond his annuity of £10 from John of Gaunt.

In July 1389, after John of Gaunt had returned to England, and the king had taken the government into his own hands, Chaucer was appointed clerk of the works at various royal palaces at a salary of two shillings a day, or over £31 a year, worth upwards of £500 present value. To this post was subsequently added the charge of some repairs at St George's Chapel, Windsor.

He was also made a commissioner to maintain the banks of the Thames between Woolwich and Greenwich, and was given by the Earl of March (grandson of Lionel, Duke of Clarence, his old patron) a sub-forestership at North Petherton, Devon, obviously a sinecure. While on the king's business, in September 1390, Chaucer was twice robbed by highwaymen, losing £20 of the king's money. In June 1391 he was superseded in his office of clerk of the works, and seems to have suffered another spell of misfortune, of which the first alleviation came in January 1393 when the king made him a present of £10.

In February 1394 he was granted a new pension of £20. It is possible, also, that about this time, or a little later, he was in the service of the Earl of Derby. In 1397 he received from King Richard a grant of a butt of wine yearly. For this he appears to have asked in terms that suggest poverty, and in May 1398 he obtained letters of protection against his creditors, a step perhaps rendered necessary by an action for debt taken against him earlier in the year.

On the accession of Henry IV a new pension of 40 marks was conferred on Chaucer (13th of October 1399) and Richard II's grants were formally confirmed. Henry himself, however, was probably straitened for ready money, and no instalment of the new pension was paid during the few months of his reign that the poet lived. Nevertheless, on the strength of his expectations, on the 24th of December 1399 he leased a tenement in the garden of St Mary's Chapel, Westminster, and it was probably here that he died, on the 25th of the following October. He was buried in Westminster Abbey, and his tomb became the nucleus of what is now known as Poets' Corner.

The portrait of Chaucer, which the affection of his disciple, Thomas Hoccleve, caused to be painted in a copy of the latter's Regement of Princes (now Harleian MS. 4866 in the British Museum), shows him an old man with white hair; he has a fresh complexion, grey eyes, a straight nose, a grey moustache and a small double-pointed beard. His dress and hood are black, and he carries in his hands a string of beads. We may imagine that it was thus that during the last months of his life he used to walk about the precincts of the Abbey.

Henry IV's promise of an additional pension was doubtless elicited by the Compleynt to his Purs, in the envoy to which Chaucer addresses him as the "conquerour of Brutes Albioun." Thus within the last year of his life the poet was still writing. Nevertheless, as early as 1393-1394, in lines to his friend Scogan, he had written as if his day for poetry were past, and it seems probable that his longer poems were all composed before this date. In the preceding fifteen — or, if another view be taken, twenty - years, his literary activity was very great, and with the aid of the lists of his works which he gives in the Legende of Good Women (lines 414-431), and the talk on the road which precedes the "Man of Law's Tale" (Canterbury Tales, B. 46-76), the order in which his main works were written can be traced with approximate certainty,[1] while a few, both of these and of the minor poems, can be connected with definite dates.

The development of his genius has been attractively summed up as comprised in three stages, French, Italian and English, and there is a rough approximation to the truth in this formula, since his earliest poems are translated from the French or based on French models, and the two great works of his middle period are borrowed from the Italian, while his latest stories have no such obvious and direct originals and in their humour and freedom anticipate the typically English temper of Henry Fielding. But Chaucer's indebtedness to French poetry was no passing phase. For various reasons — a not very remote French origin of his own family may be one of them — he was in no way interested in older English literature or in the work of his English contemporaries, save possibly that of "the moral Gower." On the other hand he knew the Roman de la rose as modern English poets know Shakespeare, and the full extent of his debt to his French contemporaries, not merely in 1369, but in 1385 and in 1393 (the dates are approximate), is only gradually being discovered.

To be in touch throughout his life with the best French poets of the day was much for Chaucer. Even with their stimulus alone he might have developed no small part of his genius. But it was his great good fortune to add to this continuing French influence, lessons in plot and construction derived from Boccaccio's Filostrato and Teseide, as well as some glimpses of the higher art of the Divina Commedia. He shows acquaintance also with one of Petrarch's sonnets, and though, when all is said, the Italian books with which he can be proved to have been intimate are but few, they sufficed. His study of them was but an episode in his literary life, but it was an episode of unique importance. Before it began he had already been making his own artistic experiments, and it is noteworthy that while he learnt so much from Boccaccio he improved on his originals as he translated them.

Doubtless his busy life in the service of the crown had taught him self-confidence, and he uses his Italian models in his own way and with the most triumphant and assured success. When he had no more Italian poems to adapt he had learnt his lesson. The art of weaving a plot out of his own imagination was never his, but he could take what might be little more than an anecdote and lend it body and life and colour with a skill which has never been surpassed.

The most direct example of Chaucer's French studies is his translation of Le Roman de la rose, a poem written in some 4000 lines by Guillaume Lorris about 1237 and extended to over 22,000 by Jean Clopinel, better known as Jean de Meun, forty years later. We know from Chaucer himself that he translated this poem, and the extant English fragment of 7698 lines was generally assigned to him from 1532, when it was first printed, till its authorship was challenged in the early years of the Chaucer Society. The ground of this challenge was its wide divergence from Chaucer's practice in his undoubtedly genuine works as to certain niceties of rhyme, notable as to not rhyming words ending in -y with others ending -ye. It was subsequently discovered, however, that the whole fragment was divisible linguistically into three portions, of which the first and second end respectively at lines 1705 and 5810, and that in the first of these three sections the variations from Chaucer's accepted practice are insignificant. Lines 1-1705 have therefore been provisionally accepted as Chaucer's, and the other two fragments as the work of unknown translators (James I of Scotland has been suggested as one of them), which somehow came to be pieced together. If, however, the difficulties in the way of this theory are less than those which confront any other, they are still considerable, and the question can hardly be treated as closed.

While our knowledge of Chaucer's Romaunt of the Rose is in this unsatisfactory state, another translation of his from the French, the Book of the Lyon (alluded to in the "Retraction" found, in some manuscripts, at the end of the Canterbury Tales), which must certainly have been taken from Guillaume Machault's Le Dit du lion, has perished altogether. The strength of French influence on Chaucer's early work may, however, be amply illustrated from the first of his poems with which we are on sure ground, the Book of the Duchesse, or, as it is alternatively called, the Deth of Blaunche. Here not only are individual passages closely imitated from Machault and Froissart, but the dream, the May morning, and the whole machinery of the poem are taken over from contemporary French conventions. But even at this stage Chaucer could prove his right to borrow by the skill with which he makes his materials serve his own purpose, and some of the lines in the Deth of Blaunche are among the most tender and charming he ever wrote.

Chaucer's A.B.C., a poem in honour of the Blessed Virgin, of which the stanzas begin with the successive letters of the alphabet, is another early example of French influence. It is taken from the Pelerinage de la vie humaine, written by

Guillaume de Deguilleville about 1330. The occurrence of some magnificent lines in Chaucer's version, combined with evidence that he did not yet possess the skill to translate at all literally as soon as rhymes had to be considered, accounts for this poem having been dated sometimes earlier than the Book of the Duchesse, and sometimes several years later. With it is usually moved up and down, though it should surely be placed in the 'seventies, the Compleynt to Pity, a fine poem which yet, from its slight obscurity and absence of Chaucer's usual ease, may very well some day prove to be a translation from the French.

While Chaucer thus sought to reproduce both the matter and the style of French poetry in England, he found other materials in popular Latin books. Among his lost works are renderings of "Origenes upon the Maudeleyne," and of Pope Innocent III on "The Wreced Engendring of Mankinde" (De miseria conditionis humanae). He must have begun his attempts at straightforward narrative with the Lyf of Seynt Cecyle (the weakest of all his works, the second Nun's Tale in the Canterbury series) from the Legenda Aurea of Jacobus de Voragine, and the story of the patience of Grisilde, taken from Petrarch's Latin version of a tale by Boccaccio. In both of these he condenses a little, but ventures on very few changes, though he lets his readers see his impatience with his originals.

In his story of Constance (afterwards ascribed to the Man of Law), taken from the Anglo-Norman chronicle of Nicholas Trivet, written about 1334, we find him struggling to put some substance into another weak tale, but still without the courage to remedy its radical faults, though here, as with Grisilde, he does as much for his heroine as the conventional exaltation of one virtue at a time permitted. It is possible that other tales which now stand in the Canterbury series were written originally at this period. What is certain is that at some time in the 'seventies three or four Italian poems passed into Chaucer's possession, and that he set to work busily to make use of them. One of the most interesting of the poems reclaimed for him by Professor Skeat is a fragmentary "Compleynt," part of which is written in terza rima. While he thus experimented with the metre of the Divina Commedia, he made his first attempt to use the material provided by Boccaccio's Teseide in another fragment of great interest, that of Quene Anelida and Fals Arcyte. More than a third of this is taken up with another, and quite successful, metrical experiment in Anelida's "compleynt," but in the introduction of Anelida herself Chaucer made the first of his three unsuccessful efforts to construct a plot for an important poem out of his own head, and the fragment which begins so well breaks off abruptly at line 357.

For a time the Teseide seems to have been laid aside, and it was perhaps at this moment, in despondency at his failure, that Chaucer wrote his most important prose work, the translation of the De Consolatione Philosophiae of Boethius. Reminiscences of this helped to enrich many of his subsequent poems, and inspired five of his shorter pieces (The Former Age, Fortune, Truth, Gentilesse and Lak of Stedfastnesse), but the translation itself was only a partial success. To borrow his own phrase, his "Englysh was insufficient" to reproduce such difficult Latin. The translation is often barely intelligible without the original, and it is only here and there that it flows with any ease or rhythm.

If Chaucer felt this himself he must have been speedily consoled by achieving in Troilus and Criseyde his greatest artistic triumph. Warned by his failure in Anelida and Arcyte, he was content this time to take his plot unaltered from the Filostrato, and to follow Boccaccio step by step through the poem. But he did not follow him as a mere translator. He had done his duty manfully for the saints "of other holinesse" in Cecyle, Grisilde and Constance, whom he was forbidden by the rules of the game to clothe with complete flesh and blood. In this great love-story there were no such restrictions, and the characters which Boccaccio's treatment left thin and conventional became in Chaucer's hands convincingly human. No other English poem is so instinct with the glory and tragedy of youth, and in the details of the story Chaucer's gifts of vivid colouring, of humour and pity, are all at their highest.

An unfortunate theory that the reference in the Legende of Good Women to "al the love of Palamon and Arcyte" is to a hypothetical poem in seven-line stanzas on this theme, which Chaucer is imagined, when he came to plan the Canterbury Tales, to have suppressed in favour of a new version in heroic couplets, has obscured the close connexion in temper and power between what we know as the "Knight's Tale" and the Troilus.

The poem may have been more or less extensively revised before, with admirable fitness, it was assigned to the Knight, but that its main composition can be separated by several years from that of Troilus is aesthetically incredible. Chaucer's art here again is at its highest. He takes the plot of Boccaccio's Teseide, but only as much of it as he wants, and what he takes he heightens and humanizes with the same skill which he had shown in transforming the Filostrato. Of the individual characters Theseus himself, the arbiter of the plot, is most notably developed; Emilie and her two lovers receive just as much individuality as they will bear without disturbing the atmosphere of romance.

The whole story is pulled together and made more rapid and effective. A comparison of almost any scene as told by the two poets suffices to show Chaucer's immense superiority. At some subsequent period the "Squire's Tale" of Cambuscan, the fair Canacee and the Horse of Brass, was gallantly begun in something of the same key, but Chaucer took for it more materials than he could use, and for lack of the help of a leader like Boccaccio he was obliged to leave the story, in Milton's phrase, "half-told," though the fragment written certainly takes us very much less than half-way.

Meanwhile, in connexion (as is reasonably believed) with the betrothal or marriage of Anne of Bohemia to Richard II (i.e. about 1381-1382), Chaucer had brought to a successful completion the Parlement of Foules, a charming sketch of 699 lines, in which the other birds, on Saint Valentine's day, counsel the "Formel Egle" on her choice of a mate. His success here, as in the case of the Deth of Blaunche the Duchesse, was due to the absence of any need for a climax; and though the materials which he borrowed were mainly Latin (with some help from passages of the Teseide not fully needed for Palamon and Arcyte) his method of handling them would have been quite approved by his friends among the French poets. A more ambitious venture, the Hous of Fame, in which Chaucer imagines himself borne aloft by an eagle to Fame's temple, describes what he sees and hears there, and then breaks off in apparent inability to get home, shows a curious mixture of the poetic ideals of the Roman de la rose and reminiscences of the Divina Commedia.

As the Hous of Fame is most often remembered and quoted for the personal touches and humour of Chaucer's conversation with the eagle, so the most-quoted passages in the Prologue to the Legende of Good Women are those in which Chaucer professes his affection for the daisy, and the attack on his loyalty by Cupid and its defence by Alceste. Recent discoveries have shown, however, that (besides obligations to Machault) some of the touches about the daisy and the controversy between the partisans of the Flower and of the Leaf are snatches from poems by his friends Froissart and Deschamps, which Chaucer takes up and returns to them with pretty compliments, and that he was indebted to Froissart for some of the framework of his poem. Both of the two versions of the Prologue to the Legende are charming, and some of the tales, notably that of Cleopatra, rank with Chaucer's best work. When, however, he had written eight and part of the ninth he tired of his scheme, which was planned to celebrate nineteen of Cupid's faithful "saints," with Alcestis as their queen. With his usual hopefulness he had overlooked the risk of monotony, which obviously weighed heavily on him ere he broke off, and the loss of the other ten stories is less to be regretted than that of the celebration of Alceste, and a possible epilogue which might have exceeded in charm the Prologue itself.

Chaucer's failure to complete the scheme of the Legende of Good Women may have been partly due to the attractions of the Canterbury Tales, which were probably taken up in immediate succession to it. His guardianship of two Kentish wards, his justiceship of the peace, his representing the county in the parliament of 1386, his commissionership of the river-bank between Greenwich and Woolwich, all make it easy to understand his dramatic use of the merry crowds he saw on the Canterbury road, without supposing him to have had recourse to Boccaccio's Decamerone, a book which there is no proof of his having seen. The pilgrims whom he imagines to have assembled at the Tabard Inn in Southwark, where Harry Bailey was host, are said to have numbered "wel nyne and twenty in a company," and the Prologue gives full-length sketches of a Knight, a Squire (his son), and their Yeoman; of a Prioress, Monk, Friar, Oxford Clerk, and Parson, with two disreputable hangers-on of the church, a Summoner and Pardoner; of a Serjeant-at-Law and a Doctor of Physic, and of a Franklin, or country gentleman, Merchant, Shipman, Miller, Cook, Manciple, Reeve, Ploughman (the Parson's brother) and the ever-famous Wife of Bath. Five London burgesses are described in a group, and a Nun and Priest[3] are mentioned as in attendance on the Prioress.

Each of these, with Chaucer himself making the twenty-ninth, was pledged to tell two tales, but including one second attempt and a tale told by the Yeoman of a Canon, who overtakes the pilgrims on the road, we have only twenty finished stories, two unfinished and two interrupted ones. As in the case of the Legende of Good Women, our loss is not so much that of the additional stories as of the completed framework. The wonderful character sketches of the Prologue are carried yet farther by the Talks on the Road which link the different tales, and two of these Talks, in which the Wife of Bath and the Pardoner respectively edify the company, have the importance of separate Tales, but between the Tales that have come down to us there are seven links missing,[4] and it was left to a later and weaker hand to narrate, in the "Tale of Beryn," the adventures of the pilgrims at Canterbury.

The reference to the Lyf of Seynt Cecyle in the Prologue to the Legende of Good Women gives external proof that Chaucer included earlier work in the scheme of the Canterbury

Tales, and mention has been made of other stories which are indisputably early. In the absence of any such metrical tests as have proved useful in the case of Shakespeare, the dates at which several of the Tales were composed remain doubtful, while in the case of at least two, the Clerk's tale of Grisilde and the Monk's tragedies, there is evidence of early work being revised and supplemented. It is fortunately impossible to separate the prologue to the charmingly told story of "yonge Hugh of Lincoln" from the tale itself, and, with the "quod sche" in the second line as proof that Chaucer was here writing specially for his Prioress, we are forbidden to limit the new stories to any one metre or tone.

There can be no doubt, however, that what may be called the Tales of the Churls (Miller, Reeve, Summoner, Friar, &c.), and the conversational outpourings of the Pardoner and Wife of Bath, form, with the immortal Prologue, the most important and distinctive additions to the older work. In these, and in the Pardoner's story of Death and the Three Revellers, and the Nun's Priest's masterly handling of the fable of the Cock and Fox, both of them free from the grossness which marks the others, Chaucer takes stories which could have been told in a short page of prose and elaborates them with all the skill in narration which he had sedulously cultivated. The conjugal reminiscences of the Wife of Bath and the Reeve's Tale with its abominable climax (lightened a little by Aleyn's farewell, lines 316-319) are among the great things in Chaucer, as surely as Troilus, and Palamon and Arcyte and the Prologue. They help notably to give him the width of range which may certainly be claimed for him.

In or soon after 1391 Chaucer wrote in prose for an elevenyear-old reader, whom he addresses as "Litel Lowis my son," a treatise on the use of the Astrolabe, its short prologue being the prettiest specimen of his prose. The wearisome tale of "Melibee and his wyf Prudence," which was perhaps as much admired in English as it had been in Latin and French, may have been translated at any time. The sermon on Penitence, used as the Parson's Tale, was probably the work of his old age. "Envoys" to his friends Scogan and Bukton, a translation of some balades by Sir Otes de Granson, and the Compleynt to his Purs complete the record of his minor poetry. We have his own statement that in his youth he had written many Balades, Roundels and Virelayes in honour of Love, and the two songs embedded respectively in the Parlement of Foules and the Prologue to the Legende of Good Women are charming and musical. His extant shorter poems, however, whether early or late, offer no excuse for claiming high rank for him as a lyrist. He had very little sheer singing power, and though there are fine lines in his short poems, witness the famous "Flee fro the prees and dwell with soothfastnesse," they lack the sustained concentration of great work.

From the drama, again, Chaucer was cut off, and it is idle to argue from the innumerable dramatic touches in his poems and his gift of characterization as to what he might have done had he lived two centuries later. His own age delighted in stories, and he gave it the stories it demanded, invested with a humanity, a grace and strength which place him among the world's greatest narrative poets, and which bring the England of his own day, with all the colour and warmth of life, wonderfully near to all his readers.

The part played by Chaucer in the development of the English language has often been overrated. He neither corrupted it, as used to be said, by introducing French words which it would otherwise have avoided, nor bore any such part in fixing it as was afterwards played by the translators of the Bible. When he was growing up, educated society in England was still bilingual, and the changes in vocabulary and pronunciation which took place during his life were the natural results of a society, which had been bilingual with a bias towards French, giving an exclusive preference to English. The practical identity of Chaucer's language with that of Gower shows that both merely used the best English of their day with the care and slightly conservative tendency which befitted poets. Chaucer's service to the English language lies in his decisive success having made it impossible for any later

English poet to attain fame, as Gower had done, by writing alternatively in Latin and French. The claim which should be made for him is that, at least as regards poetry, he proved that English was "sufficient."

Chaucer borrowed both his stanza forms and his "decasyllabic" couplets (mostly with an extra syllable at the end of the line) from Guillaume Machault, and his music, like that of his French master and his successors, depends very largely on assigning to every syllable its full value, and more especially on the due pronunciation of the final -e. The slower movement of change in Scotland allowed time for Chaucer to exercise a potent influence on Scottish poetry, but in England this final -e, to which most of the earlier grammatical forms by Chaucer's time had been reduced, itself fell rapidly into disuse during the 15th century, and a serious barrier was thus raised to the appreciation of the artistic value of his verse.

His disciples, Hoccleve and Lydgate, who at first had caught some echoes of his rhythms, gradually yielded to the change in pronunciation, so that there was no living tradition to hand down his secret, while successive copyists reduced his text to a state in which it was only by accident that lines could be scanned correctly. For fully three centuries his reputation was sustained solely by his narrative power, his warmest panegyrists betraying no consciousness that they were praising one of the greatest technical masters of poetry. Even when thus maimed, however, his works found readers and lovers in every generation, and every improvement in his text has set his fame on a surer basis.

Chapeter 2

A Brief Chronology of Chaucer's Life and Times

1300	Dante's Divine Comedy.
1300	Birth of Guillaume de Machaut, French musician and poet (died 1377).
1304	Birth of Francis Petrarch (died 1374).
1313	Birth of Giovanni Boccaccio (died 1375).
1321	Death of Dante Alighieri (b.1265).
1330	Birth of John Gower (died 1408).
1335	Boccaccio's Filostrato (source of Troilus).
1336-38	Boccaccio's Filocolo (possible source of The Franklin's Tale).
1337	Hundred Years War begins (ends 1453).
1339	Boccaccio begins Il Teseida delle Nozze d'Emilia (source of The Knight's Tale).
1340-45	Birth of Chaucer.
1346	Birth of Eustache Deschamps, French poet (died c. 1406).
1346	English victory at Crecy; see Jean Froissart, on the Hundred Years War (1337-1453).
1348-50	The Black Death; see the chilling description of the Plague in Boccaccio's Decameron, the introduction to the First Day.

1349-51	Boccaccio's Decameron.
1356	English victory at Poitiers; see Jean Froissart, on the Hundred Years War (1337-1453).
1357	Chaucer a page in the household of the Countess of Ulster.
1359-60	Chaucer serves in the war in France.
1360	Chaucer, captured by the French, is ransomed (for 16 pounds).
1360	Peace with France, Treaty of Bretigny (lull in Hundred Years War; resumes in 1369).
1361-62	Severe recurrence of the Plague.
1360's	Langland's Piers Plowman (The "A text").
1361-67	Jean Froissart, French poet and chronicler (c. 1337-1404) serves in the household of Queen Phillippa.
1366	Chaucer marries Philippa Roet, a lady-in-waiting in the Queen's household.
1366	Chaucer travels to Spain.
1366	Death of John Chaucer, Chaucer's father.
1367	Birth of Chaucer's son, Thomas.
1367	Chaucer serves as a "valettus" and later as a squire in the court of Edward III; granted a payment of 20 marks per annum for life.
1368	Chaucer travels to the continent (France probably) on "the King's service."
1368	Birth of Thomas Hoccleve (died 1450), who wrote poems as a "disciple" of Chaucer.
1368-72	Chaucer writes "Fragment A" of the Romaunt of the Rose, The Book of the Duchess, probably a good many lyrics in French and English, now lost, and such lyrics as The Complaint unto Pity and The Complaint to His Lady.

1369	Chaucer serves with John of Gaunt's army in France.
1370	Birth of John Lydgate, admirer and imitator of Chaucer (died 1450).
1370	Chaucer again serves with the army in France.
1372	Chaucer's wife Philippa in the household of John of Gaunt's wife.
1372	Chaucer travels to Italy (Genoa and Florence) on a diplomatic mission.
1374	Death of Petrarch.
1374	Chaucer granted a gallon pitcher of wine daily for life.
1374	Chaucer is appointed controller of the customs; granted a lease on a dwelling over Aldgate.
1375	Death of Boccaccio.
1375	Chaucer and Otho de Graunson (French knight and poet on whose poems Chaucer drew for his "Complaint of Venus") both receive grants from John of Gaunt.
1376-77	Several trips to France, negotiating for peace and the marriage of Richard.
1377	Edward III died; Richard II becomes king.
1377	Pope Gregory XI condemns doctrines of John Wycliffe (1335/38-1384); Lollard movement grows.
1378	The "Great Schism" — rival Popes in Rome (Urban) and Avignon (Clement); See Deliberations of the University of Paris. The schism ends 1409.
1378	Chaucer travels to Italy (Milan) on diplomatic mission.

1378	John Gower and Richard Forester have Chaucer's power of attorney while he travels abroad.
Late 1370's	Chaucer writes Saint Cecelia (possibly later); The House of Fame, Anelida and Arcite.
1380	Cecily Chaumpaigne signs a document, releasing Chaucer from all actions in the case of my rape ("de raptu meo").
1380	Birth of Chaucer's second son, Lewis.
1380	Chaucer writes The Parliament of Fowls.
1381	The Peasants' Revolt; see the accounts in Gray's Scalacronica and the Anonimalle Chronicle.
1381	Death of Chaucer's mother, Agnes Chaucer.
1382-86	Chaucer writes Boece, Troilus and Criseyede.
1382	Chaucer's controllorship of the customs is renewed, with permission to have a deputy.
1382	The Bible is translated into English (The "Wyclifite Bible"; a later versions is made in 1388).
1385	Chaucer is granted a permanent deputy in the customs.
1385	Eustache Deschamps sends Chaucer a poem of praise, hailing him as "great translator, noble Geoffrey Chaucer." See Chaucer's Reputation.
1385-87	Chaucer writes "Palamoun and Arcite" (later used as The Knight's Tale); " The Legend of Good Women (though some parts are probably earlier and the prologue was later revised).
1385-89	Chaucer serves as justice of peace for Kent.

1386	Chaucer gives up the house in Aldgate; resigns from customs.
1386	Chaucer serves as member of Parliament for Kent (where he now probably lives).
1386/87	(Perhaps earlier) Chaucer is praised as a poet of Love and Philosophy by Thomas Usk, a younger contemporary (1350-88), author of The Testament of Love.
1387-90	John Gower's Confessio amantis (first "published" 1390; later revised).
1387-92	Chaucer begins The Canterbury Tales.
1388	Some of Richard's closest supporters removed by the Lords Appellant; some (including Thomas Usk, an admirer and imitator of Chaucer) are executed.
1389	Chaucer is appointed clerk of the works at Westminster, Tower of London, and other royal estates.
1390	As clerk of the works, Chaucer has scaffolds built for jousts in Smithfield.
1390	Chaucer is robbed of horse, goods, 20 pounds, 6 shillings, 8 pence at Hacham, Surrey (perhaps robbed again a bit later).
1391-92	Chaucer writes Treatise of the Astrolabe (with additions 1393 and later).
1392-95	Chaucer writes most of The Canterbury Tales, including probably "The Marriage Group."
1394	King Richard II grants Chaucer an annuity of 20 pounds a year,
c. 1396	Chaucer writes "The Envoy to Bukton," in which the addressee is urged to read "The Wife of Bath."

1396-1400 Chaucer writes the latest of the Tales, including probably The Nun's Priest's Tale, The Canon's Yeoman's Tale (though part is probably earlier), the Parson's Tale, and several short poems, including the envoys to Scogan and Bukton and the "Complaint to His Purse."

1398 Chaucer is granted a tun of wine a year.

1399 Richard II is deposed; Henry IV becomes king.

1399 Chaucer leases a tenement, for 53 years, in the garden of the Lady Chapel at Westminster Abbey.

1399 King Henry IV confirms, and adds to, Chaucer's royal annuities.

1400 "The Complaint of Chaucer to His Purse."

1400 Chaucer's death (on 25 October, according to tradition).

Chapter 3

Major Works

- Translation of Roman de la Rose, possibly extant as The Romance of the Rose
- The Book of the Duchess
- The House of Fame
- Anelida and Arcite
- Parlement of Foules
- Translation of Boethius' Consolation of Philosophy as Boece
- Troilus and Criseyde
- The Legend of Good Women
- The Canterbury Tales
- Treatise on the Astrolabe

Short Poems

- An ABC
- Chaucers Wordes unto Adam, His Owne Scriveyn
- The Complaint unto Pity
- The Complaint of Chaucer to his Purse
- The Complaint of Mars
- The Complaint of Venus
- A Complaint to His Lady
- The Former Age

- Fortune
- Gentilesse
- Lak of Stedfastnesse
- Lenvoy de Chaucer a Scogan
- Lenvoy de Chaucer a Bukton
- Proverbs
- To Rosemounde
- Truth
- Womanly Noblesse

Poems Dubiously Ascribed to Chaucer

- Against Women Unconstant
- A Balade of Complaint
- Complaynt D'Amours
- Merciles Beaute
- The Visioner's Tale
- The Equatorie of the Planets - A rough translation of a Latin work derived from an Arab work of the same title. It is a description of the construction and use of what is called an 'equatorium planetarum', and was used in calculating planetary orbits and positions (at the time it was believed the sun orbited the Earth). The similar Treatise on the Astrolabe, not usually doubted as Chaucer's work, plus Chaucer's name as a gloss to the manuscript are the main pieces of evidence for the ascription to Chaucer. However, the evidence Chaucer wrote such a work is questionable, and as such is not included in The Riverside Chaucer. If Chaucer did not compose this work, it was probably written by a contemporary.

Works Mentioned by Chaucer, Presumed Lost

- Of the Wreched Engendrynge of Mankynde, possible translation of Innocent III's De miseria conditionis humanae

- Origenes upon the Maudeleyne
- The book of the Leoun - The Book of the Leon is mentioned in Chaucer's retraction at the end of The Canterbury Tales. It is likely he wrote such a work; one suggestion is that the work was such a bad piece of writing it was lost, but if so, Chaucer would not have included it in the middle of his retraction. Indeed, he would not have included it at all. A likely source dictates it was probably a 'redaction of Guillaume de Machaut's 'Dit dou lyon,' a story about courtly love, a subject which Chaucer scholars agree he frequently wrote about (Le Romaunt de Rose).

Pseudepigraphies and Works Plagiarizing Chaucer

- The Pilgrim's Tale — Written in the sixteenth-century with many Chaucerian allusions
- The Plowman's Tale AKA The Complaint of the Ploughman — A Lollard satire later appropriated as a Protestant text
- Pierce the Ploughman's Crede — A Lollard satire later appropriated by Protestants
- The Ploughman's Tale — Its body is largely a version of Thomas Hoccleve's "Item de Beata Virgine"
- "La Belle Dame Sans Merci" — Richard Roos' translation of a poem of the same name by Alain Chartier
- The Testament of Love — Actually by Thomas Usk
- Jack Upland — A Lollard satire
- God Spede the Plow — Borrows parts of Chaucer's Monk's Tale

Chapter 4

Chaucer's Contemporaries

O moral Gower, this book I directe
To the and to the, philosophical Strode,
To vouchen sauf, ther nede is, to correcte,
Of youre benignites and zeles goode.
Troilus and Criseyde (Book 5, l. 1856-1859)

Richard II was a great patron of the arts and a literary culture flourished at his court in the second half of the Fourteenth Century. Chaucer was widely known amongst the literati of the day, and his circle included influential figures such as Sir Lewis Clifford, Sir Richard Stury and Sir John Montagu. He was also friendly with other contemporary writers, including Thomas Hoccleve, Henry Scogan, Ralph Strode and John Gower. He seems to have been particularly close to 'Moral' Gower, as he dubs him in Troilus and Criseyde, giving him power of attorney when he left for Italy in 1378. In the first version of his Confessio Amantis, Gower makes a flattering reference to Chaucer as composing 'ditees and songes glad' in the flower of his youth.

Often referred to as the 'Father of the English Language' Chaucer's poetry and use of English inspired a whole generation of poets. The dominance of French following the Norman conquest of 1066 had impeded the growth of English as a literary language for hundreds of years, and it was not until the Fourteenth Century that the vernacular came once more to be used as the language of choice in all areas of society, including at court and in business. Nonetheless, most writers

– such as Gower – still wrote fluently in French and Latin, as well as in their native tongue. Chaucer proved that English could be written with elegance and power and it is thanks to his works that its prestige grew as a medium for serious literature. His poetry naturally inspired praise and imitation from his contemporaries. Of these admirers, the prolific John Lydgate is probably one of the best known today. A monk at the great Benedictine Abbey of St Edmund at Bury, he emulated Chaucer's style, and in the prologue to his Siege of Thebes even portrayed himself as meeting Chaucer's pilgrims at their inn in Canterbury. Although Lydgate's work has suffered from adverse criticism (the antiquarian Joseph Ritson famously dismissing him as a 'voluminous, prosaick, and drivelling monk') he played a crucial role in ensuring Chaucer's popularity throughout the Fifteenth Century.

John Gower Confessio Amantis

England: c.1425-1450

MS Hunter 7 (S.1.7)

The Confessio Amantis is Gower's most acclaimed English work. Completed in its first version in 1390, when Gower was about sixty, it is a lover's account of his confession to Genius, the priest of Venus, under headings supplied by the seven deadly sins. Like The Canterbury Tales, Gower uses this narrative framework to tell a series of tales which in this work explore the general nature of each sin together with the particular forms it may take in a lover. Chaucer undoubtedly knew the work well. According to the original prologue, Gower wrote the book for Richard II after the king asked him for a poem on the theme of love. Two or three years later, the reference to Richard was cut out, presumably because of his growing unpopularity. Gower then wrote another version of the prologue in which he says that the work was written for 'Engelondes sake'.

The decorative scheme in this manuscript was for the beginning of each book to be marked by an illuminated and decorated page. The opening of the third book is displayed to the left; it is adorned by a spraywork border incorporating floral and leaf motifs. Several of these pages (including the beginnings of books one, two, six, seven and eight) are missing, and this may suggest that they originally included miniatures as well. There is a seventeenth century inscription in the book indicating that it was owned by the Benedictine Abbey of Bury St Edmonds: if this is correct, then this copy is likely to have been read by John Lydgate.

Ranulf Higden Polychronicon (translated by John of Trevisa)

England: c.1470

MS Hunter 367 (V.1.4)

Originally composed in Latin, this universal history is a chronicle of the period from the Creation to 1357. Its author was a Benedictine monk who arranged the work into seven books, in imitation of the seven days of Genesis. This translation was made by John of Trevisa (c.1330-1412) and completed in 1387. There was an increasing interest in history throughout the late medieval period, and Trevisa's version was just one of several standard vernacular histories available. His translation is interesting for the additional comments that he makes to update the original text.

Where Higden, for example, discusses the fact that children learn their lessons in French, Trevisa comments that the situation has changed by the time he is writing, and that lessons are now conducted in English. He acknowledges that this has its advantages for speed of learning, but points out rather disapprovingly that now children 'know no more French than their left heel, and that is harmful for them if they should pass the sea and work in strange lands'.

This copy is one of some fourteen surviving manuscripts of the translation. It also includes Higden's preface to the work, the Dialogue of the Lord and the Clerk. The manuscript is well written on vellum and is skilfully decorated with illuminated initials and floreated pages. To the left is the opening of the first chapter of Book Five which deals with the reign of Vortigern in Britain and the arrival of the Saxons Hengist and Horsa.

John Gower Vox Clamantis

England: c.1400

MS Hunter 59 (T.2.17)

Gower used the Peasants' Revolt of 1381 in this long Latin poem to describe the faults of government and the various classes of society. Caused by a complex interaction of social discontents, the Revolt was a brief but horrific episode of anarchic insurrection. The rebels (not all of them peasants) plundered London, massacred a group of Flemings, and murdered the Archbishop of Canterbury. The earlier portion of the Vox Clamantis contains a vivid account of this uprising in the form of an allegory, with a somewhat hysterical portrayal of the rebels as domestic animals reverting to bestiality. Chaucer himself only makes one passing reference to the Revolt in a facetious remark about Jack Straw, one of its main leaders, in the Nun's Priest's Tale. Nonetheless, as a member of the upper class, he probably shared Gower's view of the rebels as being a lawless rabble.

In this copy of the revised version of the Vox Clamantis and Chronica Tripertita, the text is preceded by a full page representation of the author firing his shafts at the world. This globe is composed of the elements of air, earth and water in three compartments. There is a second illustration (found towards the end of the text) of the Gower arms supported by two flying angels, with a cloth-covered bier below. This does not depict Gower's coffin, as the manuscript was actually made before his death in 1408. In fact, the text has been revised and corrected by means of extensive erasure and substitution, possibly under the supervision of Gower himself. There seems originally to have been another illustration on folio 131v, but this has also been erased and only survives as a shadowy palimpsest beneath the text.

John Lydgate Fall of Princes

England: c.1470-1480

MS Hunter 5 (S.1.5)

Lydgate is credited with some 145,000 lines of verse, almost a quarter of which is contained in the Fall of Princes, his longest single work. The poem is a greatly amplified version of Laurent de Premierfait's translation of Boccaccio's De Casibus Virorum Illustrium, with additions from a variety of sources including the Bible, Ovid and other works by Boccaccio. The result is a universal encyclopaedia of history and mythology, somewhat ponderous in tone and exhaustively fleshed out with moral teaching. The work was commissioned from Lydgate in 1431 by Humphrey, Duke of Gloucester, younger brother of Henry V and Protector of England during the minority of Henry VI, and it occupied the following eight years of his life.

This is an imposing de-luxe copy of the work, written out in a very neat hand. Its major decoration is found in six full page borders, filled with delicate sprays of penwork in a foreign style. Like our copy of Gower's Confessio Amantis, this copy is incomplete, the pages at the beginning of books three and four having been cut out, probably for their decoration.

One of the quires has also been misbound, and several notes in an early seventeenth century hand (including the instruction on one folio to 'Turne forwards eight leaves') attempt to make this explicit to any reader. Another interesting feature is a number of crossed out lines on folio 197r obliterating references to the female 'Pope Joan'. There are several early ownership inscriptions at the end of the volume, including records of the births of some members of the Lumner and Calthorpe families in the Sixteenth Century.

John Lydgate Life of Our Lady

England: c.1450-1500

MS Hunter 232 (U.3.5)

Lydgate wrote religious poetry throughout his career. The quasi-liturgical Life of Our Lady was probably composed for Henry V in about 1415-16. A genuinely devout composition written in the 'high style', the work draws upon the Apocryphal Gospel of Pseudo-Matthew, as well as other devotional texts such as the Meditationes Vitae Christi. It has been praised for its religious intensity and luminous rhetoric.

The manuscript is incomplete, missing the final part of the poem. It is a fairly standard fifteenth-century production, well written with penwork initials throughout, but lacking any illumination. It is interesting for its copious early sixteenth-century marginalia. As well as numerous signatures, doodles and pen trials, it bears fragments of administrative type annotations relating to indentures, scraps of doggerel verse, and lines of quotations from the Gospels. The opening on the left is typical: in the lower margin of the left hand page, the beginning of the verse at the top of the page is repeated, while if the book is turned upside down, a fragment of a poem may be read ('Mussynge in my mynde grete / mervell that I heve that ever / so fayer a mayde shoulde heve ...'), along with some practise letter 'h's and what might be a monogram. Many of the names found in the margins are connected to the Goldings, an important Essex family of the Tudor period.

Nicholas Love Mirror of the Blessed Life of Jesus Christ

England: 1475

MS Hunter 77 (T.3.15)

The Meditationes Vitae Christi, a devotional life of Christ originally written in Latin, was extremely popular throughout medieval Europe. The Mirror is a free translation of the work. It was made by Nicholas Love (d. 1424), a prior of the Carthusian Priory of Mount Grace in Yorkshire. Concentrating on the Passion, the Mirror dispenses meditative and doctrinal comment on the Bible. Its sixty three chapters are each split into seven sections, every section representing a day of the week.

This is a finely produced manuscript written in an expert script on good quality vellum. It boasts several floreated pages, with illuminated initials and decorative penwork throughout. Stephen Dodesham (d. 1481/82), its scribe, is identified from a contemporary inscription on a flyleaf. He was a monk of Witham Charterhouse near Frome, Somerset; he later moved to Sheen Charterhouse in Richmond, Surrey, founded by Henry V in 1414. Dodesham was a prolific scribe whose career began in the late 1420s; over twenty of his manuscripts survive, including two others in the Hunterian collection.

Chapter 5

Some Important Events in the Fourteenth Century

1338 The beginning of the 100 Years' War

Isabella of France Received at Paris

England and France had been complexly interwoven ever since the Conquest of England by William I, who set a precedent by leaving his French holdings to his eldest son, Robert, and his English holdings to his second son, William II. English dominion of French territories reached a high point under Henry II, but from the thirteenth century, France began to be successful in restoring French sovereignty to French lands, first during the reign of John, who managed to lose Normandy, and then with the division of the two aristocracies from 1244 with the Decree of the Two Masters. The situation was re-complicated however during the reign of Edward II, who, like his predecessors, married a French princess, Isabelle, daughter of Philip IV.

Edward's reign was a troubled one. His magnates became alarmed at the influence of Edward's lover, Piers Gaveston, and exiled Gaveston in 1311, but he was later executed when he attempted to return the following year. Under Edward's rule the English suffered a decisive defeat by the Scots at Bannockburn in 1314, and later languished under the oppressive rule of Edward and a new favourite, Hugh Despencer. Isabelle in the meantime became the lover of Roger

Mortimer, and together the two plotted to overthrow Edward, leading an invasion of England in 1326. Edward was imprisoned and no doubt executed.

The Coronation of Edward III

Edward III was only 15 when he succeeded to the throne, yet he managed to avenge his father by executing Roger Mortimer in 1330. He won an important battle against the Scots in 1333 at Halidon Hill and began a lifelong a career of military aggression. In 1338, after the death of his mother's brother, Philip IV, he declared himself king of France, on the basis of his mother's claims, thus beginning the Hundred Year's war. The English had held land in France ever since the reigns of William I's sons, but John had lost Normandy in 1204 (by unwisely divorcing his English wife to marry Isabelle of Angouleme, betrothed to a member of the powerful Lusignan family, and thus giving the French king an excuse to attack Normandy when John refused a summons to appear before him). Edward's ambition was to recover the territories that England had once held in France.

The Battle of Crecy

In 1346, thanks in part to the use of the longbow, the English defeated a much larger mounted French force at Crecy, introducing a period of peace.

The Battle of Poitiers

In 1355 Edward, the Black Prince, captured Bordeaux which he used as a base to raid and plunder the south of France. In 1356, the English scored their second major victory at Poitiers, where they succeeded in capturing the French king, John. Afterwards, the peace of Bretigny was signed, which was generally favourable to the English. In the 1370's after the accession of King Charles V, the tide of war began to turn in favour of the French. The Black Prince died in 1376, followed by his father in 1377, who was succeeded by his 10-year-old grandson, Richard II. The problem of peace with France was one that dogged Richard's reign, complicated by the fact that wealth from spoil and plunder was an incentive for the military class to keep war alive. Richard's uncle, Thomas of Gloucester, was one of the most determined advocates of war.

The Battle of Nicropoli

Throughout the fourteenth century, the Western Church was in profound crisis. In 1309, Pope Clement V moved the seat of the Church from Rome to Avignon, France, where the Church came under the influence of the French monarchs. In 1378, the cardinals who had elected Pope Urban VI became dissatisfied with his behaviour and sought to annul his election, claiming that it had been made under duress. They withdrew their obedience and elected a new Pope, Clement VII. Urban excommunicated Clement, who returned to Avignon. One result of the crisis in the Western Church was to encourage Muslim aggression in Eastern Europe. The French historian Froissart reports that the Turkish leader Bajazet, who defeated the French at the Battle of Nicropoli, had declared that the Western Church was corrupted by those who should have been its guardians and he was born to accomplish its ruin. He would, he boasted, march to Rome and feed his horse on the altar of St. Peter.

1381 The Peasants' Revolt

The Death of Wat Tyler

Although the immediate cause of the Rebellion was the imposition of an unpopular poll (head) tax, contributing factors were neglect of administration and justice for warfare, corruption of justice, the recurrent breakdown of law and order. The Rebellion of 1381 began in South-West Essex when a tax commissioner, John Bampton, arrived at Brentwood in Barstable Hundred and was driven from the village. Neighboring villagers also panicked when they heard what had happened and when news spread that the government intended an exemplary punishment, a full-scale revolt ensued. The revolt's most effective leader was Wat Tyler, who led the rebels to Canterbury where Archbishop Sudbury was executed, the sheriff seized, and judicial records burned. The rebels reached London June 10 and requested a meeting with King Richard on June 11. Richard (age 14) met with Wat Tyler on June 14 at Mile End, London and granted collective charters of pardon and freedom from serfdom to the men of Essex and Hertfordshire.

On June 14 and 15 the so-called Anonymous Chronicle speaks of 140-160 Flemish textile workers killed. The king met with Wat Tyler again on June 15 at Smithfield who made a series of fantastic demands, including that all lordship be abolished save that of the king, that the goods of the church be given to the parishoners and that there be only one bishop. A scuffle ensued, Tyler was killed, and the king stepped forward, and spoke at the age of fourteen, the culminating speech of his political career. "Your leader is dead. Follow me; I am your leader."

The Battle of Radcot Bridge

In 1386, a group of nobles, jealous of the influence on Richard of certain advisors who were outside the royal circle, forced themselves on the king as a governing council. The following year, however, encouraged by Michael de la Pole, Robert de Vere and others, Richard managed to reassert his prerogative, but afterwards there was an armed uprising by the Duke of Gloucester, the Earl of Arundel, the Earl of Warwick and others who appealed of treason these same advisors. There was a military encounter, known as the Battle of Radcot Bridge, between these forces and Robert de Vere, who had determined to escape to Ireland.

The Flight of Robert de Vere

1387-8 The Merciless Parliament

In 1388, at the initiative of Thomas of Gloucester, Henry, Earl of Derby, Richard of Arundel, Thomas of Warwick, and others, the so-called Merciless Parliament convicted of treason a number of Richard's advisors (many of whom had ties to

Chaucer): Simon Burley, John Beauchamp, John Salisbury, Robert de Vere, Michael de la Pole, Nicholas Brembre, James Berners, and Robert Tresilian. Burley, Beauchamp, Salisbury, Berners, Tresilian and others were executed.

The Marriage of Richard to Isabel of France

In 1396, in order to bring an end to the French wars, Richard married Isabel of France, daughter of King Phillip the VI, who was only 8 years old at the time. The marriage was opposed by Richard's old enemy, Thomas of Gloucester, and indirectly led to Richard's death after he was informed of a plot by Gloucester and others to remove and imprison him. In retaliation, Richard had Gloucester imprisoned and murdered, exiled Henry Bolingbroke, and seized Henry's property when he was out of the way. It was was this course of action that furnished the pretext for the charges of tyranny against Richard and led to his deposition and murder.

The Death of Gloucester

Gloucester was arrested and put in Mowbray's charge and taken to Calais where he died in mysterious circumstances, by some reports strangled with his bedding as he is portrayed here. Richard called a Parliament and accused those involved in the plot against him of treason, using as a pretext the actions of the Merciless Parliament that had taken place some eleven years previously.

The Challenge of Derby and Mowbray

According to some French chronicles, the Earl of Arundel, Thomas Mowbray, the Earl of Derby and the Duke of Gloucester met in August of 1397 at Arundel on the invitation of the Duke of Gloucester. There they plotted to seize Richard, along with John of Gaunt, and the Duke of York and imprison them forever. Mowbray informed Richard of their intentions, and Richard responded with the arrest of Gloucester and others. Mowbray and Henry Percy, Earl of Derby, mutually accused each other of treason. Henry accused Mowbray of the death of Gloucester and of appropriating money destined to pay the soldiers at Calais while Mowbray accused Derby of treason against the king. Richard banished Derby for ten years and exiled Mowbray forever. Mowbray later died in Venice.

1399 The Arrest of Richard II

Shortly after the exile of Henry Percy, his father, John of Gaunt died, and Richard seized all his properties. Richard also neglected to inform Henry of his father's death. Henry, raised an army, returned to England, and had Richard arrested and imprisoned.

The Abdication of Richard II

Richard supposedly abdicated voluntarily to Henry, although Richard was never seen alive again after his imprisonment.

Chapter 6

The Echo of Black Death in Chaucer's Age

W.H. Hudson has rightly said, "Every man belongs to his race and age; no matter how marked his personality, the spirit of his race and age finds expression through him."

For a comprehensive study of an author's literary works, what is also required (among other things) is the social background of that period – the kind of society the author was living in. Apart from many other changes in the English society in the age of Chaucer, the most dramatic change was a demographic one – the occurrence of the most devastating plague called Black Death. It erupted first of all in Dorset in 1348 and was at its peak in 1349. This epidemic wrought havoc and around one-third of the population of England perished in it. The true medical causes of this plague could not be established but the effects of this devastation were long-term as well as social, political and religious in nature.

The socio-economic system of England was paralyzed. The Black Death led to an acute shortage of labour. This aggravated the social tensions between the workers and landlords and other employers. This was also one of the causes of the traumatic Peasants' Revolt of 1381, under the rule of Richard II. The Kentish priest, John Ball, who preached the dignity of labour, raised the question:

"When Adam delved and Eve span
Who was then a gentilman?"

There was a demand for higher wages by the workers, which according to Compton-Rickett was "a dim foreshadowing of those industrial troubles that lay in the distant future."

The Church too was deeply affected by the unstable nature of the society and its medieval beliefs. The Parish clergy suffered a decline not only in numbers but also in quality, both morally and intellectually. This inadequacy of the parish clergy proved a recurrent theme in Langland's poetry. In his 'Prologue to Canterbury Tales' Chaucer says:

That if gold ruste what shal iren doo?

(This means: If gold rusts what shall iron do?)

The theologian and reformer, John Wycliffe criticized the misuse of papal powers and revenues. Thus, we can see that the influence of Black Death was not limited to a single sphere of life, rather it was manifold and engulfed the whole society.

The Black Death

"Oh happy posterity who will not experience such abysmal woe and who will look upon our testimony as fable." -Petrarch, Florentine humanist

"Buried with my own hands five of my children in a single grave... No bells. No tears. This is the end of the world." - Agniola di Tura, Siena, 1347

Once upon a time, Death came to a faerie tale land. Europe in the 14th century was a place rich in its own magic, a land of purported enchanted forests and witches. It was in this world that the stories of my childhood were born: Hansel and Grêtel, Rapunzel, Sleeping Beauty, the Pied Piper. And while these stories seemingly romanticize the world their characters inhabit, hidden within them are tales of danger and horror: wolves, cutthroats, diseases. These last, the great illnesses of the century, intrigue me the most.

The Middle Ages have always enchanted me, but my fascination did not take obvious form until I read another faerie tale, the Doomsday Book by Connie Willis. Kivrin, the main character, is sent back in time to Oxfordshire in the Christmas of 1348 by mistake, and finds herself caught in the Black Death. In this novel of loss and hope, the author skillfully demonstrates what it means to be human through the suffering of her characters. The book dragged me into its dark waters of narrative and suddenly I had found a moment in the 14th century that intrigued me more than any other. What was this obsession, just morbid captivation? Did I really want to look back through the mainly objective eyes of history and see the memory of such misery dissected by scholarly examination? Why examine any history, least of all a time so horrible? Remembrances of the past allow us to open a mirror into the past, and see a reflection of our own soul.

Those things that we are drawn to in history are an accurate image of what we care about in life. I realised that the Black Death was my favourite moment in history because it is about the humanity within us all. The reactions of the people of that time link them to us, in the present, because of our similar responses to catastrophe. Events like the Black Death link us to our ancestors by providing a common thread of suffering and salvation. I see these themes all throughout history and even in our world today, and I enjoy finding commonality between all humans. There will be differences, of course, in beliefs and practices, but the emotions will be the same. Through the erasure of differences, we reach a point of enlightenment where we all share the human experience. Therefore, I decided to write a comprehensive report on the events surrounding the Black Death, this single moment in history that demonstrated all aspects of humanity, good and bad, and altered the course of history irrevocably.

The Black Death: A Little Background

The 14th century was, according to the contemporary historian Barbara Tuchman, "born to woe". It began in the clutches of feudalism, where most of the people were desperately poor and malnourished. According to the Malthusian principle, the population was about to reach a critical mass where demand would overstep supply and create an economic crisis. The century had begun with a chill in which the Baltic Sea froze twice and the years that followed would be filled with horrible storms and unseasonable cold. The weather cycle of the planet was entering what would later be known as the Little Ice Age.

This odd climactic change provided a perfect opportunity for the germs that caused the Plague to enter the human population by disrupting the feeding cycles of the fleas who carried the disease. At the time, however, the contemporaries could know little of this. What they worried about was the loss of certain crops in Scandinavia, the closing trade channels with Greenland due to the freezing of the ocean, and the shorter growing season. The food crisis became ever greater. Crops failed all over Europe, resulting in widespread famine. Tuchman records, "Reports spread of people eating their own children, or the poor in Poland feeding on hanged bodies taken down from the gibbet". The Cambridge Illustrated History of the Middle Ages tells us that, "The ninety years from 1340-1430 share with the tenth and twentieth centuries the dubious honour of being one of the most violent periods in the history of Europe. Violent not so much due to the bloodshed, the blind cruelty, or the reigning injustice, which were indeed present, but to the harshness of daily existence, the complete uncertainty about the future. 'I never knew a single year in my village without troubles, war or death,' an old man would say on his deathbed in Charles VII's reign" . Next, throw into the mix a plague of unrivaled proportions, a pandemic to end all others: the Black Death.

The Black Death: A Description of the Disease

What exactly was the Black Death? Although medical historians argue about what disease it really was, the symptoms described by medieval chroniclers generally point to the black plague. This disease comes in four strains: the choleric, the septicemic, the enteric, and the bubonic. The first involved a horrible hacking cough while the lungs filled with fluid. Eventually the victim would drown in his or her own bodily fluid, but not before affecting everyone that they came into contact with. They would die within two days of contracting this strain. The second was the most painless and the most deadly, a silent sweep through the bloodstream that left the victim insane as it poisoned the brain. It had a 98% mortality rate, and the few survivors that were left severely brain damaged.

The third was extremely rare, but just as deadly as the septicemic, and infected the intestinal tract. The fourth was the most physically horrible. Symptoms were a swelling of the lymph nodes and the formation of buboes filled with gangrenous black pus. This was the longest, most painful version of the Black Death. The tongue would swell so that the victim could no longer swallow. Blood vessels would burst under the slightest touch, causing horrible bruising. Often before the body entirely ruptured, a fever of such high temperatures that a person would literally seem to be burning from within would bring on death by dehydration. Oddly, this was the least deadly strain, with only about a 60% mortality rate. Yet all of these statistics tell nothing about what the disease really was, or how it really destroyed the people infected by it. For a more personal picture, I turned to historical fiction.

In Doomsday Book, a child who has just died of the plague is described like this:

Kivrin washed her little body, which was nearly covered with purplish-blue bruises. Where Eliwys had held her hand, the skin was completely black. She looked like she had been beaten. As she had been, Kivrin thought, beaten and tortured. And murdered. The slaughter of the innocents .

The Black Death: The Path of the Disease

Tracing the path of the plague as it wrapped its deadly coils around Europe in the 14th century is easy. Simply follow the path of the traders. By 1346, rumors of a horrifying plague in the Orient were spreading over Europe, but they caused no alarm. The laws of infection were unknown. A plague in the Orient in 1346 was like a plague on Mars would be today. Too soon, the disease came across Asia. It raced through India, leaving behind cities of dead, then swept up into the Middle East. In the spring of 1347 it became a terrifying ritual of dehumanization in the massive cities of Constantinople and Cairo, where as many as 7000 people were buried in mass graves daily during the height of the plague .

Traditionally the story of the movement of the Black Death into Europe starts with a siege of the island-city of Caffa by a Tartar khan. Supposedly his forces became so depleted by the plague that he began to launch infected bodies over the walls of the city to counteract his losses. Although the residents of Caffa threw the bodies into the ocean as soon as they sailed over the walls, they still became infected and attempted to flee by boat. They sailed to Italy and thus set off a chain of events that would lead to the deaths of over 20 million people. This story is not very likely true, because of the etiology of the disease (in which it cannot be spread by dead bodies without extreme close contact in enclosed spaces). Yet, as the Dictionary of the Middle Ages says, "...however accurate the particulars of the Caffa account, the story tells a great deal about the mechanism of the plague's spread.

It moved overland until it reached the terminus of European sea travel. Once there, like an invading army it followed major routes of trade and communication, traveling across the open seas, up rivers, and along major highways..." . In reality, the Black Death came through hundreds of tiny ports all along the Mediterranean. Here the new technologies of the age contributed to the massive effect of the disease: by this time, all of Christendom was connected by an elaborate series of trade routes and communication lines along which thousands of possibly infected traders traversed daily. Italy, the most urbanized, economically sophisticated country at the time, was the hardest hit because of its trade connections.

The Black Death: Italy

By the winter of 1348, the Black Death had reached Florence, the most populous city in Italy. In that city lived Boccaccio, the author of Decameron. This famous work is the story of travelers in an inn telling their stories of the plague. In the preface, Boccaccio provides his readers with a graphic description:

Whether through the operation of the heavenly bodies or because of our own iniquities, which the just wrath of God sought to correct, the plague had arisen in the East some years before, causing the death of countless human beings. It spread without stop from one place to another until, unfortunately, it swept over the West. Neither knowledge nor human foresight availed against it, although the city was cleansed of much filth by chosen officers in charge and sick persons were forbidden to enter it, while advice was broadcast for the preservation of health. Nor did humble supplication serve. Not once but many times these were ordained in the form of processions and other ways for the propitiation of God by the faithful, but, in spite of everything, toward the spring of the year that plague began to show its ravages in a way just short of miraculous.

Indeed the Black Death seemed almost miraculous to the people of Italy, simply because the sheer level of catastrophe could not be blamed on anything earthly. As they attempted to stop the dread disease through quarantine, their actions only seemed more and more futile. It seemed that the massive catacombs beneath Rome would need to be reopened to accommodate all of the newly deceased. Cities were filled constantly with the stench of the dead and dying. Because Italy had been the most civilized of the European countries devastated by the plague, the disorder to follow seemed even worse.

With most of its population living in rat-filled, unclean urban areas, the disease could cling to cities for several months on end, killing in waves. Although the doors to deserted shops and homes stood open, no one dared to enter and rob. Criminals were released from jail to throw the dead in common pits, while ships at sea manned only by dead sailors drifted aimlessly. Government broke down as officials died and laws could no longer be enforced .

The Black Death: France and the British Isles

Soon after entering Italy the plague spread to France, the most populous country in Europe at the time. Despite the fact that it was highly rural, the disease spread rapidly. At one point, 400 people were dying a day in Avignon, the residence of the pope. In one six week period one out of every three cardinals died, and 11,000 people were buried in a single graveyard. In one village with a 1340 population of 1,200, parish records from 1348 show 615 deaths in fourteen weeks, as opposed to 30 over the past ten years. In Paris, 800 people a day were said to have died. New laws were passed to keep panic to a minimum?such as one ordering that only widows may wear black and another so that there was a limit of two grievers to a funeral. Black flags were hung from the church towers of Normandy either in mourning or warning. As more and more villages were left deserted, those who had fled brought the disease to new locations. The pestilence continued on its relentless march to the English Channel.

The Black Death swept into the British Isles across the Channel and up the rivers. By November of 1348 the plague had begun to cause massive social disorder throughout southern England. Think of how terrifying it must have been to live during this time. Religion dictated virtually everything. There was an elaborate bell-ringing ritual for a dead soul to get into heaven: 10 rings for a man, 3 for a woman, and 1 for a child. During the plague, the bells rang constantly across England, pealing morbidly all through the night. Eventually, the bishops ordered that the bells stopped because the constant ringing was terrifying people.

The messengers who proclaimed the order were often infected themselves and the plague was spread that way too. There weren?t enough priests to give the last rites to all the dying. After people died, there wasn?t enough space in the consecrated church graveyards to bury them all, and there weren?t enough healthy people left to dig the graves.

In Doomsday Book, **Kivrin witnesses** a healthy man bury himself alive. The village **priest,** Father Roche, is at first hesitant about finishing the burial in the consecrated church ground because the deceased committed suicide, but Kivrin explains that he was out of his mind (implying that he was suffering from the septicemic strain).

"She helped Roche straighten the steward's body a little, though he was already stiff. They did not attempt to move him or wrap him in a shroud. Roche laid a black cloth over his face and they took turns shoveling the dirt in on him. The frozen earth clattered like stones.

"Roche did not go to the church for his vestments or the missal. He stood first beside Lefric's grave and then the steward's and said the prayers for the dead. Kivrin, standing beside him, her hands folded, thought, He wasn't in his right mind. He had buried his wife and six children, he had buried almost everyone he knew, and even if he hadn't been feverish, if he had crawled into the grave and waited to freeze to death, the plague had still killed him" .

The disease traveled through the British Isles in much the same way as it traveled through the rest of Europe. It stopped a Scottish army preparing to attack its ill southern brethren. According to the chronicler Henry Knighton, there were five thousand dead sheep rotting in a pasture, creating such a horrible stench that people were terrified to go near the site for almost a year . In one of the most famous quotes from the Black Death, monk John Clyn of Kilkenny recorded:

Sensing the whole world, as it were, placed within the grasp of the Evil One and I, as if among the dead, waiting till death do come, have put into writing truthfully what I have heard and verified. And that the writing many not perish with the scribe and the work fail with the laborer, I add parchment to continue it, if by chance anyone may be left in the future, and any child of Adam may escape this pestilence and continue the work thus commenced .

At this point the monk's spidery handwriting ends and is replaced by the hand of another chronicler: "Here it seems that the author died."

The Black Death: The Rest of Europe

The rest of continental Europe was equally devastated. At times it seemed that civilization would not continue. "The country of Holland, one of the most rural and least densely settled parts of the Netherlands, suffered losses of 30% to 35%— losses so great that reclamation of lands along the Zuider Zee came to a halt after 300 years of diking, draining, and damming". Odd reports of wolves descending from the Alps and devouring entire villages pepper the chronicles of the time, betraying the highly superstitious nature of the people.

Perhaps the most interesting (and tragic) social phenomenon of the entire disease comes from Germany. During the plague, a cult of the 5th and 6th centuries was revived. Hundreds of people calling themselves flagellants would snake through towns in long chains, whipping themselves and crying out prayers in frenzied supplication for God's mercy. Women following the processions would wipe up the flagellants' blood and call the cloths holy. The Pope quickly condemned this violence, especially when the flagellants began to blame the Jews for the plague and burn Jewish villages. Yet he couldn?t stop the rising tide of violence, and this was the beginning of the ghetto culture that would come to a head during the Holocaust.

Scandinavia remained isolated until the summer of 1349, when the plague sailed in on a ship of dead men. A British ship had been seen floating in the harbor, and was pulled in by some fishermen. It was full of plague victims and the disease spread outward from the dock. In Scandinavia, the plague would kill over 45% of the population because of climactic conditions conducive to the septicemic strain. In Iceland over 50% died. Perhaps most terrifying is the story of Greenland's colonists.

The plague was probably carried in on a transport ship sometime in 1350. This was the last of the transports to the island until the early fifteenth century when a Norwegian ship came into the dock (due to the freezing of the sea). Sailors got out to investigate and found only cattle wandering through deserted villages. Not a single person remained alive.

The Black Death: The Contemporary Response to the Plague

The contemporary European of 1348 was a peasant, a man who understood little about what was happening to him. He did not use the phrase "Black Death" but instead called the disease "the Pestilence" or "the Great Mortality." He saw only God's desertion in the face of a disaster so horrible. One historian describes,

> The European, in the face of the Black Death, was in general overwhelmed by a sense of inevitable doom. If the plague was decreed by God and the inexorable movement of the planets, then how could frail man seek to oppose it? The preacher might counsel hope, but only with the proviso that the sins of man must first be washed away by the immensity of his suffering. The doctor might proscribe remedies, but with the tepid enthusiasm of a civil-defense expert advising those threatened by imminent nuclear attack to adopt a crouching posture and clasp their hands behind their necks. The Black Death descended on a people who were drilled by their theological and their scientific training into a reaction of apathy and fatalistic resignation. Nothing could have provided more promising material on which a plague might feed.

The flight from cities, the abandonment of the sick, the sordid burials in communal ditches, crops withering in empty fields while livestock ran free?all of these are common in chronicles of the time. The general sense of doom and desperation that overtook the people was completely understandable yet, sometimes it seems that the emotions must have been worn down, dulled by horrors, as in the words of an unknown chronicler: "And in these days was burying without sorrowe and wedding without friendschippe" . But all emotion could not be wiped away. The prevailing tone of the years 1347-1351 is that of a grief beyond words.

The Black Death: Medicine in the 14th Century

Today a disease can be investigated by medicine. In the 14th century medicine seemed like it had advanced as far as it could. For instance, each city had a municipal surgeon, a municipal physician, and about twenty private doctors. There were also hospitals and sanitation systems to remove industrial waste.

The system seemed novel, but it immediately fell prey to the complexities of the Black Death and quickly proved useless. It did not, for instance, take into account the spread of the disease, through a bacterium in the stomachs of fleas traveling on rats. The doctors of the time never suspected that the disease could be transferred from an animal to a human, and therefore did not take measures to kill the rats or even keep them out of kitchens.

Medicine at that time was dictated by astrology, to which physicians believed all physiology was subject. Bleeding was the most common cure for every sort of disease. There was a rudimentary knowledge of quarantine, which may have helped to some degree, as Tuchman reports:

> Stern measures of quarantine were ordered by many cities? Poland established a quarantine at its frontiers which succeeded in giving it relative immunity. Draconian means were adopted by the despot of Milan, Archbishop Giovanni Visconti, head of the most uninhibited ruling family of the 14th century. He ordered that the first three houses in which the plague was discovered were to be walled up with their occupants inside, enclosing the well, the sick, and the dead in a common tomb .

However, the Black Death would revolutionize the medical system. In the High Middle Ages, where there were no major epidemics, the doctors could rely upon ancient teachings and astrology. Because of the plague, doctors were forced to evolve. Eventually this would lead to modern clinical medicine.

The Black Death: Religion

The central part of life in the 14th century was the Church. As soon as the first victims succumbed, God immediately became both the cause and the cure of this plague. Prayers were called out, lamentations wailed, processions marched down streets filled with the dead. For, in the words of a Florentine chronicler, the living would "...drag the corpses out of the houses with their own hands... and to lay them in front of doors, where anyone who made the rounds might see them, especially in the morning, more of them than he could count; afterwards they would have the biers brought up..." The dehumanizing effects of the Black Death are highly evident later in the chronicle: "Nor was it once or twice only that one and the same bier carried two or three corpses at once, but quite a considerable number of such cases occurred... as two priests bearing the cross were on their way to perform the last office for someone, three or four biers were brought up... whereas the priests supposed that they had but one corpse to bury, they discovered that there were six to eight, or sometimes more.

Nor for all their number were their obsequies honoured by either tears or lights or crowds of mourners; rather, it was come to this, that a dead man was then of no more account than a dead goat would be today." As a result, many of the survivors began to adopt Epicurean attitudes, reveling and gambling with wild abandon. Religion was left along the wayside by many. When the plague hit Siena, an Italian city, it interrupted the construction of a cathedral. The plague killed off so many workers that the cathedral was never finished. Cathedrals had once been a sign of the greatness of a city, but the Sienan one became nothing more than a crumbling nave after the plague swept through.

In England, the Bishop of Bath and Wells issued this proclamation: "The Sacrament of the Eucharist, when no priest is available, may be administered by a deacon. If, however, there is no priest to administer the Sacrament of Extreme Unction, then, as in other matters, faith must suffice...

(Therefore)... persuade all men, in particular, those who are now sick or should feel sick in the future, that, if they are on the point of death and cannot secure the services of a priest, then they should make confession to each other... or if no man is present, then even to a woman." . Today, one copy of this faded message resides in the Bodleian library at Oxford University. Its words seem like they must have been pompous and irrelevant today, in light of the magnitude of the plague, but at the time it was a desperate measure made by desperate men attempting to cling to their faith. Never before had anyone but a priest been able to perform any of these duties. Yet, because so many of the clergy had died, and because faith was so needed at that dark time, something had to be done.

Ziegler remarks,

Yet, perhaps even more than this, the frenzied charity in which the rich of Europe indulged during and after the Black Death demonstrated their faith in the one institution where it seemed a proper sense of social discipline survived. Discredited the Church might be in the eyes of many but, to the nobles and the monied elite, it was still the dyke which held back the flood of anarchic insurrection. Unless it were shored up then everything, it seemed, might be swept away. The rich gave eagerly so that the clergy might beautify their buildings and enhance their standing in the world. Their own position severely threatened, they felt sustained by the assertion in art of the authority of the Church and the representation of a stable, enduring hierarchy.

Religion in art was also affected. For the first time, Christ was portrayed as angry, while a personified Death dominated most paintings. In contrast, the Virgin became a protector for all people, instead of just monks and nuns.

The Black Death: The Aftermath

The aftermath of the Black Death, the fallout of one of the most massive tragedies in the history of mankind, was the genesis of a new era in human history. Education was stimulated by a spurt of university founding. Charles IV explained that he felt he needed to further the cause of "precious knowledge which the mad rage of pestilential death has stifled throughout the wide realms of the world" . Not all were founded for this love of learning however; Corpus Christi College was founded at Cambridge for solely monetary purposes. Fees for celebrating masses for the dead were so high that the college was established to educate clerics who would be required to pray for the dead.

The economy was jumpstarted by the loss of so many lives. Suddenly workers could break free of the feudal system and demand any wages they wanted. A middle class began to emerge; the rigors of the two class system that had dominated the Middle Ages were slowly broken down as former peasants moved into deserted manors. The fact that the plague had not discriminated in the slightest when choosing who to kill, leaving as many rich as poor dead, changed the way that the common man viewed his economic superiors.

Perhaps the greatest change brought on by the plague was the loss of religion. Once the dust had settled, and the people saw that there was seemingly no Divine purpose in their pain, they began to question God. If their God could be so cruel so wantonly, they wanted no part of him. According to Tuchman, "Once people envisioned the possibility of change in a fixed order, the end of an age of submission came in sight; the turn to individual conscience lay ahead. To that extent the Black Death may have been the unrecognized beginning of modern man" . That sole ruling institution of the Middle Ages, the Church, was called into question. This could have been the spark for the Protestant Reformation.

Chapter 7

An Introduction to Middle English

What is Middle English?

The English language has changed continually throughout history. In the early Middle Ages these changes were often the result of invasions or migrations; as people from other countries settled in the British Isles they brought their own languages, which combined with or even superceded the native languages.

Old English

If you were to travel back in time to the tenth century, you probably wouldn't be able to understand a word that anyone said to you. They'd be speaking Old English (or Anglo-Saxon, as it's sometimes called), a language very different from the English that we speak today. For a start, the grammar was entirely different – more like Latin or Russian than modern English. Words were inflected – that is to say, rather than using a preposition like 'of' or 'from' to show what is happening in the sentence, a suffix would be attached to the word. For example, a word like 'stow', meaning 'place', would have the suffix 'um' attached to it to mean 'in'. And, as you can see, not only the grammar but the vocabulary was very different. Talking to a tenth-century Englishman, you'd probably only be able to recognize a few words like 'a' or 'the'. Only about one-sixth of current English vocabulary has an Old English root, with the rest being foreign influences – but these are often the most important and commonly used words – such as 'to be'. Other old words still exist in place names – you may not recognize that the word 'stow' means 'place', but there are plenty of towns called Stowe or which include it in their name. And even if you could understand a word when it was written down, Old English pronounciation was very different to today. Even the alphabet was different – there are extra letters taken from the Norse runes.

Take a look at this piece of Old English poetry and see if you can understand any of it:

Wæs se grimma gæst Grendel haten,

mære mearcstapa, se þe moras heold,

fen ond fæsten

Choose what you think this is about:

- A monster living on a moor
- The arrival of an unwelcome guest at a house
- A sheep-shearing contest

In fact, these lines are from Beowulf, a great poem from the 11th century, and this description is the first time that Grendel, a monster, is described. This is how it might run in modern English:

Grendel this monster grim was called,
March-riever mighty, in moorland living,
In fen and fastness (trans R.I.Altman)

There are a few words you might recognize – 'grimma' is 'grim', 'moras' is 'moorland' and 'fen' is 'fen'. A 'march-riever' is someone who sneaks over a border to steal from and harass the inhabitants. Some words make sense if you think about them a little more – 'gaest' is an evil spirit or monster, and our word 'ghost' is its descendent. Other words you might guess from your knowledge of foreign languages – 'haten' does not mean 'hate', but 'called' or 'named', like the German 'heissen'.

The Changing Language

So why did the language change? There are a number of reasons, but a major factor was the Norman invasion of Britain in 1066. The Normans spoke an early form of French, which quickly became the 'official' language of England, overtaking the native language for governmental administration and legal matters. But the Normans and the English had to communicate somehow, and their struggles to speak changed the English language.

New French vocabulary was introduced to Old English, and the English grammar gradually became simplified as the Normans struggled with it. (As well as French and English, Latin was also an important language in the Middle Ages. It was used for some government business, for education and during religious worship in church.)

Gradually Old English turned into the Middle English that Chaucer writes in – but still the official language of England was French! It was only in 1362, during Chaucer's lifetime, that English was used at the opening of Parliament for the first time. During the same year a law called the 'Statute of Pleading' was passed, making English the official language of the courts and in Parliament (and even then, it took a while to get everyone to speak English). In 1399, King Henry IV became the first king of England since the Norman Conquest whose mother tongue was English.

However, English was a still a language of low status – especially when it came to writing poetry and literature. During the 14th century, the Italians and French were experiencing an explosion of creativity – great poets like Dante, Petrach and Boccaccio were writing in entirely new ways. But English had no such great writers.

This was where Chaucer made a difference – he took the language of the man in the street and turned it into a series of masterpieces. Chaucer proved that poetry written in English could be every bit as good as books in Latin or French.

Chaucer's Middle English and Regional Dialects

To see how different Middle English is from Old English, take a look at this passage from Chaucer's famous book The Canterbury Tales. Unlike Beowulf, you shouldn't have any problems understanding it, even though it still looks a bit odd compared with Modern English.

A Knight there was, and that a worthy man,
That fro the tyme that he first bigan
To riden out, he loved chivalrie,
Trouthe and honour, fredom and curteisie.

This is the description of the Knight, one of the group of pilgrims described in The Canterbury Tales; later we'll look at this passage more closely as we work through some ways of understanding Middle English. But if you compare this with the extract from Beowulf, you can see how English had changed between the 11th and the 14th centuries.

However, this is only one Middle English dialect; The Canterbury Tales were written in the English spoken by Londoners. In fourteenth-century England, it was far more difficult to travel around than it was today, since the only way to travel was by horse, boat, or on foot. With little contact between people from different regions, regional dialects became noticeably different. Someone from the North, for example, might find a Londoner almost incomprehensible. Caxton, the man who brought the printing press to Britian, tells a famous story about a man trying to buy eggs:

In my days it happened that certain merchants were in a ship in Thames for to have sailed over the sea into Zeland, and for lack of wind they tarried atte foreland, and went to land for to refresh them. And on of them named Sheffield, a mercer, in-to an house and asked for meat, and especially he asked after eggs. And the good wife answered, that she could speak no French. And the merchant was angry, for he also could speak no French, but would have eggs, and she undestood him not. And then at last another said that he would have eyren? Then the good wife said that she undestood him well. Lo, what should a man in these days now write, eggs or Eiern, certainly it is hard to please every man, by cause of diversity and change of language.

The English we speak today developed from the English that was spoken in London, so although we can understand most of Chaucer's language, Middle English from the north is much more difficult. Try taking a look at these lines (again, you'll see þ, which is 'th', so 'þe' is spelt 'the' today; ' is a sort of 'yuh' sound, like the 'gh' in 'night')

Þis kyng lay at Camylot vpon Krystmasse
With mony luflych lorde, ledez of þe best,
Rekenly of þe Rounde Table alle þo rich breþer,
With rych reuel ory't and rechles merþes.

The words 'Camylot' and the 'Rounde Table' should give you a clue as to this poem. These lines are taken from Sir Gawain and the Green Knight, written at about the same time as The Canterbury Tales, but by an author whose name is now forgotten. Here's a translation into modern English:

King Arthur lay at Camelot upon a Christmas-tide, with many a gallant lord and lovely lady, and all the noble brotherhood of the Round Table. There they held rich revels with merry talk and jokes.

As you can see, the language of Gawain is half-way between Old English and Chaucer's English. The other thing you'll notice is that Chaucer writes rhyming poetry, as they did in Europe, whereas the Gawain poet uses alliteration, in the old English tradition that we also saw in Beowulf.

We can get some idea of how important this different language was from Chaucer's own words - Chaucer ends his long poem Troilus and Criseyde (about the Trojan war) with a plea that his poem will be understood in different parts of Britian.

And for ther is so gret diversite [great diversity]

In English and in writyng of oure tonge, [tongue – i.e. language]

So prey I God that non myswrite thee, [miswrite – i.e. copy it out wrongly]

Ne thee mysmetre for defaute of tonge; [mismetre – i.e. get the rhythm wrong because their language isn't very good]

And red whereso thow be, or elles songe, [red = read; elles = else; songe = sung]

That thow be understonde, God I beseche! [understonde = understool]

Of course, the English language has continued to change since Chaucer's day - for example, Shakespeare's English is quite different from Chaucer's - and is still changing now. Until just a few years ago, 'C U L8R' was just a string of letters and numbers, but now most people know what it means!

Reading Middle English - Woring Out the Meaning

Although Middle English can look quite tricky to start with, it isn't difficult to work out what it means. In this section we'll take a look at an example of Chaucer's English, taken from the Prologue to *The Canterbury Tales,* and suggest some ways in which you can work through it to gain a clearer understanding of the language.

A knyght ther was, and that a worthy man,
That fro the tyme that he first bigan
To riden out, he loved chivalrie,
Trouthe and honour, fredom and curteisie.
Ful worthy was he in his lordes were,
And therto hadde he riden, no man ferre,
As wel in cristendom as in hethenesse,
And evere honoured for his worthynesse.

As you look at this, you will realise that you already recognise many of the words - most of the first line, for example, is made up of modern words, and you'll also recognise 'first', 'loved' and 'honour'. Some other words look quite familiar, although the spelling isn't what you expect - 'knyght', for example, instead of 'knight', and 'fredom' instead of 'freedom'. But there are some words that look a bit trickier - 'bigan', 'riden' and 'trouthe', perhaps. So how can you work out what they mean?

Working out the Meaning - reading Aloud

One of the best ways to understand Middle English is to try reading it aloud. Often a word will look strange, but will sound perfectly normal when spoken. So if you read these eight lines out, you'll find that 'bigan' actually sounds like the modern English word 'began' - and in fact it is exactly the same word, just spelled differently.

Working out the Meaning - change the Spelling

This leads us to another way to work out Middle English. Often a Middle English word is very similar to a modern English word, but the spelling is different. So try thinking about the spelling - can you change or remove some letters from the Middle English word to make it more like modern English? The word 'trouthe' looks hard - but if you take away the 'o' and the 'e' it becomes 'truth'.

Working out the Meaning - context

There are also some Middle English words which don't really have a modern English equivalent - for example, 'cristendom' and 'hethenesse'. When you look at the first of these words you might notice that it begins with 'crist', which looks very much like 'Christ', and in fact 'cristendom' is an old-fashioned word meaning 'the countries where people are Christians'. This may help to provide some context for the other word, 'hethenesse'. The poem says that the knight had 'riden' (ridden on horseback) 'As wel in cristendom as in hethenesse'. This seems to suggest that 'cristendom' and 'hethenesse' are contrasted in some way; are they opposites, perhaps? Could 'hethenesse' be the countries where people are *not* Christians? In fact, this is absolutely correct, and if you look again at the word, you may now think that 'hethen' looks like the modern word 'heathen'.

Working out the Meaning - tricky Words

Just occasionally there will be Middle English words that you can't work out at all, because the word has no modern English equivalent. In these cases you will need to use some other way of finding out the meaning. In books of Chaucer's poetry there is often a mini-dictionary or glossary in the back; this can help out with tricky words. If this doesn't help, you will need to look at a specialist dictionary of Middle English words, like the *Middle English Dictionary.* You can access this on the Internet at http://ets.umdl.umich.edu/m/med/ - the easiest way to use it is to click on 'Lookups' and then type in the word. There are also some other websites with Chaucer glossaries and dictionaries - see the Web Links and Resources section below.

Some other Points

References to other Texts, etc

Chaucer's poetry can seem difficult because he sometimes mentions the names of people or places you haven't heard of. Often these are people from Greek mythology, or from history or literature. It doesn't always matter if you don't know exactly who he's talking about; you can usually enjoy the poetry anyway. In some cases, however, it can make the poem more enjoyable if you find out more about the person he mentions. The poem may have some notes attached to it, explaining - or you can do a search on the Internet.

The Order of Words

Chaucer often changes the usual order of words around, just as modern poets sometimes do. For example, he says 'A knyght ther was' instead of 'There was a knight'. Sometimes he uses very long sentences, spread over several lines, which can make it tricky to work out exactly what he's saying. But there's no need to worry; you can usually get the 'gist' of it quite easily, and it doesn't take very long to get used to unravelling Chaucer's long sentences.

Double Negatives

Your teachers or parents may have told you that you shouldn't use the 'double negative'; in other words, you shouldn't say, for example, 'I don't want nothing', because 'don't' and 'nothing' are both negatives. They may have told you that these two negatives cancel each other out, making a positive - so 'I don't want nothing' really means 'I do want something'. This may be true as far as modern English is concerned, but in medieval times the opposite was true; poets and other writers used double negatives all the time to add emphasis to a negative statement. In fact, sometimes they used a triple negative, when they wanted to make a point really strongly! E.g. 'He nevere yet no vileynye ne sayde' means 'he very definitely never said anything bad at all'.

The Pronunciation of Chaucer's Middle English

English has never had a prettier sound than it had — apparently — in Chaucer's day, and every serious student of Chaucer's poetry will eventually want to master the fine details of its phonology. There are various readily available books which treat, among other things, pronunciation of Chaucer's dialect. For introductory purposes, the best are (for American readers) the standard American editions of Chaucer's work, that is, especially, the editions of F.N. Robinson, D.W. Robertson, Jr., and Albert C. Baugh. Another excellent, very brief introduction is that of E. Talbot Donaldson in the Norton Anthology of English Literature.

In all such introductions one repeatedly encounters such phrases as "It is important to maintain the distinction between such-and-such and so-and-so," for instance between "open o," as in broth (or aw, shucks), and "close o," as in note. Nothing could be truer, but when one listens to distinguished Chaucerians deliver scholarly papers at medieval conventions, or when one listens to the records made by great Chaucerians past and present, one discovers surprising differences of opinion about how things ought to be pronounced. For instance, some specialists make consonants sound much like consonants in modern English, except clearer, more precise, while other specialists speak consonants as they would in Danish or, God help us, German. For the beginner there's a valuable lesson in this: Chaucer's Middle English is relatively easy to fake. What follows here are some notes on how to fake it convincingly, so that one gets pretty clearly the sound of Chaucer's verse, making people who know the correct pronunciation believe momentarily that perhaps they've learned it wrong.

1. Read aloud or recite with authority, exactly as when speaking Hungarian — if you know no Hungarian — you speak with conviction and easy familiarity. This easy authority, however fake, gets the tone of the language, its warmth and, loosely, outgoing character — not pushy like low-class German, not jaundiced or intimate-but-weary, like modern French, and not, above all, slurred to a mumble, like modern American. Make Middle English open-hearted, like Mark Twain's jokes.

2. Pronounce the vowels like vowels in modern European languages, especially French, German, or Italian (but resist the temptation to drag in the consonant sounds of those languages). Thus a is ah, as in "Ah, so there you are!"; e is ay, as in "Say there!"; I is ee, as in "Gee, it's Marie!"; o is Oh as in "O!"; and u is, for the most part, oo, as in "Who?" That is, the vowels, a e I o u are, basically, ah ey ee oh ooh. Make them long or short exactly as you would in modern English. To be extra expressive, add the following complications:

3. Distinguish between "close e" (e with the throat closed, like the sound of an oboe) and "open e" (e wide-throated, like the sound of a clarinet); that is, distinguish between the tight e of "eek" or meet, and the easy, breathy e of there when there is pronounced with a touch of Irish, to rhyme with air. (In Middle English, any e followed by r rhymes with air.) For

purposes of faking it is fair to say that if a word is spelled ea in modern English (as in sea or beast), it had and open e in Middle English; if spelled ee in modern English (as in see or sleet), it was a close e for Chaucer. And the same goes for close and open o; words now pronounced like note or stone were open for Chaucer, like the o in our word cloth; words now pronounced like mood or good (modern o either long or short) were close o for Chaucer, like the o in our so. If this is too confusing, try to follow, in general, the pronunciation of the Cisco Kid: "Boot hombray, thees es nut yoor pesstol." For the sound al, very common in Chaucer, say ahl, as in "Ah'll be seeing you."

4. Final e: Many words in Chaucer have a pronounced final e, as in knowe, fewe, etc. . . . Pronounce the e like the a in sofa. In a line of verse, this e is silent if the word which follows it begins with a vowel but pronounced if the word which follows it begins with a consonant (except h and sometimes w or y). So that in the line, "That, by my trouthe, I take no kepe," the final e in trouthe is silent, the final e in take pronounced.
5. Diphthongs (that is, two vowels together, as in cause) can be a problem for the faker. For instance, for Chaucer fewe and newe are not quite rhymes. Short of learning Anglo-Saxon (which is behind the annoyance) or picking up the sounds by ear through listening to recordings, the faker can only depend on these two principles: (a) that au and aw are always ow, as in cow so that cause = cowzuh, drawe = drowwuh, daunger = downjer; and (b) when pronouncing any other diphthong, take the Middle English sounds of the words separately and squeeze them together, so that iu becomes ee + oo = yew. This works about have the time, which is good odds.
6. As for consonants, the rule is simple, pronounce every one of them except when you're positive the

word is French (one can swallow the g in sign, for instance) or when the consonant is an initial h. With g or gg, pronounce the same word in modern English (e.g., juggen, modern judge, has the dj, but frogges, modern frogs, has the sound gg).

7. For consonant clusters like th or gh, all you really need is this: Like any consonant or consonant cluster that can be either voiced or unvoiced (z is voiced, sss is unvoiced), the th tends to be unvoiced at the beginning and ends of words but voiced in the middle (between vowels). (F in Middle English is always unvoiced, v always voiced.) Thus that is unvoiced (like the th in thin) but bathed is voiced (like the the in then). Similarly, s is unvoiced (or hissed) in saw and was but voiced in resoun (ray-zoon). The gh sound is slightly but not excessively German, as in ich or nach; and ch, even in French words like chivalrie, is almost always pronounced as in church.

8. Some words in Middle English are accented in peculiar places — for example, coráge or solémpnely — and some can be accented as the poet pleases, as in náture and natúre. Take the pronunciation that makes the rhythm feel right, not, of course, that every line has to be rigidly iambic. In most doubtful cases, no one can really prove you wrong. For instance one may read either, "For thére is phisícién but oón," or, "For there is phisícién but oón," or even, "For thére is phisicién but oón" (slightly hovering over the first two syllables of phisicien) and the solemnest phonologiest can only muse that he himself would read it somewhat differently. There are of course downright ridiculous readings, but it's comforting to notice that most of them have been urged, from time to time, by reputable scholars.

9. One last word about e's. Don't say nay for nuh (as in "I ne have," that is, "I haven't"), thay for thuh (as in "the cat"). Say thay when Middle English the

means the pronoun thee (as in "thee, thou cat"). And watch for occasional long e's at the ends of words, as in beaute (bay-oh-tay, i.e., "beauty").

If you do all this, or some of it, and at the same time put across the sense of the lines you read, only pedants and people of mean spirit will notice your errors. You will, of course, make errors. Practice, both alone and with sympathetic friends; list to records; if you feel desperate, take a good course and, thereafter, blame your teacher.

Chapter 8

Introduction: The Canterbury Tales

The Canterbury Tales is a collection of stories written by Geoffrey Chaucer in the 14th century (two of them in prose, the rest in verse). The tales, some of which are originals and others not, are contained inside a frame tale and told by a collection of pilgrims on a pilgrimage from Southwark to Canterbury to visit the shrine of Saint Thomas Becket at Canterbury Cathedral. *The Canterbury Tales* are written in Middle English. Although the tales are considered to be his magnum opus, some believe the structure of the tales are indebted to the works of *The Decameron,* which Chaucer is said to have read on an earlier visit to Italy.

The Prologue and Individual Tales

The characters, introduced in the General Prologue of the book, tell tales of great cultural relevance. The first part of the prologue begins with "Whan that Aprill with his shoures soote" indicating the start of spring and the end of a brutal winter. The themes of the tales vary, and include topics such as courtly love, treachery, and avarice. The genres also vary, and include romance, Breton lai, sermon, beast fable, and fabliaux. Though there is an overall frame, there is no single poetic structure to the work; Chaucer utilizes a variety of rhyme schemes and metrical patterns, and there are also two prose tales. The Tales include some of the tales are serious and others comical. Religious malpractice is a major theme as well as focusing on the division of the three estates. Most of the tales are interlinked with similar themes running through them and some are told in retaliation for other tales in the form of an argument. The work is incomplete, as it was originally intended that each character would tell four tales, two on the way to Canterbury and two on the return journey. This would have meant a possible one hundred and twenty tales which would have dwarfed the twenty-four tales actually written.

People have sought political overtones within the tales, particularly as Chaucer himself was a significant courtier and political figure at the time, close to the corridors of power. There are many hints at contemporary events, and the theme of marriage common in the tales has been presumed to refer to several different marriages, most often those of John of Gaunt. Aside from Chaucer himself, Harry Bailly of the Tabard Inn was a real person, and it is considered quite likely that the cook was Roger Knight de Ware, a contemporary London cook.

The Complete Work

The work began some time in the 1380s but Chaucer stopped working on it in the late 1390s. It was not written down fully conceived: it seems to have had many revisions with the addition of new tales at various times. The plan for one hundred and twenty tales is from the general prologue. It is announced by Harry Bailey, the host, that there will be four tales each (two on the way to Canterbury, two on the way back to the tavern). This is not necessarily the opinion of Chaucer himself, who appears as the only character to tell more than one tale. It has been suggested that the unfinished state was deliberate on Chaucer's part. It had a total of 646 pages!

The structure of *The Canterbury Tales* is a frame narrative and easy to find in other contemporary works, such as *The Book of Good Love* by Juan Ruiz and Boccaccio's *Decameron*, which may have been one of Chaucer's main sources of inspiration. Chaucer indeed adapted several of Boccaccio's stories to put in the mouths of his own pilgrims, but what sets Chaucer's work apart from his contemporaries' is his characters. Compared to Boccaccio's main characters - seven women and three men, all young, fresh and well-to-do, and given Classical names - the characters in Chaucer are of extremely varied stock, including representatives of most of the branches of the middle classes at that time. Not only are the participants very different, but they tell very different types of tales, with their personalities showing through both in their choices of tales and in the way they tell them.

The idea of a pilgrimage appears to have been mainly a useful device to get such a diverse collection of people together for literary purposes. In fact, the Monk would probably not be allowed to undertake the pilgrimageand some of the other characters would be unlikely ever to want to attend. Also all of the pilgrims ride horses, so there is no suggestion of them suffering for their religion. None of the popular shrines along the way are visited and there is no suggestion that anyone attends mass, so that it seems much more like a tourist's jaunt.

Chaucer does not pay much attention to the progress of the trip. He hints that the tales take several days but he does not detail any overnight stays. Although the journey could be done in one day this speed would make telling tales difficult and three to four days was the usual duration for such pilgrimages. The 18th of April is mentioned in the tales and Walter William Skeat, a 19th century editor, determined 17 April 1387 as the probable first day of the tales.

Scholars divide the tales into ten fragments. The tales that make up a fragment are directly connected, usually with one character speaking to and handing over to another character, but there is no connection between most of the other fragments. This means that there are several possible permutations for the order of the fragments and consequently the tales themselves. The above listing is perhaps the most common in modern times, with the fragments numbered I-X, but an alternative order lists them A-G, with the tales from the Physician's until the Nun's Priest's placed before the Wife of Bath's. The exception to the independence between fragments are the last two. The Manciple's tale is the last tale in IX but fragment X starts with the Parson's prologue by saying that the Manciple had finished his tale. The reason that they are kept as two different fragments is that the Manciple starts his short tale in the morning but the Parson's tale is told at four in the afternoon. It is assumed that Chaucer would have amended his manuscript or inserted more tales to fill the time.

Significance

It is sometimes argued that the greatest contribution that this work made to English literature was in popularising the literary use of the vernacular, English, rather than French or Latin. English had, however, been used as a literary language for centuries before Chaucer's life, and several of Chaucer's contemporaries—John Gower, William Langland, and the Pearl Poet—also wrote major literary works in English. It is unclear to what extent Chaucer was responsible for starting a trend rather than simply being part of it. It is interesting to note that, although Chaucer had a powerful influence in poetic and artistic terms, which can be seen in the great number of forgeries and mistaken attributions (such as The Flower and the Leaf which was translated by John Dryden), modern English spelling and orthography owes much more to the innovations made by the Court of Chancery in the decades during and after his lifetime.

In 2004, Professor Linne Mooney was able to identify the scrivener who worked for Chaucer as an Adam Pinkhurst. Mooney, then a professor at the University of Maine and a visiting fellow at Corpus Christi College, Cambridge, was able to match Pinkhurst's signature, on an oath he signed, to his lettering on a copy of *The Canterbury Tales* that was transcribed from Chaucer's working copy.

The Canterbury Tales can also tell modern readers much about "the occult" during Chaucer's time, especially in regards to astrology and the astrological lore prevalent during Chaucer's era. There are hundreds if not thousands of astrological allusions found in this work; some are quite overt while others are more subtle in nature.

While some readers look to interpret the characters of "The Canterbury Tales" as historical figures, other readers choose to interpret its significance in less literal terms. After analysis of his diction and historical context, his work appears to develop a critique against society during his lifetime. Within a number of his descriptions, his comments can appear complimentary in nature, but through clever language, the statements are ultimately critical of the pilgrim's actions. It is unclear whether Chaucer would intend for the reader to link his characters with actual persons. Instead, it appears that Chaucer creates fictional characters to be general representations of people in such fields of work. With an understanding of medieval society, one can detect subtle satire at work.

Antisemitism

Edward I of England expelled all Jews from England in 1290, but antisemitism did not disappear in the absence of Jews. In 1385, Geoffrey Chaucer published his *Canterbury Tales* which included an account of Jews murdering a deeply pious and innocent Christian boy ('The Prioress's Tale'). This blood libel became a part of English literary tradition.[2] Jeremy Cohen contends in this regard: "from Chaucer to Margery Kempe, from the cycles of Corpus Christi Day miracle plays to the poetry of the seventeenth century, European literature retained its picture of the Jewish Christ killer, who inflicted violence on that which was most sacred to the culture and society of Western Christianity."

The Pilgrims' Route and Real Locations

The City of Canterbury has a museum dedicated to *The Canterbury Tales*.

The postulated return journey has intrigued many and continuations have been written as well, often to the horror or (occasional) delight of Chaucerians everywhere, as tales written for the characters who are mentioned but not given a chance to speak. The *Tale of Beryn* is a story by an anonymous author within a 15th century manuscript of the work. The tales are rearranged and there are some interludes in Canterbury, which they had finally reached, and Beryn is the first tale on the return journey, told by the Merchant. John Lydgate's *Siege of Thebes* is also a depiction of the return journey but the tales themselves are actually prequels to the tale of classical origin told by the Knight in Chaucer's work.

Influences

The title of the work has become an everyday phrase and been variously adapted and adopted; for example Margaret Atwood's *The Handmaid's Tale*, and others. Recently an animated version of some of the tales has been produced for British television. As well as versions with Modern English dialogue, there have been versions in the original Middle English and Welsh.

Many literary works (both fiction and non-fiction alike) have used a similar frame narrative to the *Canterbury Tales* as an homage. Science Fiction writer Dan Simmons wrote his Hugo Award winning novel *Hyperion* based around an extra-planetary group of pilgrims. Evolutionary biologist Richard Dawkins used *The Canterbury Tales* as a structure for his 2004 non-fiction book about evolution - *The Ancestor's Tale: A Pilgrimage to the Dawn of Evolution*. His animal pilgrims are on their way to find the common ancestor, each telling a tale about evolution.

Stage and Film Adaptations

The Two Noble Kinsmen, by William Shakespeare and John Fletcher, a retelling of The Knight's Tale, was first published in 1613 or 1614 and published in 1634.

- 1944, A Canterbury Tale, a film jointly written and directed by Michael Powell and Emeric Pressburger, is based on the narrative frame of Chaucer's tales - that is, a group of strangers, each with his or her own story and in need of some kind of redemption, making their way to Canterbury together. The movie opens with a scene showing a group of medieval pilgrims journeying by foot and on horseback through the Kentish countryside as a narrator speaks the opening lines of the Tales' prologue. This scene makes a now-famous transition to the time of World War 2. The film's story takes place in an imaginary town in Kent and ends with the main characters arriving at Canterbury Cathedral, bells pealing and Chaucer's words again resounding. A Canterbury Tale is recognized as one of the Powell-Pressburger team's most poetic and artful films. It was produced as wartime propaganda, using Chaucer's poetry, referring to the famous pilgrimage, and offering stirring photography of Kent to remind the public of what made Britain so special and worth fighting for. One scene in the film centers on a local historian lecturing his audience of British soldiers about the pilgrims of Chaucer's time and the vibrant history of England.

- Pasolini
- 1961, Erik Chisholm completed his opera, *The Canterbury Tales*. The opera is in three acts: The Wyf of Bath's Tale, The Pardoner's Tale and The Nun's Priest's Tale.
- 2004, BBC, modern re-tellings of selected tales.
- 2005, Royal Shakespeare Company, translation by Mike Poulton
- 2001, *A Knight's Tale* took its name from "The Knight's Tale," with a fictionalized Chaucer portrayed as a friend to the knight. At one point Chaucer declares he will use his verse to vilify two church officials who cheated him; they are a summoner and a pardoner. However the film actually has very little to do with the tale. In a deleted scene included on the DVD release, Chaucer is also seen with his wife, who comments that his new companions are better than the pilgrims he befriended earlier.

Chapter 9

List of Characters: The Canterbury Tales

CHARACTER LIST

The Host

He is the proprietor of the Tabard Inn where the pilgrims to Canterbury stay and travels with them on their journey. It is the Host who devised the scheme of the tales, proposing that each tell two tales on the way to Canterbury, and he frequently mediates arguments between pilgrims and suggests who shall tell the next story.

The Knight

A noble fighter who served in the Crusades, he travels with his son, the Squire. The Knight tells the first tale, a romantic tale of a love triangle between two knights and a woman they both love.

The Squire

A 'lusty bachelor' of twenty, the Squire is the son of the Knight. He tells an incomplete tale concerning the gifts that a mysterious knight brings to the court of Tartary.

The Knight's Yeoman

The Yeoman is the second servant who travels with the Knight. He does not tell a tale.

The Prioress

A delicate, sentimental woman, the Prioress weeps over any small tragedy such as the death of a mouse. She attempts to appear refined, but her refinement is superficial. Her tale concerns the murder of a small child at the hands of Jews who loathe the child for singing about the Virgin Mary.

The Second Nun

The secretary to the Prioress, the Second Nun tells as her tale the biography of Saint Cecilia.

The Monk

A robust and masculine man, the Monk travels with the Prioress and Second Nun. He tells the tale of a hen and her 'husband,' a rooster who prophesies misfortune.

The Friar (Hubert)

He is an immoral man concerned largely with profit rather than turning men away from sin. His tale is an attack on the wickedness of summoners.

The Merchant

He is an arrogant man obsessed with profit margins. His story is a comic tale concerning an elderly blind man who takes a young wife who proves unfaithful.

The Clerk

The Clerk is a student at Oxford, and his lack of an actual profession leaves him impoverished. Although educated, his intellectual pursuits have left him virtually unemployable. He tells a tale of the humble Griselde, who marries a man of high status who cruelly tests her devotion to him.

The Man of Law

The lawyer tells a religiously inspired tale concerning Constance, a woman who suffers a number of tragedies but is at each turn saved by her devotion to her Christian beliefs.

The Franklin

He travels with the Man of Law. The Franklin is a man who takes delight in all simple pleasures, most prominently culinary ones. His story is that of a woman who promises to have an affair with a man if he can do something she deems impossible that would nevertheless save her husband.

The Weaver

One of the five guildsmen who travel with the pilgrims to Canterbury, he does not tell a tale.

The Dyer

One of the five guildsmen who travel with the pilgrims to Canterbury, he does not tell a tale.

The Carpenter

One of the five guildsmen who travel with the pilgrims to Canterbury, he does not tell a tale.

The Tapestry-Maker

One of the five guildsmen who travel with the pilgrims to Canterbury, he does not tell a tale.

The Haberdasher

One of the five guildsmen who travel with the pilgrims to Canterbury, he does not tell a tale.

The Cook

A lewd and vulgar man, the Cook often engages in violent and contentious behaviour. He tells a tale that appears to be a fabliau. However, this tale does not exist in a completed form.

The Shipman

He tells the tale of a woman who agrees to have an affair with a monk who will pay her so that she can repay a debt to her husband, but this monk borrows this money from the husband himself.

The Physician

The Physician tells a tale about a father who, in order to protect his daughter from scoundrels who contrive to rape her, murders his daughter.

The Wife of Bath

The most ostentatious of the travelers, the Wife of Bath has been married five times and is currently searching for another man to marry. The Wife of Bath is opinionated and boisterous, and her tale, which centers around the question "what do women want?," promotes her view that women wish to have authority over men.

The Parson

The Parson is a man devoted to his congregation, decent and principled. His tale is a long dissertation on the definition of sin and its various forms.

The Miller

A large man with an imposing physique, the Miller is rude and contemptuous of his fellow travelers. His tale is a comic story of a devious student who contrives to have an affair with the wife of a dimwitted carpenter.

The Manciple

Also trained in the law, the Manciple tells a fable that attributes the dark appearance and unpleasant sound of crows to the actions of a white crow who told the god Phoebus of his wife's infidelity.

The Reeve

A slender man with a fiery temper, he tells a tale in response to the Miller's Tale. His tale concerns a villainous Miller who is humiliated by two Oxford students.

The Summoner

The profession of the summoner is to issue summons for people to appear in front of the Church court, and in this the

Summoner is quite unfair. He tells a tale in response to the Friar's diatribe against summoners that parodies the Friar's profession.

The Pardoner

An effeminate and shamelessly immoral man, the Pardoner is intensely self-loathing yet devoted to his task of defrauding people of their money by making them believe that they have sinned and need to buy pardons. His tale is an allegory about three rioters who find death through their avarice. The Pardoner uses this tale as an attempt to sell false relics to the travelers.

The Canon

A mysterious and threatening figure, he and his Yeoman are not original travelers with the pilgrims to Canterbury. They seek out the party when they learn about the tales that they have been telling. When the Canon's Yeoman reveals too much about his master's profession, the Canon suddenly disappears.

The Canon's Yeoman

The assistant to the Canon, he speaks openly about his master's tricks as an alchemist, prompting the Canon to leave the pilgrims. The Yeoman then admits that he regrets the deceptions of his master, and tells a tale that details the methods of a canon's fraud.

Arcite

Theban knight who is imprisoned in Athens but released on the intervention of his friend Pirithous, he and his friend Palamon both fall in love with Emelye. He prays to Mars for aid in his duel with Palamon for Emelye, and although he wins the battle, he suddenly is killed in an earthquake upon his victory.

Palamon

Theban knight who is imprisoned in Athens. Both he and Arcite fall in love with Emelye. Before the duel for her hand in marriage, Palamon prays to Venus, the goddess of love, to win Emelye as a wife. Although he loses the battle, he wins Emelye as a wife when Arcite dies.

Emelye

The sister of Hippolyta, she is a pawn within the struggle between Arcite and Palamon, both who have fallen in love with her. Although she wishes to remain chaste in honour of the goddess, Diana, she accepts that she must marry one of the two knights.

Theseus

The King of Athens, he wages war upon Thebes in response to the injustice of the Theban king, and imprisons Arcite and Palamon. He sets the rules and regulations of their duel for Emelye.

Hippolyta

The Queen of Scythia, she is the husband of Theseus, King of Athens, and the sister of Emelye.

Pirithous

A prince and childhood friend of Theseus, he intervenes to have Arcite released from prison on the condition that he never return to Athens.

Lycurgus

The king of Thrace, he fights with Palamon during his duel with Arcite.

Emetreus

The king of India, he fights with Arcite during his duel with Palamon.

John

An oafish carpenter, he is an older man who marries the much younger Alison. He foolishly believes Nicholas' prediction that a second great flood is coming, and hides in a kneading bucket on his roof in preparation for it.

Alison

The crafty wife of John the carpenter, Alison is much younger than her husband. She has an affair with Nicholas, a boarder who stays with her and her husband.

Nicholas

An Oxford student who boards with John and Alison, Nicholas claims to study astronomy. He has an affair with Alison and conspires to have a day of privacy with her, but proves himself less crafty than he believes when he falls prey to Absolon's prank.

Absolon

A delicate, courtly lover who pursues Alison, he is a skilled musician and an unabashed romantic. He suffers humiliation at the hands of Alison, but gets revenge on Nicholas.

Symkyn

A vulgar, dishonest and foolish miller, Symkyn repeatedly cheats his customers out of grain. He receives his comeuppance when two Cambridge students that he has cheated seduce his wife and daughter then steal their grain back from him.

Aleyn

A Cambridge student who seduces the miller's daughter, Molly, when he and John stay at the miller's house.

John (2)

A Cambridge student who seduces the miller's wife when he and Aleyn stay at the Miller's house.

Molly

The daughter of the Miller, she is a somewhat unattractive young woman, yet Aleyn nevertheless seduces her when the two students stay at the miller's home.

Constance

The daughter of the Roman emperor, she is given to be married to the Sultan of Syria after he agrees to convert to Christianity, but when his mother opposes this, she narrowly escapes an assassination attempt and ends up in England, where she marries King Alla and, escaping treachery once more, is sent back to Rome. She is a devoted Christian whose faith aids her throughout all of her travails.

The Sultan

The King of Syria, he agrees to convert to Christianity to marry Constance, but his actions infuriate his mother, who has him assassinated.

The Sultana

Villainous mother of the Sultan, she refuses to convert from Islam on the orders of her son and plots his assassination.

Dame Hermengild

The wife of the Warden of the Northumberland region where Constance lands in England, she converts to Christianity through the influence of Constance. A devious knight murders her in an attempt to frame Constance.

The Warden

The husband of Dame Hermengild, he watches over the castle of Northumberland while King Alla is at war. He converts to Christianity along with his wife.

King Alla

The English king of Northumberland, he marries Constance but is separated from her because of the machinations of his mother, Lady Donegild.

Lady Donegild

The treacherous mother of King Alla, she contrives to have Constance and her child banished from England. King Alla murders her for her evil actions.

Mauritius

The son of King Alla and Constance, he becomes the emperor of Rome when Constance's father realises his royal lineage.

Jankin

The fifth husband of the Wife of Bath, he was much younger than she and prone to reading misogynist religious texts that offended his wife. When he hurt her out of anger, he realised his error and submitted to her authority, after which he and his wife had a perfectly happy marriage.

The Knight (2)

After raping a young woman, the knight is sentenced to death, but spared by the queen, who decides that the knight will receive mercy if he can answer the question "what do women want?"

The Old Woman

This elderly woman tells the Knight what women really desire on the condition that he will marry her. When he grants her the authority in marriage, the old woman transforms into a beautiful young woman.

The Summoner (2)

The summoner, who is given no proper name, is a typical representation of his profession, according to the Friar. He meets the devil and shares trade secrets, and is cast into hell for his sinful behaviour.

Satan:

Introducing himself as a yeoman, he and the summoner become compatriots until he finally casts the summoner into hell.

The Friar

This boorish friar is rude and presumptuous, oblivious to the conditions of Thomas and his wife, who take him in as a boarder. Although ostensibly polite and refined, the friar callously begs Thomas for money.

Thomas

Owner of a home where the Friar stays, his infant child had recently died and he himself has taken ill. When the Friar begs him for money, Thomas pays him with the 'gift' of a fart.

Griselde

A woman of low status, she marries Walter, the marquis of Saluzzo, but is subjected to a number of trials that her husband devises to prove her worth. She handles each of these trials honourably, proving herself dedicated and steadfast in the face of any tragedy.

Walter

The marquis of Saluzzo, he is a dedicated bachelor until the people of his region insist that he takes a wife. When he marries Griselde, he subjects her to a number of trials meant to prove her worth, each of them cruel and heartless.

Janicula

The father of Griselde. She returns to him after she has been cast out of her home by Walter.

January

A wealthy knight and perpetual bachelor, at the age of sixty this blind man decides to take a young wife. When he marries May, he bores her with his insistent sexual desire, leading her to have an affair. He regains his sight when Pluto and Proserpina find May having sex with Damian in his presence.

May

The young wife of January, she soon tires of his persistent and monotonous sexual desire and has an affair with January's squire, Damian. When January regains his sight and sees her engaged in a tryst with Damian, she insists that he should not believe his eyes.

Damian

January's squire, he has an affair with May.

Placebo

The brother of January, he argues with his brother against the merits of marrying a young woman at such an elderly age, yet finally relents to his brother's wishes when January insists on finding a bride.

Pluto

The king of the fairies, he and his wife stumble upon January, May and Damian when the latter two have a sexual encounter. He restores January's sight.

Proserpina

She is the wife of Pluto.

Canacee

The daughter of the King of Tartary, she receives the gift of knowing the language of animals and the healing properties of every herb.

Cambyuskan

The King of Tartary. A mysterious knight brings him a mechanical horse that can transport him anywhere across the globe.

Arviragus

A devoted knight and husband to Dorigen, he travels to Britain to engage in war, causing great grief to his wife. He gives up his wife so that she may preserve her honour.

Dorigen

The wife of Arviragus, she becomes intensely depressed when he leaves for Britain, fearing for his life. She promises to have an affair with Aurelius if he can make the rocks that obstruct the shore on which Arviragus will land disappear.

Aurelius

A young squire who falls in love with Dorigen, he pays the Orleans student to make the rocks off of the Brittany shore disappear so that Dorigen will have an affair with him, but gives her up when he realises the pain that it would cause her.

The Orleans Student

A law student skilled in creating apparitions, he contrives to have the rocks off of the Brittany shore disappear, but when Aurelius does not engage in an affair with Dorigen, he forgives Aurelius of his debt for creating the apparition.

Virginius

An honourable and well-loved knight, he murders his daughter when Appius and Claudius scheme to have her raped.

Virginia

The daughter of Virginius, her incomparable beauty leads Appius to lust after her and scheme to have her raped.

Appius

A corrupt judge who governs the town where Virginius resides, he contrives to have Claudius claim that Virginius had stolen his slave from him, and claims that that slave is Virginia. When his scheme is revealed, he is taken to jail where he commits suicide.

Claudius

A churl who schemes with Appius, he claims that Virginia is his slave and that Virginius stole her from him. When his treachery is revealed, he is banished.

The Three Rioters

Three indistinguishable troublemakers who engage in all sorts of lewd behaviour, they go on a search for Death and end up finding it in the form of gold coins.

The Old Man

An aged man who cannot die, he wishes to trade his body with a younger man. He tells the three rioters where they may find Death.

The Merchant (2)

A devoted entrepreneur, he is somewhat stingy but dedicated to his business and to thrifty behaviour. He insists that his wife repay one hundred francs that he lent her, leading her to seek the sum from Dan John.

Dan John

This monk claims to be a cousin of the merchant. He agrees to lend the merchant's life one hundred francs if she has an affair with him, then borrows the sum from the husband that she intends to repay.

The Wife

A dissatisfied wife, she claims that her husband, the merchant, is a stingy man who does not satisfy her. Displeased that her husband wants her to repay a one hundred franc debt, she agrees to an affair with Dan John for that sum. When the merchant offers that he has been repaid in his own money, she tells him that she will repay him through sex.

Melibee

A mighty and rich ruler, his enemies rape his wife and attack his daughter, leading him to strive for a war of retribution, yet his wife implores him to be merciful.

Prudence

The wife of Melibee, she is raped by his enemies, but wishes to grant them mercy.

Sophie

The young daughter of Melibee, she is left for dead by his enemies when they wound her in five places, but nevertheless barely survives.

Chanticleer

This rooster, peerless in his crowing, has seven companions, the most honoured of which is Pertelote. He dreams that he will be chased by a fox, a prophesy that comes true, and is a strong believer in this prophetic power of dreams.

Pertelote

The most favoured of Chanticleer's companions, this hen is essential his 'wife.' She dismisses his idea that dreams predict future events, claiming that his ill temper stems from stomach maladies, but her advice to find healing herbs leads to the fulfillment of his prophecy.

Cecilia

Devout elite Roman woman who dies for her adherence to Christianity.

Valerian

Eventual husband of Cecilia who converts to Christianity upon the influence of Pope Urban. He is executed for his beliefs.

Pope Urban

Christian leader who baptizes Valerian and Tibertius and claims that Cecilia is a saint.

Tibertius

The brother of Cecilia, he converts to Christianity, but is executed with Valerian for his Christian beliefs.

Almachius

Roman prefect who ordered the deaths of Cecilia, Valerian and Tibertius for their Christian beliefs.

Maximus

Roman sergeant who claimed to see the spirits of Valerian and Tibertius ascending to heaven when they are executed, prompting many to convert to Christianity.

Phoebus

Deity who, when he lived on earth, took a wife who was unfaithful to him, despite his insistence on watching her. He teaches his prized white crow to speak the language of humans.

The Crow

This beautiful white crow can speak the language of humans, having been taught by Phoebus, but when he tells Phoebus that his wife had an affair, Phoebus plucks him and curses him, condemning all crows to be forever black and harsh of voice.

Chapter 10

The Canterbury Tales: Plot Overveiw

The Canterbury Tales begins with the introduction of each of the pilgrims making their journey to Canterbury to the shrine of Thomas a Becket. These pilgrims include a Knight, his son the Squire, the Knight's Yeoman, a Prioress, a Second Nun, a Monk, a Friar, a Merchant, a Clerk, a Man of Law, a Franklin, a Weaver, a Dyer, a Carpenter, a Tapestry-Maker, a Haberdasher, a Cook, a Shipman, a Physician, a Parson, a Miller, a Manciple, a Reeve, a Summoner, a Pardoner, the Wife of Bath, and Chaucer himself. These travelers, who stop at the Tabard Inn, decide to tell stories to pass their time on the way to Canterbury. The Host of the Tabard Inn sets the rules for the tales. Each of the pilgrims will tell two stories on the way to Canterbury, and two stories on the return trip. The Host will decide the best of the tales. They decide to draw lots to see who will tell the first tale, and the Knight receives the honour.

The Knight's Tale is a tale about two knights, Arcite and Palamon, who are captured in battle and imprisoned in Athens under the order of King Theseus. While imprisoned in a tower, both see Emelye, the sister of Queen Hippolyta, and fall instantly in love with her. Both knights eventually leave prison separately: a friend of Arcite begs Theseus to release him, while Palamon later escapes. Arcite returns to the Athenian court disguised as a servant, and when Palamon escapes he suddenly finds Arcite. They fight over Emelye, but their fight is stopped when Theseus finds them. Theseus sets the rules for a duel between the two knights for Emelye's affection, and each raise an army for a battle a year from that date. Before the battle, Arcite prays to Mars for victory in battle, Emelye prays to Diana that she may marry happily, and Palamon prays to Venus to have Emelye as his wife. All three gods hear their prayers and argue over whose should get precedence, but Saturn decides to mediate. During their battle, Arcite indeed is victorious, but as soon as he is crowned victor, an earthquake occurs that kills him. Before he dies, he reconciles with Palamon and tells him that he deserves to marry Emelye. Palamon and Emelye marry.

When the Knight finishes his tale, everybody is pleased with its honourable qualities, but the drunken Miller insists that he shall tell the next tale. The Miller's Tale is a comic table in which Nicholas, a student who lives with John the carpenter and his much younger wife, Alison, begins an affair with Alison. Another man, the courtly romantic Absolon, also falls in love with Alison. Nicholas contrives to spend a day with Alison by telling John that a flood equal to Noah's flood will come soon, and the only way that he, Nicholas and Alison will survive is by staying in separate kneading tubs placed on the roof of houses, out of sight of all. While John remained in this kneading tub, Nicholas and Alison left to have sex, but were interrupted by Absolon, who demanded a kiss from Alison. She told him to close his eyes and he would receive a kiss. He did so, and she pulled down her pants so that he could kiss her nether region. The humiliated Absolon got a hot iron from a blacksmith and returned to Alison. This time, Nicholas tried the same trick, and Absolon burned him on the ass. Nicholas shouted for water, awakening John, who was asleep on the roof. He fell off the roof, hurting himself, and all were humiliated.

The pilgrims laughed heartily at this tale, but Oswald the Reeve took offense, thinking that the Miller meant to disparage older men. In response, The Reeve's Tale told the story of a dishonest Miller, Symkyn, who repeatedly cheated his clients, which included the college at Cambridge. Two Cambridge students, Aleyn and John, went to the miller to buy meal and corn, but while they were occupied Symkyn let their horses run free and stole their corn.

They were forced to stay with Symkyn for the night. That night, Aleyn seduced the miller's daughter, Molly, while John seduced the miller's wife. When Aleyn told John of his exploits, Symkyn overheard and fought with him. The miller's wife hit Symkyn over the head with a staff, knocking him unconscious, and the two students escaped with the corn that Symkyn had stolen.

The Cook's Tale was intended to follow the Reeve's Tale, but this tale only exists as an incomplete fragment of no more than fifty lines. Following this tale is the Man of Law's Tale. The Man of Law's Tale tells the story of Constance, the daughter of a Roman emperor who becomes engaged to the Sultan of Syria on the condition that he converts to Christianity. Angered by his order to convert his country from Islam, the mother of the Sultan assassinates her son and Constance barely escapes. She is sent on a ship that lands in Britain, where she is taken in by the warden of a nearby castle and his wife, Dame Hermengild. Both of them soon convert to Christianity upon meeting her. A young knight fell in love with Constance, but when she refused him, he murdered Dame Hermengild and attempted to frame Constance.

However, when King Alla made the knight swear on the Bible that Constance murdered Hermengild, his eyes burst. Constance marries King Alla and they have a son, Mauritius, who is born when Alla is at war in Scotland. Lady Donegild contrives to have Constance banished by intercepting the letters between Alla and Constance and replacing them with false ones. Constance is thus sent away again, and on her voyage her ship comes across a Roman ship. A senator returns her to Rome, where nobody realises that she is the daughter of the emperor. Eventually, King Alla makes a pilgrimage to Rome, where he meets Constance once more, and the Roman emperor realises that Mauritius is his grandson and names him heir to the throne.

The Wife of Bath begins her tale with a long dissertation on marriage in which she recounts each of her five husbands. Her first several husbands were old men whom she would hector into providing for her, using guilt and refusal of sexual favours. However, the final two husbands were younger men, more difficult to handle. The final husband, Jankin, was a twenty-year-old, half the Wife of Bath's age. He was more difficult to handle, for he refused to let the Wife of Bath dominate him and read literature that proposed that women be submissive. When she tore a page out of one of his books, Jankin struck her, causing her to be deaf in one ear. However, he felt so guilty at his actions that from that point in the marriage, he was totally submissive to her and the two remained happy.

The Wife of Bath's Tale is itself a story of marriage dynamic. It tells the tale of a knight who, as punishment for raping a young woman, is sentenced to death. However, he is spared by the queen, who will grant him freedom if he can answer the question "what do women want?" The knight cannot find a satisfactory answer until he meets an old crone, who promises to tell him the answer if he marries her. He agrees, and receives his freedom when he tells the queen that women want sovereignty over their husbands. However, the knight is dissatisfied that he must marry the old, low-born hag. She therefore tells him that he can have her as a wife either old and ugly yet submissive, or young and beautiful yet dominant. He chooses to have her as a young woman, and although she had authority in marriage the two were completely happy from that point.

The Friar asks to tell the next tale, and asks for pardon from the Summoner, for he will tell a tale that exposes the fraud of that profession. The Friar's Tale tells about a wicked summoner who, while delivering summons for the church court, comes across a traveling yeoman who eventually reveals himself to be the devil himself. The two share trade secrets, and the devil tells him that they will meet again in hell if the summoner continues to pursue his trade. The summoner visits an old woman and issues her a summons, then offers to accept a bribe as a payment to prevent her excommunication. The old woman believes that she is without sin and curses the summoner. The devil then appears and casts the summoner into hell.

The Summoner was enraged by the Friar's Tale. Before he begins his tale, he tells a short anecdote: a friar visited hell and was surprised to see that there were no other friars. The angel who was with him then lifted up Satan's tail and thousands of friars swarmed out from his ass. The Summoner's Tale is an equally vitriolic attack on friars. It tells of a friar who stays with an innkeeper and his wife and bothers them about not contributing enough to the church and not attending recently. When the innkeeper tells him that he was not recently in church because he has been ill and his infant daughter recently died, the friar attempted to placate him and then asked for donations once more. Thomas the innkeeper promised to give the friar a 'gift,' and gives him a loud fart.

The Clerk, an Oxford student who has remained quiet throughout the journey, tells the next tale on the orders of the Host. The Clerk's Tale tells about Walter, an Italian marquis who finally decides to take a wife after the people of his province object to his longtime status as a bachelor. Walter marries Griselde, a low-born but amazingly virtuous woman whom everybody lo'es. However, Walter decides to test her devotion. When their first child, a daughter, is born, Walter tells her that his people are unhappy and wish for the child's death. He takes away the child, presumably to be murdered, but instead sends it to his sister to be raised.

He does the same with their next child, a son. Finally, Walter tells Griselde that the pope demands that he divorce her. He sends her away from his home completely naked, for she had no belongings when she entered his house. Each of these tragedies Griselde accepts with great patience. Walter soon decides to make amends, and sends for his two children. He tells Griselde that he will marry again, and introduces her to the presumed bride, whom he then reveals is their daughter.

The family is reunited once more. The Clerk ends with the advice that women should strive to be as steadfast as Griselde, even if facing such adversity is unlikely and perhaps impossible.

The Merchant praises Griselde for her steadfast character, but claims that his wife is far different from the virtuous woman of the Clerk's story. He instead tells a tale of an unfaithful wife. The Merchant's Tale tells a story of January, an elderly blind knight who decides to marry a young woman, despite the objections of his brother, Placebo. January marries the young and beautiful May, who soon becomes dissatisfied with his constant sexual attention to her and decides to have an affair with his squire, Damian. When January and May are in their garden, May sneaks away to have sex with Damian. The gods Pluto and Proserpina come upon Damian and May and restore January's sight so that he may see what his wife is doing. When January sees what is occurring, May tells him not to believe his eyes, and he believes her.

The Squire tells the next tale, which is incomplete. The Squire's Tale begins with a mysterious knight arriving at the court of Tartary. This knight gives King Cambyuskan a mechanical horse that can transport him anywhere around the globe and return him within a day and gives Canacee, the daughter of Cambyuskan, a mirror that can discern honesty and a ring that allows the wearer to know the language of animals and the healing properties of all herbs. Canacee uses this ring to aid a bird who has been rejected in love, but the abruptly ends.

The Franklin's Tale that follows tells of the marriage between the knight Arviragus and his wife, Dorigen. When Arviragus travels on a military expedition, Dorigen laments his absence and fears that, when he returns, his ship will be wrecked upon the rocks off the shore. A young man, Aurelius, falls in love with her, but she refuses to return his favours. She agrees to have an affair with Aurelius only on the condition that he find a way to remove the rocks from the shore, a task she believes impossible. Aurelius pays a scholar who creates the illusion that the rocks have disappeared, while Arviragus returns. Dorigen admits to her husband the promise that she has made, and Arviragus tells her that she must fulfill that promise. He sends her to have an affair with Aurelius, but he realises the pain that it would cause Dorigen and does not make her fulfill the promise. The student in turn absolves Aurelius of his debt. The tale ends with the question: which of these men behaved most honourably?

The Physician's Tale that follows tells of Virginius, a respected Roman knight whose daughter, Virginia, was an incomparable beauty. Appius, the judge who governed his town, lusted after Virginia and collaborated with Claudius, who claimed in court that Virginia was his slave and Virginius had stolen her. Appius orders that Virginia be handed over to him. Virginius, knowing that Appius and Claudius did this in order to rape his daughter, instead gave her a choice between death or dishonour. She chooses death, and Virginius chops off his daughter's head, which he brings to Appius and Claudius. The people were so shocked by this that they realised that Appius and Claudius were frauds. Appius was jailed and committed suicide, while Claudius was banished.

The Pardoner prefaces his tale with an elaborate confession about the nature of his profession. He tells the secrets of his trade, including the sale of useless items as saints' relics, and admits that his job is not to turn people away from sin, but rather to frighten them to such a degree that they pay for pardons. The Pardoner's Tale concerns three rioters who search for Death to vanquish him. They find an old man who tells them that they may find Death under a nearby tree, but under this tree they only find a large fortune. Two of the rioters send the third into town to purchase food and drink for the night, for they intend to escape with their fortune, and while he is gone they plan to murder him. The third rioter poisons the drink, intending to take all of the money for himself. When he returns, the two rioters stab him, then drink the poisoned wine and die themselves. The three rioters thus find Death in the form of avarice. The Pardoner ends his tale with a diatribe against sin, imploring the travelers to pay him for pardons, but the Host confronts him.

The next story, The Shipman's Tale, is the story of a thrifty merchant who demands that his wife repay a one hundred franc debt that she owed him. The dissatisfied wife complained about this to Dan John, a monk who stayed with him, and he agrees to pay her the sum if she has an affair with him. She consents to this, and Dan John procures the one hundred francs by borrowing it from the merchant himself. However, the merchant realises that he has been paid with money that he had lent to the monk. The wife therefore tells him that she can repay the debt to her husband in bed.

The Prioress' Tale tells the story of a young Christian child who lived in a town in Asia that was dominated by a vicious Jewish population. When the child learned Alma redemptoris, a song praising the Virgin Mary, he traveled home from school singing this. The Jews, angry at his behaviour, took the child and slit his throat, leaving him in a cesspool to die. The boy's mother searched frantically for her son. When she found him, he was not yet dead, for the Virgin Mary had placed a grain on his tongue that would allow him to speak until it was removed. When this was removed, the boy passed on to heaven. The story ends with a lament for the young boy and a curse for the Jews who perpetrated the heinous crime.

Chaucer himself tells the next tape, The Tale of Sir Thopas, a florid and fantastical poem in rhyming couplets that serves only to annoy the other pilgrims. The Host interrupts Chaucer shortly into this tale, and tells him to tell another. Chaucer then tells The Tale of Melibee, one of the few tales that is in prose format. This tale tells about Melibee, a powerful ruler whose enemies rape his wife, Prudence, and nearly murder his daughter, Sophie. When deciding whether to declare war on his enemies, Prudence advises him to remain merciful, and they engage in a long debate over the appropriate course of action. Melibee finally gives his enemies the option: they can receive a sentence either from him or from his wife. They submit to Melibee's judgment, and he intends to disinherit and banish the perpetrators. However, he submits to his wife's plea for mercy.

The Monk's Tale is not a narrative tale at all, but instead an account of various historical and literary figures who experience a fall from grace. These include Adam, Samson, Hercules, King Pedro of Spain, Bernabo Visconti, Nero, Julius Caesar, and Croesus. The Knights interrupts the Monk's Tale, finding his listing of historical tragedies monotonous and depressing.

The Nun's Priest's Tale tells the story of the rooster Chanticleer and the hen Pertelote. Chanticleer was ill one night and had a disturbing dream that he was chased by a fox. He feared this dream was prophetic, but Pertelote assured him that his dream merely stemmed from his illness and that he should find herbs to cure himself. Chanticleer insists that dreams are signifiers, but finally agrees with his wife. When he searches for herbs, Chanticleer is indeed chased by a fox, but is saved when Pertelote squawks, alerting the woman who owns the farm where the two fowl live and causing her to chase the fox away.

Chaucer follows this with The Second Nun's Tale. This tale is a biography of Saint Cecilia, who converts her husband and brother to Christianity during the time of the Roman empire, when Christian beliefs were illegal. Her brother and husband are executed for their beliefs, and she herself is cut three times with a sword during her execution, but does not immediately die. Rather, she lingers on for several more days, during which time she orders that her property be distributed to the poor. Upon her death Pope Urban declared her a saint.

After the Second Nun finishes her tale, a Canon (alchemist) and his Yeoman join the band of travelers. The Canon had heard how they were telling tales, and wished to join them. The Yeoman speaks incessantly about the Canon, telling fantastical stories about his work, but this annoys the Canon, who suddenly departs. The Yeoman therefore decides to tell a tale himself. The Canon's Yeoman's Tale is a story of the work of a canon and the means by which they defraud people by making them think that they can duplicate money.

The Host tells the Cook to tell the next tale, but he is too drunk to coherently tell one. The Manciple therefore tells his story. The Manciple's Tale is the story of how Phoebus, when he assumed mortal form, was a jealous husband. He monitored his wife closely, fearing that she would be unfaithful. Phoebus had a white crow that could speak the language of humans and could sing beautiful. When the white crow learns that Phoebus' wife was unfaithful, Phoebus plucks him and curses the crow. According to the Manciple, this explains why crows are black and can only sing in an unpleasant tone.

The Parson tells the final tale. The Parson's Tale is not a narrative tale at all, however, but rather an extended sermon on the nature of sin and the three parts necessary for forgiveness: contrition, confession, and satisfaction. The tale gives examples of the seven deadly sins and explains them, and also details what is necessary for redemption. Chaucer ends the tales with a retraction, asking those who were offended by the tales to blame his rough manner and lack of education, for his intentions were not immoral, while asking those who found something redeemable in the tales to give credit to Christ.

Chapter 11

Introduction: Pardoner's Tale

The Pardoner's Tale and the Unredeemed Dead

The Pardoner's Tale is rife with allusions to the doctrine of the resurrection of the body, and conversely to the association between the unredeemed dead and the corruption of the body. One way of looking at the quest of the three rioters may be as a search for eternal death, that is, death without any possibility of resurrection. Such a death represents the triumph of body over spirit, or the reduction of man to his bodily component alone, not susceptible to resurrection.The bodily resurrection of the dead was one of the doctrines that most concerned theologians from the origins of Christianity throughout the middle ages.

In the first centuries of Christianity, the doctrine of the resurrection of the dead was that which most clearly separated Christianity from pagan religions such as Docetism (the idea that Christ's body was somehow unreal or metaphorical) and Gnosticism which saw the body as separate and distinct from the soul and denied the redeemable nature of the body. In its most extreme form, Gnosticism understood the resurrection in terms of a moral and spiritual regeneration that could take place on earth. Pagan critics of Christians who found the idea of the bodily resurrection of the dead to be both ridiculous and revolting forced Christian thinkers to respond to such questions as the destiny of aborted fetuses or amputated body parts or fingernail parings as well as the state of the body at the time of resurrection. Would people be resurrected with all the signs of their bodily infirmities? What age would people be at the time of resurrection?

According to Tertullian:

> If God raises not men entire, He raises not the dead. For what dead man is entire, although he dies entire? Who is without hurt, that is without life? What body is uninjured, when it is dead, when it is cold, when it is ghastly, whin it is stiff, when it is a corpse? Thus for a dead man to be raised again amounts to nothing short of his being restored to his entire condition. God is quite able to remake what He once made. Thus our flesh shall remain even after the resurrection—so far indeed susceptible of suffering, as it is the flesh, and the same flesh too; but at the same time impassible, in as much as it has been liberated by the Lord for the very end and purpose of being no longer capable of enduring suffering.

Most Christian thinkers tried to reconcile the idea of the perfection of the body in paradise with the identity of its composition on earth. According to Tertullian, the resurrected body maintains all the bodily organs but defects and mutilations are repaired.

> Now if the death of the whole person is rescinded by its resurrection, what must we say of the death of a part of him? If we are changed for glory, how much more for integrity? Any loss sustained by our bodies is an accident to them, but their entirety is their natural property . . . To nature, not to injury, are we restored.

The basic concept underlying the doctrine of bodily resurrection was the belief in the identity between body and self. Thinkers such as Athanagoras argued that the human being cannot be said to exist when body is divided and scattered.

Although very late, St. Bonaventure's statements about the bodily assumption of Mary illustrate the belief in the essential identity between body and self. If Mary ascended into heaven before dying, she MUST have ascended into heaven corporally because body and self are inseparable.

Her happiness would not be complete unless she were there personally. The person is not the soul' it is a composite. Thus it is established that she must be there as a coomposite, that is, of soul and body. Otherwise she would not be there in perfect joy; for (as Augustine says) the minds of the saints are hindered, because of their natural inclination for heir bodies, from being totally borne into God.

Thus, resurrection required that God reunite the fragments that had been divided, even in cases in which the body had been divided up among many animals. The ultimate threat to bodily integrity was in fact represented by the digestive process. On the one hand, digestion makes one being a part of another threatens to turn humans into that which they eat, and on the other being eaten incorporates the substance of one individual into the substance of another.

Since the resurrection of the body was conceived of as a reassemblage of the parts of the body, being eaten (by wild animals, or more inevitably, by worms) threatened the identity and continuity of the discreet parts. Caroline Walker Bynum has shown how eating metaphors expressed medieval concerns about death, in particular anxiety about the disintegration, change, and decay of the body and the resulting loss of identity. Eating expressed both the threat to bodily integrity and continuity that comes about through the risk that we become what we eat (thus Athanagoras took pains to explain that humans were incapable of digesting human flesh and that human matter passed through their digestive tracts unabsorbed, as the thinness of cannibals illustrates), or, being eaten, we become a part of something else.

A solution to this problem was offered by the model of the Eucharist. The paradox of the Eucharistic feast that did not threaten the bodily integrity of the risen Jesus offered a model for all Christians who were endangered in their bodies. Ignatius of Antioch, writing about, argued that martyrdom, which would transform the individual into a type of Eucharist, offered a means of union with Christ:

"Let me be the food of wild beasts through whom it is possible to attain God; I am the wheat of God, and I am ground by the teeth of wild beasts that I may be found pure bread; instead, entice the wild beasts that they may become my tomb and leave behind no part of my body that when I fall asleep, I may burden no one."

". . . Fire and cross, and packs of wild beasts, the wrenching of bones, the mangling of limbs, the grinding of my whole body, evil punishments of the devil—let these come upon me, only that I may attain Jesus Christ."

Irenaeus argued that just as the flesh of Jesus survives digestion by humans in the mass, so the human flesh is capable of surviving digestion. We eat the flesh of Christ, and by eating his flesh we become Christ but without consuming Christ. The fact that we become Christ guarantees our resurrection:

And just as a cutting from the vine planted in the ground fructifies in its season, or as a corn of wheat falling into the earth and becoming decomposed rises with manifold increase, and then becomes the Eucharist; so also our bodies, being nourished by it, and deposited in the earth, and suffering decomposition there, shall rise at their appointed time, the Word of God granting them resurrection.

Hell as Digestion

In later medieval iconography, despite the doctrinal belief in the bodily resurrection of all people, the difference between the saved and the damned was often expressed by portraying the damned as separated, disjoined, fragmented while the saved were represented as whole. Likewise, a frequent conception of hell was as a devouring mouth, a metaphor that conveyed the idea that to be damned was to be digested and thus to lose bodily identity. The illustration on the left from a fifteenth century book of hours made for Catherine of Cleves shows hell as a series of concentric mouths which swallow the damned.

The illustration on the right is a thirteenth century mosaic from the cupola of the Baptistry of the Duomo of Florence in which Satan is depicted greedily gobbling up the damned.

Note the many avenues by which the damned are eaten: through Satan's mouth, through beasts emerging from his ears as well as through beasts emerging from his throne.

Many portrayals of death emphasize in particular the stink of rot and decomposition, a characteristic that links it to the sin of sodomy. In this illustration taken from the Hours of Jeanne D'Evreux, Saint Louis is seen collecting the skulls of those who died after the massacre of Christians by the Saracens at Sidon in 1253. On the one hand, collecting and burying the bones expresses faith in the resurrection, but the details emphasize the stink of rot and bodily corruption, as all the characters hold their noses and avert their faces. One of the disturbing features about the Pardoner's Old Man is that he views death not in terms of bodily resurrection and ascendancy to heaven but as an entry into the earth. Moreover, his flesh is disappearing even before he is dead, further suggesting complete and utter dissolution without any possibility of resurrection.

Oaths

Swearing oaths on Christ's body signifies a lack of faith in the resurrection of Christ and thus of the resurrection of the world to come. Oaths were popularly equated with attacks on Christ himself, as this exemplum from the Fasciculus Morum makes clear:

Lo, what happened in London. A certain Lombard by the name of Hubert de Lorgo, who is buried among the Domenicans in London, reported that he had a squire who, whenever he spoke, swore terrible oaths by Christ's members, such as his heart, eyes, teeth, and all wounds together, that it was awful to hear him. At last, when he was ill, he saw in a vision a most beautiful lady enter his room, carrying in her arms the sweetest child, who was most cruelly wounded. "Dearest lady," he said, "is this your son?" And she answered with somber voice: "Yes, this is my son." And he replied: "Whoever has mistreated him thus would be worthy of the greatest punishment, wounding an innocent child this way."

When she heard this, she turned to him sharply and said: "You, wretch, are the one who have thus torn my child through your oaths, which often were even false. And now he will be your judge who has said to y, 'May it happen to you as you have said.' " And with these words she disappeared, whereas the squire, returning to his senses, cried out and told those present what had happened. And then he added: "I shall go to the devils." And with these words he expired at once.

A fourteenth-century confessional manual, *Handlyng Synne* has this to say about swearing oaths on Christ's body:

yf þou were euer so fole hardy
To swere grete oþys grysly,
As we folys do all day,
Dysmembre Ihesu alle þat we may,
Gentyl men, for grete gentry
wene þat grete oþys beyn curteysy;
Noþeles, blode, fete & y en,
þey scorne Ihesu and vpbreyde hys pyn.
Of hys woundys he haþ vpbreyde,
Our shame hyt ys þat yt ys seyd;

Gluttony and Death

Although many critics have pointed out the Pardoner's "error" in considering Adam's sin to be gluttony rather than pride, in fact the Pardoner was not alone in considering Adam's sin to be gluttony. Tertullian also thought Adam's sin was gluttony, which symbolized mortality and decay. The anxiety about the perpetual state of change and disintegration of the body was evident in the medieval descriptions of the sin of gluttony which focus on excrement and vomit and in which all the disgust and fear over the corruptibility and impermanence of the body was evident.

This is the description of Glutton from Piers Plowman, which stresses the disgust at excrement.

By that time Glutton had put down more that a gallon of ale, and his guts were beginning to rumble like a couple of greedy sows. Then, before you had time to say the Our Father, he had pissed a couple of of quarts, and blown such a blast on the round horn of his rump, that all who heard it had to hold their noses, and wished to God he would plug it with a bunch of gorse.

Homosexuality

It may well be the association of homosexuality with anality and thus with feces and excrement that made homosexuality such a horrifying sin. It was associated with unredeeemed, unregenerate corruption of the body.

Homosexuality was so dangerous a sin that it could not be named even by priests for fear of leading man to temptation, even though those guilty of the sin were required to confess it to gain forgiveness. This is what Mirk's preaching manual, an early fifteenth century handbook of instruction for parish priests, had to say about homosexuality, a sin not to be mentioned by priests in their sermons for fear of imparting wicked ideas but which nonetheless the sinner was obliged to confess:

Also wryten wel I fynde,
That of synne a eynes kynde
Thow schalt thy paresch no þynge teche,
Ny of that synne no thynge preche;
But say þus by gode a-vys,
þat 'to gret synne forsoþe hyt ys,
For any mon þat bereth lyf
To forsake hys wedded wyf
And do hys kynde other way,
þat is gret synne wyþowte nay;'
But how and where he doth þat synne,
To hys schryffader he mote þat mynne.

The author of the *Fasciculus Morum,* a fourteenth-century preacher's handbook, shares the concept of homosexuality as that sin which is unspeakable. Likewise, evident in his description of the punishment of homosexuality is the emphasis on internal bodily corruption. It is significant that hell is described as the state of being swallowed up and eaten by the earth, that is, being consigned to rot, decay, and decomposition of the body. Though their bodies might appear beautiful on the outside, they enclose a sulphurous hell of unredeemable death within. The particular horror reserved for homosexuality would seem to derive from its association with digestion and excrement, and thus with the bodily corruption of death. Homosexuality is the negation of the resurrection of the flesh.

The fifth and last branch of lechery is the diabolical sin against nature called sodomy. I pass it over in horror and leave it to others to describe it. . . . Not only did fire and sulphur falling from above kill people and animals, but the earth opened its mouth and swallowed all the living. Thus it is certain that on account of the said sin they perished forever in hell. As an open sign the sea there remains dead even in our days; no living being can submerge or remain it it; and it is all for just revenge in horror of such a sin. As it is said in the book, On the Nature of Things, if a burning light is thrown into this sea, it floats on the surface and cannot drown until it is put out, as a sign that nothing alive that is done in the light of grace for those for whose sake such vengeance was taken is of any use. And a further testimony, according to writers on natural history and several moderns who have observed this with their own eyes, is that while the apples that grow on the shore of that sea are most beautiful to look at, when they are ripe and are cut open they give forth a sulphurous smoke and dusty ashes.

The same applies to the evil lechers who are devoted to the aforementioned abhorrent sins: thought they show great external beauty in their body, like green and beautiful apples, the riper they grow, the more they give forth a sickening ash in their lust that burns and smells like sulphur. Therefore, according to Augustine, "God hated this vice so much that, seeing it being committed by men before his incarnation, he almost refrained from becoming a man." And thus God did not want to entrust any angel or man with the execution of this punishment but kept its vengeance for himself, after the words: "Revenge is mine, and I will repay."

The Middle English poem *Cleanness* characterizes the sin of sodomy in terms of digestive references: the stink associated with vomit and excrement. The speech of the Sodomites is referred to in terms of its malodour:

> *What! They spewed out and spoke of such sickening filth!*
> *What! They shouted such scandalous, sin-ridden words*
> *That the wind and the world and the weather themselves*
> *Still stink from the sin that they spoke of that day!*
> (ll. 845-8)

Relics

The cult of relics of martyrs also depended on the partition of the body. Whereas the idea of death and hell played on the fear of eternal bodily division, the cult of relics was closely bound up with the idea of the identity of the partial bodily remains of the saint with the saint as a whole, blessed resurrected body. Thus in the mid-twelfth century, Peter the Venerable explains the significance of relics of saints.

> The divine dignity divides his martyr into equal parts, so that he may retain his soul for himself among the mass of the blessed and gie, with marvelous largesse, the relics of his sacred body to be venerated by the faithful still living in the flesh. . . . Therefore we know the spirits of the just will in the meanwhile live happily in the eternal life which we expect through faith, which he promises who is faithful in his words and we anticipate for them a future resurrection in their bodies with immortality and in every sense incorruptibility. For this reason we do not debase as inanimate, despise as insensate, or trample under foot like the cadavers of dumb beasts the bodies of those who in this life cultivated justice; rather we venerate them as temples of the Lord, revere tham as palaces of divinity, hoard them as pearls suitable for the crown of the eternal king, and, with the greatest devotion of which we are capable, preserve them as vessels of resurrection to be joined again to the blessed souls . . .

The reliquary, as a repository for the hand bones of the saint, serves as a metaphor for resurrection, the reliquary itself recomposing the fragments it contains into the original form of the body they composed.

As a result, sharing the possession of relics with the community of the faithful was a religious obligation. On the other hand passing off animal parts for the relics of saints could deceive men into idolatry and damnation. That the selling of animal bones as relics by pardoners was a well-known abuse can be seen by the fact that the *Fasciculus Morum* uses this misdeed to describe those who cloak their sins in excuses.

We should thus know that people who veil their sins in this fashion are like these false pardoners, who show their relics in some golden vessel that is decorated with precious gems, or else wrapped in cloths of gold and silk, so that they may look truly precious before the people. But as it often happens, when they open them up, you will find nothing but the bones from a farm animal that have been pulled out of a ditch, stinking and dried up and worthy of every abomination. IN the same say,, when such people ought to show their sins frankly and truthfully in confession, they put so many excuses around them like wrappers, as if they wanted to make of their sins relics to be worshipped whereas in truth they stink horribly before God and his angels.

Since the value of the relic lies in its identity with the resurrected body at Christ's second coming, it is not surprising that one of the qualities of the relics of saints is their incorruptibility. Sermon exempla illustrate the point both that those who conceal true relics will be found out and punished and those that have faith in the power of relics will be rewarded..

Avarice and Gluttony

Although the Pardoner's insistence on avarice as the root of all evil has been seen as a cover for his real sins of lechery and carnality, we should remember that medieval thought closely connected unnatural sexual acts, gluttony, and avarice. A striking if confused metaphor of the association between money, eating, and excrement as the antithesis of the resurrection of the body guaranteed by Jesus is found in Alain de Lille's *Complaint of Nature* (thirteenth century). Here we find two metaphors used to describe gluttony. On the one hand, gluttony is described in terms of avarice, and the extent to which the sin of gluttony is described in the vocabulary of money is striking. The stomach is a coffer controlled by a tax collector; food is the tax deposited in the coffer or the stomach; digestion is a form of robbery; vomit is the disgorging of coins in order to indulge in their possession.

Not only the aforementioned passion for drink, but also a canine greediness for eating, entices very many. The abnormal desires of such, and their gross thoughts, dream of preparations of food. While they pay too fully their due of food to the daily tax-collector, he, more than loaded, has to pay back his debtor. They prize whatever they hold in the coffer of the stomach, and although neither rust can consume that trust with the tooth of corrosion, nor the guile of the stealthy thief snatch it away, nevertheless it vanishes more ignobly in the baser robbery of digestive heat. That they may more carefully fawn upon this tax collecting stomach, they urge the purse to disgorge its treasure, the coffer to vomit its coins. Though within they enrich the belly with wealth of foods, without they are situated in sheer, naked, and lonely poverty. Now this pestilence, not contented with plebeian humility, extends itself quite deeply among prelates.

These, degrading the office of baptism, baptize in the base font of spice salmon, pike, and other fish which are exceptional in equal excellence, and have been crucified in various martyrdoms of cookery, to the end that, by coming from such a baptism, they may acquire a varied and agreeable savor. Furthermore, on the same table the beast of the earth is drowned in the flood of spice, the fish swims in it, the bird is limed in its paste. And while so many species of animals are confined in the single prison-house of a belly, the creature of the sea wonders that the tribes that go on foot and the tribes of the air are buried With it in the same sepulchre. If freedom to go out is given them, the width of the door hardly suffices for their egress.

The second metaphor used to describe gluttony, and to classify it as a particular vice of the priesthood, is that of a perversion of the death and resurrection of Christ, an obscene parody of the Eucharist. In the following illustration of gluttony taken from the *Fasciculus Morum,* fish are martyred and crucified to produce the sacrament of baptism consisting of immersion in spiced sauces, and the stomach becomes a sepulcher in which animals, birds, and fishes are promiscuously buried together so that their expulsion from the stomach through an orifice that can hardly accommodate them becomes an obscene parody of the resurrection of Jesus.

Not only the aforementioned passion for drink, but also a canine greediness for eating, entices very many. The abnormal desires of such, and their gross thoughts, dream of preparations of food. While they pay too fully their due of food to the daily tax-collector, he, more than loaded, has to pay back his debtor. They prize whatever they hold in the coffer of the stomach, and although neither rust can consume that trust with the tooth of corrosion, nor the guile of the stealthy thief snatch it away, nevertheless it vanishes more ignobly in the baser robbery of digestive heat. That they may more carefully fawn upon this tax collecting stomach, they urge the purse to disgorge its treasure, the coffer to vomit its coins. Though within they enrich the belly with wealth of foods, without they are situated in sheer, naked, and lonely poverty. Now this pestilence, not contented with plebeian humility, extends itself quite deeply among prelates. These, degrading the office of baptism, baptize in the base font of spice salmon, pike, and other fish which are exceptional in equal excellence, and have been crucified in various martyrdoms of cookery, to the end that, by coming from such a baptism, they may acquire a varied and agreeable savor. Furthermore, on the same table the beast of the earth is drowned in the flood of spice, the fish swims in it, the bird is . limed in its paste. And while so many species of animals are confined in the single prison-house of a belly, the creature of the sea wonders that the tribes that go on foot and the tribes of the air are buried with it in the same sepulchre. If freedom to go out is given them, the width of the door hardly suffices for their egress.

Chapter 12

The Pardoner's Tale: Text and Paraphrase

The Introduction to the Pardoner's Tale

The wordes of the Hoost to the Phisicien and Pardoner.

287 Oure Hooste gan to swere as he were wood;

Our Host began to swear as if he was crazy;

288 "Harrow!" quod he, "by nayles and by blood!

"Alas!" said he, "by (Christ's) nails and by (His) blood!

289 This was a fals cherl and a fals justise.

This was a false churl and a false judge.

290 As shameful deeth as herte may devyse

As shameful a death as heart can devise

291 Come to thise juges and hire advocatz!

Come to these judges and their advocates!

292 Algate this sely mayde is slayn, allas!

At any rate, this innocent maid is slain, alas!

293 Allas, to deere boughte she beautee!

Alas, too dearly she paid for her beauty!

294 Wherfore I seye al day that men may see

Therefore I say that every day men may see

295 That yiftes of Fortune and of Nature
That gifts of Fortune and of Nature

296 Been cause of deeth to many a creature.
Are cause of death to many a creature.

297 Hire beautee was hire deth, I dar wel sayn.
Her beauty was her death, I dare well say.

298 Allas, so pitously as she was slayn!
Alas, so pitifully as she was slain!

299 Of bothe yiftes that I speke of now
Of both gifts that I speak of now

300 Men han ful ofte moore for harm than prow.
Men have very often more harm than benefit.

301 But trewely, myn owene maister deere,
But truly, mine own master dear,

302 This is a pitous tale for to heere.
This is a pitiful tale to hear.

303 But nathelees, passe over; is no fors.
But nonetheless, pass over; is does not matter.

304 I pray to God so save thy gentil cors,
I pray to God so save thy gentle body,

305 And eek thyne urynals and thy jurdones,
And also thy vessels for analyzing urine and thy flasks,

306 Thyn ypocras, and eek thy galiones,
Thine ipocras, and also thy galiones (*medicines*),

307 And every boyste ful of thy letuarie;
And every container full of thy electuaries;

308 God blesse hem, and oure lady Seinte Marie!
God bless them, and our lady Saint Mary!

309 So moot I theen, thou art a propre man,
As I may prosper, thou art a proper man,

310 And lyk a prelat, by Seint Ronyan!
And like a prelate, by Saint Ronyan!

311 Seyde I nat wel? I kan nat speke in terme;
Said I not well? I can not speak in technical terms;

312 But wel I woot thou doost myn herte to erme,
But well I know thou makes mine heart to grieve so,

313 That I almoost have caught a cardynacle.
That I almost have caught a palpitation of the heart.

314 By corpus bones! but I have triacle,
By corpus' bones! unless I have medicine,

315 Or elles a draughte of moyste and corny ale,
Or else a draught of fresh and strong ale,

316 Or but I heere anon a myrie tale,
Or unless I hear right now a merry tale,

317 Myn herte is lost for pitee of this mayde.
My heart is lost for pity of this maid.

318 Thou beel amy, thou Pardoner," he sayde,
Thou fair friend (rascal), thou Pardoner," he said,

319 "Telle us som myrthe or japes right anon."
"Tell us some mirth or comic tales right away."

320 "It shal be doon," quod he, "by Seint Ronyon!
"It shall be done," said he, "by Saint Ronyon!

321 But first," quod he, "heere at this alestake
But first," said he, "here at this ale stake (tavern sign)

322 I wol bothe drynke and eten of a cake."

I will both drink and eat of a cake."

323 But right anon thise gentils gonne to crye,

But right away these gentlefolk began to cry,

324 "Nay, lat hym telle us of no ribaudye!

"Nay, let him tell us of no ribaldry!

325 Telle us som moral thyng, that we may leere

Tell us some moral thing, that we may learn

326 Som wit, and thanne wol we gladly heere."

Some useful knowledge, and then will we gladly hear."

327 "I graunte, ywis," quod he, "but I moot thynke

"I agree, indeed," said he, "but I must think

328 Upon som honest thyng while that I drynke."

About some respectable thing while I drink."

The Pardoner's Prologue

Heere folweth the Prologe of the Pardoners Tale.

Radix malorum est Cupiditas: Ad Thimotheum, 6°.

Greed is the root of evils: Paul's Epistle to Timothy, chapter 6.

329 "Lordynges," quod he, "in chirches whan I preche,

"Gentlemen," he said, "in churches when I preach,

330 I peyne me to han an hauteyn speche,

I take pains to have a loud voice,

331 And rynge it out as round as gooth a belle,

And ring it out as round as goes a belle,

332 For I kan al by rote that I telle.

For I know all by rote that I tell.

333 My theme is alwey oon, and evere was —
My theme is always the same, and ever was —
334 Radix malorum est Cupiditas.
'Greed is the root of all evil.'
335 "First I pronounce whennes that I come,
"First I pronounce from whence I come,
336 And thanne my bulles shewe I, alle and some.
And then my papal bulls I show, each and every one.
337 Oure lige lordes seel on my patente,
Our liege lord's seal on my letter of authorization,
338 That shewe I first, my body to warente,
I show that first, to protect my body,
339 That no man be so boold, ne preest ne clerk,
So that no man be so bold, neither priest nor clerk,
340 Me to destourbe of Cristes hooly werk.
To hinder me from (doing) Christ's holy work.
341 And after that thanne telle I forth my tales;
And after that then I tell forth my tales;
342 Bulles of popes and of cardynales,
Indulgences of popes and of cardinals,
343 Of patriarkes and bishopes I shewe,
Of patriarchs and bishops I show,
344 And in Latyn I speke a wordes fewe,
And in Latin I speak a few words,
345 To saffron with my predicacioun,
With which to add spice to my preaching,
346 And for to stire hem to devocioun.
And to stir them to devotion.

347 Thanne shewe I forth my longe cristal stones,
Then I show forth my long crystal stones,

348 Ycrammed ful of cloutes and of bones –
Crammed full of rags and of bones –

349 Relikes been they, as wenen they echoon.
Relics they are, as suppose they each one.

350 Thanne have I in latoun a sholder-boon
Then I have mounted in latten (brass-like alloy) a shoulder-bone

351 Which that was of an hooly Jewes sheep.
Which was of a holy Jew's sheep.

352 'Goode men,' I seye, 'taak of my wordes keep;
'Good men,' I say, 'take heed of my words;

353 If that this boon be wasshe in any welle,
If this bone be washed in any well,

354 If cow, or calf, or sheep, or oxe swelle
If cow, or calf, or sheep, or ox swell

355 That any worm hath ete, or worm ystonge,
That any worm has eaten, or worm stung,

356 Taak water of that welle and wassh his tonge,
Take water of that well and wash its tongue,

357 And it is hool anon; and forthermoore,
And it is whole right away; and furthermore,

358 Of pokkes and of scabbe, and every soore
Of pocks and of scab, and every sore

359 Shal every sheep be hool that of this welle
Every sheep shall be whole that of this well

360 Drynketh a draughte. Taak kep eek what I telle:
Drinks a draft. Take heed also what I say:

361 If that the good-man that the beestes oweth
If the householder who owns the beasts
362 Wol every wyke, er that the cok hym croweth,
Will every week, before the cock crows,
363 Fastynge, drynken of this welle a draughte,
Fasting, drink of this well a draft,
364 As thilke hooly Jew oure eldres taughte,
As that same holy Jew taught our elders,
365 His beestes and his stoor shal multiplie.
His beasts and his possessions shall multiply.
366 'And, sires, also it heeleth jalousie;
'And, sirs, it also heals jealousy;
367 For though a man be falle in jalous rage,
For though a man be fallen in jealous rage,
368 Lat maken with this water his potage,
Have his potage made with this water,
369 And nevere shal he moore his wyf mystriste,
And he shall never more mistrust his wife,
370 Though he the soothe of hir defaute wiste,
Though he knew the truth of her misdeed,
371 Al had she taken prestes two or thre.
Although she had taken two or three priests.
372 'Heere is a miteyn eek, that ye may se.
'Here is a mitten also, that you may see.
373 He that his hand wol putte in this mitayn,
He that will put his hand in this mitten,
374 He shal have multipliyng of his grayn,
He shall have multiplying of his grain,

375 Whan he hath sowen, be it whete or otes,
When he has sown, be it wheat or oats,
376 So that he offre pens, or elles grotes.
Providing that he offer pennies, or else fourpences.
377 'Goode men and wommen, o thyng warne I yow:
'Good men and women, one thing I warn you:
378 If any wight be in this chirche now
If any person be in this church now
379 That hath doon synne horrible, that he
Who has done such horrible sin, that he
380 Dar nat, for shame, of it yshryven be,
Dare not, for shame, be confessed of it,
381 Or any womman, be she yong or old,
Or any woman, be she young or old,
382 That hath ymaked hir housbonde cokewold,
Who has made her husband cuckold,
383 Swich folk shal have no power ne no grace
Such folk shall have no power nor no grace
384 To offren to my relikes in this place.
To offer to my relics in this place.
385 And whoso fyndeth hym out of swich blame,
And whoever finds himself out of such blame,
386 He wol come up and offre a Goddes name,
He will come up and offer in God's name,
387 And I assoille him by the auctoritee
And I will absolve him by the authority
388 Which that by bulle ygraunted was to me.'
Which by papal bull was granted to me.'

389 "By this gaude have I wonne, yeer by yeer,
"By this trick have I won, year after year,

390 An hundred mark sith I was pardoner.
An hundred marks since I was pardoner.

391 I stonde lyk a clerk in my pulpet,
I stand like a clerk in my pulpit,

392 And whan the lewed peple is doun yset,
And when the ignorant people are set down,

393 I preche so as ye han herd bifoore
I preach as you have heard before

394 And telle an hundred false japes moore.
And tell a hundred more false tales.

395 Thanne peyne I me to strecche forth the nekke,
Then I take pains to stretch forth the neck,

396 And est and west upon the peple I bekke,
And east and west upon the people I nod,

397 As dooth a dowve sittynge on a berne.
As does a dove sitting on a barn.

398 Myne handes and my tonge goon so yerne
My hands and my tongue go so quickly

399 That it is joye to se my bisynesse.
That it is joy to see my business.

400 Of avarice and of swich cursednesse
Of avarice and of such cursedness

401 Is al my prechyng, for to make hem free
Is all my preaching, to make them generous

402 To yeven hir pens, and namely unto me.
To give their pennies, and namely unto me.

403 For myn entente is nat but for to wynne,
For my intention is only to make a profit,
404 And nothyng for correccioun of synne.
And not at all for correction of sin.
405 I rekke nevere, whan that they been beryed,
I care not a bit, when they are buried,
406 Though that hir soules goon a-blakeberyed!
Though their souls go picking blackberries!
407 For certes, many a predicacioun
For certainly, many a sermon
408 Comth ofte tyme of yvel entencioun;
Comes often times from an evil intention;
409 Som for plesance of folk and flaterye,
Some for pleasure of folk and flattery,
410 To been avaunced by ypocrisye,
To be advanced by hypocrisy,
411 And som for veyne glorie, and som for hate.
And some for vain glory, and some for hate.
412 For whan I dar noon oother weyes debate,
For when I dare debate no other ways,
413 Thanne wol I stynge hym with my tonge smerte
Then I will sting him with my sharp tongue
414 In prechyng, so that he shal nat asterte
In preaching, so that he shall not escape
415 To been defamed falsly, if that he
To be defamed falsely, if he
416 Hath trespased to my bretheren or to me.
Has trespassed to my brethren or to me.

417 For though I telle noght his propre name,
For though I tell not his proper name,
418 Men shal wel knowe that it is the same,
Men shall well know that it is the same,
419 By signes, and by othere circumstances.
By signs, and by other details.
420 Thus quyte I folk that doon us displesances;
Thus I repay folk who make trouble for us pardoners;
421 Thus spitte I out my venym under hewe
Thus I spit out my venom under hue
422 Of hoolynesse, to semen hooly and trewe.
Of holinesses, to seem holy and true.
423 "But shortly myn entente I wol devyse:
"But shortly my intention I will tell:
424 I preche of no thyng but for coveityse.
I preach of nothing but for greed.
425 Therfore my theme is yet, and evere was,
Therefore my theme is yet, and ever was,
426 Radix malorum est Cupiditas.
'Greed is the root of all evil.'
427 Thus kan I preche agayn that same vice
Thus I can preach against that same vice
428 Which that I use, and that is avarice.
Which I use, and that is avarice.
429 But though myself be gilty in that synne,
But though myself be guilty of that sin,
430 Yet kan I maken oother folk to twynne
Yet I can make other folk to turn away

431 From avarice and soore to repente.
From avarice and bitterly to repent.

432 But that is nat my principal entente;
But that is not my principal intention;

433 I preche nothyng but for coveitise.
I preach nothing but for greed.

434 Of this mateere it oghte ynogh suffise.
Concerning this matter this ought to be enough.

435 "Thanne telle I hem ensamples many oon
"Then I tell them illustrative tales many a one

436 Of olde stories longe tyme agoon.
Of old stories from long time ago.

437 For lewed peple loven tales olde;
For ignorant people love old tales;

438 Swiche thynges kan they wel reporte and holde.
Such things they can well repeat and hold in memory.

439 What, trowe ye, that whiles I may preche,
What, do you suppose, that while I can preach,

440 And wynne gold and silver for I teche,
And win gold and silver because I teach,

441 That I wol lyve in poverte wilfully?
That I will live in poverty voluntarily?

442 Nay, nay, I thoghte it nevere, trewely!
Nay, nay, I never thought it, truly!

443 For I wol preche and begge in sondry landes;
For I will preach and beg in various lands;

444 I wol nat do no labour with myne handes,
I will not do any labour with my hands,

445 Ne make baskettes and lyve therby,
Nor make baskets and live thereby,
446 By cause I wol nat beggen ydelly.
Because I will not beg idly.
447 I wol noon of the apostles countrefete;
I will imitate none of the apostles;
448 I wol have moneie, wolle, chese, and whete,
I will have money, wool, cheese, and wheat,
449 Al were it yeven of the povereste page,
Although it were given by the poorest servant boy,
450 Or of the povereste wydwe in a village,
Or by the poorest widow in a village,
451 Al sholde hir children sterve for famyne.
Even though her children should die of hunger.
452 Nay, I wol drynke licour of the vyne
Nay, I will drink liquor of the vine
453 And have a joly wenche in every toun.
And have a pretty wench in every town.
454 But herkneth, lordynges, in conclusioun:
But listen, gentlemen, in conclusion:
455 Youre likyng is that I shal telle a tale.
Your desire is that I shall tell a tale.
456 Now have I dronke a draughte of corny ale,
Now I have drunk a draft of strong ale,
457 By God, I hope I shal yow telle a thyng
By God, I hope I shall tell you a thing
458 That shal by reson been at youre likyng.
That shall, for good reason, be to your liking.

459 For though myself be a ful vicious man,
For though myself be a very vicious man,
460 A moral tale yet I yow telle kan,
Yet I can tell you a moral tale,
461 Which I am wont to preche for to wynne.
Which I am accustomed to preach in order to profit.
462 Now hoold youre pees! My tale I wol bigynne."
Now hold your peace! My tale I will begin."

The Pardoner's Tale

Heere bigynneth the Pardoners Tale.

463 In Flaundres whilom was a compaignye
In Flanders once was a company
464 Of yonge folk that haunteden folye,
Of young folk who practiced folly,
465 As riot, hasard, stywes, and tavernes,
Such as debauchery, gambling, brothels, and taverns,
466 Where as with harpes, lutes, and gyternes,
Where with harps, lutes, and guitars,
467 They daunce and pleyen at dees bothe day and nyght,
They dance and play at dice both day and night,
468 And eten also and drynken over hir myght,
And also eat and drink beyond their capacity,
469 Thurgh which they doon the devel sacrifise
Through which they do the devil sacrifice
470 Withinne that develes temple in cursed wise
Within that devil's temple in cursed manner

471 By superfluytee abhomynable.
By abominable excess.
472 Hir othes been so grete and so dampnable
Their oaths are so great and so damnable
473 That it is grisly for to heere hem swere.
That it is grisly to hear them swear.
474 Oure blissed Lordes body they totere —
Our blessed Lord's body they tore in pieces —
475 Hem thoughte that Jewes rente hym noght ynough
They thought that the Jews did not tear him enough
476 And ech of hem at otheres synne lough.
And each of them laughed at the other's sin.
477 And right anon thanne comen tombesteres
And right away then come dancing girls
478 Fetys and smale, and yonge frutesteres,
Elegantly shaped and slim, and girls selling fruits,
479 Syngeres with harpes, baudes, wafereres,
Singers with harps, bawds, girls selling wafers,
480 Whiche been the verray develes officeres
Which are the very devil's officers
481 To kyndle and blowe the fyr of lecherye,
To kindle and blow the fire of lechery,
482 That is annexed unto glotonye.
That is joined unto gluttony.
483 The hooly writ take I to my witnesse
The Bible I take as my witness
484 That luxurie is in wyn and dronkenesse.
That lechery is in wine and drunkenness.

485 Lo, how that dronken Looth, unkyndely,
Lo, how that drunken Lot, unnaturally,
486 Lay by his doghtres two, unwityngly;
Lay by his two daughters, unwittingly;
487 So dronke he was, he nyste what he wroghte.
So drunk he was, he knew not what he did.
488 Herodes, whoso wel the stories soghte,
Herod, whoever should seek well the histories (would learn),
489 Whan he of wyn was repleet at his feeste,
When he was filled with wine at his feast,
490 Right at his owene table he yaf his heeste
Right at his own table he gave his command
491 To sleen the Baptist John, ful giltelees.
To slay John the Baptist, full guiltless.
492 Senec seith a good word doutelees;
Seneca says a good word, doubtless;
493 He seith he kan no difference fynde
He says he can find no difference
494 Bitwix a man that is out of his mynde
Between a man that is out of his mind
495 And a man which that is dronkelewe,
And a man that is drunk,
496 But that woodnesse, yfallen in a shrewe,
Except that madness, fallen in an evil person,
497 Persevereth lenger than doth dronkenesse.
Lasts longer than does drunkenness.
498 O glotonye, ful of cursednesse!
O gluttony, full of cursedness!

499 O cause first of oure confusioun!
O first cause of our ruin!
500 O original of oure dampnacioun,
O origin of our damnation,
501 Til Crist hadde boght us with his blood agayn!
Until Christ had bought us with his blood again!
502 Lo, how deere, shortly for to sayn,
Lo, how dearly, shortly to say,
503 Aboght was thilke cursed vileynye!
Was bought that same cursed villainy!
504 Corrupt was al this world for glotonye.
Corrupt was all this world for gluttony.
505 Adam oure fader, and his wyf also,
Adam our fader, and his wife also,
506 Fro Paradys to labour and to wo
From Paradise to labour and to woe
507 Were dryven for that vice, it is no drede.
Were driven for that vice, there is no doubt.
508 For whil that Adam fasted, as I rede,
For while Adam fasted, as I read,
509 He was in Paradys; and whan that he
He was in Paradise; and when he
510 Eet of the fruyt deffended on the tree,
Ate of the forbidden fruit on the tree,
511 Anon he was out cast to wo and peyne.
Immediately he was cast out to woe and pain.
512 O glotonye, on thee wel oghte us pleyne!
O gluttony, on thee well we ought to complain!

513 O, wiste a man how manye maladyes
O, if a man knew how many evils
514 Folwen of excesse and of glotonyes,
Follow of excess and of gluttony,
515 He wolde been the moore mesurable
He would be the more moderate
516 Of his diete, sittynge at his table.
Of his diet, sitting at his table.
517 Allas, the shorte throte, the tendre mouth,
Alas, the short throat, the tender mouth,
518 Maketh that est and west and north and south,
Makes that east and west and north and south,
519 In erthe, in eir, in water, men to swynke
In earth, in air, in water, men work
520 To gete a glotoun deyntee mete and drynke!
To get a glutton dainty food and drink!
521 Of this matiere, O Paul, wel kanstow trete:
Of this matter, O Paul, well can thou treat
522 "Mete unto wombe, and wombe eek unto mete,
"Food unto belly, and belly also unto food,
523 Shal God destroyen bothe," as Paulus seith.
God shall destroy both," as Paul says.
524 Allas, a foul thyng is it, by my feith,
Alas, a foul thing it is, by my faith,
525 To seye this word, and fouler is the dede,
To say this word, and fouler is the deed,
526 Whan man so drynketh of the white and rede
When man so drinks of the white and red

527 That of his throte he maketh his pryvee

That he makes his privy of his throat

528 Thurgh thilke cursed superfluitee.

Through that same cursed excess.

529 The apostel wepyng seith ful pitously,

The apostle weeping says full piteously,

530 "Ther walken manye of whiche yow toold have I —

"There walk many of whom I have told you —

531 I seye it now wepyng, with pitous voys —

I say it now weeping, with piteous voice —

532 They been enemys of Cristes croys,

They are enemies of Christ's cross,

533 Of whiche the ende is deeth; wombe is hir god!"

Of which the end is death; belly is their god!"

534 O wombe! O bely! O stynkyng cod,

O gut! O belly! O stinking bag,

535 Fulfilled of dong and of corrupcioun!

Filled with dung and with corruption!

536 At either ende of thee foul is the soun.

At either end of thee the sound is foul.

537 How greet labour and cost is thee to fynde!

How great labour and cost it is to feed thee!

538 Thise cookes, how they stampe, and streyne, and grynde,

These cooks, how they pound, and strain, and grind,

539 And turnen substaunce into accident

And turn substance into outward appearance

540 To fulfille al thy likerous talent!

To fulfill all thy gluttonous desire!

541 Out of the harde bones knokke they
Out of the hard bones they knock
542 The mary, for they caste noght awey
The marrow, for they throw nothing away
543 That may go thurgh the golet softe and swoote.
That may go through the gullet softly and sweetly.
544 Of spicerie of leef, and bark, and roote
Of seasonings of leaf, and bark, and root
545 Shal been his sauce ymaked by delit,
Shall his sauce be made for delight,
546 To make hym yet a newer appetit.
To make him yet a newer appetite.
547 But, certes, he that haunteth swiche delices
But, certainly, he who habitually seeks such delicacies
548 Is deed, whil that he lyveth in tho vices.
Is dead, while he lives in those vices.
549 A lecherous thyng is wyn, and dronkenesse
A lecherous thing is wine, and drunkenness
550 Is ful of stryvyng and of wrecchednesse.
Is full of striving and of wretchedness.
551 O dronke man, disfigured is thy face,
O drunken man, disfigured is thy face,
552 Sour is thy breeth, foul artow to embrace,
Sour is thy breath, foul art thou to embrace,
553 And thurgh thy dronke nose semeth the soun
And through thy drunken nose the sound seems
554 As though thou seydest ay "Sampsoun, Sampsoun!"
As though thou said always "Sampson, Sampson!"

555 And yet, God woot, Sampsoun drank nevere no wyn.

And yet, God knows, Sampson never drank any wine.

556 Thou fallest as it were a styked swyn;

Thou fallest like a stuck pig;

557 Thy tonge is lost, and al thyn honeste cure,

Thy tongue is lost, and all thy care for decency,

558 For dronkenesse is verray sepulture

For drunkenness is truly the sepulcher

559 Of mannes wit and his discrecioun.

Of man's wit and his discretion.

560 In whom that drynke hath dominacioun

In whom drink has domination

561 He kan no conseil kepe; it is no drede.

He can keep no secrets; there is no doubt.

562 Now kepe yow fro the white and fro the rede,

Now guard yourself from the white and from the red,

563 And namely fro the white wyn of Lepe

And namely from the white wine of Lepe

564 That is to selle in Fysshstrete or in Chepe.

That is for sale in Fishstreet or in Cheapside.

565 This wyn of Spaigne crepeth subtilly

This wine of Spain creeps subtly

566 In othere wynes, growynge faste by,

Into other wines, growing near by,

567 Of which ther ryseth swich fumositee

Of which there rise such bodily vapors

568 That whan a man hath dronken draughtes thre,
That when a man has drunk three drafts,
569 And weneth that he be at hoom in Chepe,
And supposes that he is at home in Cheapside,
570 He is in Spaigne, right at the toune of Lepe –
He is in Spain, right at the town of Lepe –
571 Nat at the Rochele, ne at Burdeux toun –
Not at La Rochelle, nor at Bordeaux town –
572 And thanne wol he seye "Sampsoun, Sampsoun!"
And then will he say "Sampson, Sampson!"
573 But herkneth, lordynges, o word, I yow preye,
But listen, gentlemen, one word, I pray you,
574 That alle the sovereyn actes, dar I seye,
That all the great deeds, I dare say,
575 Of victories in the Olde Testament,
Of victories in the Old Testament,
576 Thurgh verray God, that is omnipotent,
Through true God, who is omnipotent,
577 Were doon in abstinence and in preyere.
Were done in abstinence and in prayer.
578 Looketh the Bible, and ther ye may it leere.
Look in the Bible, and there you can learn it.
579 Looke, Attilla, the grete conquerour,
Consider how Attila, the great conqueror,
580 Deyde in his sleep, with shame and dishonour,
Died in his sleep, with shame and dishonour,
581 Bledynge ay at his nose in dronkenesse.
Bleeding ever at his nose in drunkenness.

582 A capitayn sholde lyve in sobrenesse.

A captain should live in sobriety.

583 And over al this, avyseth yow right wel

And beyond all this, consider right well

584 What was comaunded unto Lamuel –

What was commanded unto Lamuel –

585 Nat Samuel, but Lamuel, seye I;

Not Samuel, but Lamuel, I say;

586 Redeth the Bible, and fynde it expresly

Read the Bible, and find it explicitly

587 Of wyn-yevyng to hem that han justise.

About giving wine to those that have the duty of doing justice.

588 Namoore of this, for it may wel suffise.

No more of this, for it may well suffice.

589 And now that I have spoken of glotonye,

And now that I have spoken of gluttony,

590 Now wol I yow deffenden hasardrye.

Now I will forbid you gambling.

591 Hasard is verray mooder of lesynges,

Dicing is the true mother of lies,

592 And of deceite, and cursed forsweryngs,

And of deceit, and cursed perjuries,

593 Blaspheme of Crist, manslaughtre, and wast also

Blasphemy of Christ, manslaughter, and waste also

594 Of catel and of tyme; and forthermo,

Of possessions and of time; and furthermore,

595 It is repreeve and contrarie of honour

It is a disgrace and contrary to honour

596 For to ben holde a commune hasardour.
To be considered a common dice player.

597 And ever the hyer he is of estaat,
And ever the higher he is of estate,

598 The moore is he yholden desolaat.
The more is he considered abandoned (to shame).

599 If that a prynce useth hasardrye,
If a prince plays at dicing,

600 In alle governaunce and policye
In all governance and policy

601 He is, as by commune opinioun,
He is, by common opinion,

602 Yholde the lasse in reputacioun.
Held the less in reputation.

603 Stilboun, that was a wys embassadour,
Stilboun, who was a wise ambassador,

604 Was sent to Corynthe in ful greet honour
Was sent to Corinth in very great honour

605 Fro Lacidomye to make hire alliaunce.
From Sparta to make their alliance.

606 And whan he cam, hym happede, par chaunce,
And when he came, it happened, by chance,

607 That alle the gretteste that were of that lond,
That all the greatest men that were of that land,

608 Pleyynge atte hasard he hem fond.
Playing at dice he found them.

609 For which, as soone as it myghte be,
For which, as soon as it could be,

610 He stal hym hoom agayn to his contree,
He stole home again to his country,
611 And seyde, "Ther wol I nat lese my name,
And said, "There I will not lose my reputation,
612 Ne I wol nat take on me so greet defame,
Nor will I take on me so great infamy,
613 Yow for to allie unto none hasardours.
To ally you unto any dice-players.
614 Sendeth othere wise embassadours;
Send other wise ambassadors;
615 For, by my trouthe, me were levere dye
For, by my troth, I would rather die
616 Than I yow sholde to hasardours allye.
Than I should ally you to dice-players.
617 For ye, that been so glorious in honours,
For you, that are so glorious in honours,
618 Shul nat allyen yow with hasardours
Shall not ally yourselves with dice-players
619 As by my wyl, ne as by my tretee."
By my will, nor by my negotiation."
620 This wise philosophre, thus seyde hee.
This wise philosopher, thus said he.
621 Looke eek that to the kyng Demetrius
Consider also that to the king Demetrius
622 The kyng of Parthes, as the book seith us,
The king of Parthia, as the book tells us,
623 Sente him a paire of dees of gold in scorn,
Sent him a pair of dice of gold in scorn,

624 For he hadde used hasard ther-biforn;
Because he had played at dicing before that;
625 For which he heeld his glorie or his renoun
For which he held his glory or his renown
626 At no value or reputacioun.
At no value or esteem.
627 Lordes may fynden oother maner pley
Lords may find other sorts of play
628 Honest ynough to dryve the day awey.
Respectable enough to pass the time.
629 Now wol I speke of othes false and grete
Now will I speak of oaths false and great
630 A word or two, as olde bookes trete.
A word or two, as old books treat them.
631 Gret sweryng is a thyng abhominable,
Great swearing is an abominable thing,
632 And fals sweryng is yet moore reprevable.
And false swearing is yet more worthy of reproof.
633 The heighe God forbad sweryng at al,
The high God forbad swearing at al,
634 Witnesse on Mathew; but in special
Witness on Matthew; but in special
635 Of sweryng seith the hooly Jeremye,
Of swearing says the holy Jeremiah,
636 "Thou shalt swere sooth thyne othes, and nat lye,
"Thou shall swear truly thine oaths, and not lie,
637 And swere in doom and eek in rightwisnesse";
And in judgement and also in righteousness";

638 But ydel sweryng is a cursednesse.
But idle swearing is a cursed thing.

639 Bihoold and se that in the firste table
Behold and see that in the first three

640 Of heighe Goddes heestes honurable,
Of high God's honourable commandments,

641 Hou that the seconde heeste of hym is this:
How the second of his commands is this:

642 "Take nat my name in ydel or amys."
"Take not my name in vain nor amiss."

643 Lo, rather he forbedeth swich sweryng
Lo, he forbids such swearing rather

644 Than homycide or many a cursed thyng;
Than homicide or many a cursed thing;

645 I seye that, as by ordre, thus it stondeth;
I say that, so far as order is concerned, thus it stands;

646 This knoweth, that his heestes understondeth,
He who understands his commandments knows this,

647 How that the seconde heeste of God is that.
How that is the second command of God.

648 And forther over, I wol thee telle al plat
And furthermore, I will tell thee flatly

649 That vengeance shal nat parten from his hous
That vengeance shall not part from his house

650 That of his othes is to outrageous.
Who of his oaths is too excessive.

651 "By Goddes precious herte," and "By his nayles,"
"By God's precious heart," and "By his nails,"

652 And "By the blood of Crist that is in Hayles,
And "By the blood of Christ that is in Hales Abbey,
653 Sevene is my chaunce, and thyn is cynk and treye!"
Seven is my number, and thine is five and three!"
654 "By Goddes armes, if thou falsly pleye,
"By God's arms, if thou falsely play,
655 This daggere shal thurghout thyn herte go!" —
This dagger shall go throughout thy heart!" —
656 This fruyt cometh of the bicched bones two,
This fruit comes of the two cursed dice,
657 Forsweryng, ire, falsnesse, homycide.
Perjury, anger, falseness, homicide.
658 Now, for the love of Crist, that for us dyde,
Now, for the love of Christ, who for us died,
659 Lete youre othes, bothe grete and smale.
Leave your oaths, both great and small.
660 But, sires, now wol I telle forth my tale.
But, sirs, now will I tell forth my tale.
661 Thise riotoures thre of whiche I telle,
These three rioters of whom I tell,
662 Longe erst er primé rong of any belle,
Long before prime rang of any bell,
663 Were set hem in a taverne to drynke,
Had set themselves in a tavern to drink,
664 And as they sat, they herde a belle clynke
And as they sat, they heard a bell clink
665 Biforn a cors, was caried to his grave.
Before a corpse, which was carried to its grave.

666 That oon of hem gan callen to his knave:
The one of them did call to his servant:
667 "Go bet," quod he, "and axe redily
"Go quickly," he said, "and ask at once
668 What cors is this that passeth heer forby;
What corpse is this that passes by here;
669 And looke that thou reporte his name weel."
And see that thou report his name correctly."
670 "Sire," quod this boy, "it nedeth never-a-deel;
"Sir," said this boy, "that is not at all necessary;
671 It was me toold er ye cam heer two houres.
It was told me two hours before you came here.
672 He was, pardee, an old felawe of youres,
He was, indeed, an old fellow of yours,
673 And sodeynly he was yslayn to-nyght,
And suddenly he was slain last night,
674 Fordronke, as he sat on his bench upright.
Completely drunk, as he sat on his bench upright.
675 Ther cam a privee theef men clepeth Deeth,
There came a stealthy thief men call Death,
676 That in this contree al the peple sleeth,
Who slays all the people in this country,
677 And with his spere he smoot his herte atwo,
And with his spear he struck his heart in two,
678 And wente his wey withouten wordes mo.
And went his way without more words.
679 He hath a thousand slayn this pestilence.
He has slain a thousand (during) this pestilence.

680 And, maister, er ye come in his presence,
And, master, before you come in his presence,
681 Me thynketh that it were necessarie
It seems to me that it would be necessary
682 For to be war of swich an adversarie.
To beware of such an adversary.
683 Beth redy for to meete hym everemoore;
Always be ready to meet him;
684 Thus taughte me my dame; I sey namoore."
Thus taught me my mother; I say no more."
685 "By Seinte Marie!" seyde this taverner,
"By Saint Mary!" said this tavern-keeper,
686 "The child seith sooth, for he hath slayn this yeer,
"The child says truth, for he has slain this year,
687 Henne over a mile, withinne a greet village,
Over a mile from here, within a great village,
688 Bothe man and womman, child, and hyne, and page;
Both man and woman, child, and laborer, and servant boy;
689 I trowe his habitacioun be there.
I suppose his habitation is there.
690 To been avysed greet wysdom it were,
It would be great wisdom to be forewarned,
691 Er that he dide a man a dishonour."
Before he did a man any harm."
692 "Ye, Goddes armes!" quod this riotour,
"Yea, God's arms!" said this rioter,
693 "Is it swich peril with hym for to meete?
"Is it such peril to meet with him?

694 I shal hym seke by wey and eek by strete,

I shall seek him by path-way and also by street (everywhere),

695 I make avow to Goddes digne bones!

I make a vow to God's honourable bones!

696 Herkneth, felawes, we thre been al ones;

Listen, fellows, we three are all agreed;

697 Lat ech of us holde up his hand til oother,

Let each of us hold up his hand to other,

698 And ech of us bicomen otheres brother,

And each of us become the others' brother,

699 And we wol sleen this false traytour Deeth.

And we will slay this false traitor Death.

700 He shal be slayn, he that so manye sleeth,

He shall be slain, he who slays so many,

701 By Goddes dignitee, er it be nyght!"

By God's dignity, before it be night!"

702 Togidres han thise thre hir trouthes plight

Together have these three pledged their troths

703 To lyve and dyen ech of hem for oother,

To live and die each of them for other,

704 As though he were his owene ybore brother.

As though he were his own born brother.

705 And up they stirte, al dronken in this rage,

And up they leaped, all drunken in this rage,

706 And forth they goon towardes that village

And forth they go towards that village

707 Of which the taverner hadde spoke biforn.

Of which the tavern-keeper had spoken before.

708 And many a grisly ooth thanne han they sworn,
And many a grisly oath then have they sworn,
709 And Cristes blessed body they torente –
And Christ's blessed body they tore to pieces –
710 Deeth shal be deed, if that they may hym hente!
Death shall be dead, if they can catch him!
711 Whan they han goon nat fully half a mile,
When they have gone not fully half a mile,
712 Right as they wolde han troden over a stile,
Right as they would have stepped over a fence,
713 An oold man and a povre with hem mette.
An old and poor man met with them.
714 This olde man ful mekely hem grette,
This old man full meekly greeted them,
715 And seyde thus, "Now, lordes, God yow see!"
And said thus, "Now, lords, may God look after you!"
716 The proudeste of thise riotoures three
The proudest of these three rioters
717 Answerde agayn, "What, carl, with sory grace!
Answered in reply, "What, churl, bad luck to you!
718 Why artow al forwrapped save thy face?
Why art thou all wrapped up except for thy face?
719 Why lyvestow so longe in so greet age?"
Why live thou so long in such old age?"
720 This olde man gan looke in his visage,
This old man did look in his face,
721 And seyde thus: "For I ne kan nat fynde
And said thus: "Because I can not find

722 A man, though that I walked into Ynde,
A man, though I walked to India,
723 Neither in citee ne in no village,
Neither in city nor in any village,
724 That wolde chaunge his youthe for myn age;
That would change his youth for my age;
725 And therfore moot I han myn age stille,
And therefore I must have my age still,
726 As longe tyme as it is Goddes wille.
As long a time as it is God's will.
727 Ne Deeth, allas, ne wol nat han my lyf.
Nor Death, alas, will not have my life.
728 Thus walke I, lyk a restelees kaityf,
Thus I walk, like a restless wretch,
729 And on the ground, which is my moodres gate,
And on the ground, which is my mother's gate,
730 I knokke with my staf, bothe erly and late,
I knock with my staff, both early and late,
731 And seye 'Leeve mooder, leet me in!
And say 'Dear mother, let me in!
732 Lo how I vanysshe, flessh, and blood, and skyn!
Lo how I waste away, flesh, and blood, and skin!
733 Allas, whan shul my bones been at reste?
Alas, when shall my bones be at rest?
734 Mooder, with yow wolde I chaunge my cheste
Mother, with you would I exchange my strongbox
735 That in my chambre longe tyme hath be,
That in my chamber long time has been,

736 Ye, for an heyre clowt to wrappe me!'
Yea, for an hair shirt to wrap me!'
737 But yet to me she wol nat do that grace,
But yet to me she will not do that favour,
738 For which ful pale and welked is my face.
For which full pale and withered is my face.
739 "But, sires, to yow it is no curteisye
"But, sirs, to you it is no courtesy
740 To speken to an old man vileynye,
To speak rudeness to an old man,
741 But he trespasse in word or elles in dede.
Unless he trespass in word or else in deed.
742 In Hooly Writ ye may yourself wel rede:
In Holy Writ you may yourself well read:
743 'Agayns an oold man, hoor upon his heed,
'In the presence of an old man, gray upon his head,
744 Ye sholde arise;' wherfore I yeve yow reed,
You should rise;' therefore I give you advice,
745 Ne dooth unto an oold man noon harm now,
Do no harm now unto an old man,
746 Namoore than that ye wolde men did to yow
No more than you would want men to do to you
747 In age, if that ye so longe abyde.
In old age, if you live so long.
748 And God be with yow, where ye go or ryde!
And God be with you, wherever you walk or ride!
749 I moot go thider as I have to go."
I must go thither where I have to go."

750 "Nay, olde cherl, by God, thou shalt nat so,"
"Nay, old churl, by God, thou shall not so,"

751 Seyde this oother hasardour anon;
Said this other dice-player quickly;

752 "Thou partest nat so lightly, by Seint John!
"Thou depart not so quickly, by Saint John!

753 Thou spak right now of thilke traytour Deeth.
Thou spoke right now of that same traitor Death.

754 That in this contree alle oure freendes sleeth.
That slays all our friends in this country.

755 Have heer my trouthe, as thou art his espye,
Have here my pledge, as thou art his spy,

756 Telle where he is or thou shalt it abye,
Tell where he is or thou shall pay for it,

757 By God and by the hooly sacrement!
By God and by the holy sacrament!

758 For soothly thou art oon of his assent
For truly thou art in league with him

759 To sleen us yonge folk, thou false theef!"
To slay us young folk, thou false thief!"

760 "Now, sires," quod he, "if that yow be so leef
"Now, sirs," said he, "if you are so eager

761 To fynde Deeth, turne up this croked wey,
To find Death, turn up this crooked way,

762 For in that grove I lafte hym, by my fey,
For in that grove I left him, by my faith,

763 Under a tree, and there he wole abyde;
Under a tree, and there he will wait;

764 Noght for youre boost he wole him no thyng hyde.
He will not in any way hide himself because of your boast.

765 Se ye that ook? Right there ye shal hym fynde.
Do you see that oak? Right there you shall find him.

766 God save yow, that boghte agayn mankynde,
God save you, He who redeemed mankind,

767 And yow amende!" Thus seyde this olde man;
And amend you!" Thus said this old man;

768 And everich of thise riotoures ran
And every one of these rioters ran

769 Til he cam to that tree, and ther they founde
Until he came to that tree, and there they found

770 Of floryns fyne of gold ycoyned rounde
Of fine round florins of coined gold

771 Wel ny an eighte busshels, as hem thoughte.
Well nigh eight bushels, as they thought.

772 No lenger thanne after Deeth they soughte,
No longer then after Death they sought,

773 But ech of hem so glad was of that sighte,
But each of them was so glad of that sight,

774 For that the floryns been so faire and brighte,
Because the florins are so faire and bright,

775 That doun they sette hem by this precious hoord.
That they set themselves down by this precious hoard.

776 The worste of hem, he spak the firste word.
The worst of them, he spoke the first word.

777 "Bretheren," quod he, "taak kep what that I seye;
"Brethren," he said, "take heed of what I say;

778 My wit is greet, though that I bourde and pleye.
My wit is great, though I jest and play.

779 This tresor hath Fortune unto us yiven
Fortune has given this treasure unto us

780 In myrthe and joliftee oure lyf to lyven,
In mirth and jollity to live our life,

781 And lightly as it comth, so wol we spende.
And as easily as it comes, so will we spend it.

782 Ey, Goddes precious dignitee! Who wende
Ah, God's precious dignity! Who would have supposed

783 To-day that we sholde han so fair a grace?
To-day that we should have such good fortune?

784 But myghte this gold be caried fro this place
But if this gold could be carried from this place

785 Hoom to myn hous, or elles unto youres —
Home to my house, or else unto yours —

786 For wel ye woot that al this gold is oures —
For well you know that all this gold is ours —

787 Thanne were we in heigh felicitee.
Then we would be in great happiness.

788 But trewely, by daye it may nat bee.
But truly, it may not be (done) by day.

789 Men wolde seyn that we were theves stronge,
Men would say that we were arrant thieves,

790 And for oure owene tresor doon us honge.
And for our own treasure have us hanged.

791 This tresor moste ycaried be by nyghte
This treasure must be carried by night
792 As wisely and as slyly as it myghte.
As wisely and as slyly as it can be.
793 Wherfore I rede that cut among us alle
Wherefore I advise that among us all straws
794 Be drawe, and lat se wher the cut wol falle;
Be drawn, and let's see where the lot will fall;
795 And he that hath the cut with herte blithe
And he who has the shortest straw with happy heart
796 Shal renne to the town, and that ful swithe,
Shall run to the town, and that very quickly,
797 And brynge us breed and wyn ful prively.
And very secretly bring us bread and wine.
798 And two of us shul kepen subtilly
And two of us shall carefully guard
799 This tresor wel; and if he wol nat tarie,
This treasure well; and if he will not tarry,
800 Whan it is nyght, we wol this tresor carie,
When it is night, we will carry this treasure,
801 By oon assent, where as us thynketh best."
By mutual agreement, where we think best."
802 That oon of hem the cut broghte in his fest,
That one of them brought the straws in his fist,
803 And bad hem drawe and looke where it wol falle;
And commanded them to draw and see where it will fall;
804 And it fil on the yongeste of hem alle,
And it fell on the youngest of them all,

805 And forth toward the toun he wente anon.
And forth toward the town he went right away.
806 And also soone as that he was gon,
And as soon as he was gone,
807 That oon of hem spak thus unto that oother:
The one of them spoke thus unto that other:
808 "Thow knowest wel thou art my sworen brother;
"Thou knowest well thou art my sworn brother;
809 Thy profit wol I telle thee anon.
Thy profit will I tell thee straightway.
810 Thou woost wel that oure felawe is agon.
Thou knowest well that our fellow is gone.
811 And heere is gold, and that ful greet plentee,
And here is gold, and that a full great quantity,
812 That shal departed been among us thre.
That shall be divided among us three.
813 But nathelees, if I kan shape it so
But nevertheless, if I can arrange things so
814 That it departed were among us two,
That it were divided among us two,
815 Hadde I nat doon a freendes torn to thee?"
Had I not done a good turn to thee?"
816 That oother answerde, "I noot hou that may be.
That other answered, "I know not how that can be.
817 He woot that the gold is with us tweye;
He knows that the gold is with us two;
818 What shal we doon? What shal we to hym seye?"
What shall we do? What shall we say to him?"

819 "Shal it be conseil?" seyde the firste shrewe,
"Shall it be (our) secret plan?" said the first scoundrel,
820 "And I shal tellen in a wordes fewe
"And I shall tell in a few words
821 What we shal doon, and brynge it wel aboute."
What we shall do, and bring it well about."
822 "I graunte," quod that oother, "out of doute,
"I agree," said that other, "without doubt,
823 That, by my trouthe, I wol thee nat biwreye."
That, by my troth, I will not betray thee."
824 "Now," quod the firste, "thou woost wel we be tweye,
"Now," said the first, "thou knowest well we are two,
825 And two of us shul strenger be than oon.
And two of us shall be stronger than one.
826 Looke whan that he is set, that right anoon
Look, when he has set down, right away
827 Arys as though thou woldest with hym pleye,
Arise as though thou would with him play,
828 And I shal ryve hym thurgh the sydes tweye
And I shall stab him through the two sides
829 Whil that thou strogelest with hym as in game,
While thou struggle with him as in game,
830 And with thy daggere looke thou do the same;
And with thy dagger see that thou do the same;
831 And thanne shal al this gold departed be,
And then shall all this gold be divided,

832 My deere freend, bitwixen me and thee.
My dear friend, between me and thee.
833 Thanne may we bothe oure lustes all fulfille,
Then we both can fulfill all our desires,
834 And pleye at dees right at oure owene wille."
And play at dice just as we wish,"
835 And thus acorded been thise shrewes tweye
And thus these two scoundrels are agreed
836 To sleen the thridde, as ye han herd me seye.
To slay the third, as you have heard me say.
837 This yongeste, which that wente to the toun,
This youngest, who went to the town,
838 Ful ofte in herte he rolleth up and doun
Very often in heart he rolls up and down
839 The beautee of thise floryns newe and brighte.
The beauty of these florins new and bright.
840 "O Lord!" quod he, "if so were that I myghte
"O Lord!" he said, "if it would be that I might
841 Have al this tresor to myself allone,
Have all this treasure to myself alone,
842 Ther is no man that lyveth under the trone
There is no man that lives under the throne
843 Of God that sholde lyve so murye as I!"
Of God that should live so merrily as I!"
844 And atte laste the feend, oure enemy,
And at the last the fiend, our enemy,
845 Putte in his thought that he sholde poyson beye,
Put in his thought that he should buy poison,

846 With which he myghte sleen his felawes tweye;
With which he might slay his two fellows;
847 For-why the feend foond hym in swich lyvynge
Because the fiend found him in such a manner of living
848 That he hadde leve him to sorwe brynge.
That he had leave bring him to sorrow.
849 For this was outrely his fulle entente,
For this was utterly his full intention,
850 To sleen hem bothe and nevere to repente.
To slay them both and never to repent.
851 And forth he gooth, no lenger wolde he tarie,
And forth he goes, no longer would he tarry,
852 Into the toun, unto a pothecarie,
Into the town, unto an apothecary,
853 And preyde hym that he hym wolde selle
And prayed him that he would sell him
854 Som poyson, that he myghte his rattes quelle;
Some poison, that he might kill his rats;
855 And eek ther was a polcat in his hawe,
And also there was a polecat in his yard,
856 That, as he seyde, his capouns hadde yslawe,
That, as he said, had slain his capons,
857 And fayn he wolde wreke hym, if he myghte,
And he would gladly revenge himself, if he could,
858 On vermyn that destroyed hym by nyghte.
On vermin that ruined him by night.
859 The pothecarie answerde, "And thou shalt have
The apothecary answered, "And thou shall have

A thyng that, also God my soule save,
A thing that, as God may save my soul,
In al this world ther is no creature
In all this world there is no creature
That eten or dronken hath of this confiture
That has eaten or drunk of this concoction
Noght but the montance of a corn of whete,
Only so much as the amount of a seed of whe
That he ne shal his lif anon forlete;
That he shall not immediately lose his life;
Ye, sterve he shal, and that in lasse while
Yea, he shall die, and that in less time
Than thou wolt goon a paas nat but a mile,
Than thou will go at a walk but only a mile,
This poysoun is so strong and violent."
This poison is so strong and violent."
This cursed man hath in his hond yhent
This cursed man has in his hand taken
This poysoun in a box, and sith he ran
This poison in a box, and then he ran
Into the nexte strete unto a man,
Into the next street unto a man,
And borwed [of] hym large botelles thre,
And borrowed [of] him three large bottles,
And in the two his poyson poured he;
And in the two he poured his poison;
The thridde he kepte clene for his drynke.
The third he kept clean for his drink.

874 For al the nyght he shoop hym for to swynke
For all the night he intended to work
875 In cariynge of the gold out of that place.
In carrying of the gold out of that place.
876 And whan this riotour, with sory grace,
And when this rioter, bad luck to him,
877 Hadde filled with wyn his grete botels thre,
Had filled his three big bottles with wine,
878 To his felawes agayn repaireth he.
He goes back again to his fellows.
879 What nedeth it to sermone of it moore?
What needs it to preach of it more?
880 For right as they hadde cast his deeth bifoore,
For right as they had planned his death before,
881 Right so they han hym slayn, and that anon.
Right so they have him slain, and that immediately.
882 And whan that this was doon, thus spak that oon:
And when this was done, thus spoke that one:
883 "Now lat us sitte and drynke, and make us merie,
"Now let us sit and drink, and make us merry,
884 And afterward we wol his body berie."
And afterward we will bury his body."
885 And with that word it happed hym, par cas,
And with that word it happened to him, by chance,
886 To take the botel ther the poyson was,
To take the bottle where the poison was,
887 And drank, and yaf his felawe drynke also,
And drank, and gave his fellow drink also,

888 For which anon they storven bothe two.
For which straightway they died, both of the two.

889 But certes, I suppose that Avycen
But certainly, I suppose that Avicenna

890 Wroot nevere in no canon, ne in no fen,
Wrote never in any authoritative book, nor in any chapter,

891 Mo wonder signes of empoisonyng
More wondrous symptoms of poisoning

892 Than hadde thise wrecches two, er hir endyng.
Than had these two wretches, before their ending.

893 Thus ended been thise homycides two,
Thus ended are these two homicides,

894 And eek the false empoysonere also.
And also the false poisoner as well.

895 O cursed synne of alle cursednesse!
O cursed sin of all cursedness!

896 O traytours homycide, O wikkednesse!
O treacherous homicide, O wickedness!

897 O glotonye, luxurie, and hasardrye!
O gluttony, lechery, and dicing!

898 Thou blasphemour of Crist with vileynye
Thou blasphemer of Christ with churlish speech

899 And othes grete, of usage and of pride!
And great oaths, out of habit and out of pride!

900 Allas, mankynde, how may it bitide
Alas, mankind, how may it happen

901 That to thy creatour, which that the wroghte
That to thy creator, who made thee

902 And with his precious herte-blood thee boghte,
And with his precious heart's blood redeemed thee,

903 Thou art so fals and so unkynde, allas?
Thou art so false and so unnatural, alas?

904 Now, goode men, God foryeve yow youre trespas,
Now, good men, God forgive you your trespass,

905 And ware yow fro the synne of avarice!
And guard yourselves from the sin of avarice!

906 Myn hooly pardoun may yow alle warice,
My holy pardon can cure you all,

907 So that ye offre nobles or sterlynges,
Providing that you offer gold coins or silver pennies,

908 Or elles silver broches, spoones, rynges.
Or else silver brooches, spoons, rings.

909 Boweth youre heed under this hooly bulle!
Bow your head under this holy papal bull!

910 Cometh up, ye wyves, offreth of youre wolle!
Come up, you wives, offer some of your wool!

911 Youre names I entre heer in my rolle anon;
Your names I enter here in my roll immediately;

912 Into the blisse of hevene shul ye gon.
Into the bliss of heaven you shall go.

913 I yow assoille, by myn heigh power,
I absolve you, by my high power,

914 Yow that wol offre, as clene and eek as cleer
You who will offer, as clean and also as clear (of sin)

915 As ye were born. — And lo, sires, thus I preche.
As you were born. — And lo, sirs, thus I preach.

916 **And Jhesu Crist, that is oure soules leche,**
And Jesus Christ, that is our souls' physician,
917 **So graunte yow his pardoun to receyve,**
So grant you to receive his pardon,
918 **For that is best; I wol yow nat deceyve.**
For that is best; I will not deceive you.
919 **But, sires, o word forgat I in my tale:**
But, sirs, one word I forgot in my tale:
920 **I have relikes and pardoun in my male,**
I have relics and pardons in my bag,
921 **As faire as any man in Engelond,**
As fine as any man in England,
922 **Whiche were me yeven by the popes hond.**
Which were given to me by the pope's hand.
923 **If any of yow wole, of devocion,**
If any of you will, of devotion,
924 **Offren and han myn absolucion,**
Offer and have my absolution,
925 **Com forth anon, and kneleth heere adoun,**
Come forth straightway, and kneel down here,
926 **And mekely receyveth my pardoun;**
And meekly receive my pardon;
927 **Or elles taketh pardoun as ye wende,**
Or else take pardon as you travel,
928 **Al newe and fressh at every miles ende,**
All new and fresh at every mile's end,
929 **So that ye offren, alwey newe and newe,**
Providing that you offer, again and again,

930 Nobles or pens, whiche that be goode and trewe.
Gold coins or silver pennies, which are good and true.

931 It is an honour to everich that is heer
It is an honour to every one that is here

932 That ye mowe have a suffisant pardoneer
That you may have a pardoner with sufficient power

933 T' assoille yow in contree as ye ryde,
To absolve you in the countryside as you ride,

934 For aventures whiche that may bityde.
For accidents that may happen.

935 Paraventure ther may fallen oon or two
Perhaps there may fall one or two

936 Doun of his hors and breke his nekke atwo.
Down off his horse and break his neck in two.

937 Looke which a seuretee is it to yow alle
Look what a safeguard is it to you all

938 That I am in youre felaweshipe yfalle,
That I happen to be in your fellowship,

939 That may assoille yow, bothe moore and lasse,
Who can absolve you, both more and less (every one),

940 Whan that the soule shal fro the body passe.
When the soul shall from the body pass.

941 I rede that oure Hoost heere shal bigynne,
I advise that our Host here shall begin,

942 For he is moost envoluped in synne.
For he is most enveloped in sin.

943 Com forth, sire Hoost, and offre first anon,
Come forth, sir Host, and offer first right now,
944 And thou shalt kisse the relikes everychon,
And thou shall kiss the relics every one,
945 Ye, for a grote! Unbokele anon thy purs."
Yea, for a fourpence coin! Unbuckle thy purse right now."
946 "Nay, nay!" quod he, "thanne have I Cristes curs!
"Nay, nay!" he said, "then I will have Christ's curse!
947 Lat be," quod he, "it shal nat be, so theech!
Let it be," he said, "it shall not be, as I may prosper!
948 Thou woldest make me kisse thyn olde breech,
Thou would make me kiss thine old underpants,
949 And swere it were a relyk of a seint,
And swear it was a relic of a saint,
950 Though it were with thy fundement depeint!
Though it were stained by thy fundament!
951 But, by the croys which that Seint Eleyne fond,
But, by the cross that Saint Helen found,
952 I wolde I hadde thy coillons in myn hond
I would I had thy testicles in my hand
953 In stide of relikes or of seintuarie.
Instead of relics or a container for relics.
954 Lat kutte hem of, I wol thee helpe hem carie;
Have them cut off, I will help thee carry them;
955 They shul be shryned in an hogges toord!"
They shall be enshrined in a hog's turd!"
956 This Pardoner answerde nat a word;
This Pardoner answered not a word;

957 So wrooth he was, no word ne wolde he seye.
So angry he was, no word would he say.
958 "Now," quod oure Hoost, "I wol no lenger pleye
"Now," said our Host, "I will no longer joke
959 With thee, ne with noon oother angry man."
With thee, nor with any other angry man."
960 But right anon the worthy Knyght bigan,
But immediately the worthy Knight began,
961 Whan that he saugh that al the peple lough,
When he saw that all the people laughed,
962 "Namoore of this, for it is right ynough!
"No more of this, for it is right enough!
963 Sire Pardoner, be glad and myrie of cheere;
Sir Pardoner, be glad and merry of cheer;
964 And ye, sire Hoost, that been to me so deere,
And you, sir Host, who are so dear to me,
965 I prey yow that ye kisse the Pardoner.
I pray you that you kiss the Pardoner.
966 And Pardoner, I prey thee, drawe thee neer,
And Pardoner, I pray thee, draw thyself nearer,
967 And, as we diden, lat us laughe and pleye."
And, as we did, let us laugh and play."
968 Anon they kiste, and ryden forth hir weye.
At once they kissed, and rode forth their way.

Heere is ended the Pardoners tale.

Chapter 13

Summary and Analysis: The Pardoner's Tale

Prologue to the Pardoner's Tale

The Host thinks that the cause of Virginia's death in the previous tale was her beauty. To counter the sadness of the tale, the Host suggests that the Pardoner tell a lighter tale. The Pardoner delays, for he wants to finish his meal, but says that he shall tell a moral tale. He says that he will tell a tale with this moral: the love of money is the root of all evil. He claims that during his sermons he shows useless trifles that he passes off as saints' relics. He proudly tells about how he defrauds people who believed they have sinned. He states explicitly that his goal is not to save people from sin, but to gain money from them. The Pardoner says that he will not imitate the apostles in their poverty, but will have food, comfort, and a wench in every town.

Analysis

Among the various pilgrims featured in the Canterbury Tales, the Pardoner is one of the most fully realised characters. The only character to whom Chaucer gives greater detail is the Wife of Bath. The Pardoner is a fraudulent huckster who shows no qualms about passing off false items as the relics of saints, but he also demonstrates a great sense of self-loathing. The Pardoner shifts from moments of direct honesty to shameless deceit, openly admitting the tricks of his trade to the travelers but nevertheless attempting to use these various methods on these travelers who are aware of his schemes. The Pardoner is in many senses a warped character, unable to hold to any consistent code of moral behaviour. Even in his physicality he is deformed. The General Prologue, suggesting that the Pardoner resembles a 'gelding or a mare,' hints that the Pardoner may be a congenital eunuch or, taken less literally, that he is a homosexual. In his deformity the Pardoner becomes a shell of a person. Although he is one of the most developed characters, he is the character perhaps most defined by his profession. The Pardoner has substituted a system of values with a rote performance, which conforms to his profession, which substitutes a meaningless monetary transaction for penance for sin. The Pardoner therefore suggests a traditional Vice character who behaves strictly out of the most impure motives, but where he departs from vice characters, who shamelessly commit misdeeds for their own pleasure, is that he lacks the necessary amoral quality. The Pardoner is not a moral man, but he nevertheless has a moral system to which he most certainly does not adhere.

The Pardoner's Tale

There once lived in Flanders a group of three rioters who did nothing but engage in irresponsible and sinful behaviour. They were blasphemous drunkards who, while in a tavern one night, witnessed men carrying a corpse to its grave. A boy told the rioters that the dead man was one of their friends, slain by an unseen thief called Death. They remark that Death has slain thousands, and vow to slay Death themselves. The three drunken men go off to find Death, but only come across an ancient man shrouded in robes. He claims that Death will not take him, and says that they can find Death underneath a nearby oak tree. When they found the tree they only found bushels of gold. They decide to take the treasure and divide it evenly, but realise that if they immediate went into town with it they would be presumed robbers. They therefore draw lots; the one with the shortest straw shall go into town and fetch food and drink for them. They shall stay in the forest with the gold until they can leave in the middle of the night. The youngest drew the shortest lot and was sent into town. The two that remain decide to murder the third once he returns, for they would then be able to divide the gold by two instead of three. However, while the third rioter was in town, he bought poison from an apothecary which he poured into the wine bottle. When he returned, the two rioters stabbed the third, murdering him. They then drank the poisoned wine and died themselves.

The Pardoner interrupts the end of his tale with a diatribe against the sin of avarice, then launches into a sermon in which he attempts to sell relics to the other travelers. The Host argues with him, telling him that the only relic he would want from the Pardoner is his testicles enclosed in a hog's turd. The knight mediates the conflict.

Analysis

The Pardoner's Tale is a direct extension of the personality of the narrator, an overtly moralistic tale that serves primarily to elicit a specific response. It is a particularly shameless tale, a condemnation of avarice that stems from the avarice of its narrator; by condemning the sin, the Pardoner hopes to motivate the travelers to pay the Pardoner to absolve their sins. The character of the Pardoner is omnipresent throughout the tale, which is told in an intimidating oratorical style that intends to create a sense of horror at the consequences for sinful action. Throughout the tale the narrator drifts in and out from the story, as the Pardoner occasionally leaves the plot of the tale to launch into sermons against sin. Finally, at the conclusion of the tale, he reveals the rationale for this authorial intervention, preaching against avarice for the sole intention of selling phony relics to the travelers. The tale is thus less of a fully formed narrative than a performance given by the Pardoner in which he never submerges his presence in the story.

The importance of the narrator is reflected in the relative unimportance of the characters in the story. The three rioters are anonymous hoodlums to whom the narrator gives no distinctive characteristics. The one distinction that the Pardoner makes among the three is that the rioter who is sent for food and drink is younger than the other two. Their characteristics are uniformly negative, but relatively broad - they are avaricious, but also drunkards and murderers, which gives the Pardoner opportunity to condemn a vast array of sins.

The old man that points the rioters in the direction of death is the single developed character in the story, a grotesque figure who waits to die out of extreme weariness for life. When he tells the rioters that he wishes to die, he claims that he walks on the ground, his 'mother's gate,' and asks to return to the earth (in the form of a decayed corpse). This conforms to the idea of rebirth, as the old man asks to return to the earth (his mother's womb) presumably to be born once again. However, for the old man this is only his second choice. He would prefer to exchange bodies with a young man, but can find no man willing to trade. He suffers the misery of a man who does sees no hope for redemption. He does not consider the possibility of heaven and Christian redemption, but rather adheres to ideas of earthly reincarnation. Quite significantly, this is the only expression of any spirituality contained in the Pardoner's Tale. The Pardoner has little concern with actual religious matters and makes no real reference to Christianity. His concern is money, and the Christian religion is only the means to achieve this end.

The Tale itself is a relatively simplistic moral fable that hinges on the distinctions between literal and figurative language. The initial personification of death that the young child uses as a metaphor and euphemism leads to the actual physical manifestation of Death as a tangible object: the piles of gold that the three rioters find. The plot of the tale derives from the rioters' literal interpretation of euphemism - since death has taken their friend, they must find death. This personification of death finally becomes metaphor once again when the piles of gold represent the death that they find.

Chapter 14

The Pardoner's Performance

The Pardoner's Performance, or How Do We Know What We Know about the Pardoner?

Chaucer's innovation in the Pardoner's performance tests our concept of dramatic irony by suggesting information regarding the Pardoner's sexuality, gender identity, and spirituality, major categories in the politics of identity, without confirming that information. Our presumed understanding of the Pardoner as a character lacks substantiation. As we learn about the Pardoner through the narrator's eyes and ears, we look to fit the "noble ecclesiaste" into the figure shaped by our own prejudices and perceptions, as any active reader must do. But the Pardoner, ever aware of his audience, does not offer clear clues to his personality. This break between what the other characters say about the Pardoner and what the Pardoner says about himself has been a major source of tension for all readers of the Tales and especially critics who search for substantiation of their views beyond the Chaucer's own language. The general tone of the Canterbury Tales is comic. After all, the pilgrims are traveling to the shrine St. Thomas Beckett in a public act of holy reverence, but the Tales take a darker turn when the Pardoner is brought to the foreground. The whole Canterbury Tales is a collected set of performances, stories told about telling stories. As Joseph Ganim has written, theatricality, by which he means "a governing sense of performance, an interplay among the author's voice, his fictional characters, and his immediate audience," is "a paradigm for the Chaucerian poetic" . This paper shall endeavor to show that the major effect of the Pardoner's presence in the Tales is to focus the reader's attention to questions of performance and performativity, literary perception, and the unstable relations between language, and more specifically art, and the self. This essay will be as much a critical discussion of Chaucerian criticism as an interpretation of the Pardoner for much of our current understandings of the Pardoner and his performance come from nearly six hundred years of scholarship on the subject.

What exactly do we now about the Pardoner? Much of our understanding of him as a literary human being rests on several key descriptive statements in the text, most about his appearance. They fail, however, to paint as full a portrait as we would like, but these descriptions amount to a generally negative picture. The General Prologue offers a first impression of the Pardoner which has affected his interpreted characterization to this day. The narrator, having met with each of the pilgrims and learned something of their characters, offers a portrait of each of them before the tales begin. In his description of the Pardoner, the narrator notes his traveling companion, his most prominent physical features (including his questionable sexuality), his "newe jet" fashion, his relics, and his professional status.

One focus of much criticism of the past fifty years has been the Pardoner's sexuality/gender identity. The narrator explicitly uses animal imagery in his portrait of the Pardoner, comparing him to a "hare", "a goot", and "a geldying or a mare", suggesting that the Pardoner is "something subhuman". These animals were also figuratively indicative of sexual abnormality in medieval times. The most troubling line is the narrator's: "I trowe he were a gelding or a mare" . The line is troublesome because the words do not gloss easily. Benson notes the line's complex mixture of subjective interpretation of gendered signs, metaphorical assertion (the Pardoner is like a neutered horse...), and contradiction ("he is either a eunuch or a homosexual") . Critics have been quick to take the narrator at his word on this point while recognizing his equivocation and irony when describing other pilgrims. The Pardoner's indeterminate sexual nature begs the question of the reliability of the narrator. The narrator "appears" to be a disinterested, unbiased observer of the pilgrims in their journey, faithfully trying to make clear his plan "To telle yow al the condicioun/ Of ech of hem", but his humble qualification that the portrait he paints is "as it semed me" emphasizes the obfuscation that exists between the perception and the use of language to convey the perception.

He is the tales' first performer. The narrator, who "hadde . . . spoken with hem everichon", acts as the sieve through whom we come to know the characters. His tale is his own retelling of his perceptions of the pilgrims, not an objective portrait of the motley lot. His three categories of description - each pilgrim's general circumstance, attire, and social status - limit his role to observer of appearances. And the Pardoner, as a master performer cunningly aware of his audience, was figuratively born to supply an appearance that will earn as much monetary reward as possible. Huppé calls the narrator's line "gossiping curiosity" and notes that "he is not aroused to any personal comment on the Pardoner's evil ways" . In fact, as we will later find, the Pardoner is quite willing to reveal his own sins to his pilgrim audience.

As several critical studies have shown, his interpretation of the Pardoner's sexuality is at best ambiguous. Rather than investigate the origins of the Host's and the narrator's (mis)readings of the Pardoner, critics have accepted their comments as indicative of the Pardoner's sexual deviance, either physical or social. All of the phrases interpreted as evidence of the Pardoner's sexuality and sex are ambiguous in the context of the language of the poem itself. The phrase "beel amy" of line 318 is regularly regarded as a homophobic jibe at the Pardoner, but the phrase also means simply "rascal" or "knave" .

Despite the diversity of interpretations, we can say that the text does convey some sense of sexual abnormality about the Pardoner. As Helen Cooper indicates, "Chaucer himself implies abnormality or perversion but refuses to predicate any specific ï¿½reality' behind it" . Whether he is a hermaphrodite, a homosexual, an overzealous ("effeminate") heterosexual, or a eunuch, the text fails to fully disclose. In this sense, we can say the Pardoner is sexually abject or queer. There is not enough textual evidence to determine whether he is any of these and all are attractively argued today. His perceived sexual abnormality has been an attractive topic of critical inquiry in the field of gender/queer studies for this reason. As with such matters in popular culture, we ache to know sexual secrets of celebrities, and the Pardoner is no less a celebrity in literature as political candidates on their pilgrimage to office.

The narrator's naming of his sexual abnormality is his misreading of the culturally determined signs that his culture interprets as such. "In any event," writes Gordan Hall Gerould, "Chaucer pretends to no expert knowledge. His surmise was based on appearance: the effeminacy of the Pardoner's smooth yellow hair and his dress, the quality of his voice" . Sedgewick concurs in his assertion that the Pardoner is a eunuch: "this is what everybody, medieval or modern, would ï¿½trowe' him to be from his appearance and voice alone" .

Similarly, Monica McAlpine argues that "the physical description, once it is set in the context of medieval sexual theory, seems to me to provide the strongest evidence of the Pardoner's possibly homosexuality, which in turn helps us both to recognize a possible implication of his association with the Summoner and to gloss ï¿½mare'" . Carolyn Dinshaw interprets the Pardoner as a eunuch and extends this interpretation of physical lack to his social relations and his delivery of his tale. "The Pardoner," she writes, "is defined by absence - he's a not-man or not even that - and it is in this fundamental sense that I shall take him to be a eunuch, a figurative one if not in fact a literal one as well. His sense of his own lack informs his social behaviour, his interactions with other; his incompleteness, moreover, informs the very thematics and narrative strategies of his Tale" .

Most critics fail to realise that in medieval times effeminacy connotes rambunctious heterosexuality in men, an excessive interest in and desire for women. Following this line, another critic offers another perspective on the Pardoner's sexuality. Richard Green argues that Chaucer's use of the legend of the soiled pants confused with a holy relic was present in several medieval tales throughout Europe and the overwhelming suggestion that these tales make is that the owner of these pants is excessively heterosexual, a cleric pursuing adulterous relations with parishioners: "If Chaucer, consciously or otherwise, is making the Host echo an incident from the story of The Friar's Pants' when he launches into his diatribe against the Pardoner, it is difficult to avoid the conclusion that the Pardoner is here being cast mentally in the role of philanderer".

We also have the Pardoner's own reference to his having "a joly wenche in every toun" in his Prologue. Huppé writes that "The boast is curious; does he expect thereby to hide from his audience his infirmity? Or is he simply exacerbating his sore by arrogantly calling attention to what might otherwise pass without comment? It is possible that he is doing both - pretending to himself, but knowing that it is pretense" . We demand that the Pardoner "be" homosexual while we ignore contradictory or ambiguous textual evidence. In a well-argued study that at times breaks with much of twentieth century Chaucerian criticism by not beginning with an overtly homophobic prejudice, Monica McAlpine notes that the infamous line is not the narrator's only comment on the Pardoner and that his profession, his appearance, and his talent for preaching are equally important to our understanding of his character:

"The narrator sets an example of not reducing the Pardoner to his sexuality, an example that at other levels of response Chaucer means us to emulate" . Rather than accuse the narrator of rabid homophobia, a response anachronistic to the text at hand, McAlpine believes "he is rather like the modern person who has not mastered the distinctions among homosexuals, bisexuals, transvestites, and transsexuals", again reemphasizing the distance between what one sees and what one is. As we can see, the question of the Pardoner's sexuality remains unanswered.

Chaucer's Pardoner joins a list of fictional persons throughout Western literature, including Mary Magdalene of the Bible, Viola of Twelfth Night, Coleridge's Christabel, the Tiresias of "The Waste Land," and Nabakov's Humbert Humbert, whose vivacity and power lie in the tense relation of sexuality and morality that forms their characters. One of the most striking peculiarities of the Pardoner's character, according to Sedgewick, has been Chaucer's "combination of pardoner and eunuchus in one person" . The Pardoner is also a "noble ecclesiaste" who draws in the faithful to repentance while committing deception and fraud upon them. The social figure of the Pardoner elicits the stock response of suspicion, disgust, and moral outrage among medieval and modern audiences alike. As a trope for ecclesiastical deviance, the historical pardoner stained the pristine dogma of the medieval Christian church, voiding the sacred heart of the Church's work for material gain.

On the way "fro the court of Rome", his first act in the narrator's tale is to sing the refrain of a popular song, immediately confirming the reader's suspicions of this stock figure. The Pardoner and the Summoner, spiritual con men both, offer up their appearances for the narrator's imagination. He is excessively preoccupied with his appearance, as well he should be as a performer. In order to be a good performer, he must look like a good performer. He must stand out in his crowd. Perhaps taking advantage of the sexual abnormality which has drawn the narrator's comment "I trowe he were a geldying or a mare," he adorns himself with attractive attire, and indeed with holy relics, so as to indulge even more attention. His dress, merely one feature of his performative nature, overcompensates for the mysterious lack, physical, sexual, or spiritual, from which he has suffered in the critical mind.

His clothing is another critical trope for the deceptive appearance of the Pardoner. Carolyn Dinshaw finds a great deal of existential meaning in her interpretation of the Pardoner's fashion consciousness: "the Pardoner opens out another - unnerving - possible hermeneutic significance of the image of the body swaddled in veils: there is perhaps nothing underneath those cloaks of representation. There might be nothing but veils and letters covering a fundamental absence, a radical lack of meaning or truth" . I tend to regard such an interpretation as melodramatic for surely the Pardoner, as the source of such radical misreadings, is not nothing.

Chaucer makes clear the nature of the Pardoner's Tale as a performance, not only as one of the fifty-eight tales the pilgrims will tell on their journey to and from Canterbury, but as the Pardoner's own recreation of a performance he may give on any other occasion to make his living. As Robert Jordan has noted, "More than any of the other Canterbury pilgrims, the Pardoner encourages the realist assumption that the pilgrims are ï¿½alive' and existentially distinct from the tales they tell" . The Pardoner makes his performance known explicitly and even proudly early in his Prologue. He warns his audience that, despite "A voys . . . as small as hath a goot", he takes pains to speak loudly so that all may hear the sermons that "I kan al by rote" . Calling further attention to his efforts at performance, he reveals the theme of all his sermons: "Radix malorum est Cupiditas" . Warren Ginsberg warns that "the Pardoner is an avaricious man, and his many words confess the fact more than he knows" .

The Pardoner's naming of his own sin, his own avaricious intentions, and his own crafty methods recalls the standard mode of the morality play's Vice figure, as Helen Cooper notes . The difference is the Pardoner's self-revelation is entirely for his own gain and has nothing to do with his audience's salvation. Indeed, he does not care if, when the poor souls die, "hir soules goon a-blakeberyed" .

Critics such as Harold Bloom locate Chaucer's strength as a poet in his vivid creation of character who create themselves through language: "What they say to others, and to themselves, partly reflects what they already are, but partly engenders also that they will be" .

One of the major points of contention in today's Chaucerian criticism is the dispute between linguistically- and rhetorically-oriented interpretations of the characters as rhetorical effects of Chaucer's conscious manipulation of language and psychologically-oriened studies that treat the pilgrims as dramatic characters. Beginning in this century with Kittredge, we find the critics responding to the Pardoner and indeed all the pilgrims as personalities that can be separated from the context of the tales. As member of the rhetorical critics, Marshall Leicester argues that "the tales must be treated not as the performances of preexisting selves but as texts. They are not written to be spoken, like a play, but written to be read as if they were spoken" (13). Part of the allure of great literature, however, is its capacity to approximate an image of ourselves through creative characterization. We respond more passionately and intimately to fictional people than we do to mere words and sentences, however finely woven.

A great deal has been written on the meaning of the Pardoner's Prologue and Tale. I shall leave the interpretations to others and focus my attention on their other function as performance by the Pardoner. I would, however, like to point out several features of the Prologue and Tale which inform my discussion of the Pardoner's performativity. The dominant feature of the Prologue is its superfluity. Packed with lists, laments, threats, and famous names, the first part's form connotes urgency and speed, Benson suggests . The Pardoner's delivery of the Prologue is fragmentary and disconnected, never allowing his audience a moment to reflect on what he has said. We can expect that non-verbal signals would accompany such a performance. Unable to think on the Pardoner's words, we must respond emotionally. His language in preparing his audience for his mock-sermon and tale emphasize a concern with his performance as a performance. Stephen Knight admits "this tale demands" performance "more than most . . .". The overarching theme of the Pardoner's

Prologue and Tale, as stated in my thesis, is the distinction between the performer and the performance, a distinction which Yeats problematizes between "the dancer and the dance". Our knowledge of the Pardoner's avaricious intentions, told by himself, gives away to the oratorical extravagance of his work. At the heart of the Pardoner's Tale, Leicester notes, is "a failure or refusal to distinguish carefully and consistently between literal and spiritual levels of meaning and discourse" . The melodramatic lamentations that colour his Tale are emotional icing to the simple, yet effective story of the three rioters:

> *O glotonye, ful of cursednesse!*
> *O cause first of oure confusioun!*
> *O original of oure dampnacioun . . . (ll. 490-500)*
> *O glotonye, on thee wel oghte us pleyne!*
> *O, wiste a man how manye maladyes*
> *Folwen of excesse and of glotonyes . . . (ll. 512-3)*

"These sudden bursts of mechanical emotionalism," Benson argues, "contain little moral seriousness or artistic taste, but they might well arrest the attention of an unsophisticated audience" . Most of the Pardoner's presentation lacks the substance necessary to achieve his desired results, and so he turns to the delivery of the presentation itself The strength of the Pardoner's verbal project is its forcefulness rather than its substance.

The Pardoner concludes the Tale with the much-cited claim "I wol yow nat deceyve", a deliberately ambiguous statement that perfectly fits the Pardoner's character and performance for the statement is both true and false in its diversity of connotations on multiple performative levels. The statement is not the "very paroxysm of agonized sincerity" that Kittredge famously claims, but is the exact point at which the Pardoner's character and his performance converge. In this moment, the statement is truth and falsehood, appearance and reality, performer and performance are devoid of any intellectual meaning. The emotive impact of the statement, the verbal climax of the Pardoner's performance in the Canterbury

Tales, renders the pilgrims silent with a mixture of horror and contempt. The line has had a similar effect on critics unable to find a definite meaning. Helen Cooper describes the Pardoner as "a character within his own tale", introducing himself as a weak speaker who must strain his voice to be heard .By introducing himself as the speaker of his own tale, the Pardoner clears the way to manipulate himself in front of the audience's gullible eyes and ears. In describing his own actions and intentions in his Prologue, the Pardoner becomes "the first exegetical critic of his own tale" .

Many critics have tried to interpret the Pardoner's Sermon and Exemplum in terms of the literary tradition of the sermon. But the Pardoner is not following the sermon tradition. He is instead manipulating that tradition, using its conventions and rhetorical strategies to further his ultimate goal of cheating the "lewed" audience out of their money. "Even though the Pardoner's sermon on the tavern sins echoes phrases, imagery, and themes from authoritative medieval works, we should not therefore conclude that Chaucer meant us to read it as a serious exposition of Christian thought" . The Pardoner sounds more like an actor reciting lines remembered from previous performances than a true Church official offering a moral lesson. He employs his skill in employing the features and conventions of the medieval sermon tradition to his own obsessive ends, all the while becoming "more conscious of himself and more aware of both his power and his powerlessness" . His power in this case is his power of persuasion, the dangerous use of language against which Plato warns. His powerlessness is the instability of the performance, the constant threat that his performance will be seen for the lie that it is.

Besides being "a moral thyng" with meaning unto itself, the Tale is also a vehicle for the Pardoner's self-revelation. So many studies have explored the aspects of the Pardoner to be found in the tale that it is unnecessary for me to offer my insights. One example that Leicester offers for our purposes is the way the sermon "keeps associating the sins it describes with the Pardoner, showing that he is guilty of them" . The

Old Man, perhaps one of the most diversely interpreted figures in all of literature, has long been seen by many to be an embodiment of the Pardoner and his sin of cupiditas. The anonymity and impersonality of the rioters reinforces the poem's theme throughout, the evasion of identity through performance. To name someone or something is an attempt at stability and permanence, the locating of an essential nature to human personality. The Pardoner's sermon, his tale, and his character, as described by the narrating pilgrim, all speak to the evasiveness and illusion of identity as a social concept. The conclusion of the Tale, the violent result of the Pardoner's telling of the Tale, and the general literary reaction to the Pardoner's occupation emphasize the danger inherent to unstable identity

We must not forget that the Pardoner makes his living by his ability to perform. He is thereby at a distinct advantage in the story-telling competition set up by the Host. He is no amateur at delivering a convincing sermon, as he boasts in the Prologue. He has a set routine he follows in delivering his performances: first, he tells from whence he has come; then, he shows his papal bulls as evidence of his religious authority; he might flavor his already notable appearance with "a wordes fewe" "in Latyn" to paint him as a learned man; then, she offers his relics for the audience's inspection (for a price). If the Pardoner has faith, it is a faith in the rhetorical force of his own performance, as he demonstrates when he reveals his other-than-holy intentions to defraud his listeners of their "pens, or elles grotes" . "As I create myself through language," he believes, "so do I shape my sinful listener into a believer by making him aware of his own sinfulness through making my own sinful self the subject of my sermon." He is a professional magician of words who suffers muted outrage when the truth of his conjuring is discovered. I read the Pardoner's Prologue and Tale as a routine performance of his job duties. On this particular occasion, however, the Pardoner is caught up in his own performance. His over-confidence in his own talents, his greed, and his negative self-concept culminate in a terrible moment when the performance moves beyond his control. Leonard Koff suggests that "The Pardoner may not be evil so much as bold - bold with language because he is bold with the idea of language as skill, and performance as making. He distinguishes motive from deed and forthrightly raises the question fo the moral efficacy of language considered as technique pure and simple". Manipulated by the Pardoner, language is a weapon.

The conclusion of the tale of the three rioters, of course, should not be read as the end of his performance. The real end of his performance is the presentation of relics and the collection of money, but the boisterous Host steps up to deny the Pardoner his final glory. The Pardoner is so angry with the Host because the Host refuses to participate in the Pardoner's self-conscious performance.

The Pardoner's raison d'etre is his capacity to perform for an audience and the effects of this performance are the audience's responses to this preaching, their purchase of pardons and their fee for touching the relics. The bold Host recognizes the Pardoner to be too slick for his own game and violently refuses to play. Following the spoiling of his story, the Pardoner slinks away in Iago-like silence. Without his performance, the Pardoner is nothing. The Pardoner concludes the Tale with the much-cited claim "I wol yow nat deceyve", a deliberately ambiguous statement that perfectly fits the Pardoner's character and performance for the statement is both true and false in its diversity of connotations on multiple performative levels.

The statement is not the "very paroxysm of agonized sincerity" that Kittredge famously claims, but is the exact point at which the Pardoner's character and his performance converge. In this moment, the statement is truth and falsehood, appearance and reality, performer and performance are devoid of any intellectual meaning. The emotive impact of the statement, the verbal climax of the Pardoner's performance in the Canterbury Tales, renders the pilgrims silent with a mixture of horror and contempt. The line has had a similar effect on critics unable to find a definite meaning.

Chaucer blesses the Pardoner with a distinct performative style and technique. What was once considered "the monstrous cynicism of the Pardoner's confessions" is now more generally recognized as the rhetorical effect of his performance. The Pardoner's abject, spectacular life offer the raw material for the emotional force of his tale. Forced to live by what he swindles from the faithful, he probably has performed this and similar sermons many times in his life. Consumed by greed, he refines his talents to yield greater fruits from his listeners' repentance. Like an actor who studies the habit and condition of the character he is to portray, the Pardoner is versed in at least a basic understanding of Christian theology, classic learning, and rhetorical strategies.

As a socially recognizable sexually abnormal person in a most despised occupation, the Pardoner is no doubt aware of the effects and the extent of evil and malice. At the extreme of negative assessments of the Pardoner, Ruth Nevo claims "the Pardoner stands at the outer pale of Chaucer's tolerance for humanity. He is a concentrate of the maximum hypocrisy. He is parasite of parasites". His selfishness, coupled with a knowledge of evil drawn perhaps from his personal experience, "works to enable him not to choose the good but to exploit it" among his listeners. The Pardoner reveals his fundamental sin is cupiditas, always the subject of his preaching. His great talent is his ability to weave a fabulous tale from his own sinful despair. The Pardoner's cupiditas finds active expression in the rioters, writes Benson, discovering two terrible effects: "the revelers' separation from God and from each other (the opposite of Jesus's twin commands to love God and one's neighbor) . . ." .

The Pardoner is a practical rhetorician, mastering diverse ways of persuading an audience to act as he wishes. "The essence of his being," Benson argues, "is his misuse of the art of preaching for profit" . When called to tell his tale, the pilgrims, fearful of his acknowledged power with language, bid him "Telle us som moral thyng" (l. 325). No amateur, he is ready to preach at the first scent of financial reward and his decision to drink "a draughte of moyste and corny ale" while he "thynke/ Upon som honest thyng" is purely intended for theatrical effect. Like a good showman, he knows the value of the dramatic pause. "He knows plenty of moral things," Sedgewick believes, "but to tell one as such is completely out of his character and habit; and what is more, he knows the Pilgrims know that also" .

A look at The Pardoner in Geoffrey Chaucer's Canterbury Tales

What effect does the Pardoner have on us as readers? The Pardoner has many audiences: the "lewed peple" (l. 437) who pay him for pardons, his fellow Canterbury pilgrims, the reader of Chaucer's poem. The Pardoner adapts his presentation with each re-reading to the benefit of his audience. In Leicester's view, "Chaucer conceives and represents the act of storytelling as the encounter of a subject with an institution" . In the present case, the institutions are the Holy Church itself and the sermon tradition. Because the knowledge of the boundaries and definitions of these institutions are already in the minds of his audience, the Pardoner can easily tailor his performances to his audience's expectations for maximum profit. Despite making clear his avaricious intentions, the Pardoner nevertheless convinces some of the veracity of his words and the dire need for repentance. Otherwise, he would not last long as a Pardoner. I agree with H. Marshall Leicester's assertion that "the Canterbury tales are individually voiced, and radically so - that each of the tales is primarily (in the sense of ï¿½first,' that is, the place where one starts) an expression of its teller's personality and outlook as embodied in the unfolding ï¿½now' of the telling" . The Tale has the feel of an impromptu performance in which the speaker shapes the details as he goes along, reacting to and reinforcing audience responses as they catch his attentive eye. Following Bloom, Leicester locates the source of the reader's understanding of the characters in the tales they tell: "The tales are examples of impersonated artistry because they concentrate not on the way preexisting persons create language but on the way language creates people" . The

Pardoner is as much a product of his own self-expression and adaptation to his own self-expression as a conduit for Chaucer's intentional meaning. In the violent dissociation between the speaker's intention and the speech's effect, Chaucer demonstrates "the potential power art has to affect an audience, an essential quality even Christian literature must have to succeed, though here used for all the wrong reasons" .The substance of the Pardoner's message is never questioned by his audience, only the truth of the Pardoner.

The Pardoner, his Prologue, and his Tale are evocative emotionally, spiritually, morally, aesthetically, and as literature. The only certainty we can claim about the Pardoner is that his presence and story provoke a strong response. Koff states "I can think of no other ars poetica that links art and its use, its social value and its morality, as engagingly as the Pardoner's Prologue and Tale. We can hardly avoid the concern of the tale - the condition of our souls" . In reading the Tales, we are invited into dialogue with the ideas, presumptions, and beliefs it presents. Chaucer anticipates that the intellect will not so much check as augment by tempering - be being itself - whatever responses are necessarily felt, whatever responses are left to us only after the narrative ï¿½has happened'" . The Noble Ecclesiaste's fictive power is his powerful hold over our imaginations as readers. He confuses critics with a clever self-awareness that suggest our own. As Koff puts it, the Pardoner knows he is only pretending and "we are expected, indeed invited, to see through him". What we see behind that fictive veil is left to the reader's imagination. There can be no doubt that the rich diversity of meanings which countless critics have drawn from the Pardoner are possible only because of Chaucer's masterfully woven creation. The figure of the Pardoner forces us to contemplate the performances we enact in our own lives.

Chapter 15

Study Questions

Q.1. Analyse Chaucer's Pardoner, The Scriptural Eunuch, and The Pardoner's Tale

Or

Q. Explain Augustinian theology in Chaucer's Pardoner

A recent article in Speculum suggested that Chaucer's Pardoner may best be understood in terms of Augustinian theology. It is possible that the principles discussed there may be profitably elaborated. The intent of this paper is to indicate that the tradition of which St Augustine was perhaps the most influential expositor provides more than a general climate of idea: specifically, that Scriptural imagery, utilized by Chaucer in the portrait and tale of the Pardoner, serves to illuminate quite precisely the nature of the man and the "moralite" of his sermon.

We are learning that the mediaeval author sought to build up the surface or cortex of his work in such a way as to indicate some particular nucleus, or inner meaning. For this purpose he had at his command two main sources of material: the Book of Nature or God's Creation — the data of sense perception, and another Book — the Bible — which offered the unperceived data of revelation. Both "Books" provided the opportunity to achieve by study and interpretation a better knowledge of their Author. The Old Testament foreshadowed the "New Law" of charity under a series of types or figures, and was consequently to be reinterpreted in this light. Both the Bible and the Book of Nature provided a type of surface reality-a series of which, if properly understood, reflected the will and the law of God.

The "compaignye" created by Geoffrey Chaucer for the most famous fourteenth-century literary pilgrimage has been almost microscopically examined by the modern scholar in the effort to arrive at the most satisfactory understanding possible of the text of the Canterbury Tales. The characters are so firmly conceived that attempts have been made to identify the actual prototypes whom Chaucer may himself have known; and considerable study has been devoted to the various mediaeval sciences which provided details of psychological or physiognomical characteristics. It is surprising, however, to find scholarly effort directed so intensively upon what the mediaeval author called the cortex of his work, without an equally persistent effort to discover what nucleus might lie beneath. What we now call realism was of itself only a point of departure in a world where man's sensible experience consistently reflected the presence and nature of his Creatorwhere reality itself lay beneath the sign.

The criterion of ulterior signification is, in fact, a hallmark of literature as a mode of expression. We expect the "cortex" to set forth a "nucleus" which is not denotable by scientific description. The reality of literature in any age may be said to lie beneath the sign, although the complexity of signification may not, perhaps, be as extensive or as arbitrary as that afforded the mediaeval artist by a highly developed system of conventional Scriptural symbolism.

Surface realism, however, even in the Middle Ages, was desirable insofar as it did not obscure the real issue of a particular work; and there is ample justification for historical study of the "realistic" details of mediaeval literature by which its inner sense is communicated to the reader. We have tended, nevertheless, to minimize the importance of the main source of mediaeval symbolic expression: that is, the Bible which, as the Word of God, provided, along with the Book of God's other works, the means for ulterior knowledge. Even if enigmatic, the words of the Bible could not be doubted, and here too, as with the Book of nature, interpretation demanded insight. With respect to either, the letter killed, while the spirit gave life.

In his analysis of the Pardoner and his "secret" eunuchry, Professor Curry has adequately demonstrated that Chaucer's account is "scientifically correct." But, although he approaches an inner equivalent for the detail he examines, Curry clarifies only the "letter" of this provocative characteristic. It would be strange indeed if Chaucer had intended his characters to be recognizable as particular living individuals, or as scientific phenomena, and nothing more. In this paper I wish first to indicate the literary purpose of the detail of eunuchry used in the description of the Pardoner — the nucleus beneath this element of the cortex. The detail may be shown to apply, not particularly to an individual quaestor of the House of Rouncevale, but to any pilgrim on his earthly pilgrimage. The Pardoner's "secret" may thus hold the secret of his literary existence. It will be my purpose to show how Chaucer, in making his Pardoner a eunuch, intended to expose and to stress the essential nature of this Canterbury pilgrim. It should be understood that this paper does not attempt to establish sources for idea or phraseology, except generally in Biblical context. For the present purpose it has been necessary to limit severely the associations connected with various Scriptural images, and citations of patristic writers have usually been minimized to offer an indicative selection of statements which may be found repeated in different ways elsewhere.

I

The last of all the pilgrims described in the General Prologue, the Pardoner is pictured as riding along singing a duet with that other "noble ecclesiaste," the Summoner. These two compeers, whose business in theory is to increase and multiply the congregation of the faithful in the Church, are ironically singing a popular song of carnal, rather than spiritual, love -of cupidity (to use the conventional mediaeval distinction) rather than of charity. Like January in his garden, the Pardoner tries to put on a gay and new exterior: with his hood folded in his wallet, "Hym thoughte he rood al of the newe jet." Chaucer does not fail to note, however, that, despite his "newe" appearance and the lecherous look in his eye, this man is somewhat less than he seems.

Swiche glarynge eyen hadde he as an hare. . . 684
A voys he hadde as smal as hath a goot.
No berd hadde he, ne nevere sholde have;
As smothe it was as it were late shave. 690
I trowe he were a geldying or a mare.

The images of the hare, goat and horse — all common symbols of lechery — do not prevent notice that this man is also described as a eunuch. In choosing this descriptive detail Chaucer may have had in mind a concept used in several Biblical texts and dealt with by many patristic commentators. In such terms the rather extraordinary detail of eunuchry may be shown not to be haphazard.

The symbol of the eunuch receives noteworthy Scriptural treatment in three separate texts: Deuteronomy xxiii, 1, Isaiah, lvi, 3-5, and Matthew, xix, 12. They are sometimes considered independently in Biblical commentaries, but more often the texts are referred to each other for clarification and exposition. Thus Rupertus, in a very full consideration of the prohibition of eunuchs under the Old Law, cites all three texts:

'A eunuch. . . shall not enter into the church of the Lord' . In Isaias we read: 'And let not the eunuch say, Behold, I am a withered tree. For thus says the Lord to eunuchs: If they shall keep my sabbaths, and do my will, and hold fast my covenant, in my house and in my walls I shall give them a place. . .' Are, then, the Law and the Prophet contradictory, that the Law should say, 'A eunuch shall not enter into the church of the Lord,' while in the Prophet the Lord says the opposite?. . . Now, the meaning of the term 'eunuch is not the same in both quotations. In the former it is to be understood literally, in the latter spiritually.

Let us then enumerate the species of eunuchs. In the Gospel the Lord declares: 'There are eunuchs who were born so from their mother's womb, and there are eunuchs who have been made so by men, and there are eunuchs who have made themselves such for the kingdom of heaven'. This third eunuchry, because it is not achieved with a cutting instrument but rather through a purposeful chastity, is to be called spiritual, though not entirely so, because celibacy is made manifest in the flesh. And these, without doubt, are those laudable eunuchs to whom, according to the aforesaid Prophet, the Lord will give 'a place in his house and in his walls'. . .

. . . He continues with an interpretation of the letter of the Law:

Of all these types one cannot truly say that none enters the church of the Lord, but only that canonical authority forbids the sacred honours of the altar to the maimed and the castrate. We must therefore ask what kind of eunuch it is who may not enter into the church of the Lord. To those who ask this, another quotation offers itself: 'Cursed is every male who does not produce seed in Israel.' Neither quotation can rightly be understood without the other; though the words are different, the sense is the same. Thus, the eunuch who may not enter into the church of the Lord, who does not produce seed in Israel, and who ought to be cursed because he has not produced seed in Israel, is the man who, though able to edify his neighbor with his words, has kept silent, or who, though lie has known good and useful things, loves idle and vain ones. Such a man is the opposite of the man who has made himself a eunuch for the kingdom of heaven's sake. The latter is to be praised because, having the natural power to beget sons, he is continent of his flesh for the kingdom of heaven. . . . The former is in the same degree detestable because, having had committed to him the talent of God's word, which he could invest well and barter usefully for the edification of many men, he lies idle and neglects the grace he has undeservedly received.

This exposition may be valuable for an understanding of Chaucer's use of the idea of eunuchry in his description of the Pardoner. . . . Besides eunuchry thought of as voluntary I chastity, we are presented with another figurative type which Rupertus characterizes as detestabilis, the antithesis of the laudable spiritual eunuchry. This eunuchry is also the result of an act of will, but of an opposite act in that this man, in full knowledge of the bona et utilia, chooses the worse part: the otiosa. . . et vana. This man, possessing the ability to inform his neighbor, remains silent; knowing the value of good works, he chooses idleness. Instead of cutting himself off from evil works, he cuts himself off from good works. He refuses offered grace. In short, he is the presumptuous man who, by his act of will, commits the unpardonable sin, not for the sake of, but in despite of, the kingdom of heaven. He holds a position in Babylon exactly equivalent to that held by his opposite in Jerusalem. . . .

Besides the significant treatment of the idea by Rupertus, it is not difficult to find equally suggestive statements in other places. The Glossa Ordinaria itself reflects the opposition already noted. In the second class of eunuchs it places those false religious who deceptively put on the guise of religion, but in reality are not chaste: the wolves in sheep's clothing. "Inter hos computantur etiam hic qui specie religionis simulant castitatern." Consonant with these remarks is also the opposition by Paschasius Radbertus between the eunuchus Dei and the eunuchus non Dei. Rabanus Maurus gives a most significant account of the eunuchi qui facti sunt:

> Man-made eunuchs are produced by philosophers, or are softened into women for the worship of idols, or under the spell of heresy they simulate charity in order to counterfeit the truth of religion. But none of these will attain the kingdom of heaven; only the man who has made himself a eunuch for Christ.

The eunuchus non Dei — the perverted, or perverse, churchman — is he who, according to Deuteronomic law, non intrabit in ecclesiam Domini. Commentaries on Deuteronomy xxiii, 1 also describe this type of eunuchry with clarity. The Glossa Ordinaria explains the prohibition thus: "All who live effeminately and do not do manly work cannot remain in the congregation of the saints, nor are they fit to enter the kingdom of heaven. . . ." The false eunuch is the man who lives at ease (vacat otio, in Rupertus' words), and does not carry out "manly" works. That is to say, he is sterile in good works, impotent to produce spiritual fruit. Bruno Astensis is more specific yet: "By this is signified that no one will enter into the heavenly homeland who, sterile in good works, does not have the organs of spiritual generation and fertility."

We may carry the metaphor one step farther. The spiritual fruits, or progeny, which the upright produce are, traditionally, as Bruno suggests, virtues or good works. St Augustine refers several times to the analogy by which good works represent spiritual offspring. For this idea the most obvious Scriptural basis is Genesis, i, 28, in which the Lord, having created man in His own image, male and female, "blessed them and said: Increase and multiply and fill the earth. . . ." This benediction is usually distinguished from that given the beasts which was a precept for physical multiplication only. While man was granted the necessity of such increase, his blessing referred also to the soul by which he was superior to the beasts. For man, then, the precept instituted the state of honourable marriage, but further prescribed for the soul the multiplication of virtues by spiritual fertility.

Common also is the interpretation according to which man is thus commanded to "increase and multiply" the congregation of the faithful that the number of the elect might be fulfilled. With respect to the concept of spiritual "multiplication" reference is also frequently made to Psalm cxxxvii, 3: "Multiplicabis me in anima mea, virtute' By increase in good works and multiplication in virtues, or by augmenting the number of the faithful, the eunuchus, Dei may properly be said to be fecund. "In the third kind of eunuchry, hope of the heavenly kingdom, engendered by faith, is brought forth by charity, by which many more children are begotten than by the flesh." It is in just such spiritual multiplication that the eunuchus non Dei is sterile. As Rupertus said, he deliberately refuses to perform good works, and wilfully turns away from virtue.

If we look at Chaucer's Pardoner in terms of the Christian concept of eunuchry, both the utility of the image and the true character of this "noble ecclesiaste" are illuminated. According to these terms we should indeed expect him to be a eunuch. That is, the ecclesiastic is figuratively supposed to be the third type of eunuch distinguished in Matthew – one who by his own will has cut himself off from temporal pleasures. Castration or circumcision by the word of God is equivalent to cutting away the vetta homo that the novus homo might live: 13 this eunuch's will, says Radbertus, is "newly begotten in the Holy Spirit."

The Pardoner, according to his own boast, is by no means a eunuch in this sense. The opposite, however, implicit in the developed Christian concept of eunuchry, provides a sense quite appropriate to the man as he presents himself in his prologue and tale; and this opposition itself implies a biting and bitter satire directed at the type of churchman he represents. It is evident that by his act of will he has cut himself off from virtue and good works, and that this act has been performed, not through charity, but through its antithesis, cupiditas. The animal symbols of lechery with which he is associated immediately suggest that, although he is perhaps physically frustrated, the inner man hardly "abides in chastity." If the eunuchus Dei is the novus homo of Scripture, the Pardoner, having cut away this possibility, lives impenitently the life of the vetus homo.

Upon such oppositions, basic to Scriptural imagery and exegesis, the portrait of the Pardoner is developed by Chaucer. The song of cupidity with which he is introduced, for example, strongly suggests the vetus canticum sung by the vetus homo, itself the reverse of the canticum novum which the new man sings.

More definite, however, is the comparison provided between the Pardoner and the parson whom he is said to gull with his false relics.

But with thise relikes, whan that he fond
A povre person dwellynge upon lond,

Upon a day he gat hym moore moneye
Than that the person gat in monthes tweye;
An thus, with feyned flaterye and japes,
He made the person and the peple his apes.

The comparison seems to be purposefully introduced in order to play off the character of the Pardoner against that of the "povre Persoun of the Toun" who yet was rich "of hooly thought and werk" — that is, of virtue and good deeds, the spiritual progeny of the true eunuch. The Parson, we recall, "also a lerned man, a clerk, That Cristes gospel trewely wolde preche," preaches in churches for motives other than cupiditas; his interest, as it should be, is in increasing and multiplying the congregation of the faithful: To drawen folk to hevene by fairnesse, By good ensample, this was his bisynesse.

He is a shepherd, not a mercenary. Of all these traits the Pardoner possesses the opposite, by his own rather proud admission. The Parson who with his "brother" may be said to live in "parfit charitee," like the true eunuch who has devoted his life to others propter regnum coelorum and thus multiplies spiritually, is a perfect foil to the Pardoner. By spiritual standards the best of all the pilgrims, he is ironically compared with one who, in his perfect cupidity, is possibly the worst of the lot.

The Pardoner does better the Parson in one respect: "he gat hym moore moneye." But to do this he subverts the Parson and all that he stands for. The analogy of his "Com hider, love," in Church, is the "offertorie," the purpose of which he reverses by applying it to his own benefit rather than to God's. Like the song he sings with the Summoner, this is the vetus canticum of cupidity rather than the canticum novum of charity. The increase of his money is typical of the Pardoner's multiplicatio. Sterile in the spiritual multiplication of heavenly treasure, he lays up his treasure on earth. Since Deuteronomy stated that such eunuchs shall not enter in ecclesiam Domini, it is ironic that the Pardoner is said to conduct most of his business "in chirches," 15 Here he advertises his own variety of multiplications with a calculated propaganda. The goodman who uses his 'sholdre-boon, Which that was of a hooly Jewes sheep," with the proper magic ritual, "As thilke hooly Jew our eldres taughte," (suggestive of the Old Law) will find "His beestes and his stoor shal multiplye." His marvellous mitten, equally useful to the man who wishes to get ahead in the world, will provide "multiplying of his grayn." The formula here is the offering of "pens, or elles grotes."

The Pardoner thus makes of the Church a kind of medicine show, and will promise to multiply earthly and material things, a function singularly appropriate to the particular type of sterility he represents.

'Multiplication' can be taken in many senses. There is that of earthly begetting, in accordance with that first blessing our nature received. . . . And such multiplication plainly is fruitful and comes only from the Lord's blessing. What of other multiplications? One man is multiplied in respect to gold; another, silver; another, cattle; another, his family; another lands; another, all of these. . . . And men are multiplied with burdens in their soul. He in whom vices are multiplied is multiplied in his soul. One is sensual only; another avaricious, proud, sensual: he is multiplied in his soul, but by his own evil. This is a multiplication of poverty, not of richness.

Multiplicationes terrenae, the increase of earthly treasure, are those at which the spiritually sterile excel. The Pardoner in this activity uses his "relikes" to turn the mind of the goodman not to God through charity, but to his personal material wealth through cupidity: a reversal insidiously perverse with regard to his victim's eternal well-being. The increase he offers (and even this is "feyned") is that of the vetus homo-the opposite of the multiplyings of the novus homo. So far as the latter are concerned, the Pardoner is wilfully a sterile man. . . .

If the Pardoner may be analysed in terms of the eunuchus non Dei, his nature and status among the pilgrims of the Canterbury Tales may be further clarified in terms of its equivalent — the vetus homo. The term " Old Man" is Paul's who also calls him the "body of sin." As an aspect of the nature of man, the vetus homo represents the flesh and its manifold lusts, opposed to the novits homo: that is, the spirit and reason, by which these are subdued. In terms of the Biblical history of man, the Old Man, in any human being, is the image of fallen Adam, unregenerate in accepted grace and unredeemed by Christ, Who is called the "New Man."

As the result of original sin, all men are said to be born in the image of the vetus Adam. By baptism, however, we are said to die to sin and to be reborn in the image of Christ; and he who adopts this image is termed the New Man (sometimes the Young Man). As Christ's flesh was crucified and buried that the Old Law might be overthrown, so should the vetus homo, or the flesh, be crucified and buried, first in baptism and later in penance, by a similar free act of will. Through this death man achieves life under the New Law, as the eunuchus Dei, by an analogous act, achieves spiritual potency.

This brief account of the vetus homo is intended to suggest a common cluster of ideas also utilized by Chaucer in his description of the Pardoner. Although this man thinks he deceives his fellows by putting on external "newness," his "newe jet" does not completely disguise the Old Man, sterile in charitable works, beneath. That in his perfect cupidity, he typifies the vetus homo (an identification strengthened by verbal hints) would have sufficiently condemned the Pardoner in the more perceptive minds of Chaucer's audience. What is worse, the man knows and freely admits the evil of his character. And worse yet, besides knowing the evil of cupidity and still practicing it, he is proud, even boastful, of his abilities. Acting out of neither ignorance nor frailty, he is recognizable as the man impenitent in sin. Thus there is no hesitation in the confession of his prologue:

But shortly myn entente I wol devyse;
I preche of no thing but for coveitise.
Therefore my theme is yet, and evere was,
Radix malorum est cupiditas.
Thus can I preche agayn that same vyce
Which that I use, and that is avarice.

It is not difficult to recognize the theological type after which the Pardoner is figured. . . . His eunuchry, his vetustas and his pride, would easily have identified him as a man sinning vigourously against the Holy Ghost.

Presumption, or peccatum in Spiritum sanctum, is the one sin which is irremissible, since it involves the refusal of grace. St Augustine stressed final impenitence as the irremissible sin, for God is said not to pardon where penitence is absent. This sin is usually described in terms of malice, the opposite or absence of charity. The less serious sin against the Father arises through frailty (absence of power), and that against the Son through ignorance (absence of wisdom). Impenitence, or other aspects of this sin, are absolutely opposed to the remission of sins which is appropriated to the Holy Ghost. It refuses profferred grace, without which there can be no pardon. The grace of the Holy Ghost precedes contrition, the first requisite of penitence, as the Pardoner knows. Of the: last requisite, penance, he sells partial indulgence.

Again the contrast with the Parson, whose tale is a penitential manual, is evident. According to their offices, both the Pardoner and the Parson are media through which grace may be brought to the faithful; but the Pardoner, like Rupertus' eunuchus detestabilis, "acceptam indigne gratiam negligit" ["neglects the grace he has undeservingly received"]. A type of the impenitent man, the Pardoner accumulates temporal wealth by making a mockery of penitence and pardon. Like the eunuchs described by Rabanus Maurus, who "persuasione haeretica simulant charitatem, ut mentiantur religionis veritatem" ["simulate charity through heretical persuasion in order to counterfeit the truth of religion"], he knowingly perverts the function of his office.

According to St Augustine, the duplicity characteristic of the sinner in Spiritum sanctum is likely to appear in a discrepancy between words and deeds — a concept which elsewhere forms part of his definition of a lie." 20 This characteristic obviously applies to the Pardoner, who stirs his hearers to devotion in order to increase his sales. In the bragging confession of his misdeeds there in not a sign of contrition. The same distinction, highly conventional, also forms part of the traditional exegesis of the lignum aridum with which Isaiah compared the eunuch. Of the sterile tree St Augustine remarks in another place, "It had only leaves; fruit it did not have. . .: even so are those who have words and have not deeds."

I have tried thus far to indicate that the three terms suggested for identifying the character of the Pardoner — that is, consideration of the man as the conventional eunuchus non Dei, as the vetus homo, and as the sinner in Spiritum sanctum — are merely different emphases with respect to the same spiritual phenomenon. The eunuch is the vetus homo, who by wilfully cutting himself off from grace presumptuously sins against the Holy Spirit. Chaucer suggests this spiritual state by using the image of eunuchry, reinforcing his point by allusions to the concept of the veteres homines who, according to Paul, "have given themselves up to lasciviousness, unto the working of all uncleanness, unto covetousness"

The significance of the concept of the vetus homo for an understanding of the character of the Pardoner can be grasped only by examination of all of Paul's statements in their full Scriptural and exegetical context. However, a few details' may be mentioned with regard to the statement in Ephesians, iv, 17 ff. A specific reference to this text indicates its importance. To Paul's exhortation to those who have "put off the Old Man": "he that stole,. . . let him labor, working with his hands. . . that he may have something to give the needy" (iv, 25), the Pardoner retorts, "I wol nat do no labour with myne handes," and engages rather in thievery of spiritual offerings. . . .

In portraying the Pardoner of Rouncevale, then, Chaucer provides the cortex of his description with details which individualize his character, but which also expose for the reader a nucleus of deeper significance. By recalling the conventional concepts of the false eunuch and of the vetus homo, they help to identify the nature and enormity of the Pardoner's sin. He emerges as a type of the false ecclesiastic.

Among the pilgrims of the Canterbury Tales he stands at the opposite pole from the Parson, the true leader in the Church, who strives.

To shewe you the wey, in this viage, Of thilke parfit glorious pilgrimage That highte Jerusalem celestial:

that is, the straight and narrow "wey" which Christ identifies with Himself. On the other hand, the Pardoner, dealing as he does with spiritual merchandise, commits the most vicious and dangerous hypocrisy possible. Of the characters on the pilgrimage to Canterbury he is the representative of the false leader within the Church, who "having had committed to him the talent of God's work, which he could invest well and barter usefully for the edification of many men, lies idle and neglects the grace he has undeservedly received." He will not make baskets nor counterfeit the apostles. Cloaked in the outward aspects of his office, he wilfully misdirects those whom he can move. As he says, he "saffrons" his speech with Latin . . . for to strike hem to devocioun. Than sbewe I forth my longe crystal stones. . .

The shift in intent expressed between these two lines dramatizes his tactics, the gap between his verba and facta — his "handes" and his "tonge." It parallels significantly his concluding effort with Harry Bailly. The relics in those "stones" turn the love of his victim from God and into amor sui, reversing the proper ladder of love, for they claim to provide increase in temporal or earthly treasure. As a selling technique he makes his hearers "soore to repente."

The "wey," therefore, that the Pardoner shows "in this viage" is the opposite to that pointed out by the Parson. The Parson's way is through penitence; the Pardoner's, although he knows the better path, through impenitence in evil. Sterile in good works, wilfully sinning against the Holy Ghost, he remains boastfully impenitent in full knowledge of his sin. Chaucer has produced a daring and effective irony in creating as his Pardoner the eunnuch who presumptuously glories in the one unpardonable sin.

Rupertus' method in analyzing the concept of the eunuch may be applied to a great variety of signs, with much the same results. A case in point is Professor Robertson's illustration of the mediaeval treatment of gardens, trees, flowers and related symbols. As he says, "similar studies might be made of names, numbers, animals, stones, or other things," 23 and they might be similarly documented. When the more familiar Scriptural images appear literally in the cortex of Christian art, they immediately suggest one of their spiritual analogies which are themselves usually twofold, referring to their significance in both Jerusalem and Babylon. We may often determine the exact spiritual analogy only from context, since the opposite spiritual equivalent is usually implied. Concepts such as the concept of Death may be considered literally, as the rioters themselves do in the tale, still preserving the spiritual opposition-in this case, death to sin or death to Christ or life 24 To use pertinent terms, the concepts of either the death of the vetus homo or the death of the novus homo may be symbolized by physical death. Thus, taking an example from the Pardoner's Tale, the literal image of the treasure suggests the spiritual opposites of Matthew, vi, 19. In the context of the tale we recognize that the rioters do not find the "true" treasure (in which the "povre" Parson is "rich") they should have laid up in heaven, but the "false" earthly treasure which is itself the death they seek — as was understood by the hermit of the analogue in the Cento Antiche Novelle. The concept of the heavenly treasure, strongly implied, stresses how far down the "croked" way the rioters have gone.

In these terms I wish now to outline briefly an interpretation of the tale itself, in which the calculated description of the Pardoner may be seen to be functionally appropriate. Recognizing the importance of the form of the sermon (one of the effects of which is to throw the Pardoner into bolder contrast with the Parson) and of the theological subdivisions of its expositio for a detailed analysis of the Pardoner's Tale, I confine my attention here almost exclusively to the exemplum intended to illustrate his exposition of the theme: Radix malorum est Cupiditas. One of the best conceived stories in all literature, this exemplum possesses an undeniable universality, provocative despite any change in systems of values. I feel, however, that an interpretation based on Chaucer's use of Scriptural imagery, without precluding others, provides an additional dimension of philosophical importance.

The Pardoner — this quaestor — himself a seeker after the false treasure, tells a tale of seekers after Death. We should remember that the basic concern of the exemplum is Death. Death in the tale is the literal result of each of the aspects of cupiditas distinguished in the expositio. The tale is first an example showing the evils of drunkenness, that "verray sepulture Of mannes wit and his discrecioun." The rioters' day begins in drink, to the solemn background of their "fordronke" comrade's funeral bell, and ends in death, brought to two of the three in a bottle of wine. They swear, furthermore, an oath of brotherhood, the breaking of which leads directly to death. After they find their treasure they draw lots to decide who is to bring back the "breed and wyn," and hasardrye becomes involved in all the murders.

Ironically, the Pardoner, of course, is himself a chief offender with regard to most of the vices he treats in his sermon. He will not tell his tale until he has eaten and drunk his fill.

> *"It shal be doon," quod he, "by Seint Ronyan*
> *! But first," quod he, "heere at this al-stake*
> *I wol bothe drynke, and eten of a cake."*

He is a man of many oaths (Ronyan, in both French and English a word for the "coillons," is an appropriate saint for a eunuch to swear by). More generally, as the vetus homo and the aridum lignum of spiritual eunuchry, he is the literal embodiment of cupiditas, the larger theme of his sermon.

> *Therfore my theme is yet, and evere was,*
> *Radix malorum est Cupiditas.*

Death is conceived in the exemplum in the variety of senses implicit in Christian thought. Death of either the vetus homo or the novus homo is the modus vivendi of the other: a phenomenon suggested by Chaucer's metaphor of eunuchry, and expressed by the Pardoner himself:

But, certes, he that haunteth swiche delices
Is deed, whil that he lyveth in tho vices 548

In attempting to "slay" Death, then, the rioters do not engage in an entirely meaningless quest. Adam's fall brought death, both physical and spiritual, into the world, and all men after, born in his image, have been mortal. The virtuous man should slay Death, the inheritance of the Old Man. By crucifixion and burial of this "earthly image" — the "body of sin" — the soul may put on the image of Christ and achieve its heavenly treasure in eternal life, the inheritance of the New Man. As Christ slew Death upon the Cross, so his followers can gain eternal life and cause the death of Death.

The symbolic quest of the rioters to cause their version of the death of Death is significantly introduced.

In Flaundres whilom was a compaignye
Of yonge folk that haunteden folye,
As riot, hasard, stywes, and tavernes
Where as with harpes, lutes, and gyternes,
They daunce and pleyen at dees bothe day and nyght,
And eten also and drynken over hir myght,
Thurgh which they doon the devel sacrifise
Withinne that develes temple, in cursed wise,
By superfluytee abhomynable.

Like the Pardoner himself, they are classed ironically as "yonge folk." That these men are literally but not spiritually young" is apparent from Chaucer's compact exposition. Dancing the "olde daunce," subjecting themselves to fortune in their play, engaging in the false banquet of sense, "they doon the devel sacrifise Withinne that develes temple."

And right anon thanne comen tombesteres
Fetys and smale, and yonge frutesteres 478
Syngeres with harpes, baudes, wafereres, —

the purveyors of the "olde daunce," the false feast, the vetus canticum —"Whiche been the verray develes officeres." Into this atmosphere of spiritual death is introduced the spectre of physical death: "they herde a belle clynke Biforn a cors, was caried to his grave."

The irony of the situation is now heightened. One of the rioters tells his "knave" to ask the corpse's name. The "boy" provides not only this information, but also some suitable advice.

"And, maister, et ye come in [Death's] presence,
Me thynketh that it were necessarie
For to be war of swich an adversarie.
Beth redy for to meete hym everemoore;
Thus taughte me my dame; I sey namoore."
"By seinte Mariel" seyde this taverner
"The child seith sooth. . . .
To been avysed greet wysdom it were
, Er that he dide a man a dishonour."

The advice of the "child" can be duplicated endlessly in sermons and moral tracts. One should be ready to meet death at all times in view of the judgment after death. The "truth" of the young man's assertion has been recognized, however, by few other than the taverner. As a point of departure for the tale the false "yonge folk" literalize (and thus pervert) the word of the true "young man," [26] whose "dame" is the Church, the source of such doctrine. They set out to seek a literal Death.

Having perverted the counsel of the novus homo, the rioters turn for advice to a mysterious "olde man" who directs them on their way. Their search is not fruitless. The Death they discover, however, is no literal "traytour," but spiritual death which their spiritual blindness prevents them from recognizing: the gold which turns their hearts from the life of their souls. It is clear that this is the false "treasure" — almost eight bushels of earthly treasure; the opposite of the eternal treasure which should be laid up in heaven. The quest of Death personified and the resultant physical death of the revellers emphasize the real spiritual death found under the oak tree to which the old man guides them. Physical death comes to all; but spiritual death is the root of all evil.

The circumstances in which the treasure is discovered reinforce this identification. Although he says that he seeks Death himself, the old man points the way.

"Now, sires," quod he, "if that ye be so leef
To fynde Decth, turne up this croked wey,
For in that grove I lafte hym, by my fey,
Under a tree, and there he wole abyde;
Noght for youre boost he wole him no thyng hyde."

Death, he says, lies up the "croked wey" — the opposite of the straight and narrow; "in that grove" — that is, in the false paradise of cupidity, wid "under a tree" — in medio ligni, where Adam and Eve lost their true Eden and found Death first. In terms of mediaeval Christian imagery, this is surely the way to find death, but not the way to slay him. Furthermore, if the exemplum as a whole illustrates the Pardoner's theme, in a sense the oak tree under which the gold is discovered literally exemplifies the words of his text, Radix malorum est Cupiditas. For this tree may itself be regarded as the arbor malorumthe tree of evil (or of death) — whose root is cupidity symbolized by the golden earthly treasure. This tree, whose radix is cupiditas, is also a version of the symbolic sterile tree to which the eunuch is compared by Isaiah.

It is finally appropriate that the director on the "croked wey" should be the old man, who thus assumes a position in the tale suggestively analogous to that of the teller. Spiritual death is arrived at by failing to follow the counsel of the novus homo in preference to that of the vetus homo. The cupidinous desires of the fallen aspect of man not only point out the way of perdition, the false paradise and the tree of death, but in a sense create them. In the tale the figure of the old man stands as a symbolic opposite to that of the tavern boy.

Like the youth, the old man refers to his mother:
Thus walke I, lyk a restelees kaityf,
And on the ground, which moodres gate,

I knokke with my staf, bothe erly and late,
And seye "Leeve mooder, leet me in!"

In contrast to the youth, he is of the generation of the earth, earthy. There is a broad suggestion of the "earthly image" of Adam, the vetus homo, the antithesis of the imago Christi, or novus homo. Like the wandering Jew, the Old Man of whom Paul wrote cannot die, and will not die so long as human nature does not change. Significantly the revellers refer to him as a spy of Death, an ally of Death, and he is dressed in a shroud — "al forwrapped" save his face: for the vetus homo represents the state of spiritual death. He desires "an heyre clowt to wrappe" himself in — i.e. the hair shirt of penance, and he wishes to be buried: for the Old Man must be crucified and buried that the New Man may live. The vetus homo may die only by the assumption of the novus homo. This familiar concept lies behind a significant passage which previous discussions of the old man have avoided: his response to the question of the rioters:

"Why lyvestow so longe in so great age?"
This olde man gan looke in his visage
And seyde thus, "For I ne kan nat fynde
A man, though that I walked into Ynde,
Neither in citee ne in no village,
That wolde chaunge his youthe for myn age;
And therfore moot I han myn age stille,
As longe tyme as it is Goddes wille."

Like the Pardoner, this old man can quote Scripture to his own purpose; his mouth is full of verbal holiness. Like the Pardoner, too, in full knowledge he points the way to spiritual death, directing the "riotoures" up the "croked wey" into the garden of cupidity, just as the desires of the vetus homo lead any soul astray. Lacking that peace which passeth understanding, he wanders, a "restelees kaityf," in a manner reminiscent of a description provided by the Parson with respect to the Judgment of the veteres homines:

Right so fareth the peyne of helle; it is lyk deeth for the horrible angwissh, and why? For it peyneth hem evere, as though they sholde dye anon; but certes, they shal nat dye. / For, as seith Seint Gregorie, "To wrecche caytyves shal be deeth withoute deeth, and ende withouten ende, and defaute withoute failynge. / For hir deeth shal alwey lyven, and hir ende shal everemo bigynne, and hir defaute shal nat faille." / And therfore seith Seint John the Evaungelist: "They shullen folwe deeth, and they shul nat fynde hym; and they shul desiren to dye, and deeth shal flee fro hem."

The result of the old man's direction is death, both spiritual and physical. . . . The convivium under the oak, with its reversed sacramental "breed and wyn," serves to symbolize the subjection of these Cain-like "brothers" to their earthly treasure; and recalls the Pardoner's own repast at the "alestake." The exemplum pictures the discovery and the effect of the "root of all evil."

The extraordinarily tight-knit organization of the Pardoner's Tale does not permit full explication in a limited space. Other details of the cortex might be shown to be similarly significant. What should be clear however, is the consistent philosophical pattern artistically presented through the manipulation of Scriptural images, the main points of which have here been suggested rather than defined. The import of the nucleus is thus a consistent exemplification of the Pardoner's text.

It should also be more evident how the Pardoner's Tale fits generally into a scheme of opposition between Charity and Cupidity in the Canterbury Tales as a whole. The extreme maliciousness of the Pardoner as a person sets him at the far end of the scale among the pilgrims. As a type he is even more definitely evil. He is the false eunuch who stands and points the way up the wrong road. He represents the way of cupidity, malice, impenitence, spiritual sterility — just the opposite of the way of the Parson and his spiritual brother, the Plowman. He is that Old Man as he lives and exerts his influence in the great pilgrimage of life. And as the vetus homo he is to be opposed to the Christlike figure of the novits homo, the true guide-the "povre Persoun of a Toun." . . .

Behind Chaucer's conception of the Pardoner and his tale lies the familiar Christian thesis that all men should be quaestores — not, like the Pardoner, for the material treasure, but for what the Pardoner should seek, the spiritual "offertorie." They should seek not the false pardons of which the Pardoner's wallet is so "bret-ful," but that pardon which Chaucer cannot forbear mentioning albeit in the words of the Pardoner: that is, the Pardon of "Jesu Crist, that is oure soules leche." Important also is the concept that all should be seekers of Death, too — but the death of that Old Man, through whose burial Death is really conquered; and who must be put down before we cease to find confusio, or disorder, such as that which literally breaks out between the Pardoner and Harry Bailly at the end of this tale. And it is clear that this is a spiritual matter. All the worthy Knight can do as representative of the temporal arm of the law is to make a temporary peace-an earthly equivalent of the visio pacis. But the Old Man still goes on wandering through the world, glaring with sterile; lust out of his hare-like eyes.

Q.2. Discuss Chaucer's representation of the Pardoner as a womanizer.

or

Q. Analyse The hints of effeminacy to be found in Chaucer's portrait of the Pardoner

The hints of effeminacy to be found in Chaucer's portrait of the Pardoner should not be taken to indicate either homosexuality or a physical condition (whether that of a eunuch or a hermaphrodite), but rather an inordinate preoccupation with women. To be effeminate in the Middle Ages, suggested, was primarily the mark of a womanizer. This position has recently been endorsed by H. A. Kelly, who has adduced a plethora of evidence from theological, legal, and physiological texts to support it. The purpose here is merely to add a brief footnote to Kelly's characteristically learned and exhaustive survey, one intended to point out that the idea of the womanizing effeminate was not restricted to the schoolroom and the cloister, but can also be found in a milieu with which Chaucer himself is likely to have been familiar. Robert S. Sturges has taken me to task for offering evidence from 'the wrong period', so it is gratifying to be able to offer confirmation of my position from a pair of literary texts written during the first phase of the Hundred Years War (1337-6), when Chaucer was a young man.

The charge of effeminacy seems in fact to have been rather commonly employed by the English in polemical attacks on their French opponents at this time. A long poem titled 'An invective against France' by Thomas Wright (but more simply 'Crecy' by A. G. Rigg in a recent edition) begins, 'Francia, feminea, pharisea, vigour is ydea' ('France, effeminate, divided, a mere shadow of strength'), alludes to the French king's fighting like a woman (line 51), and compares him to that well-known type of the effeminate King Sardanapalus (line 149.3). Even more interesting for our purposes, however, are a pair of poems that Wright titles 'A dispute between an Englishman and a Frenchman'. Together they form a miniature flyting, though as they now stand in the unique manuscript (London, British Library, MS Cotton Titus A. their order appears to have been reversed: the Frenchman's speech makes rather more sense as a rebuttal of the Englishman's points than (as it is there presented) as the stimulus for them.

After four lines in which the Englishman asks how the Frenchman can have had the effrontery to challenge him to battle, he launches into an extended attack (lines 5-22) on his opponent's effeminate behaviour. Since this passage, particularly with Wright's punctuation, is far from straightforward (and at one point (line 12) clearly corrupt), it may be helpful to reproduce it here emended and repunctuated:

Parce viris! Societ mulierem lis mulieri:
Impar certamen cum muliere mari.
Quicquid agas gestu, quocunque feraris, eidem
Semper inest aliquid quod tibi crimen emat.
Si caput aspicias, compto dum crine superbit,
Nescio qua reliquos suspicione trahit;

Si capitis motum, nunc hac nunc vertitur illac:
Discu[ti]es tanquam non velit esse tuum;
Si faciem, Veneris vitio praedante ruborem,
Eloquitur vitium pallida forma tuum;
Si linguam, mollit pulsum ne forte palatum
Obstrepat, et mulier fatur in ore viri;
Si gressum, tumidas suspendis in aere plantas,
Vix pede degustans anteriore vias;
Si partes alias, muliebrem cedis in usum,
Femineo gestu dissimulante virum.
Sed quia femineos castravit Gallica Gallos,
Gallinae, Galle, nomen et omen habe.

A particular difficulty is presented by the poet's switching between second and third person singular in this passage while at the same time addressing two distinct audiences, the reader and his French enemy. In the translation that follows I have tried to simplify this by rendering the address to the reader (i.e. 'si aspicias') in the third person ('if one considers'), while retaining the second person (i.e. 'quicquid agas') where the poet is addressing the Frenchman ('whatever you do'):

Spare the men! Let the quarrel join woman and woman: unequal is the contest of a man with a woman. Whatever you do by way of gesture, wherever you may be borne, there is always something in it that may earn you blame. If one considers the head, while it boasts an elegant coiffure, it drags the rest into God knows what suspicion; if [one considers] the movement of the head, it turns now this way, now that: you will shake it about as if it did not want to belong to you; if [one considers] the face, from which the vice of Venus has robbed the blush of shame, [its] pale complexion proclaims your own vice; if [one considers] the speech, [the tongue] softens its force lest it strike strongly against the palate, and a woman speaks in a man's mouth; if [one considers] the gait, you suspend your proud feet in the air, with the foremost foot scarcely grazing the path; if [one considers] other parts, you yield to feminine manners, concealing the man with womanish gesture. But because French womanhood has emasculated the effeminate French, take on the name and style of 'capon', Frenchman!

The Frenchman responds to each point in turn (lines 9-24), but the general thrust of his argument is that his cultivated behaviour is the external sign of an inner virtue which only a vicious mind could misconstrue as vice.

What is important about the Englishman's attack, then, is not simply that he describes his French opponent as effeminate but that he gives a detailed physical description of this effeminacy and assigns it a clear cause.

Some of the details he lists correspond to those in Chaucer's portrait of the Pardoner: the Frenchman has elegant hair ('compto crine'), for instance, and a feminine voice ('mulier fatur in ore viri'); others, such as the tossing of his head ('capitis motum'), his pale complexion ('pallida forma'), and his mincing gait ('vix pede degustans anteriore vias'), are peculiar to this text. More importantly, there is no evidence that such marks of effeminacy are meant to be read as signs of either homosexuality or physical abnormality: the Frenchman's pallor, for example, is due to his indulgence in the vice of Venus ('vitio Veneris'), and in a striking final couplet he is reviled as a 'capon' ('gallinae nomen habe'), castrated by French womanhood ('castravit Gallica'). We could scarcely ask for more convincing evidence that Chaucer's line, 'I trowe he were a geldyng or a mare', might be taken by contemporaries as a sign of effeminizing heterosexuality.

Q.3. Discuss Preaching and Avarice in the Pardoner's Tale

or

Q. Analyse the statement' The Pardoner himself, it is true, certainly owes something to Faux-Semblant of the *Roman de la Rose*'

Unlike the tales of the Knight and the Clerk, no literary ancestor lies behind the Pardoner's Tale which can help to account for certain elements in Chaucer's creation that continue to puzzle and delight us. The Pardoner himself, it is true, certainly owes something to Faux-Semblant of the *Roman de la Rose,* and the tale he tells has numerous analogues, but the personification of Jean de Meung's poem hardly reflects the complexity of the Preacher of Rouncivale, nor has any exemplum yet discovered aroused the controversy his sermon has. Yet in the absence of a direct source, other medieval documents can offer insight into Chaucer's creation. The Pardoner, after all, does declare himself a preacher, and the subject he preaches about is avarice: both the occupation and the sin were much discussed in the Middle Ages. One shall therefore draw upon medieval treatises on preaching, together with homiletic material on avarice and pertinent exegetical traditions, in order to reexamine the Pardoner and the remarkable tale he tells.

One say reexamine because some work has already been done. Since the Pardoner does preach, his sermon has been analysed to see whether it follows the suggestions found in contemporary artes praedicandi. These works set forth the rationale of medieval homilies, commenting on such matters as how and where the preacher should divide his sermon; not surprisingly the *Pardoner's Tale* seems to conform to these dicta. Yet, if the mechanics of sermon-making have been noted, what these manuals and other sources have had to say about the kind of man a preacher should be has not. This is unfortunate, for a glance at any number of works that discuss preaching might have offered an answer to one of the more celebrated cruces of the *Pardoner's Tale.*

Since Kittredge, critics have wondered why the Pardoner must stop to think of "som honest thyng" to tell the pilgrims; in a recent article, John Halverson has summarized the commentators' bewilderment:

> It is inconceivable that a professional homilist like the Pardoner should need time to recall a moral tale, his stock in trade.

Then, like many critics before him, Halverson offers a "psychological" explanation: "the inference seems inescapable that he is reacting ironically to the implied derogation [of the *gentils'* request for a moral tale]. " Appealing as this interpretation may be, I think more than psychological inference may guide us here. In a passage of the *De Doctrina Christiana* which was to have great influence, Augustine advises the orator of God's word to prepare himself in the following manner:

> Ipsa hora iam ut dicat accedens, priusquam exerat proferentem linguam, ad deum leuet animam sitientem, ut ructet quod biberit, uel quod impleuerit, fundat.

When the hour in which he is to speak approaches, before he begins to preach, he should raise his thirsty soul to God, in order that he may give forth what he shall drink, or pour out what shall fill him.

Furthermore, Augustine continues, let the man who would both know and teach learn everything which should be taught, and acquire "a skill in speaking appropriate to an ecclesiastic," but when the time comes for speech itself, the preacher should follow the advice of Matthew:

> Take no thought how or what to speak: for it shall be given you in that hour what to speak. For it is not you that speak, but the Spirit of your Father that speaketh in you.

In the later Middle Ages this advice was not forgotten, though direct illumination by divine wisdom became less frequent; therefore a typical *ars praedicandi* by the thirteenth-century French preacher Astazius, while honouring the precept, nevertheless counsels prelates to prepare their sermons beforehand:

> Advertendum quod sancti doctores qui in Ecclesia praecesserunt sine sumpto themate praedicabant nec praedicationis materiam ordinabant, quia non indigebant aliquo directivo, cum praedicarent Spiritu Sancto inspirante. Unde praedicabant prout Spiritus Sanctus dabat eis. Sed moderni qui non stint sancti nec divina scientia illustrati, primo antequam praedicent, praedicantionis materiam ordinare debent.

We should note that the holy doctors who have preceded us in the Church used to preach without a prepared text, nor did they arrange the material they preached. For they did not need an ordering method, since they would preach with the Holy Spirit inspiring them. Thus they preached as the Holy Spirit gave them. But today, preachers who are not saints nor illuminated by divine knowledge should, before they preach, first arrange the material of their sermon.

The passage in Chaucer now becomes clear. When he grants the pilgrims' request, the Pardoner's words seem almost a direct parody of Augustine's formula:

> *"I graunte, ywis," quod he, "but I moot thynke*
> *Upon som honest thyng while that I drynke."*

Eucharist. This interpretation gains added force when we recognize that Corny ale is the Pardoner's draught, not spiritual illumination, and when he later describes how he spits out his venom "under hewe / Of hoolynesse, to semen hooly and trewe" thePardoner literally pours out, in the manner Augustine has described, the poison that fills him. Some have seen the cake and ale which the Pardoner consumes as an ironic reference to thethe Pardoner is mocking the very act of preaching itself. His inspiration is not the Holy Ghost's, but is his own, and inevitably it will fail.

Even before he speaks, Chaucer has alerted us that the Pardoner's spiritual insight is suspect; yet as dispensator of sound doctrine, the Christian preacher should, indeed must, be alive to the spiritual sense of Scripture. If he is not, if he is a man of the letter and desires worldly wealth rather than his spiritual treasure in heaven, he is then one who adulterates God's word, and he will fall into temptation and the devil's snare. This verse from the First Epistle to Timothy ("But those who desire to become rich, fall into temptation, and into the snare of the devil") was interpreted by Nicholas of Lyra, among others, as referring specifically to preachers. And this verse is especially significant for the Pardoner, as it immediately precedes the sentence he has taken for his theme, *Radix malorum est cupiditas.*

Indeed, the very text in which this sentence appears, Paul's First Epistle to Timothy, was regarded in the Middle Ages as a biblical directive which authorized the use of allegorical interpretation. As a group, the Epistles of Paul to Timothy and Titus came to be known as the *epistolae pastorales*, for, as A. Médèbielle explains, "Elles tracent les règles à suivre pour diriger et instruire le peuple fidèle et pour le choix des ministres sacrés." In this regard the Letters were especially important for Augustine and subsequent preachers in that they taught the disciples what and how they should teach others. Any man, Augustine writes, who teaches in Church should have these three Epistles before his eyes. The substance of what the pastor should teach may be summarized as sound doctrine; to determine what that doctrine was, however, the preacher had to discern the hidden meaning of the text. The whole of the *De Doctrina Christiana*, as well as many other texts, had just this purpose: to teach preachers how to discover the spiritual sense.

Particular scriptural passage of Now the Pardoner himself "was in chirche a noble ecclesiaste," (A. 708), and therefore should know how to read a text spiritually; furthermore, the allegorical exposition of thethe day was always a common feature in medieval sermons, one which a preacher of the Pardoner's experience certainly would have known and used. Yet because he is a self-confessed, unrepentant sinner, the Pardoner is incapable of admitting anything more than the literal sense of what he says. Thus when he introduces figures such as a dove or an Old Man, figures that seem to call for an allegorical interpretation, we find his dove has nothing to do with the Holy Spirit, but rather is a barnyard purveyor, and the Old Man's too solid flesh blurs whatever symbolic significance he seems to demand. The Pardoner is not a spiritual man, and the very manner of the fiction he tells reveals his lack of faith. In the words of Rabanus Maurus, following Paul, *Symbolum fidei et spei nostrae non scribitur in charta et atramento, sed in tabulis cordis carnalibus.* [The symbol of our faith and hope is not written on paper with ink, but on the fleshly tablets of the heart.] His ghostly heart empty, the

Pardoner wears his corporeal heart on his sleeve; an act of audacity and defiance, but ultimately the act of an inwardly hollow man.

That a man as unconcerned with the evils of gluttony and "dronkenesse" as the Pardoner is should eat and drink before he inveighs against these vices seems quite in character. Yet we remember Augustine's exhortation that the preacher give forth what he shall drink. The Pardoner drinks ale, and we may be certain that no thought of that spiritual wine that was a common symbol for divine preaching ever crossed his mind. *"Vinum dicitur divina praedicatio,"* says Alain de Lille; but those who preach "with an eye to human favour or worldly gain" are frauds: they are like the hucksters and innkeepers who Isaiah says "mix wine with water":

Unde Isaias): Caupones vestri miscent vinum aqua. Ille doctor vel praedicator miscet vinum aqua qui docet vel praedicat intuitu favouris humani vel terreni emolimenti.

Preachers of this sort are especially insidious, for, as Alain notes in his *Summa de Arte Praedicantium,* the "silly and scurrilous words they use have the effect of making their audience somewhat effeminate":

In illa praedicatione est aqua vino mista in qua puerilia et scurrilia verba, et animos quodammodo effeminantia ponuntur.

Thus with the Pardoner the spiritual draught that fills the good preacher's vessel has not been diluted but actually transformed into the moist and corny ale he guzzles by the wayside; furthermore, those who partake with him are in danger of becoming like him. If his sermon has had the effect the Pardoner intended, he will have made each listener his "ape"): not only will the avaricious preacher have fired the pilgrims' desire for his money-increasing relics, but the Pardoner will also have had each buyer mimic him in all his effeminacy. There could hardly be an insult more stinging to the Host, the first customer approached, than to be compared to the effeminate Pardoner. Our innkeeper will have none of it; he reacts violently, and by revealing the Pardoner's wanting virility, he appropriately exposes a symbol of this preacher's spiritual sterility as well.

When the Pardoner compares himself to a dove, the creature he has in mind is similarly of this world, not the next. For when he preaches, the Pardoner takes pains

to strecche forth the nekke,
And est and west upon the peple I bekke,
As dooth a dowve sittynge on a berne.

This image is so effective precisely because it is vividly literal, because it steadfastly refuses to be symbolic. The dove was so common an emblem for the Holy Ghost (and indirectly the spirit that informs the good preacher) in the Middle Ages, one might have seen even "lewed" folks' eyebrows rise when the Pardoner appropriates it for himself. Yet the man is consistent: spiritual understanding is absent, the tangible reality is all.

Both the ale the Pardoner drinks and the dove he compared himself to tell us something about the kind of man the Pardoner is. So too, I think, does the oak tree of his *Tale,* under which the rioters find their just reward. This oak seems to have been Chaucer's invention; at least it exists in none of the printed analogues, where one searches in vain for mention of any tree, much less an oak. Usually the treasure is found in a forest or grove, in a cave or river. The oak certainly locates the scene more specifically, yet the tree's allegorical significance also seems a telling comment on the Pardoner and rioters alike.

The Old Man advises the rioters that, if they "be so leef / To fynde Deeth," they should

Turne up this croked wey,
For in that grove I lafte hym, by my fey,
Under a tree, and there he wole abyde;
Noght for youre boost he wole him no thyng hyde.
Se ye that ook? Right there ye shal hym fynde.

As Death is given an increasingly specific location, from grove, to tree, to oak, to the gold the sinners will soon discover, the Old Man at the same time scores the rioters' increasingly dogged determination to find that "privee theef." The tension thus created is enough to guarantee the scene's success, yet the scene is heightened if the oak symbolizes *duritia desperationis,* the obduracy of despair, as it does in an exegetical tradition, or if we associate it with the idea of hardness and determination, as Chaucer does elsewhere in his work; we sense that the very landscape reflects the inner condition of these men.

That avarice, as the root of all evil, was sometimes pictured as the trunk of the tree of the seven deadly sins strengthens our conviction that this oak is not so much a locational marker as it is a signpost. But the rioters do not perceive that the setting in which they find the gold constitutes a warning: to them, the tree is nothing more than a tree. In this they resemble the Pardoner, who also is unaware of any symbolic meaning; they neither see nor understand as they should, nor is this surprising, for their spiritual blindness, as I shall now show, is the result of avarice.

If medieval discussions of preachers and their sermons provide insights into the Pardoner and his Tale, what the commentators had to say about the sin of avarice also ought to prove illustrative. After all, the Pardoner declares himself a covetous man, and the only theme he preaches constitutes the chief condemnation of the vice in Scripture. Avarice was attacked in many tracts and exempla written during the Middle Ages; among these one in particular immediately relates to the Pardoner's spiritual vacuity. In his *Summa de Exemplis,* John of San Giminiano compared the covetous man to a shadow for seven reasons: the third had to do with that shadow which led to inner barrenness:

Tertio quorum umbra sterilitatis inductiva, quia nihil quasi crescit ubi est continua umbra.

Sic semina divinorum verborum non possunt crescere et fructus producere ubi est avariciaet divitiarum cura sollicita.

The third is the shadow that induces sterility, since almost nothing grows where there is continuous shade.

Thus the seeds of divine words cannot grow and produce fruit where there is avarice and anxiety-ridden studying after riches.

Avarice, then, can well be the ultimate cause of the Pardoner's subservience to the letter. It is an especially pernicious sin for a preacher to be guilty of, since it is "the ax of preaching," as Guilelmus Peraldus puts it in his *Summa de virtutibus et vitiis*, that must eradicate this sin:

Ad avariciam quasi ad radicem omnium malorum praecipue adhibenda esset securis praedicationis. Frustra laboratur in extirpatione malorum si rami amputantur et radix ista relinquitur.

The ax of preaching must be applied to avarice especially as though to the root of all evil. He labors in vain to uproot evil if the branches are cut and this root remains.

What exactly was this sin, and what were its effects? The questions are important, for their answers will affect our evaluation of the Pardoner's Tale.

One might begin with the implications of the text the Pardoner knows by heart: "*Radix malorum est cupiditas.*" *Cupiditas*, as the *Glossa Ordinaria* and many other sources tell us, translates the Greek *philargyria*, which strictly means the love of money; not surprisingly, some commentators, including Augustine, read the verse as *radix omnium malorum avaritia*. From this narrow definition avarice quickly grew to have the meaning of any immoderate desire for more than is necessary, be it money or "external goods." Thus avarice was the specific sin of *pecuniae amor*, as it appears in lists of the seven deadly sins, and the sin of excessive avidity for things in general. Using this distinction, the Church fathers were able to reconcile the statement in Timothy with Ecclesiasticus 10:15: The beginning of all sin is pride. Every sin was understood to involve a twofold action: the soul turned away from God in pride, and towards a created thing through avarice. Pride and avarice thus became inseparably linked: whenever the chapter in Timothy was mentioned, a discussion of its relation to the verse from Ecclesiasticus was sure to follow. Some critics have thought the Pardoner overweeningly proud; it would be remarkable were he not so.

As one might expect, avarice was accounted a very grave sin; John of San Giminiano notes how it leads to "spiritual death":

Similiter, avaricia veneno cupiditatis extinguit vitalem calorem charitatis, et ita est causa mortis spiritualis.

Similarly, avarice extinguishes the vital warmth of charity with the venom of cupidity, and thus is the cause of spiritual death.

We remember the Pardoner's telling threat:
Thus spitte I out my venym under hewe
Of hoolynesse, to semen hooly and true.

and realise that the certain victim of the Pardoner's poison is the Pardoner himself.

Peraldus also thought avarice as bad an infirmity of the spirit as there could be:

Inter infirmitates spirituales ipsa est pessima, vel una de peioribus.

Among spiritual infirmities this [i.e., avarice] is the worst, or one of the worst.

Part of the illness, Peraldus continues, is that the avaricious man refuses to be cured: he holds Christ, the *celestis medicus,* as though he were danger itself: he judges *"tantus medicus quasi ad mortem."* At the climax of his Tale, the Pardoner prays that Christ, "oure soules leche," grant the pilgrims His pardon, "For that is best, I wol yow nat deceyve" (C. 916-18): the statement is utterly true, and the irony arising from its inapplicability to the Pardoner almost unendurable.

To St. Paul, however, the most pernicious effect of avarice was that, as the root of all evil, it drew men from the faith (1 Tim. 6:10). When the commentators elaborated on this verse, they isolated one further consequence: cupidity leads men into vain and empty speech. Hugh of St. Cher's comment is typical:

> A quibus [faith and good conscience] aberrantes, conversi sunt in vaniloquium.
>
> Wandering from which, they deal in empty speech.

Bromyard agrees, and in a sermon on the circumcision of the spirit, Bonaventure quotes St. Bernard on 1 Timothy 6:10:

> Habentes victum et vestitum, his contenti simus, spiritualis etiam circumcisio debet esse in omnibus sensibus corporis nostri, videndo, audiendo, gustando, tangendo, paucitate utamur, et maxime in loquendo.... Loquacitasest vitium pessimum, et Deo et hominibus odiosum et displicibile: unde debemus esse circumcisi lingua, id est pauca et utilia loqui.
>
> We have food and clothing: let us be content with these, for one ought to be spiritually circumcised in all our bodily senses. In seeing, hearing, tasting, touching, let us be sparing, and especially in speaking. Loquacity is a most miserable vice, hateful and displeasing to both God and man. Therefore we ought to be circumcised in speech, that is, speaking little and to the point.

Critics have wondered for many years why the Pardoner, his magnificent Tale brought to its moving conclusion, presses on, indulging in what Kittredge called "a wild orgy of reckless jesting." Chaucer, I think, would have replied, "But it is his nature to talk too much"; the Pardoner is an avaricious man, and his many words confess the fact more than he knows.

The Pardoner is literal, and he is literal because he is avaricious. Not only his story, but the very manner in which he tells it, points to his spiritual condition. The subject of the Pardoner's exemplum is, of course, avarice; as we shall now see, the most arresting figure in that Tale, the Old Man, is, with the Pardoner himself, Chaucer's greatest embodiment of the effects of that sin.

The Old Man in the Pardoner's Tale has become something of a *cause célèbre*; so famous, in fact, that he has not only been the subject of articles, but articles on these articles have appeared. The Old Man has been many things to many people: a symbol of Death, Death's Messenger, the Wandering Jew to some, to others Paul's *Vetus Homo,* Old Age, Odin, or literally just an old man. What has caused this embarrassment of interpretation? One reason, it seems to me, lies in the fact that Pardoner presents this figure in exactly the same manner each of his other figures has been presented. Everything about the man seems to cry out for an allegorical interpretation; as a man who lives and dies by the letter, however, the Pardoner has refused to allow him anything but a literal sense. For the reader, the effect is astonishing: we are given no answer; we are left to see for ourselves.

We may follow the Old Man's directions blindly, as the rioters do, or we may come to see through their experience that his "wey" is "croked" as Dante's via is diritta. Yet in any attempt to fathom the meaning of this mysterious guide, there are two considerations at least which I think should guide us. One is that pains of avarice and has since repented.

As such he is a walking text on as the man's "greet age" is stressed, we should not be surprised to find him exhibiting some signs of senectitude. The other and more important is that since he appears in what is essentially a sermon on avarice, we might therefore reasonably expect him either to represent the sin or warn us against it. The Old Man does both: in appearance and speech, this figure embodies the vice he speaks against. The Old Man is not Avarice, just as he is not Old Age or any other single state or thing, but it seems he is a man who has suffered thethe evils of avarice; understanding him, however, seems to he the reader's prerogative.

What do we know of the Old Man? He appears to be Chaucer's invention, this figure, completely wrapped, save his face, who is asked to justify his existence. "Why lyvestow so longe in so greet age?" the proudest of the three seekers after death demands. The Old Man's answer is his history:

"For I ne kan nat fynde
A man, though that I walked into Ynde,
Neither in citee ne in no village,
That wolde chaunge his youthe for myn age;
And therfore moot I han myn age stille,
As longe tyme as it is Goddes wille.
Ne Deeth, allas! ne wol nat han my lyf
Thus walke I, lyk a restelees kaityf,
And on the ground, which is my moodres gate,
I knokke with my staf, bothe erly and late,
And seye, 'Leeve modder, leet me in!
Lo how I vanysshe, flesshe, and blood, and skyn!
Allas, whan shul my bones been at reste?
Mooder, with yow wolde I chaunge my cheste
That in my chambre longe tyme hath be,
Ye, for an heyre clowt to wrappe in me!'
But yet to me she wol nat do that grace,
For which ful pale and welked is my face."
(C. 721-38)

Let us begin with the chest. Robinson assures us that this is a clothes chest, not a coffin; recently, however, commentators have suggested that it might be a money chest, "filled with the florins that he has been hoarding." This I think an exceedingly tempting interpretation, for it provides a strong structural link between the Old Man and the gold (he has left it by the oak, rather than has discovered it there), and it lends, as we shall see, great power and meaning to his words. Unfortunately, evidence to support this claim has been, for the most part, conjecture; some will ask, with Alfred David, "Where is this chamber with the chest full of possessions that he says he would exchange for a hair-cloth?" Once again, medieval sermon books suggest an answer.

Among the many exempla that illustrated the addicting power of avarice, one seems to have particularly appealed to preachers. The version given here is the liveliest, and was reported by Owst in his *Literature and Pulpit in Medieval England:*

When a certain very rich rustic, who was hard-hearted both to the poor and towards his own soul, had amassed so much wealth that he had a chest filled with money and other treasures, he had it set in front of him as he lay sickening on his deathbed. By the time that the priest could be summoned to make his Will, the sick man had already lost power of speech. The priest, accordingly, suggested a plan to his wife and brother, whereby a "Ha!" from the patient might be taken to indicate approval of what was proposed to him, and silence as the mark of disapproval. Having won agreement for his plan, our priest said to the testator—Do you wish to bequeath your soul to God after your decease, and your body to Mother Church for burial?, and the latter replied, "Ha!" Then the priest said to him—Do you wish to leave twenty shillings to the fabric of your church, where you have chosen to be buried? But the other made no reply and kept a complete silence. Forthwith the priest pulled him violently by the ear, whereat the man cried—"Ha!" Then the priest said— Write down twenty shillings for the church fabric: for see, he has granted it with his "ha!" After that the priest pondered how he could get for himself the chest with the aforesaid treasure. So he said to the sick man—I have some books, but I have no chest to keep them in.

That coffer over there would be most useful to me. Would you like me, therefore, to have that coffer to put my books in? But the other said nothing whatever to these remarks. Then the priest pinched his ear so hard that those who were present declared afterwards that the pinch drew blood from the man's ear. Then the enfeebled rustic, in a loud voice, said to the priest before them all—O you greedy priest, by Christ's death, never shall you have from me as much as a farthing of the money which is in that chest! Having spoken thus, he turned to his devotions and expired. Accordingly, his wife and relatives divided the money between them. This happened in England, so it is said.

Bromyard tells a similar story of a dying man who had lost his power to speak. The priests who were standing about him saw he was near death, and urged him to think of his soul.

They shouted in his ears that if he wished to receive the sacraments, he should at least make some sign with his hands, mouth, or face, but they were unable to get any sign from him. Then a certain associate of the fellow said:

> Ego cito habebo ab eo signum et apposuit manum ad cistam que erat ad pedes eius in qua erat pecunia sua et cor suum et thesaurus suus quasi volens eam aperire vel apportare et statim quasi expergefactus et quasi nitens caput erigere et voce et vultu triste signum vite ostendit.

I will quickly get a sign from him, and he placed his hand on the chest which was by his feet, as though he wished to open it or carry it away. In this chest was the fellow's money and his heart and his treasure, and immediately, as if startled from sleep and striving to raise his head, he speedily gives a sign with sad face and voice.

In another story, Bromyard speaks of a man who, when he was to be given extreme unction, hid his right hand from sight. The priest asked him where his hand was and why he did not bring it forth, and the man replied, "*Sub me teneo in ea clavem ciste mee.*"

This is the kind of chest, then, that the Old Man offers to change for a "heyre clowt"; before all else, we should realise the magnitude of the transaction. A "clowt" is a piece of cloth, next to nothing; indeed, the words began to acquire this figurative meaning in Middle English, a userer "wold not gyff þerfor þe valour of a sh[red] clowte." Yet the Old Man would willingly exchange his chest for it. If the chest were filled with treasure, he would indeed be giving up all that he had. Unlike the dying men in the exempla, it seems our venerable figure has renounced the sin of avarice; by wishing to clothe himself in a hair-shirt, a traditional emblem for penance, he indicates that he would like to do satisfaction for his sin.

The Old Man's affinities with the Wandering Jew would indicate that, in Dewey Faulkner's phrase, "like the Jew, he is being forced to wander eternally for having offended God grievously in some way." Avarice, I submit, has been the offense, and the Old Man's wandering, his penance.

But why does the Old Man offer to exchange his chest with his mother, the earth? John Steadman has noted that commentators writing against cupidity would frequently portray the earth as the mother a man must return to stripped of his worldly possessions. Due to the nature of the sin, the earth often chides the avaricious man: "Hear," cries Alain de Lille against the miserly man, "hear what the elements declare against you, and especially the earth, your mother. Why dost thou do injury to your mother, why bearing violence against me, who produced you from my bowels?" Chaucer reverses the situation: the Old Man pleads with the earth, and the sincerity of his petition makes us feel that his repentance has been long-standing and heartfelt.

If we look at the Old Man in this way, as a repentant sinner, we can also see why he is old. Chaucer might have gotten the idea from the sixth chapter of the Epistle to Timothy, the same chapter that gave him the Pardoner's theme. The Old Man quotes Paul's precepts to the rioters, though without much effect. Innocent III's *De Contemptu Mundi* might also have contributed to the character's formation. At least since Seneca, however, avarice has been the bane of the old: *Caeteris vitiis in homine senescentibus, sola avaritia juvenescit* [When the other vices in man have grown old, avarice alone flourishes]. Bromyard's explanation of this fact is novel, but symptomatic. He notes that as a man more eagerly clutches his own goods when other men come near him, so does an old man amass temporal goods when he sees many men like him who are nearing death and the loss of their goods. Chaucer himself, in the Reeve's Prologue, specifically links old age and avarice:

Foure gleedes han we, which I shal devyse,—
Avauntyng, liyng, anger, coveitise;
Thise foure sparkles longen unto eelde.
(ll. 3883-85)

It seems natural enough, then, that Chaucer chose to make this man old. But in doing so, Chaucer also realised how powerful the associations that would accompany such a figure would be. No longer just a repentant miser, the Old Man becomes an archetype, a reminder to every man who covets wealth that terrible beyond measure is the affliction this sin brings against the soul. For the Old Man has wandered to the ends of the earth seeking expiation for his sin, and with it the peace of Death. And as of now, he has not found it. But this changes before our eyes, for even the object of the Old Man's search, the exchange of youth for old age, may be seen in terms of avarice. For if longevity is one of the vice's qualities, this does not mean that the young are therefore immune: *Avaritia enim non parcit sent nec iuveni.*

In the young rioters I think the Old Man finds three who *figuratively* would exchange their youthful desire for his former passion. Thus we might see the Old Man as a distinguished player in an ancient drama, an expiation myth which requires some sort of exchange to effect the protagonist's release. In Chaucer's version, expiation is wedded to Christian notions of repentance, satisfaction, and understanding. We see the Old Man at the moment of exchange and release; it is a timeless moment that recurs whenever the soul is struck by greed.

The Old Man is perfectly honest with rioters and readers alike; what separates us from them is our greater understanding of his words. Death, Old Age, no matter what signification we assign him, the Old Man should be seen within the context of Chaucer's sermon on avarice. He is a figure who delights, who instructs, but who most of all leaves very few unmoved. He is a different guide, another text, from the Pardoner.

Old Man, This essay has dealt with the Pardoner and the telling of his Tale. As a preacher who scorns God, the Pardoner lacks spiritual insight, and therefore is excessively literal. His inspiration is his own, and the conclusion of the Tale vividly demonstrates how his inspiration fails. Like the Old Man, the Pardoner is a victim of the sin of avarice; unlike thethe Pardoner remains defiant. He is a remarkable figure in a remarkable Tale, one that will continue to delight and puzzle us the more we understand.

Q.4. Do you think the Pardoner exposes himself with unnaturally frank cynicism.

Or

Q. Analyse if The character of the Pardoner is in part a reproduction of the False Semblant of Roman de la Rose

Chaucer, the critics tell us, possessed a genius eminently dramatic, and a matchless talent for story-telling, but frequently allowed his mediaeval love of moralizing to defeat, for the moment, his narrative powers, and now and then grossly violated dramatic propriety, whether carelessly or from the exigencies of satire. As instances of the first of these sins are usually cited the self-satisfied speech of Nature in the Doctor's Tale, and the long soliloquizing excursus on free will and predestination in the Troilus. The most flagrant offense under the second head is commonly supposed to be the harangue of the Pardoner.

In The Doctor's Tale, Nature is produced in person, exhibiting her artistic masterpiece Virginia, and boasting of her in a showmanlike address to the public. The device may be granted absurd, and it certainly interferes with the flow of the narrative. But there is a further consideration, the character of the doctor. The doctor is a very formal person, from whom a degree of prosiness is to be expected. It was Chaucer's artistic duty, in the Canterbury Tales, — as it has clearly been his purpose, — not only to select stories appropriate to the several pilgrims, but to make the method of delivery correspond to the character of the teller.

The offending passage in the Troilus must be justified, if at all, on other grounds. A long soliloquy on the foreknowledge of God, absolute necessity, necessity conditional, and free will is not quite what one expects from a Trojan prince whose love is going to the Grecian camp. But though a great anachronism, and though rather unskillfully brought in, the soliloquy is by no means an impertinence. The idea of fate is subtly insistent throughout the poem, — it is perhaps even the key to

Cressida's character; and surely, at this juncture, if ever, Troilus may have his thoughts about the mysterious inevitableness that is governing his life.

These and other considerations make it worth while to look with some scrutiny at what passes for Chaucer's great sin against dramatic propriety, the confession of the Pardoner.

The Pardoner, it is said, exposes himself with unnaturally frank cynicism. He might properly indulge in a sly sneer at the pretenses of his vocation; but to proclaim that his relies are a sham; to declare that his

"Intent is only for to win,
And nothing for correction of sin,"

and that when once the penitents' money in his pouch he does not care if their "souls go a-blackberrying" after death; to avow in a coolly casual way that he is himself "a full vicious man," — all this is dramatically impossible. But this not all: after the tale is finished, the Pardoner, according to the usual view, is so foolish as to try his impostures on very audience which he has just enlightened as to his own vices and the tricks of his trade.

An attempt is sometimes made to account for these absurdities by a reference to the Roman de la Rose. The character of the Pardoner is in part a reproduction of the False-Semblant of that poem, and False-Semblant, as an allegorical personage, is not bound by dramatic law. It is a convention of satire, illustrated in a drastic way by Garnet's speech in Oldham, to make an odious character describe himself unsparingly, — a trick absurd in itself, but no more absurd than such conventions as the long " aside " in the drama. This defense, or explanation, has always been felt to be unsatisfactory. Chaucer is not a reformer.

He is not even, if rightly taken, a satirist. His aim is not to reconstruct the Church or to amelioratehumanity, but to depict certain characters, and to let them tell stories. He has no right to resort to conventions which, permissible to one who depicts a character ad hoc, are unjustifiable in one who depicts a character for its own sake. It is an equally weak defense to allege that the Pardoner is drunk. One draught of ale, however "moist and corny," would never fuddle so seasoned a drinker. Besides, he manifests none of the signs of intoxication. Unless, then, it can be shown that the character of the Pardoner is consistent with itself and with nature, the poet has blundered; and the gravity of his blunder is increased by the excellence of the Pardoner's Tale, perhaps the best short narrative poem in the language. In general, Chaucer shows exquisite delicacy in fitting the various Canterbury tales to the characters of the tellers. In the present case, we have a beautiful story, wonderfully told, put into the mouth of a vulgar, prating rascal, not only destitute of moral and intellectual dignity, but so lacking in common sense that he cannot hold his tongue about his own impostures.

Yet the prologue, the tale, and the epilogue all show Chaucer at the height of his powers. It is possible that an explanation of the problem may be found by considering all the available evidence as to the Pardoner's character. It may appear from such an examination that his character is consistent throughout, and of a kind to make the apparent impropriety of the introductory confession in conformity to nature.

In the first place, then, we may be sure that the Pardoner is a thorough-paced scoundrel. His bulls of popes and cardinals may be genuine, — it would in any case not do for him to confess to the felony of forging the pope's seal, but his relics are counterfeit, and he has no illusions about the holiness of his mission. He preaches for money, and has no concern for the reformation of morals or for genuineness of repentance on the part of those who offer to his relics, and receive his absolution. He is skillful at his business: it has brought him in a hundred marks (almost seven hundred pounds in our values) a year since be first took it up. Like all clever impostors, he is proud of his dexterity. Under ordinary circumstances, prudence would constrain him to suppress the exhibition of this pride; but the circumstances are not ordinary. He is not on his rounds. The pilgrims are a company associated by chance, and likely never to assemble again after their return supper at Harry Bailly's. If they repeat his words, it will not much matter. He cannot labour in his vocation while he is with them, and none of them are likely to cross his path in the future. They are not of the kind among whom he is used to ply his arts. His best field is the country village. To be sure, the parson and the ploughman are from the country; but the character of the parson makes the parish which he administers a forbidden region to such loose fish as the Pardoner. One of the ordinary restraints on freedom of self-revelation, then, is wanting: he need fear no disagreeable consequences.

Farther, the unsoundness of the Pardoner's morals is known to the company before he begins his cynical confessions. He may pose as a holy man when he is swindling the peasantry of some remote hamlet; but hypocritical airs and graces would be absurdly futile among his present companions. That there has been no attempt at such posturing is made clear enough by the host, the gentles, and the Pardoner himself.

The host calls on the Pardoner for a merry tale; the Pardoner assents with an alacrity which warrants vehement suspicion, and the gentles protest that they want no ribaldry, and insist on something elevated and instructive. This is significant enough of the impression the Pardoner has made on his traveling companions. The Pardoner easily adapts himself tothe temper of his audience. It is his business to know moral tales. He has his sermons by heart, and most of these, as a matter of course contain an exemplum, an anecdote which can be "improved " to the edification of a church-ful of laymen. But before beginning he feels the need of refreshment.

'I graunte ywis,'quod he,'but I moot thynke
Upon som honest thyng whil that I drynke.'

Not that he has "to think awhile before he can recollect some decent thing," as has been suggested. He is honestly thirsty, and glad of an excuse to quench his thirst, no doubt; but, being a man of ability and eloquence, be must have plenty of "honest things" at his tongue's end.

Perhaps we have now facts enough to explain the self-revelation of the Pardoner's prologue. He knows what his fellow-travelers think of him; he has just consented to tell an over-facetious story; he is now about to preach a highly edifying sermon. There is no opportunity to pull wool over the eyes of his hearers, even if there were any motive for it. Sure that they will perceive the enormous discrepancy between his character and his teaching, the Pardoner is impatient of occupying the position of a futile hypocrite. He is too clever a knave to wish others to take him for a fool.

Hence these cynical confessions at the outset, the dramatic purpose of which is now clear. The Pardoner is, in effect, saying to the pilgrims: "I am about to tell you a moral tale. I am going to preach you one of my sermons. You will find the sentiments of this sermon unexceptionable. Do not think, however, that I expect you to believe me in earnest. You know what kind of fellow I am, and this is my trade."

With these feelings, then, the Pardoner begins his tale or sermon. Knowing it by heart, as he tells us himself, and being accustomed to preach with great unction, he is soon rapt into the same mood of conventional earnestness that he has found so effective in the pulpit. By the time he arrives at the ejaculations on the wickedness of sin and the horrors of homicide, gluttony, lechery, and gambling, which (though marked "auctor " by the officious stupidity of some scribe) form the "application " of the whole discourse, he is at a white heat of zeal. Forgetful of his surroundings, he does not stop with the "application," but goes on to the exhortation with which he regularly concludes his harangues: —

"Now, good men, God foryeve yow your trespas,
And ware yow fro the sinne of avarice!
Myn holy pardoun may yow alle wariee,
So that ye offre nobles or sterlinges,
Or elles silver broches, spones, ringes.
Boweth your heed under this holy bulle!
Cometh up, ye wyves, offreth of your wolle!
Your name I entre heer in my rolle anon,

Into the blisse of heven shul ye gon;
I yow assoile, by myn heigh power,
Yow that wol offre, as clene and eek as cleer
As ye were born. — And lo, sirs, thus I preche;
And Jesu Crist, that is our soules leche,
So graunte yow his pardoun to receyve,
For that is best, I wol yow not deceyve!"

The last four lines of this passage are particularly significant. The Pardoner's invitation to come up and offer to the relics and receive absolution is glaringly out of place in a speech to his fellow-travelers, to whom he has already made full confession of the emptiness of his pretensions. "Come up, ye wives, and offer of your wool!" has no appropriateness when addressed to the pilgrims. Perceiving the absurdity, the speaker pulls himself up with the explanatory "This is the kind of sermon I am in the habit of delivering." ("And lo, airs, thus I preche.")

So far, all is plain sailing. We might suppose the preacher carried away by professional enthusiasm, and forgetting just where he ought to have stopped. We might suppose, on the other hand, that he wished to give his hearers acomplete specimen of his discourses, final invitation and all. But what shall we think of his next words? —

"And lo, sirs, thus I preche;
And Jesu Crist, that is our soules leche,
So graunto yow his pardoun to receyve,
For that is best, I wol yow nat deceyve!"

It may be that these words, apparently so out of consonance with anything we have yet heard from the Pardoner, furnish the key to his character. May we not believe that the beautiful and impressive story that he has just told — a story that no one can read without emotion — has moved even him, though he has told it a thousand times before in the way of his profession? The unusual circumstances under which he has preached his sermon may have assisted in producing this effect. For once, perhaps, the hideous incongruity between his preaching and the profligate invitation to come up and be pardoned through the efficacy of his trumpery relics has appeared to him. Possibly we may venture to think that the Pardoner, moved by his own tale, went on mechanically to this professional invitation, perceived its absurd inopportuneness with a start, and thus had its hypocritical villainy suddenly projected in his own mind against the beauty and impressiveness of his tale.

This would still further increase his emotion, which, after an explanatory "And lo, sirs, thus I preche," finds vent in an ejaculation profoundly affecting in its reminiscence of the Pardoner's better nature, which he had himself thought dead long ago. "My pardon," he says, "is of no account, as you know. God grant that you receive Christ's pardon, which is better than mine. I will not deceive you, though deceit is my business."

Of course this better mood can last but a moment. There is no question of repentance or reformation, for the Pardoner is a lost soul. The reaction comes instantly, and is to the extreme of reckless jesting. Aware that the pilgrims know him thoroughly by this time, for he has even taken pains to reveal himself, he nevertheless impudently urges them to kiss the relics and make offering and receive pardon. The invitation has sometimes been taken as given in dead earnest; but this is inconceivable. It would imply superhuman folly on the speaker's part to try to deceive the pilgrims when he has just warned them against his own deceit. Besides, we have evidence that the Pardoner hurries into this strain of reckless jocularity to escape from the serious mood that has surprised him.

"But, sirs, o word forgat I in my tale,"

are the words with which he begins the closing passage, and these very words indicate his confusion. For he has not forgotten his relics. On the contrary, he has just been talking about them, and praising their efficacy. The whole passage is jocose. At the end, he turns to the host, and pointedly suggests that he begin, as being the most sinful of the company. This remark alone would suffice to indicate how little serious purpose there is in the proposition of the Pardoner. The host is the last person to yield to seductive suggestions of this sort in any case, and it would be idle to expect him to do so after the full revelation of himself that the Pardoner has made.

The host, who of course has no knowledge of the conflict of feelings through which the Pardoner is passing, naturally replies in a strain of coarse raillery. Under ordinary circumstances, the effect of this jesting on the Pardoner would be to evoke a still more scurrilous response. He must often have bandied words in all good nature with persons of the host's freedom of speech, and there is no reason to suppose that he is constitutionally thin-skinned. Under ordinary circumstances, too, so fluent a man as the Pardoner, if he got angry, would have plenty of words in which tovent his wrath. On the present occasion rage makes him dumb.

"This Pardoner answered not a word:
So wroth he was no word he wolde seye."

The inference seems to be plain. The contest of feelings in the Pardoner's mind, the momentary return to sincerity, which must have been accompanied by profound emotion, the revulsion of feeling indicated by his jesting proposition to his fellow-travelers, are too much for his equanimity. When the host replies with a scurrile jest, he is simply too angry to speak. That this is the correct interpretation of the course of events is further substantiated by the surprise which the host feels at this, to him, inexplicable anger on the part of the Pardoner. He has not noticed the Pardoner's moment of emotion; he has, therefore, supposed the jesting to be of the ordinary sort, and he feels injured that his reply is taken in ill part.

"`Now,' quod our host, 'I wol no lenger pleye
With thee, ne with no other angry man.'"

The knight makes up the quarrel, which of course neither party wishes to prolong, and the company rides on as before.

If these considerations are sound, we have in Chaucer's treatment of the Pardoner no violation of dramatic propriety, but, on the contrary, the subtlest piece of character delineation the poet has ever attempted. The Pardoner is an able and eloquent man, a friar, very likely, who had entered his order with the best purposes, or, at any rate, with no bad aims, and with possibilities of good in him, and had grown corrupt with its corruption. His debasement seems to be utter, for one must not forget the picture in the general prologue. Nothing but a ribald story appears possible from him. But, by showing us the man in a moment of moral convulsion, Chaucer has invested him with a sort of dignity which justifies the poet in putting into his mouth one of the most beautiful as well as one of the best told tales in the whole collection.

If the considerations referred to be not sound, there is no explaining away the difficulties: the cynical prologue remains a monstrous absurdity; the error in tact involved in giving a despicable fellow a magnificent tale to tell seems ultimate; the earnest remark of the Pardoner that Christ's pardon is better than his is a piece of impertinence; the Pardoner's anger at the host's jesting is improbable; the dumbness of his wrath is out of character; and the surprise of the host at his losing his temper is nugatory. The interpretation suggested seems not only to be in harmony with all the phenomena, but even to explain some phenomena otherwise inexplicable except as blunders. That a fortuitous collection of blunders should combine to make up a subtle piece of character delineation is not impossible, perhaps, but is hardly what one would expect. Is it not reasonable, then, to accept an interpretation of the prologue and the tale which brings them into harmony with what we know of Chaucer's exquisite delicacy of portraiture, and wonderful power of dramatically adapting his stories to their tellers, particularly as the Pardoner's Tale must have been written when all his powers were at their height?

Q.5. Discuss The Pardoner's hyprocrisy of his subjectivity

Or

Q. Analyse the Pardoner's tale as a his parodic reaction to the Wife of Bath's prior literary performance.

In this essay interrogation of the almost ubiquitous assumption of Chaucer's Pardoner's hypocrisy and suggest an alternative reading, one informed by recent debate over Chaucerian subjectivity, in which the Pardoner's words do not reveal anything about his morality but instead depict his parodic reaction to the Wife of Bath's prior literary performance.

In the fourteenth-century English Franciscan preacher's manual, the Fasciculus Morum, which treats at length the Seven Deadly Sins and their remedial virtues, we find a succinct description, under the topic of "Pride," of hypocrisy:

> Ypocrite autem similes sunt trutannis qui cum accessus hominum intelligerint, labia movent sanctitatem pretendentes, ut cicius a transeuntibus aliquid accipiant, set cum per transierint in dissolucionem prorumpuntur. Revera sic ypocrite in conspectu hominem orant, ieiunant, et huiusmodi faciunt ut ab hominibus videantur; set in latibulo faciunt omnia contraria, nam orant clamorose ut ab hominibus audiantur, set revera cor dissonat longe ab ore: Populus his labiis me nonorat, cor autem eorum longe, etc.

> Hypocrites are like fake beggars who, when they have noticed someone coming, move their lips in pretended holiness, in order to receive something from the passersby, but when they are gone they dissolve into laughter. Thus in the sight of men hypocrites pray, fast, and do similar works that they may be seen by people; but in secret they do all the opposite, for they pray aloud that they may be heard by people, but in fact their heart is far from their mouth.: "This people honours me with their lips, but their heart is far from me:' and so on.

The reader must immediately notice how poorly the Pardoner fits this description. He indeed "moves his lips," not in "pretended holiness," but in self-condemnation, openly claiming his own hypocrisy:

> For certes, many a predicacioun Comth ofte tyme of yvel entencioun; Som for plesance of folk and flaterye, To been avaunced by ypocrisye, And som for veyne glorie, and som for hate .... Thus spitte I out my venym under heave Of hoolynesse, to semen hooly and trewe.

The Pardoner "dissolves" not "into laughter" when his performance is over but into silence; before this his "heart" is seemingly very close to his "mouth" in that he announces his hypocritical intentions both before and after his preaching performance. In short, his performance is more a contrite repentance for a past sin of hypocrisy than an enactment of his present condition.

Chaucer well knew the definition of a hypocrite, cited above, or something close to it, for he provides a definition very similar to it in his own excursus on the Seven Deadly Sins, the Parson's Tale: "Ypocrite is he that hideth to shew hym swich as he is, and sheweth hym swich as he noght is". Again, the issue is one of hiding. Other standard treatments of hypocrisy agree. As one important instance among many, the Summa Virtutum Anime (of course, one of the sources of the Parson's Tale) includes hypocrisy as part of its treatment of humility, the remedy for pride:

Sequitur de falsa humilitate, que idem est quot simulacio uel ypocrisis, que dicitur ab "ypos," quod est falsum et "crisis," iudicium, quia falsum iudicium de se velinguit cum aliud aget et aliud astrendet.

Now we turn to false humility, which is the same as pretense of hypocrisy, which is named from "hypos," which means false and "crisis:' judgment, because it causes a false judgment of itself when it does one thing and shows forth another.

What follows in the text is a series of metaphors expounding the disjunction between outward virtue and inner corruption: a hypocrite is a whited sepulcher, a wolf in sheep's clothing, a dungheap covered with snow (sterquilinium niue tectum) . The Pardoner, of course, fails to hide his supposed hypocrisy, trumpeting aloud his intentions to all the pilgrims: "For myn entente is nat but for to wynne, / And nothyng for correccioun of synne" .

Following George Lyman Kittredge, though, Chaucerians have uniformly taken the Pardoner's words at face value, condemning him as a hypocrite. As long ago as 1914, Kittredge claimed, "The Pardoner is an abandoned wretch" characterized by "cynicism" (22, 218). He is "[t]he most abandoned character among the Canterbury Pilgrims", "the one lost soul among the Canterbury Pilgrims" . Subsequent condemnations of him abound.2 Critical response to the Pardoner, his tale, and especially his infamous appeal for money from his fellow pilgrims has, with some interesting variation, followed that of Harry Bailly, who reacts to him with startling vituperation. Venerable established theories that have long been accepted as truth are, of course, dangerous, for they masquerade as something they are not. The very dominance of the received interpretation of the Pardoner demands that it be questioned, lest we inscribe our own reading of him on Chaucer's intentions.

How does this ubiquitous condemnation square with the Pardoner's obvious failure to conceal the dungheap under the snow-or, more accurately, with his enthusiasm in revealing his sin? As the handbooks of the Seven Deadly Sins point out, it is only the truly humble who can openly confess their sins. The problem is, in other words, the Pardoner's call to the pilgrims, with Harry Bailly first in line, to donate money for indulgences. If penitent, the Pardoner still seems as interested in profit as he was in his unrevealed and presumably truly hypocritical state: "Com forth anon, and kneleth heere adoun.... / So that ye offren, alwey newe and newe, / Nobles or pens. ." (6.925, 29-30). Harry Bailly picks up, in his truculent response, the excremental nature of the dunghill-covered-with-snow metaphor: "Thou woldest make me kisse thyn olde breech, / ... though it were with thy fundement depeint!" (6.948, 50).

A possible solution to the problem is that the Pardoner's appeal is a performance whose purpose is to parody the pilgrim whose prologue and tale seem in so many odd ways to echo his own-the Wife of Bath. Indeed, almost as central to the criticism of Chaucer's Pardoner's Tale as the Pardoner's arrogance, blind hypocrisy, and sexual irregularities is his odd relationship with that other favourite of the explicator, the Wife of Bath. In this interpretation, the Pardoner is someone who emphasizes seemingly hypocritical excesses in his own character and career primarily as a means of interpreting the Wife's hypocrisy.3 He is being intentionally parodic and interpretive, and it is the pilgrims' misunderstanding of his performance that leads to Harry Bailly's violent reaction. Connections between the Pardoner and the Wife of Bath have long been recognized, but a coherent interpretation emphasizing the parodic nature of the Pardoner's performance has not yet been made.

A partial list of important connections between the Pardoner and the Wife of Bath is helpful here: The Pardoner and the Wife couple tales with long, confessional prologues. The mysterious old Loathly Lady in the Wife's Tale appears to a young knight on a quest, while the mysterious Old Man in the Pardoner's appears to three young men, also on a quest. Both tales center on surprises for their young heroes: the Loathly Lady changes her old age for youth while the Old Man (who says he cannot4.721-24) enables the rioters to find death in a very unexpected way. Both the Wife and the Pardoner are fond of quoting books, particularly the writings of St. Paul. Both go off on tangents that delay the beginning of their tales.

The Wife glories in the libidinizing effect on her of wine and dancing to a harp (3.455-59); the Pardoner condemns drinking as a sin (6.549-55) while he has the three rioters playing musical instruments— including the harp-in drunken revelry at their tavern (6.463-71). The Pardoner frequently alludes to, sometimes actually quotes, the words of the Wife, with the most obvious example being his "For myn entente is nat but for to wynne" (6.403)-a quotation and misdirection of the Wife's "For myn entente is nat but for to pleye" (3.192). This list could be lengthened considerably. These connections indicate that the Pardoner is performing a parody of the Wife in which an exaggerated and paradoxically admitted hypocrisy plays a large part.

When the Pardoner makes his appeal, it is a calculated, open parody of what the Wife has left submerged in her text:

I rede that oure Hoost heere shal bigynne, For he is moost envoluped in synne. Com forth, sire Hoost, and offre first anon,

And thou shalt kisse the relikes everychon, Ye, for a grote! Unbokele anon thy purs. (6.941-45)

He has prepared his audience for this literary critical act by earlier explaining his hypocrisy:

For myn entente is nat but for to wynne, And nothyng for correccioun of synne .... Thus quyte I folk that doon us displesances; Thus spitte I out my venym under hewe Of hoolynesse, to semen hooly and trewe. (6.403-04, 20-22)

Significant is not only his quotation of the Wife but also his adoption of the vocabulary generated in The Canterbury Tales for a rudimentary sort of literary criticism: quyte, as, for example, in the Miller's statement, "I kan a noble tale for the nones, / With which I wol now quite the Knyghtes tale" (1.3126-27). The Pardoner means for his hypocrisy to be evident to the pilgrims-as it certainly is-but with its primary meaning not the literal one but the allegorical, which is the Wife's hypocrisy.

When, having gained sovereignty over her knight, the Loathly Lady assumes both beauty and faithfulness and becomes the perfect wife, she makes the same covert appeal for the Wife herself, who, as she explains, likes to go abroad "for to se, and eek for to be seye / Of lusty folk" (3.552-53) and is ready to "[w]elcome the sixte, whan that evere he shal" (3.45). Like the Pardoner's appeal for money, this appeal is directed toward the other pilgrims. The Wife's unfaithfulness, shrewishness, violence, and increasing age, however, dismantle the meaning of her tale: her covert appeal thus is hypocritical. By carefully parodying her and appending an overt appeal to his own prologue and tale, the Pardoner is engaged not so much in self-revelation but in literary criticism-interpretive explication of the Wife's text.

We are in danger when we take his parody of another's autobiography for his own. All we know of him, after all, comes from two sources-his own words, which I suggest are not self-directed but parodic of the Wife, and the Pilgrim Chaucer's portrait of him in the "General Prologue." That portrait certainly seems to support the standard interpretation of the Pardoner: "And thus, with feyned flaterye and japes, / He made the person and the peple his apes" (1.705-06). But the assumption here is that the Pilgrim Chaucer finally has one character right after naively misunderstanding so many others (Donaldson 7). If he accepts so many of the self-congratulatory remarks of the other pilgrims at face value, thus generating that favourite concept of critics, Chaucerian irony, we have no logical grounds to assume that he does not also mistakenly accept the equally wrong self-deprecating remarks of the Pardoner. The Pardoner's silence, then, at the end of his tale reflects anger not only at the violence of the Host's attack on him but also at the literary insensitivity that would miss the point of his brilliant parodic criticism: "This Pardoner answerde nat a word; / So wrooth he was, no word ne wolde he seye" (6.956-57). The control he loses at the end is not over himself but over his audience. His only recourse, when his performative words fail to signify, is silence.

If this reading of the Pardoner has any force, the Pardoner's performance has interesting implications for the recent discussion of Chaucerian subjectivity. In their powerful readings of the Pardoner, H. Marshall Leicester and Lee Patterson have between them defined the terms of the debate over the Pardoner and his tale. For Leicester, the Pardoner is a marginalized deconstructer of his own tale and language, one "who deliberately mimes official discoveries in such a way as to bring out their underlying contradictions". He is a self-conscious voice, an "exegetical critic of his own tale" whose despair causes him to interpret "himself in traditional terms as the vetus homo," the unregenerate sinner of the Bible . The similarities between the Pardoner and the Wife of Bath lead Leicester to the conclusion that the fundamental experience of the constitution of the subject as an absence is the same in the cases of the Wife of Bath and the Pardoner. For both, the "I" is what slips away, evades definition, never settles down.

The Pardoner for Leicester is an exegetical critic whose spiritual despair leads to self-deconstruction.

Patterson, following the social theories of Anthony Giddens, is interested in a Chaucer who constitutes his own subjectivity through his text . His characters, one narrative level away from Chaucer, do the same:

In The Wife of Bath's Prologue and Tale Chaucer used the rhetoric of misogyny to construct a feminine subjectivity. In the remarkably similar Pardoner's Prologue and Tale, he deploys the rhetoric of penance for an analogous act of self-constitution.

For Patterson, the Pardoner's "performance is best understood in terms of medieval confessional habits" . The Pardoner is anxious, tormented inwardly, despairing yet impenitent . His language reveals yet conceals this despair, for although his tale "contains an accurate account of ... [his] own spiritual condition.... it is one that he is himself apparently incapable of reading" . The Pardoner's offering of the relics to his fellow pilgrims is "an elliptical and compact gesture that is as self-contradictory as the Pardoner's previous utterances".

Both Leicester and Patterson appeal to Lacanian psychoanalysis in their divergent erasures of the Pardoner's subjectivity. I do not wish to challenge their readings, the most persuasive admissions of the Pardoner we have inherited from Kittredge into the discourse of postmodern critical theory. If my reading of the Pardoner diverges yet further from theirs, it does so only to suggest a more thorough erasure of the subject than theirs and to free us at last from Kittredge's Pardoner. If the Pardoner's words signify a parodic performance rather than an autobiographical confession, and if he reads the Wife's text as an exegetical critic, allegorizing her "play" by his "win:' substituting avaricia for luxuries, money for sex as an interpretive gesture aimed at the Wife's use of the latter to gain the former, then we have almost no subject left at all. He is a trace, as Derrida might put it, rather than a presence. We cannot confidently speak of his hypocrisy, despair, eunuchry, homosexuality, or greed. The fleeting glimpse we have of him as he recedes from us is, simply, that of a parodist.

Q.6. Discuss Pardoner's Homosexuality

Or

Q. Analyse Pardoner as an enunch

The Famous pronouncement of Chaucer's narrator on Chaucer's Pardoner — "I trowe he were a geldyng or a mare" (I. 691) — poses several questions for modern readers. What are the options that it offers for the interpretation of the Pardoner? Why is the narrator unable to decide between them? To what extent does Chaucer maintain this indeterminacy about the Pardoner and require the reader, like the narrator, to remain forever undecided? Does Chaucer in any way lead the reader to a greater certitude? If so, what is the sexual status of the Pardoner? Finally, what is the moral significance of that status? These questions arise partly from the complexity of Chaucer's poetry and partly from present-day ignorance of medieval sexual concepts and terminology.

The term "mare," in particular, has proved notoriously difficult for modern readers to interpret, and even when the term is glossed, the possibility that the Pardoner may be a "mare" is often ignored in favour of the belief that he is certainly a "geldyng," or eunuch. Psychological, moral, and spiritual interpretations of the Pardoner's eunuchry and of the sterility and, less accurately, the impotence with which it is associated permeate current critical treatments of this pilgrim. A faithful reading of Chaucer's line requires that the balance be restored. We need a gloss for "mare," and we need interpretations of the Pardoner's portrait and of his prologue and tale that explore the implications of his possible status as "mare" justPardoner as a possible homosexual. In the second part, I consider the spiritual implications of the Pardoner's sexuality by redirecting attention to his bagful of pardons and relics.

The initial references to these objects occupy a significant place in the middle section of the Pardoner's tripartite portrait in the General Prologue: he is not only a "geldyng or a mare" (ll. 669-91) but also both a "pardoner" peddling false relics (ll. 692-706) and a "noble ecclesiaste" (Il. 707-14). Through an interpretation of the Pardoner as homosexual, hope to confirm what this structure suggests: that his pardons and relics constitute the essential link, the lifeline, between this sexually anomalous Christian and his church.

For many of Chaucer's readers, the narrator's pronouncement is intimately linked with certain deservedly influential commentaries on the Pardoner's sexual status, and any reconsideration of the subject must acknowledge its debt to those studies and carefully discriminate its conclusions from theirs. In his ground-breaking review of medieval texts on medicine and physiognomy, Walter Clyde Curry opened discussion of the Pardoner's physical nature.Although the point is seldom noticed, Curry interprets the narrator's pronouncement as offering a choice between impotence and effeminacy.

He treats the mention of these two sexual phenomena as serving to define a third possibility, underlying and unnamed, and then shows that the Pardoner's physical characteristics — long, fine hair; high voice; glaring eyes; and beardlessness — fit the descriptions of eunuchs offered by medieval doctors and physiognomists. All but one of Curry's sources, moreover, associate eunuchry with immorality, and some also insist that the congenital eunuch is more evil than the castrated eunuch. The sins attributed to eunuchs include dissoluteness, shamelessness, cunning, and viciousness. In what has proved the least convincing part of his argument. Curry contends that the other pilgrims. and Chaucer's audience, would have been able to go beyond the narrator's speculations to deduce that the Pardoner suffers from the (presumably rare) condition of congenital eunuchry.

Since in the view of the medieval experts the physical characteristics of all eunuchs are much the same, Curry's labeling of the Pardoner as a *congenital* eunuch is grounded not in unarguable physiognomical fact, as is sometimes believed, but in fallible literary interpretation. One argument appeals to the influence of source. Chaucer may have based his Pardoner, in part, on the characterization of a eunuch by the physiognomist Polemon (pp. 62-64), and Curry assumes that because Polemon' s eunuch was a congenital eunuch. Chaucer's must be, too. A second argument rests on Curry's own estimate of the Pardoner's character: the depth of the Pardoner's depravity is seen as justifying his classification with the more malicious congenital eunuchs rather than with the comparatively benign castrated eunuchs . Moreover, by concentrating on the moral distinction between congenital eunuchs and castrated eunuchs. a prominent distinction in his sources, Curry distracts his readers from what he himself understands to be the different distinction in the General Prologue: that between "geldyng" and "mare." While he reveals the accuracy with which Chaucer uses the stereotype of the eunuch for some of the details of the Pardoner's portrait, Curry neither proves that the Pardoner is a congenital eunuch nor definitively exhausts the implications of the narrator's pronouncement.

The relationship of the Pardoner's eunuchry to his spiritual condition and to the larger themes of Chaucer's work was first addressed in a sophisticated way by Robert Miller.Miller examines medieval biblical glosses that attempt to resolve a conflict in attitudes toward eunuchs in the Old Testament, Deuteronomy xxiii.1, reflecting a literal-minded racial and sexual perception of holiness, excludes eunuchs from the temple, while Isaiah lvi. 3-5, taking a more spiritual approach, gives assurances that righteous eunuchs are among God's people. The medieval commentators found a solution to this conflict in a statement of Christ's discriminating among congenital eunuchs, involuntary castrates, and "eunuchs who have made themselves such for the Kingdom of heaven" . Identifying the last group, the voluntary celibates in the service of God, as the eunuchs of Isaiah who will be accepted by God, the commentators go on to invent a second group of metaphorical eunuchs who will be rejected, as in Deuteronomy: those who, while capable of good works, deliberately remain spiritually sterile. Miller argues that the Pardoner's physical eunuchry is the sign of his deliberate spiritual sterility. His chosen role as *eunuchus non Dei* is seen as bitterly satiric, since he has a special responsibility as a churchman to be a *eunuchus Dei,* fruitful in good works.

If, however, Chaucer did use the Pardoner's physical condition as a sign in this way, he ran a considerable risk of undermining the very spiritual values he was attempting to communicate. Both Christ and the medieval commentators were reacting against the physical determinism of one strain of Jewish tradition. For them, involuntary eunuchry had no necessary moral significance at all; they were attempting to free the career of the soul from questions of genital competency Miller's Pardoner, in contrast, is a static figure. While Miller rightly emphasizes the free action by which the Pardoner would have become a *eunuchus non Dei,* he does not recognize in Chaucer's characterization a continuing human potential for change. Because the immutable physical fact of eunuchry is taken as the sign of the Pardoner's spiritual status, his soul cannot be allowed its own career independent of his sexual destiny.

Despite this difficulty, Miller' s study has done more than any other to establish the level of seriousness on which the problem of the Pardoner's sexuality should be addressed. Moreover, the biblical materials he has brought to our attention can now be seen as documenting one kind of consideration that medieval people gave to a question central to Chaucer's characterization of the Pardoner: What is the place of sexually different, or "deviant," persons in the scheme of salvation?

Wide acceptance of the conclusions of Curry and Miller has had the unintended side effect of dulling readers' responses to the Pardoner; this pilgrim, it seems, has been fully "explained." As Donald Howard puts it in *The Idea of the Canterbury Tales,* the theory of the Pardoner's congenital and "scriptural" eunuchry has become an excuse for not taking him seriously. In his dazzling treatment of the Pardoner as a grotesque, as a "feminoid" or "hermaphroditic" male, Howard succeeds in re-creating the strangeness of this pilgrim — his power to mystify, frighten, and fascinate. Partly from motives of anger and revenge, the Pardoner alienates himself from the community of human and divine values; in Howard's view, he becomes — like evil itself as defined in medieval philosophy, like the grotesques in manuscript illuminations, and like the very fragment of the *Canterbury Tales* in which his tale appears — something "on the periphery of the ordered world of created goodness," "marginal," "floating," "outside," "demonic" . Curiously, Howard accepts as fact the congenital and "scriptural" eunuchry that theorists have attributed to the Pardoner and claims that we know the character's sexual status while the narrator and the others do not . His discussion of the Pardoner nevertheless proceeds, rightly I think, as if we share the same general perspective as the pilgrims — that is, as if we too remain uncertain about the Pardoner's sexual status and thus experience the whole man as mysterious.

Howard fears that any interpretation of the Pardoner as homosexual would "explain" the Pardoner in the same deadening and unprofitable way as the belief in the character's eunuchry has and that the modern stereotype of the effeminate male homosexual would be anachronistically used to deny the Pardoner's mystery. While I agree that the danger of another reductive reading is real, a view of the Pardoner as homosexual would not necessarily have this effect; for the danger lies not in any particular sexual definition but in the manner of relating the Pardoner's sexuality to his spirituality.

Nor is the stereotype of effeminate male homosexuality an anachronism; it is as authentically medieval as it is modern. Indeed, the medieval confusion of homosexuality with effeminacy and, as we shall see, with other sexual phenomena indicates both that Chaucer's contemporaries tried to explain homosexuality to themselves and that they failed to dispel the mystery it presented to them. It is true, however, that I cannot produce a Pardoner quite so enigmatic as Howard's, but this difference arises not from our disagreement about the Pardoner's possible homosexuality but from my unwillingness to accept, with Howard (p. 351), the Pardoner's definition of himself as a "ful vicious man." By turning our attention from the standard glosses on the Pardoner's sexuality to the literary characterization itself, Howard has brought the Pardoner alive again; but in his valuable explication of the Pardoner as a grotesque, he accepts too fully the Pardoner's own tortured and theatrical self-image. While giving detailed consideration to the possibility that the Pardoner is isolated from his heterosexual and homophobic peers by a condition of homosexuality, I emphasize the Pardoner's identity as a pilgrim in the fellowship of other pilgrims, motivated, even in his cupidity, by the love they all seek and experiencing an anguished self-division not unlike what others suffer.

The first step in a reconsideration of the Pardoner's sexuality must be the establishment of a gloss for "mare." "Geldyng" and "mare" are homely metaphors that must have had meanings both familiar and fairly precise for Chaucer's medieval audience; modern readers, however, face difficulties in recovering those meanings. Curry's influence is registered, but often inaccurately or incompletely, in modern editions of the *Canterbury Tales*. Among recent editors, only Donald Howard glosses both "geldyng" and "mare," and he interprets the first as "castrated eunuch" and the second as "congenital eunuch."John Hurt Fisher preserves Curry's too narrow interpretation of "geldyng" as suggesting impotence, while Albert Baugh reflects what I think is the most common understanding of Curry's argument (and of the Pardoner's status): that "geldyng" means "eunuch" (without implying any differentiation of types) and that the Pardoner is a eunuch. Neither Fisher nor Baugh, however, repeats Curry's interpretation of "mare" as a reference to effeminacy or offers any alternative gloss for that word. Finally, while both the *Middle English Dictionary* and the *Oxford English Dictionary* fully document the use of "geldyng" as a term for "eunuch," neither includes any evidence for a meaning of "mare" relevant to Chaucer's context.

For many modern readers, the obvious possible translations for "mare" are "effeminate male" and "homosexual male." Until recently, though, there appeared to be no evidence that the word had been used in either of these senses. Then, in 1973, Jill Mann pointed to a Latin poem by the twelfth-century satirist Walter of Chatillon in which homosexual men, also described as effeminate, are labeled "mares": "equa fit equus" 'the horse becomes a mare' While it is not certain that Chaucer knew Walter's works, they were relatively well known in England, and the poem does add weight to the suggestion that "mare" may mean "effeminate male" or "homosexual male" or both. But even if there were no question about Chaucer's having read the poem, one supporting text would not constitute proof of his meaning.

We need not wait for the discovery of more supporting texts, however. The details of the Pardoner's portrait and the term "geldyng" create a context that suggests criteria for glossing "mare." "Mare" must be a term commonly used in Chaucer's day to designate a male person who, though not necessarily sterile or impotent, exhibits physical traits suggestive of femaleness, visible characteristics that were also associated with eunuchry in medieval times and that were thought to have broad effects on the psyche and on character. The gloss that most satisfactorily fulfills these criteria is "a homosexual." Chaucer did not know the word "homosexual," of course, since it did not enter the language until 1869 but he might have referred to what we call homosexuality by making a biblical reference (to sodomites), a mythological reference (to Ganymede or Orpheus), a historical reference (to Julius Caesar, for example), or a philosophical reference (to sinners against nature). As we shall see. the choice of "mare" has several important and related advantages: it avoids provoking an immediate response of condemnation, which other references might have invited; it focuses attention not on sexual acts but on a type of person in whose soma and psyche Chaucer apparently believed homosexuality to be deeply rooted;and it suggests an attitude on the narrator's part in keeping with his character — a mixture of sympathy, amusement, and condescension.

Since several historical accounts are available, I shall not pause to document in detail the familiarity of Chaucer's audience with male homosexuality; I should like to explore instead the situation reflected in my criteria for glossing "mare," the confusion of homosexuality with other sexual phenomena.

In using a word denoting femaleness, Chaucer reflects one ancient and widespread misunderstanding about male homosexuality, that it involves a man's becoming in some sense a woman. The concept of effeminacy provides one way of thinking about this supposed transformation, but care must be taken in interpreting references to effeminacy in the medieval setting. The *Middle English Dictionary* records only two uses of the word "effeminate," both in the sense "self-indulgent" or "unreasonable." Satires on the fop, often described as long-haired and beardless. reflect a perception of feminization of behaviour and appearance without any necessary suggestion of homosexuality. In medieval Latin, however, *effeminatus* sometimes means "homosexual," as in the Vulgate Bible, and this sense had passed into English by the time of the King James Bible. There is some evidence, moreover, that the young aristocrat who aspired to fashion had to be careful to observe the boundaries that marked off effeminacy and homosexuality. At the end of a lengthy set of instructions on conduct, dress, and grooming in Guillaume de Lorris' *Roman de la Rose,* for example, the God of Love tells the young lover:

Cous tes manches, tes cheveus pigne,
Mais ne te farde ne ne guigne:
Ce n'apartient s'as dames non,
Ou a ceus de mauvais renon,
Qui amors par male aventure
Ont trovees contre Nature.

Sew your sleeves and comb your hair, but do not rouge or paint your face, for such a custom belongs only to ladies or to men of bad repute, who have had the misfortune to find a love contrary to Nature.

(ll. 2169-74)

Just as not all effeminate males were suspected of homosexuality, so not all homosexual males were perceived as effeminate. In his translation of Dante's *Inferno,* Mark Musa notes the contrast between the effeminate speech patterns of the sodomitical clerks in Canto xv and the more robust manner of the sodomitical soldiers in xvi. Since the substance of what constitutes effeminacy in males is culturally defined and subject to change, it is not necessary to find in the Middle Ages exact replicas of our current stereotype of effeminacy in homosexual males would (including, for example, distinctive walk or hand movements): it is only necessary to show that certain types of feminized behaviour and appearance in males were sometimes interpreted as evidence of homosexuality. Thus, even if the primary meaning of "mare" was "an effeminate male," a second meaning may have been "a possibly homosexual male."

Another ancient way of conceiving the male homosexual's supposed participation in the feminine was to think of him as a hermaphrodite. In Hellenic rites and legends, the hermaphrodite is a double god, a being with the overt equipment of both sexes (i. e., male genitals and female breasts), a symbol of unity, fruitfulness, and eternal life. In Hellenistic art, however, the hermaphrodite is an extremely feminized figure; though recognizably male, representative of one ideal of homosexual beauty. Interest in this type of hermaphrodite revived during the twelfth-century resurgence of classical scholarship (Curtius, pp. 113-16). A late and perhaps unconscious reflection of this tradition, evidence of its thorough absorption into European thinking, appears in the treatment of the story of Sodom and Gomorrah in the Middle English *Purity*, a work commonly ascribed to the *Gawain* poet. The poet describes Lot's first glimpse of the angels as they pass through the crowded streets of Sodom toward his house; they are extraordinarily beautiful young men with beardless chins. rosy complexions, and luxurious hair like raw silk:

As he stared into þe strete þer stout men played,
He sy3e þer swey in asent swete men tweyne;
Bolde burnez were þay boþe, wyth berdles chynnez,
Royl rollande fax, to raw sylk lyke,
Of ble as þe brere-flor where so þe bare schew[e]d;
Ful clene watz þe countenaunce of her cler y3en;

Wlonk whit watz her wede and wel hit hem scm[e]d.
(ll. 787-93)

On one level the beauty of the angels is meant to suggest a spiritual excellence superior to all considerations and distinctions of human sexuality: but as A. C. Spearing remarks, it also explains something left unexplained in the biblical text: how the men of Sodom came to desire homosexual intercourse with the angels. It seems likely that a hermaphroditic or feminoid male would have been suspected of sexual deviance.

An alternative to thinking of the male homosexual as a woman-man was to think of him as a nonman, for homosexuality was long confused with eunuchry.In Gautier de Leu's thirteenth century fabliau "La Veuve," for example, a widow who remarries finds the vigourous sexual performance of her new husband on the wedding night nonetheless disappointing:

Nos avons caiens un bruhier,
un durfeut, un hebohet.
Ahi! con Damerdex me het
qui fui des bons vallés aquius,
et des cortois et des gentius,
si pris cest caitif par nature.
. . . .
Et cis ribaus me tient plus vil
que le femier de son cortil,
mais je sai bien, par Saint Eloi,
qu'il n'est mie de bone loi,
ains est de caus del Mont Wimer:
il n'a soing de dames amer.
What have we here? An impotent,
beardless ne'er-do-well! Ah me!
The Lord must hate me bitterly,
who turned away from fine young men,
well born, courteous, and then
wound up with this congenital bum!
. . . .
This scoundrel shows me less regard

than he does the dungheap in the yard.
However, by Saint Loy I know
his moral code is just as low
as that of those on Mount Wimer:
for woman's love he doesn't care.

The widow equates less than heroic sexual performance with impotence, impotence with beardless eunuchry, both of these with homosexuality, and all of these with heresy, for the reference to Mount Wimer concerns a large group of *bougres* who were burned to death for homosexuality and heresy in Champagne in 1239. The fabliau makes fun of the widow and her insatiable appetite, but the intended comedy of her speech must have depended partly on the pervasiveness of just such misunderstandings; at the same time, the poet who made comedy out of the widow's confusion must himself have been in some degree superior to it. Like the French poet, Chaucer may be seen as making artistic use of what he perceived to be common misunderstandings of sexual phenomena. The Pardoner's possible eunuchry may contribute to the portrait of a homosexual since medieval people apparently strove to understand homosexuality by identifying it with now one, now another, sexual anomaly.

Seen against this background, Chaucer's portrait of the Pardoner in the General Prologue emerges as a pastiche of allusions to the three distinct sexual phenomena with which homosexuality was often confused — effeminacy, hermaphroditism, and eunuchry — and thus very probably to homosexuality itself. In the order of their appearance in the portrait the allusions are the description of the Pardoner's hair — its length and fineness suggesting effeminacy, eunuchry, and hermaphroditism and his grooming of it suggesting effeminacy; the Pardoner's concern with fashion, implying effeminacy: the references to goats and hares, suggesting hermaphroditism; the high voice, connoting effeminacy and eunuchry; the glaring eyes, associated with eunuchry; and the beardlessness, a symptom of effeminacy, eunuchry, hermaphroditism, and homosexuality. Furthermore, the glaring eyes and the references to goats, hares, and mares connote extreme lechery, which is at least as suggestive of sexual deviance as of sexual inadequacy.

What this catalog shows is that most of the allusions tend to be multivalent, and the reason is that the lines between these various sexual phenomena were fluid in medieval theory. It is impossible to say whether beardlessness, for example, was more likely to suggest eunuchry or homosexuality to a medieval person. Because of this fluidity, too, references to effeminacy, hermaphroditism, and eunuchry could serve as a code for homosexuality. Finally, while the categories "effeminate," "hermaphrodite," and "eunuch" can each account for some of the Pardoner's characteristics, only the category "homosexual" can account for all of them. For example, while the Pardoner's interest in fashion can be referred directly only to effeminacy (and not to eunuchry or hermaphroditism) and the narrator's allusion to goats only to hermaphroditism, both can be referred to homosexuality through what the medieval audience regarded as the mediating concepts of effeminacy and hermaphroditism.

Thus at a minimum it seems impossible to exclude the suggestion of homosexuality from the portrait. It is also impossible for the reader not to be influenced by the opening frame for this physical description: the presentation of the Pardoner's association with the Summoner. The nature of this association has long been debated, but there is no doubt that the Pardoner is introduced to us traveling with a male "friend" and "compeer" and that the two are singing, in their contrasting voices, a love song, "Com hider, love, to me" (ll. 670-71). This tableau may be read in two ways. The Pardoner may be seen as a frustrated heterosexual who associates himself with the lecherous Summoner in order to deny his own impotence and to acquire symbolically the Summoner's virility; or he may be seen as a homosexual, ambivalent about disclosing his status, who nonetheless becomes suspect through the public display of this ambiguous friendship. These are the two possibilities that the narrator makes explicit, I believe, when he provides the closing frame for the physical description of the Pardoner: "I trowe he were a geldyng or a mare." Thus these three parts of the Pardoner's portrait — the opening-tableau, the physical description, and the closing pronouncement — fit together in a way that has not been fully appreciated. For the medieval audience, with its confused and limited lexicon of sexual terms and concepts, it was the physical description. I suspect, that was most ambiguous; the opening frame first provided implicit guidance, and the closing frame then explicit guidance, to its interpretation.

Modern readers may have a different experience, since the meaning of the Pardoner's friendship with the Summoner has been clouded by controversy and the meaning of the term "mare" has long been lost. In this situation, the physical description, once it is set in the context of medieval sexual theory, seems to me to provide the strongest evidence of the Pardoner's possible homosexuality, which in turn helps us both to recognize a possible implication of his association with the Summoner and to gloss "mare."

Given, then, that Chaucer's text explicitly and implicitly raises the issue of homosexuality, the narrator's treatment of the Pardoner seems to unfold in this way. Faced with a somewhat bewildering set of indications to interpret, the narrator rather shrewdly cuts through the complexity to suggest that the Pardoner is either a nonman, that is, a eunuch, or a woman-man, a homosexual. Indeed the phrase "I trowe," which may denote either speculation or certainty, serves to dramatize the narrator in his role as interpreter, dealing confidently yet respectfully with resistant reality. There may even be an element of self-congratulation in his announced inability to decide exactly what the Pardoner's status is; the narrator may think that the double reference to eunuchry and homosexuality displays his sophistication. Actually, though, he is rather like the modern person who has not mastered the distinctions among homosexuals, bisexuals, transvestites, and transsexuals. One consequence of the narrator's characteristically limited perception is that we initially encounter the Pardoner as a kind of puzzle to be solved rather than as a pilgrim to be judged.

The animal imagery of the narrator's pronouncement also helps temporarily to isolate the Pardoner from moral judgment. The narrator perceives the Pardoner as someone conspicuously deficient in the animal sphere of perfection, lacking integrity of sexual identity, physical intactness, or procreative competency — the amoral perfections, elaborated in various cultural forms, that the narrator admires in the Monk and Harry Bailey. Though found wanting in one sphere, the Pardoner is perceived as supremely competent in another; thus the significance of the "but" as the narrator turns to the Pardoner's work in the world: "But of his craft, fro Berwyk into Ware, / Ne was ther swich another pardoner" (ll. 692-93). Sheer expertise, unrelated to its use or purpose, is one of the narrator's chief measures of value throughout the General Prologue, and this ideal, despite its moral limitations, has a special virtue in regard to the Pardoner since it embraces more than sexuality. For the narrator, the "pardoner" and the "noble ecclesiaste" are as important as the "geldyng" or the "mare." The narrator sets an example of not reducing the Pardoner to his sexuality, an example that at other levels of response Chaucer means us to emulate.

Nevertheless we cannot be so content with the narrator's tentative diagnosis of the Pardoner as the narrator himself is. As viewed by the medieval church, eunuchry and homosexuality had very different moral statuses; pace the doctors and physiognomists, eunuchry was not in itself regarded as sinful, while homosexual acts (the concept of a homosexual condition was not recognized by the moral theologians) were considered grave sins. From this standpoint the narrator's self-satisfied conclusion that the Pardoner is one thing or the other is quite astonishing, for it reflects an essentially secular perspective. Since, however, we must view the Pardoner as a pilgrim — that is, not only as an animal being and an expert worker but also as a moral being with a spiritual destiny — we need to know more than the narrator is able to tell us. The narrator's comment on the Pardoner's sexual status preserves immutably for all time the narrator's own uncertainty about his fellow pilgrim. It does not fix to the same degree the mystery about the Pardoner himself, although the absence of any other explicit statement about his sexuality means that a choice between "geldyng" and "mare" or any extrapolation using both terms will always be an interpretation. Many critics, having chosen "geldyng," have traced the implications of their choice in readings of the Pardoner's prologue and tale; while admitting that the Pardoner may be a eunuch as well, I choose to emphasize his possible status as a "mare," or homosexual, and I should like to explore some of the consequences of my choice

It is rather widely agreed that the avarice the Pardoner boasts about is a screen sin, concealing some graver defect of body or soul or both.Like his interpreters, the Pardoner betrays an interest in degrees of sinfulness, identifying one of the rioters in his tale as the "proudeste" (I. 716), another rioter (or perhaps the same one) as the "worste of hem" (I. 776), Harry Bailey as "moost envoluped in synne" (I. 942), and himself as "a ful vicious man" (I. 459). Also, as his constant preaching text, "*Radix malorum*" (I. 334), reveals, he is obsessively interested in underlying states of sinfulness, and other evidence suggests that he finds the root of all evil in the body. Although his semihysterical discussion of the so-called tavern sins seems not to rest on any positive values, it does have a unifying theme. All the sins are developed to some degree in a way that relates them to the human body.

Gluttony, of course, has a natural relation to the body, but the Pardoner's tracing of ingested food from "the tendre mouth" to the "shorte throte" (compared to a privy) to the "stynkyng cod, Fulfilled of dong and of corrupcioun" and at last to the bowels with their "foul . . . soun" (ll. 512-35) tends to turn all eating into an obscene act. He even treats the sin of Adam and Eve as an act of gluttony, ignoring its intellectual content. Similarly, cursing is treated not as a rejection of Christ's divinity and teachings but as an attack on Christ's body; all the examples the Pardoner provides refer to Christ's body and passion, and he later says of the rioters "Cristes blessed body [they] torente" (I. 709). Finally, gambling is most dramatically presented to us in an imagined scene in which the dice are referred to as "bones" (l. 656). The treatment of these vices suggests an obsessive concern with the body as the source of sin, the instrument of sin, and the victim of sin. Significantly, avarice, the screen sin, is not presented as having an intimate connection with the body; instead it is decidedly intellectual, requiring of the Pardoner great cleverness in plying the tricks of his trade.

A key passage in the Pardoner's prologue hints more directly at what the concealed and deadly sinfulness in the body might be. The Pardoner describes one of his most ingenious tricks for persuading people to venerate his relics and offer alms:

Goode men and wommen, o thyng warne I yow:
If any wight be in this chirche now
That hath doon synne horrible, that he
Dar nat, for shame, of it yshryven be,
Or any womman. be she yong or old,
That hath ymaad hir housbonde cokewold.
Swich folk shal have no power ne no grace
To offren to my relikes in this place. (ll. 377-84)

The specificity about the woman's sin and the lack of specificity about the man's provoke interpretation. It seems likely that the unnamed sin shares a number of characteristics with infidelity: it is a sexual sin; it is peculiarly associated with one sex — with men, as culpable infidelity had long been associated with women; and it inspires a special opprobrium that arises from a cultural bias rather than from the principles of Christian ethics. Male homosexuality meets all these criteria.Most important, the shame that attends the naming of the sin even in the confessional seems a clear allusion to homosexuality. Long before homosexuality was christened by Lord Alfred Douglas "the Love that dare not speak its name," it had been commonly referred to in some variation of the formula found in Chaucer' s Parson's Tale: "thilke abhomynable synne, of which that no man unnethe oghte speke ne write

It would be wrong to seem to deny, by qualification, the intense homophobia embodied in this notorious phrase, and yet it is important to recognize that there were shadings of opinion and feeling about homosexuality. In the *Canterbury Tales* the Pardoner's behaviour and the reactions of the other pilgrims reflect a setting in which a homosexual person, while possibly aware of the severe penalties sometimes inflicted on his kind, did not feel a proximate fear for his safety. The Pardoner's flaunting of his friendship with the Summoner, though undoubtedly compulsive behaviour, is probably not undertaken without some realistic assessment of the risks. As the pilgrims' apprehension about his ribaldry and Harry's false camaraderie suggest, what the Pardoner must confront in others is not their outright condemnation of him but their discomfiture. with its varying degrees of amusement, fear, sympathy, disgust, and ambiguous tolerance.

In ministers of the church's sacraments, like Chaucer's Parson. the Pardoner would almost certainly encounter at least unthinking, if not vehement, reflections of that homophobia which the church had helped both to create and to perpetuate. In himself, the Pardoner has to contend with that self-hatred which internalizes the judgments of others. Ultimately the man who cannot confess the unnamed and unnameable sin is the Pardoner himself.

It may well be, moreover, that the Pardoner's inability to approach the confessional arises partly from his perception of the gulf between what the church was prepared to forgive and what he had to confess. As his portrait suggests, the Pardoner's homosexuality is a profound part of his being, an aspect that Chaucer could portray (and probably conceive of) only by projecting a biological cause.The Pardoner himself seems to feel that he is in a state of alienation from Christ and the church, a state that is more than the sum of his sinful acts. *Mala,* or specific evil deeds, are not his concern; the *radix,* or root condition, is. But in the matter of homosexuality, as in matters of human sexuality generally, the church' s moral theology tended to focus on acts, not on persons; and while it took account of a variety of actors, it defined them in terms of certain fixed statuses only: young or old, male or female, married or unmarried, clerical or lay. It understood homosexual acts only as the perverse behaviour of basically heterosexual persons. In other words, the church was prepared to deal with sinners like the scabby Summoner but not with the tortured Pardoner. The "inverted" Pardoner did not fit the church's definitions and could scarcely form a sincere purpose to amend a condition in himself he probably felt he had no power to change. Chaucer's study of homosexuality in the Pardoner seems to represent a deliberate intention to explore the inner reality of an outcast especially despised by his society and especially misunderstood by his church.

It is no accident that the man who cannot confess becomes a pardoner. Seizing on a theologically marginal church practice, the granting of indulgences, the Pardoner subverts the sacrament of penance he cannot use while simultaneously setting himself up as a substitute confessor. Officially, he had the power to offer almsgivers only remission of the punishment due sins already absolved by a priest. In practice, like many actual pardoners, he sold supposed absolution from sin.While some of his customers may have been naive Christians who could not appreciate the difference, others must have hoped to buy spiritual safety dishonestly, without reforming their lives. By exploiting the potential for self-deceit in those he imagines condemn him, the Pardoner attempts to convict his customers of being themselves "envoluped in synne." As he leads them away from the legitimate sacrament, it is as if he were saying, "If I cannot be truly forgiven, neither shall they be."

At the same time, the Pardoner constantly enacts in reverse the scene of absolution he longs for. As he dispenses his own brand of absolution, often arousing in his audience true contrition (vi. 430-31), it is as if he were saying, "If there is anyone the church will not forgive, I will forgive him," all the while hoping that the forgiveness he dispenses will magically flow back to cleanse himself.

This manipulation of the sacrament is one of the things the Pardoner does that tend to be obscured by what he says as he constructs a smoke screen of single-minded avarice. But his intimate association with confession betrays, beneath his practiced cynicism, the seriousness with which he regards the sacrament. Apparently he does not allow himself the easy out he offers others — the chance to buy forgiveness and satisfaction with money or specific good works. For himself the Pardoner requires true contrition, true purpose of amendment; he does believe that Christ's pardon is best.

Interestingly, it was the subversion of the sacrament, more than the misappropriation of funds, that other churchmen principally complained of in actual pardoners. But Chaucer's association of his Pardoner with false relics may be a more imaginative touch, since it is not especially characteristic of the pardoners described in contemporary documents. Perhaps nothing else about the Pardoner expresses so poignantly his anguish about his body as do the jars and bottles of old bones and bits of clothing he always carries with him. When Harry Bailey charges that the Pardoner would try to pass off his "olde breech" " with [his] fundement depeint" as a relic and proposes to enshrine the Pardoner's testicles in a hog's turd "in stide of relikes or of seintuarie" (vi. 948-55). the symbolic equivalence between the relics and the Pardoner himself becomes almost explicit. For many readers. Harry's crudity must suddenly and explosively bring to consciousness a truth they have already apprehended subliminally.

Binding himself again to a marginal expression of the church's life, the veneration of relics, the Pardoner expresses both his fear, nearing conviction, that his own body. like the tavern in his tale, is the devil's temple (1. 470) and his faint but continuing hope that this same body may yet prove to be the holy temple of God. Because he uses false relics to make money and to entice others away from true contrition, the relics become, like his body, sources of sin to himself and to others. Moreover, by offering the relics for veneration, he dupes his customers into kissing what is symbolically the instrument of that sodomitical sin he and they have learned to despise. At the same time, the Pardoner seems always to be hoping that others will repose a genuine faith in his relics, a faith that will miraculously transform his relics and the body they represent into holy things. In all his traffickings with relics, the plea for money is partly a camouflage for the plea for the redemptive kiss. The relics he uses for this purpose *must* be false. His relics must be as unholy as he thinks his body is so that the hoped-for transformation can be "real." The Pardoner will never experience such a transformation, of course, since he will never be able to respect the faith of those he deceives and corrupts.

The notorious difficulty of accounting for the Pardoner's offering to the pilgrims relics he has already admitted to be false arises in part from overemphasizing the mercenary motive. But by taking the pilgrims into his confidence to a degree, the Pardoner has developed a more intimate relationship with this audience than he usually develops with his more gullible victims. In offering relics now, he is acting under an unusually strong compulsion to acquire that personal validation he is always seeking through them. Even on this occasion, though, the Pardoner's attempt to reach out to Harry Bailey and the community he represents is doomed by the inveterate ambivalence of the Pardoner's own attitudes.

The latent aggression in the Pardoner's statement that Harry "shalt kisse the relikes everychon" (1. 944) and the latent sexual implication in his command to Harry to "Unbokele anon thy purs" (l. 945) turn the scene into one of implied seduction or even rape; the Pardoner uses his homosexuality as a weapon. In addition, by characterizing Harry as "envoluped in synne" (l. 942) and offering to pardon Harry's sins, the Pardoner contemptuously portrays the heterosexual Christian as needing the absolution of the despised sodomite. But with the same gesture with which he assaults Harry's heterosexual sensitivities, the Pardoner asks for love; and with the same gesture with which he charges another with sin. he seeks forgiveness for himself. Understandably Harry reacts to the threats to himself in the Pardoner's behaviour and does not hear the cry for acceptance. Example of natural manhood that he is, Harry retaliates by casting aspersions on the Pardoner's virility and by threatening castration (ll. 946-55). But as the reference to the true relic of Saint Helen's cross suggests, the ultimate issue is not perfection in the physical order but holiness in the spiritual order. The Pardoner's defeat lies in the clear implication of Harry's obscenity that both the Pardoner's relics and his body are *not holy*.

The goal of the final scene, as of all the Pardoner's maneuvers, is a kiss. The scene does in fact end with a kiss, of course, though not one of the sort the Pardoner was seeking. The Knight engineers a reconciliation between Harry and the Pardoner that restores a degree of mutual tolerance while avoiding all the issues. We may be thankful, though, that the Pardoner does not receive the kiss that in rage and self-contempt he wished to extort from an abased Harry. It would truly have been an obscene kiss, not because of any homosexual element, but because of its sadomasochistic nature. Left unanswered, however, is the question whether the Pardoner will ever receive the kiss that in another sense he was seeking: not a kiss mirroring his own self-contempt or a kiss of ambivalent social tolerance but a kiss expressing genuine acceptance of his humanity — in Christian terms, a kiss confirming his part in the Father's creation and in the Son's redemption.

Through his manipulation of the sacrament of penance, the Pardoner covertly seeks forgiveness for what he takes to be his sinful condition; through his manipulation of relics, he covertly seeks affirmation that he is in some sense holy. The Pardoner fives his life through the church's rituals, sacraments, and sacramentals in a way that dramatizes both the pain of exclusion and the hope for ultimate inclusion. No other pilgrim is so saturated in the life of the institutional church as this accomplished singer of the liturgy, this eloquent preacher steeped in the lore of the pulpit, and this successful entrepreneur in absolutions and relics. Though believing himself the church's rejected son, the Pardoner has done everything he can to make himself a "noble ecciesiaste."

Given the position of the medieval church on homosexuality, this interpretation of the Pardoner might seem to offer new grounds for the still current belief that the Pardoner is, among Chaucer's pilgrims, uniquely evil. In my view it does no such thing. Ideally this interpretation should help us to penetrate the Pardoner's own obfuscatory characterization of himself as "a ful vicious man," a characterization that has already begun to receive the skeptical criticism it deserves. Making a useful distinction between behaviour and state of mind, John Halverson shows that the Pardoner probably does less actual harm than the Friar and that his description of his own spiritual condition is preposterous, serving to mock those who accept it while disguising and protecting the Pardoner's true self. Halverson finds the Pardoner not evil, but deadly, "necrophiliac." While the relationship of the Pardoner to death is important and deserves the further study Halverson calls for, I think it is already possible to say that the Pardoner's manipulation of relics and pardons betrays signs of spiritual life.

Interestingly, the subject of homosexuality offers Chaucer the opportunity to distinguish between behaviour and state of mind in much the same way as Halverson does. Any physical acts in which the Pardoner expressed his homosexuality would be viewed by the medieval church as sinful, and Chaucer does not challenge this teaching. But he does challenge the belief that such sins are uniquely abhorrent, poisoning the whole character and extirpating all good and all potential for good. The Pardoner's elaborate way of relating to church and community through his relics and pardons reveals such hopeful signs as a latent belief in his own essential worthiness, a desire to be restored to God's grace, a desire to be socially useful, and a desire to give and receive love. The Pardoner's defenses, even against the best in himself, are so well entrenched, however, that the possibility of a transformation seems remote, though it cannot be denied.

The Pardoner's preaching text, *"Radix malorum est Cupiditas,"* is only one of the mottoes relevant to the judgment of this pilgrim; the other is the snatch of popular song on his lips when we first meet him, "Corn hider, love, to me." it is sometimes said that this song refers only to carnal love, and to a love made distasteful by the characters of the Summoner and the Pardoner. But just as Chaucer alludes here to that charity which is the cardinal value of his pilgrimage, so the Pardoner, however unconsciously, names this charity as the ultimate goal of his own yearnings. Cupidity and love — each reader must decide what relative weight to give to these two in judging the Pardoner, and the weighting of the balances is not obvious.

The task of judging the Pardoner, like that of judging each of the other pilgrims, makes the judges vulnerable, too, not least of all Chaucer himself. A final question cannot be evaded. Why does Chaucer treat the possibility of the Pardoner's homosexuality so allusively? Does his indirection betray some allegiance, or at least some submission, to the phobic view that homosexuality is so abhorrent it must not be spoken or written about? We must admit, on the one hand, that here Chaucer may be showing a characteristic degree of caution.

On the other hand, Chaucer's very silences can be seen as an allusion to the sin that should not be named.Such an argument runs the risk of being merely selfserving for the critic, of course; but if the glossing of "mare" as "homosexual" is accepted, then the interpretation of Chaucer's other allusions has a firm anchor in the literal meaning of the text. Moreover, what I take to be this explicit suggestion of possible homosexuality is never withdrawn or disproved.

Thus readers must engage in a work of interpretation that inescapably becomes a moral exercise. Because the facts about the Pardoner's sexuality are not given but must be established, readers cannot easily retreat into one-dimensional judgments of this pilgrim; they are forced to consider the whole character of the Pardoner in a way that should in turn contribute to a nonreductive appreciation of his sexuality and its spiritual implications.

Chaucer may have been inspired by a conviction like the one with which the Parson closes his discussion of "thilke abhomynable synne": "though that hooly writ speke of horrible synne. certes hooly writ may not been defouled. namoore than the sonne that shyneth on the mixne"). Chaucer may be seen as using his art, and especially its indirection and allusiveness, to challenge the sexual phobias of his readers, requiring them mentally to juxtapose the Pardoner's countenance with Christ's, even as the Pardoner himself has done by wearing a vernicle on his cap (1.685). The vernicle, a representation of Christ's face as it appeared on Veronica's veil, was commonly worn by Christians who had made pilgrimage to Rome.

There is nothing unusual about the Pardoner's wearing such an emblem (although another pilgrim to Rome, the Wife of Bath, is apparently not wearing one), but Chaucer's use of it is nonetheless thematically significant. The vernicle asserts the dignity of the Pardoner, whatever his sexual status, as part of Christ and reminds us that through his sexual sufferings the Pardoner participates in the crucifixion.

But most important. the vernicle asserts the necessity of each reader's responding to the Pardoner in the context of Christian love, a necessity that cannot be evaded by appeals to the values of secular society or to the prescriptions of ecclesiastical leaders. The use of the vernicle is daring, the challenge to the reader risky; Chaucer is not always cautious.

It would be wrong to overstate the special relation of the vernicle to the Pardoner, however, and thus to isolate him once again in his supposed uniqueness. The vernicle might be mentally placed on the headdresses of all the pilgrims: there is not one of them who does not challenge the observer's capacity for insight and love. The Pardoner will not be rightly judged until we also subject to judgment our own fascination with him and until we perceive what he shares with the other pilgrims as clearly as we perceive what sets him apart. Chaucer, after all, suggests the balance at the very beginning: he gives us a "compaignye, / Of sondry folk" but "pilgrimes were they alle."

Q.7. Discuss *Penitential Literature and the Pardoner*

Or

Q. Discuss the Pardoner's self-revelation in terms of either medieval convention or modern psychology

Despite a substantial critical commentary, the basic terms for the interpretation of the "Pardoner's Prologue and Tale" remain in dispute. We are typically urged to understand the Pardoner's self-revelation in terms of either medieval convention or modern psychology, and yet neither category is wholly satisfactory: the appeal to convention is too blunt a response to Chaucer's careful observations, while we cannot help but mistrust our modernity.1 But, in fact, this is a false dilemma, for there is further medieval material we can bring to bear on Chaucer's text that can preserve both its complexity and its historicity. I refer to the vast literature of instruction and exhortation that grew up around the sacrament of penance, and in particular to the discussions, both poetic and theological, of the meaning and dynamics of confession. The point is not that the Pardoner's self-display is a confession in any sacramental sense, but that the literature of confession can explain both the spiritual condition out of which he speaks and the complicated meanings he imparts.

Our problem with the Pardoner's self-revelation, after all, is less with content than with the significance of form, not so much what he says but the meaning of his act of speaking. Hence it is contemporary discussions of the act of confession itself that can perhaps provide us with guidance, As for specific texts, this means that we shall put aside works that are merely adjuncts to the sacrament, such as the numerous versions of the *forma confitendi*, in favour of those that, while originally deriving from the sacrament, move beyond it to explore the inner dynamics of the act of confession itself. In Middle English, this self-regard is found both in the penitential lyric and in the confession of the Sins in *Piers Plowman*, and it is these works that can provide for us a literary context for the "Pardoner's Prologue and Tale". Theologically, our concern is with discussions of the psychology of confession, and specifically of the penitential motive of contrition and its dark semblance of despair. And it is here that writings both patristic and medieval can furnish a terminology and an imagery that will reappear in the Pardoner's self-portrait; indeed, we shall see that Chaucer has, with typical economy, taken the defining terms of the Pardoner's character from the very penitential system of which he is an agent.

The range of the Middle English penitential lyric includes both the exemplary and the analytic. The *forma confitendi,* for example, appears both in a complete form, so that the reader can check every category, and in a more selective and subtle way as the structure of a dramatized and personal act of penitential reflection. Similarly, many of the poems are frankly instructive of doctrine or, more usually, emotion, providing the reader with a pattern of penitential feeling. But others qualify this severe impersonality with an implicit psychological dialectic: they seek not simply to arouse or even express sorrow but to show it transformed and made fruitful by confession. A good example is the Harley lyric "God, þat al þis myhtes may." By his sin, the speaker has alienated himself from God — "ichabbe be losed mony a day, / er ant late y-be by foo" (3-4) — and is now overcome with self-disgust: "when y my-self haue þourh soht, / y knowe me for þe wrst of alle" (15-16); "Ich holde me vilore ben a gyw" . His feelings, then, are perilously near to despair, but the remainder of the poem provides a rescue. These very feelings are transformed into an offering, the broken and contrite heart that, says the Psalmist, the Lord will not despise. The speaker remakes the broken relationship with God not by petition — "louerd crist, whet shal y say?" — but by assuming the language and posture of penance: having been set against God in his arrogance, the sinner now kneels before Him in humility and supplication. Seen penitentially, self-disgust becomes contrition, and hence an advocate for salvation, so that the first line of the poem that originally threatened judgment can be repeated at the end as a warrant of mercy: "In þy merci y me do, / god, þat al þis myhtes may" The poem ends, in short, in prayer: *confessio peccati* is fulfilled in *confessio laudis.*

Prayer is the most common of the resolutions towards which the speaker of the penitential lyric directs his sorrow, but moral generalization also appears frequently. By understanding his life as an instance of a moral law, the penitent not only grants it a certain significance, however dismaying, but is able to use his new understanding as a sign of his conversion from the past. The *sententia* in which he generalizes his personal experience completes both his poem and his life of sin: possessed of bitter wisdom, he is self-evidently no longer the man he once was, and in the very course of the poem he becomes less a penitent than a sage, directing his words to an audience that has not yet learned the lesson he now knows so well. Hence a poem that begins, "In my ȝowþe fulle wylde I was," and includes a carefully individualized confession can end in a tone of severe impersonality:

Man take hede what þu art!
But wormys mete þu wote wel þis!
Whanne þe erthe hath take his parte,
heven or helle wolle haue his.
Yf þu doest welle þu goest to blis;
Yf þu do eville vnto þy foo;
love þy lorde, and thynke on þis,
Or wite þy self þyn owne woo!

Most relevant to the "Pardoner's Tale" are the numerous poems in which the penitent is an old man. At times the speaker fears he has repented too late, that his profession in old age of the values he abused in youth is belated and unwelcome. As the speaker of the *Poema Morale* says,

Wel late ich habbe me þi-bouht bute god do me mylce . . . .
Ich myhte habbe bet i-do heuede ich eny selhþe
NV ich wolde and i ne may for elde ne for vnhelhþe;
Elde is me bi-stolen on er þan ich hit wiste . . . .
Þe wel nule do hwile he may ne schal he hwenne he wolde.

Age is at once a symbol of sinfulness, the sin itself,and, final irony, the punishment, a cheerless decay that stands as nature's mocking parody of the spiritual change that will now never be achieved. Here, the old man turns from his anguish into an exhortation to others to do penance; in other poems he finds relief simply by understanding his sorrow within a penitential context, by turning regret into contrition. This pattern can best be illustrated by comparing two of the best known poems, "Le Regret de Maximinn" and the so-called "Old Man's Prayer." Maximian's complaint is uncompromising in its despair. He hates not only the old man he now is but the youth that brought him to it, and the poem is an act of self-annulment, a betrayal of the past to the bitterness of the present: even if he had his youthful strength back, he can think of no other use for it than to silence his badgering wife. The most serious negation is his failure to arrive in the poem at a prospect from which his experience, however sad, can become significant. "Wat helpeþ al itold?" he asks; he has no *sententia* with which to redeem the past: "Deþ ich wolde fawe, / For I ne may tellen no sawe" . Hence, the lament lacks both structure and direction and sinks sullenly to a closing obsession with the present: retrospection is not possible for the self-absorbed mind.

While "An Old Man's Prayer" also opens in an embittered tone, it revises the feelings and materials of lament in a penitential direction. God has created man both as a lover of "murþes" and a victim of time, and the paradox baffles and grieves the poet. He used to be a man of "semly sawes" but now he does not know "whet bote is beste" . His remedy, interestingly, is not a new saw but redefinition of the "murþes" that have been lost: the speaker changes his poem from lament to a confession by describing his youth in terms of the seven deadly sins:

whil mi lif wes luþer & lees,
glotonie mi glemon wes,
wiþ me he wonede a while;
prude wes my plowe-fere,
lecherie my lauendere —
wiþ hem is gabbe & gyle —
Coueytise myn keyes bere, Niþe ant onde were mi fere,
þat bueþ folkes fyle,

Lyare wes mi latymer,
sleuthe & slep mi bedyuer,
þat weneþ me vnbe while.
(52-63)

This penitential perspective redefines both youth and age. The "murþes" of sin are now well left behind, and age is not a betrayal but a merciful respite in which the penitent can bewail his sin: "Monne mest y am to mene, / lord, þat hast me lyf to lene" (66-7). Now the poet knows both that "Murþes helpeþ me no more" (92) and "whet ys be beste bote": to "heryen him þat haht vs boht, / vre lord þat al þis world haþ wroht, / ant fallen him to fote" . The poem thus completes its transformation from lament through confession to prayer:

Nou icham to deþe ydyht,
y-don is al my dede,
god vs lene of ys lyht,
þat we of sontes habben syht
ant heuene to mede!
(103-7)

The old man's anguish is resolved, not merely by the hope of salvation, but by the prior and larger step of being understood within the penitential process in the first place: the sorrow of old age becomes the sorrow of contrition and, with the closing prayer, the poem becomes itself an act of penance.

The explicitness of "An Old Man's Prayer" helps us to recognize that contrition is at the heart of the penitential lyric as a whole, whether it is resolved into the hindsight of wisdom or the forward movement of prayer. The poems function to prevent the sorrowful mind from sinking in on itself, as in "Le Regret de Maximian," and to direct it rather towards patterns of action and language in which sorrow becomes fruitful. In the confession scene of *Piers Plowman,* the most accomplished piece of penitential literature of the fourteenth century, Langland explores the same themes, and it is worth inquiring how he disposes his inherited material in order to open up these inward areas. For in the vernacular treatises on which he draws, sinfulness is presented not as a condition of the soul but as a deed, or at most a habit: the sinner recognizes himself, not by what he is, but by what he has done.

Even when personified and allowed to describe themselves, as in Deguilleville's three *Pélerinages* or the Morality plays, the sins remain exteriors, dutifully rehearsing the things that have been said about them: their speeches are hardly more than identifications, *tituli* to stand beside the crude allegorical image. Although often they speak for no reason or in defiance of reason — Deguilleville's Treason carefully unfolds her devices to the pilgrim she is about to attack — their self-revelations are not removed from human range simply by being unmotivated. Belial's "Ho, ho, be-holde me!" for example, springs from a manic self-delight that in its consistent display throughout the play stands as sufficient motive; and Faus Semblant's self-exposure in the *Roman de la Rose* is compelled by the God of Love. But this motivation does not proceed from the sinfulness that is both embodied and expressed, so that Jean de Meun, for instance, accords to the paradox of the sincere hypocrite only a passing acknowledgement, rather than allowing it to complicate Faus Semblant's self-revelations.

The autobiography of medieval allegory, in other words, habitually severs the link between character and language that helps us to recognize the intention and ultimately the significance of human speech. In Langland's confession scene, on the other hand, the challenge of the allegorical form is accepted: he restores the link between self-revelation and the self revealed. By forcing upon the Sins the confessional occasion they are designed to serve in others, not only does he give them the best of all Christian reasons to speak, but he allows them to speak to and from their sinfulness. In a sense, Langland's innovation is simply to take the short step from confession in terms of the sins to confession by the sins; in a larger sense it is to combine the didactic and hortatory substance of one tradition with the literary purposes of another, to fuse content (the nature of Avarice) with form (have

I committed avarice?). In Langland's scene, Avarice confesses to itself, so that the well-worn literary details become now the symptoms of an inward and hopefully problematic human condition. It is from this grounding of speech in the self, rather than vividness or energy, that the force and originality of Langland's scene derive,

The scene is based on a paradox, for by confessing to itself, the Sin calls into question its very existence. "lch, Pruyde, pacientliche penaunce ich aske" but, once patient, he is no longer prideful; " `I haue ben coueytouse,' quod this caityue, `I biknowe it here' " (B.V.200), but if he was Couetyse (or coueytouse), who is he now? The scene turns not just on a quirk of the allegorical confession but on the mystery of spiritual rebirth that is at the heart of penance. As the Sin confesses, he is caught in the middle of a transformation from the old self that is extinguished in the words he speaks to the new self he hopes to become. He can, of course, speak without understanding, and it is precisely by their bland obtuseness that several Sins erode the force of their confessions: Couetyse of the B-Text, when asked if he has made restitution, proudly describes robbing merchants while they were at *rest*, and when corrected complains that he doesn't know any French. But while the Sins do on occasion play the fool, the scene as a whole is not primarily satiric in intention.

Langland stresses the anguish of sin as much as its hardened impenitence: the self-consumption of Enuye, the endless rage of Wrathe, and the despair of Sloth are traditional attributes here raised to the level of motive.The purpose is not to portray the Sins as moved by contrition but to trace the vicissitudes of contrition itself within the sinful soul. "Enuye with heuy herte asked after shrifte, / And criede `*mea culpa*' corsynge alle hus enemys" (C.VII.63-4): the sorrow for sin and desire for amendment of contrition are overwhelmed in the last half-line by the anguish and obsessions of envy.

Again, Repentauncc asks him if he is sorry: " `Ich am euere sory,' sayde Enuye, `ich am bote selde other;/ That maketh me so megre for ichne may me auenge'" (93-4). Enviousness suborns and appropriates the contrition that is its only cure; the pain caused by the sin overwhelms the pain by which sin is cleansed. The same question is asked of several of the other Sins. Can contrition survive Wrathe's fury? Is Gloton contrite or hung over? Can Couetyse worry about his soul when he has to worry about his money? Langland's scene demonstrates how sin destroys its own cure, and so condemns itself to itself. By subverting the contrition that would annul them, the Sins succeed in prolonging a life of anguish, condemning themselves to damnation, a death without death and an ending without an end.

Langland's interest in the dynamics of contrition is confirmed by the processes of his own revision. In the B-Text the comically stupid Couetyse falls into wanhope and needs the comfort of Repentaunce's words about the breadth of God's mercy. But the C-Text goes beyond this negative point to show contrition in its positive workings: the reductive humour gives place to Couetyse's own careful explanation of how the anxiety of the miser overcomes care for his soul. Having so explicitly established the power of sin to nullify its antidote, Langland then preserves the balance of the scene by similarly strengthening the claims of Repentaunce: he replaces the abstract arguments against despair with the living proof, as it were, of 3even 3eld-a3eyn and Robert the ryfeler. The effect of this revision is not only to gain vividness and persuasion but to express the ontological paradox of the literary form and of penance itself. Having demonstrated his contrition by accepting the demands of satisfaction (*Reddite quod debes*), Couetyse is freed from himself and allowed to become a man who can be saved, whether 3even or Robert.

They are arguments against despair less by their typology than by their participation in the *salus animarum* of the Christian dispensation, a dispensation from which a being who is Couetyse (or coueytouse) is forever excluded. This is, then, Langland's rendering of personal change through penance, the articulation into the inward complexities of human experience of some of the central concerns of medieval penitential theology.

At the centre of the Christian dispensation stands the idea of a radical transformation of the self, literally of its "reformation" according to the pattern (*imago Dei*) in which it was originally created and from which it has defected through sin. The process begins with the inward turn of self-confrontation. "Quid te foris circumspicis, et non intus inspicis? . . . . Intus inspice, quid transis te? Descende in te." The sinner must set himself before himself, face to face with the defilement he has become: no longer the *imago Dei* he is now the *imago terreni hominis*"This image if thou behold it wittily," says Walter Hilton, "is all belapped with black stinking clothes of sin, as pride, envy, ire, accidie, covetise, gluttony and lechery. . . . This image and this black shadow thou bearest about with thee where thou goest." A true knowledge of himself humiliates the sinner, and he cries out to the Lord, "In Thy truth Thou hast humbled me." Gratefully, he abandons his corruption to the gnawings of the worm of conscience, receiving in his present pain a warrant against eternal agony. Now is the moment for the crucifixion of the old Adam, the annihilation of the man of sin, the pulverizing force of contrition that destroys the dying to bring forth life.

Whether called *compunctio* or *contritio,* the impulse which gives rise to penance is complex and even conflicted. In the authoritative *Summa de casibus poenitentiae,* St. Raymound of Pennaforte lists the six causes of contrition:

> Causae inductiuae contritionis sunt sex, cogitatio,et ex ea pudor de peccatis commissis: detestatio vilitatis ipsius peccati: timor iudicij, et poenae gehennae: dolor de amissione patriae caelestis, et multiplici offensa Creatoris: et spes triplex, veniae, gratiae, et gloriae.

Contrition is an uneasy balance of negation and assertion, a radical self-hatred and fear of God that is paradoxically joined to *spes triplex* and a reliance on divine mercy. "Idcirco te alloquor, ut sperare doceam et timere," says Augustine to Petrarch in the *Secretum Meum,* and he warns him against excesses of both hope (*praesumptio*) and fear (*desperatio*). Presumption and despair are the Scylla and Charybdis of the spiritual life, the Devil's greyhounds, in the words of the *Ancrene Riwle,* "igedered to gederes . . . nexst þe 3ete of helle."28 Despair is both the more interesting and the more apposite of these false ways. For, while presumption removes the sinner from the penitential context entirely, despair not only arises from the self-confrontation that initiates penance but is tragically close to the genuine spiritual impulses that lead to salvation. It is not simply one of the impedimenta to contrition or even its obverse, for its terrors and self-negations are themselves an important part of the penitential motive.

Five of the six *causae* listed by Pennaforte, for instance, are also characteristics of despair; and, in his influential discussion of penance, William of Auvergne lists ten "motus virtutis confringentis veterem hominem, ac funditus, ac radicitus mortificantis:" *timor, pudor, dolor, ira, indignatio, abominatio, horror, odium, execratio, detestatio* — a virtual litany of despair.

The dangerous instability of these ncgative feelings had long been recognized by writers on the spiritual life. According to St. Paul, there are two kinds of sorrow over sin, *tristitia secundum Deum* which works repentance unto salvation and *tristitia secundum saeculum* which works death (2 Cor. 7.10). For Augustine, *tristitia* is so unstable that he admits, even in the midst of an attack on Stoic apathy, that "scrupulosior quaestio est, utrum inveniri possit in bono." And, says Cassian, whereas Godly sorrow secures for the soul all the fruits of the Holy Spirit, its obverse is "impatiens, dura, plena rancore et moerore infructuoso, ac desperatione poenali, . . . fructus spirituales evacuans, quos novit illa conferre." Warnings against the danger of contrition deteriorating into despair are common in discussions of penance,and more personal accounts in the literature of the fourteenth century show it to have been one of the hardest passages of the spiritual life.

Julian of Norwich warns that "the beholding of [our sinfulness] maketh us so sorry and so heavy, that scarsely we can find any comfort. And this dread we take sometimes for a meekness, but it is a foul blindness and a weakness."Margery

Kempe begins her autobiography and her spiritual life with the story of how her conscience and her confessor drove her from contrition to despair and then to madness. And Henry of Lancaster presents a homeopathic explanation for the double effect of *tristitia*: it is a triacle drawn from the venom of sin itself, and, while in some it cures, in those too deeply infected it adds its force to the sin already present.In sum, if the ulcerous sinner is cleansed by the worm of conscience, he may also be killed by it:

Cest de conscience le ver
Qui a les dens durs comme fer
Si cruel est et si mordant
Si poignant et si trespercant
Que sil nauoit qui le tuast
Qui le ferist ou assommast
De tant runger ne fineroit
Jusques son maistre oscist auroit.

In destroying its victims, despair operates in two ways. The most dangerous is simply the working out of its own internal dynamic. A sin not of commission but feeling — Donne's "sin of fear" — despair is efficiently self-fulfilling: thinking himself lost, the man in despair refuses to ask for mercy; refusing to ask, he cannot receive; and not receiving, he becomes lost in deed as well as thought. In practical terms this means that the man

in despair avoids confession: "Non confitetur autem qui desperat de misericordia Dei," says Gregory flatly, and the confessional manuals are virtually unanimous in warning against despair. And yet, of course, the bitterest irony is that it is only by confession that despair is finally conquered. The other way is through the excesses of desperation and final impenitence. According to Augustine, the despairing man is like a gladiator doomed to the sword: "Jam peccator sum, jam iniquus, jam damnandus, nulla veniae spes est; cur jam non faciam quidquid libet, etsi non licet? Cur non impleam, quantum possum, quaecumque desideria, si post haec non restant nisi sola tormenta?" And a well-known Gregorian text describes the hidden anxiety and inner torment of the despairing impenitent:

> Quia dum feriri se undique insidiis credit, salute desperata, semper ad nequitiam excrescit. Aliquando vero iste perversus etiam superna judicia attendit, et super se haec venire metuit. . . . Sed a malo non avertitur, ut etiam ipsa quoque ab ejus interitu valeat averti. Accusante se autem conscientia feriri metuit, sed tamen semper auget quo feriatur. Contemnit reditum suum, desperat veniam, superbit in culpa; sed tamen testem suae nequitiae intus habet timorem. Et quamvis prava videatur foris audacter agere, de his tamen apud semetipsum cogitur trepidare.

Licentiousness is a vain attempt at distraction, and beneath a reckless bravado works the anxiety of despair, tormenting the sinner with a foretaste of the eternal punishment that awaits him.

But hope must never be abandoned for the man in despair. Even if contrition does collapse into despair, the process can be reversed: in DeGuileville's language, the worm of conscience can be broken by the hammer of contrition, and the lesson of the triumph of Mercy at the close of the *Castle of Perseverance* is not so much to cast out despair as to convert it to the work of penance. The mystical writers tend to see despair as an early stage in the soul's progress towards God, the necessary *siccitas* of the dark night rather than the *accidia* of sin, and they accept its scourges and corrosion as both the punishment for sin and the pain by which the old Adam is destroyed that the Christ within may live. Although the acts of desperation to which despair gives rise are perilous in the extreme, its negations are an important part of the penitential process, and any impulse that forces upon the sinner the reality of his condition can prove in the event to have been useful.

The emotions that excite penance are complex, and no matter how refractory or self-regarding the initial motives, they can be transformed by the penitential act itself into an offering acceptable to God. Putting aside the ontological changes effected *ex opere operato*, simply at the level of psychology the movement of the sinner towards contrition is understood to be a gradual and even hesitant process. Similarly, the act of confession itself can excite in even the impenitent fruitful spiritual motions. "Multi enim accedunt indevoti," says Jacques de Vitry, "qui cum lachrymis et devotione recedunt," and according to Walter Hilton,

> Though the ground of forgiveness stand not principally in confession, but in contrition of the heart and in forethinking of sin, nevertheless I expect that there is many a soul that should never have felt very contrition, nor had full forsaking of sin, if confession had not been. For it falls oft times that in time of confession grace of compunction comes to a soul that before never felt grace, but aye was cold and dry, aud far from feeling of grace.

In the confession scene in *Piers Plowman* Langland revises earlier forms to bring into poetic focus the nature of contrition and its relation to sin, penitential concerns characteristic of medieval, and especially fourteenth-century, religious thought. In the "Pardoner's Prologue and Tale" Chaucer's revision of his inherited materials is in the same, inward direction. The one-dimensional monologue of allegory is deepened, not by functioning as the Pardoner's confession, but by becoming part of a larger sequence of involuntary self-exposure that is fulfilled only in the tale; and the tale is, in turn, transformed by the context of its telling from an *exemplum* about avarice into a psychological allegory that reveals the Pardoner as a man in despair. The confession of despair, like that of Pruyde or Couetyse, is a theoretical impossibility, and it is this paradox that requires the transformations of genre: the direct self-revelation of autobiography is distorted by strategies of manipulation and concealment, and the negatives of his condition are visible only in the displacement of fiction. It may well be that his oblique confession brings sacramental healing no closer to the Pardoner, but, if we are to understand why he speaks and what he is saying, we must recognise the penitential context.

The ironic smile with which the God of Love accepts Faus Semblant's pledge of loyalty is Jean de Meun's perfunctory gesture towards the discontinuity between character and speech implicit in the paradox of the truthful hypocrite. But the Pardoner's illegitimately-assumed role of the professional speaker places this discontinuity at the centre of his charactcrization. Language is the means by which he creates himself for others, whether it be the cocksure prattle with which he disguises his eunuchry or the witty and learned sermon, liberally embellished with impressive *exempla,* with which he establishes his authority before the "lewed peple." The "Prologue," for all its apparent candour, is part of this image-making.

Recent critics have rightly argued that the pardoner of the Prologue, a monster who cheerfully anticipates his victims' damnation and steals food from the mouths of starving children, is a gross and deliberate parody of sinfulness. At once offending the censorious gentils and titillating the raucous lower elements represented by Harry Bailly, he plays to the full the role of the diabolical sinner, the man who has chosen with open eyes the path to his own damnation. Always the rhetorician, he speaks in the uncompromising tone of allegory, sounding at times like DeGuileville's Avarice, who tells her pilgrim-victim that

Souvanteffois par le pais
Faulx sainctuaires et fainctiz
Va moustrant a la simple gent
Pour faussement tirer argent.

But the similarities are only on the surface, and the differences in detail and dramatic energy between allegorical self-exposure and the Pardoner's "Prologue" spring ultimately from a deep difference in intent. The allegorical figure speaks in order to be fully known, while the very excess of the Pardoner's revelations hide him from us: rather than being created by the conventions of medieval allegory, he himself exploits them.

This is not to say that there is no controlling convention here, but that we must find its source elsewhere. I would suggest the false or uncontrite confession of satiric literature, what in the *summae confessorum* is called the liar's confession or *confessio ficti*. Instances in Middle English include Lady Meed's confession to the friar and the Devil's confession with which Robert of Brunne closes *Handlyng Synne*, but its most common appearance is in the Renart story. In the French version Renart confesses no less than five times in all, and his habit of misusing the sacrament led at least one cleric to label the perfunctory or uncontrite confession a *confessio renardi*. The instance closest to Chaucer's poem, and one which he almost certainly knew, is Renart's confession to "frere Huberz" the kite. Desperately hungry, Renart lures the kite within striking distance by confessing, apparently truthfully, that he has in his gluttony devoured even Hubert's children. He begs the horrified kite to forgive him, but when Hubert leans forward for a kiss of peace Renart gobbles him up.

The parallels between this scene and Chaucer's poem are striking: the confession as a trap, the extravagant sinfulness, the crucial role of the kiss of peace, and the ambiguity of both confessions — in neither case can we easily separate truth from fiction. Whether this episode is a specific source for Chaucer or not, the analogies suggest that, in revising the allegorical monologue, Chaucer moved in the direction of the rogue's confession. "3a, whanne þe fox prechyth, kepe wel 3ore gees!" is a cautionary proverb that applies in the first instance to the "lewed peple"; by giving his Pardoner a confessional prologue Chaucer wittily brings it to bear upon the pilgrims as well.

By choosing as his speaker an habitual sinner like Renart, rather than a hypocrite like Faus Semblant, Chaucer has avoided the stock satire of the mendicant controversy. In his further revision, however, he also avoids the irrepressible cynicism of the *Roman de Renart*. Renart is a cheerful outcast who remains always in control of his language and his victim, but Chaucer's reaccenting of the same narrative elements creates a character.

Who is anxious and dependent. For not only does his trap close on the Pardoner himself, but the whole relationship between his real and his created selves is less controlled and deliberate than with Renart. From the pilgrims the Pardoner covets not money, but admiration: his confession is designed to extract from the *gentils* a shocked respect and from Harry Bailly and his ilk the dubious title of "a good felawe." But, in fact, he goes too far and defines himself as a man outside the human community, making his ultimate rejection inevitable and revealing a pattern of self-destruction that surfaces in the offer of the relics. More significant than this misjudgment of others' cynicism, however, is the genuineness and even vulnerability that the Pardoner reveals. While insisting early and often that his motives are brazenly simple he also claims — and repeats the claim — that he is doing good works:

But though myself be gilty in that synne,
Yet kan I maken oother folk to twynne
From avarice, and soore to repente.
. . . .
For though myself be a ful vicious man,
A moral tale yet I yow telle kan.
(429-31, 459-60)

These hints are made all the more telling by the Pardoner's own response to them. In both cases he hastily withdraws from the disturbing complications he has raised to the comforting simplicity of avarice: "But that is nat my principal entente; / I preche nothyng but for coveitise" and his moral tale is only a device "for to wynne" . And in both instances he cuts off his line of thought with a misdirected and defensive conclusion: " Of this mateere it oghte ynogh suffise" — although he himself continues to worry at the subject; and, "Now hoold youre pees! my tale I wol bigynne".

This fugitive and embarrassed self-defense shows the Pardoner acknowledging in his spirit the values he subverts in his working, a complication that appears again in the benediction with which he closes the tale. In sum, he is by no means unambiguously impenitent, and his attempt to reduce himself to the simplicity of allegorical evil is best understood as an attempt to escape from a consciousncss that is too painfully divided. The "Prologue," then, by turns derisory and hesitant, vaunting and awkwardly candid, reveals in its very lack of clarity a spirit in conflict.

In fleecing his victims, the Pardoner in fact proffers both wisdom and an opportunity to perform the penance of alms-giving; and, doubtless, the knowledge that God turns even the wicked to His purpose encourages these gingerly efforts at self-justification. But are they not simply further instances of his presumption? Our answer to this question, and indeed our final judgment of the Pardoner, depends in large part upon our understanding of his eunuchry. Current opinion generally follows Robert

Miller's exegetical reading that identifies the Pardoner as the *eunuchus non Dei*: "Instead of cutting himself off from evil works, he cuts himself off from good works, He refuses offered grace. In short, he is the presumptuous man who, by his act of will, commits the unpardonable sin, not for the sake of, but in despite of, the kingdom of heaven." This reading is uncompromising in stressing the Pardoner's damnation and encourages us to see him as an instance of pure evil, Chaucer's "one lost soul," in Kittredge's too memorable phrase. It is quite true that in this case an exegetical approach is probably the right one, especially as it accords with the larger strategies of the poem. But I would propose a different pattern of scriptural imagery, that of the *arbor infructuosa*. Not only does the symbol of the withered tree allow for a less absolute reading, but it offers distinct critical advantages.

For one thing, it is a far more common image than the *eumuchus non Dei* and has a wide currency in medieval art and literature. For another, it has a striking presence in the tale in the "ook" where the rioters find death, the *radix malorum* that bears the bitter fruit of three corpses. The appropriateness of this biblical imagery to the Pardoner is obvious. He is like the fig tree of Matthew 2 1.18-21 that offers to the hungry Lord not fruit but foliage and is withered with His curse: according to the exegetes the foliage shows that the tree glories in vain words (*pompa locutionis*), while lacking the fruit of good works The Pardoner is one of those "qui verba habent, et facta non habent,"and his need is for precisely the "fructum dignum poenitentiae"that can alone save him from the fire of judgment: "lam enim securis ad radicem arborem posita est: omnis ergo arbor quae non facie fructum bonum exciditur et in ignem mittitur" .

Yet, for all its judicial gravity, this sequence of biblical imagery includes a controlling message of mercy in the parable of the sterile fig tree The *paterfamilias* commands that the tree be uprooted and destroyed, but the cultor advises that it be ditched and dunged and given one last chance; according to the exegetes, the ditch is "humilitas poenitentis" and the dung "memoria peccatorum," "cordis luctus et lacrymarum." "Non potest arbor mala fructus bonos facere" remains an inviolable principle, but, as Augustine (among others) insists, each righteous Christian has been made a fruitful tree: "Quisquis igitur homo hodie bonus est, id est, arbor bona, mala inventa est et bona facta est." The *radix arboris*, the human will, can be changed by penance from *cupiditas* to *caritas*: "ut in semetipsum oculos convertat, in se descendat, se discutiat, se inspiciat, sc quaerat, et se inveniat: et quod displicet, necet; quod placet, optet et plantet."

Perhaps the "hogges toord" in which the Host would enshrine the Pardoner's non-existent "coillons" is a last, bitter reminder of the *cophinus stercoris* by which the sterile tree can be made fruitful, a dung also nastily brought to our attention by the Host's comment about the "fundement" with which the Pardoner is supposed to paint his "olde breech." At any rate, it is in the "Tale" that the penitential contradictions of the Pardoner's condition are most fully revealed to us, although we must avoid the temptation to misread it that the Pardoner himself puts in our way. Taken literally, as he recommends, it is an exemplum meaning *Radix malorum est cupiditas*

; but, read spiritually, it is a moral allegory about the Pardoner himself, and it figures not avarice but despair. On the one hand, the rioters enact the Pardoner's life of self-damnation. Brazenly impenitent ("And ech of hem at otheres synne lough"), they are perverse *imitatores Dei* both in symbol ("we thre been al ones", "the yongeste of hem alle" serves bread and wine) and action ("Deeth shal be deed, if that they may hym hente!" And when, like the Pardoner, they issue from their tavern to do God's work, they receive their deserts with the terrifying efficiency of final judgment. These are, as it were, the facts of the Pardoner's'case, his history both past and future. But the human meaning of that history is expressed in the emotional centre of the talc, the old man. Rather than the saintly wise man of the analogues, a philosopher or hermit or even Christ, the Pardoner presents a figure who accurately reflects his own irreducible contradictions. Like the Pardoner, the old man proffers advice both needful ("Agayns an oold man, hoor upon his heed, / Ye sholde arise" [743-44]) and perilous: "turne up this croked wey".

Also like the Pardoner, he knows the truth but is unable to use it. In the terms of the story, he knows where Death is to be found but cannot find him himself, while tropologically he has won through to a gentle wisdom that has done little to relieve his suffering: hence he too offers a closing benediction — "God save yow, that boghte agayn mankynde, / And yow amende!" — that is in the event self-excluding. For the old man's fate is to remain ever unregenerate, whether this be expressed in the fairy-tale (or allegorical) terms of exchanging age for youth or in the theological terms of exchanging the "cheste" of his worldly goods for the "heyre clowt" of penance.

As we should remember, he speaks with a voice traditional to the penitential lyric that of the sinner whose repentance has come too late and whose wisdom is bought at the price of endless anguish: "Deþ ich wilni mest, / Wi nis he me I-core?" These are "Maximian's" words in his "Regret," and it is precisely Maximianus's first elegy that Chaucer drew upon for this portrait and that directs us to the context of failed penance which helps to explain the old man. "Vivere poena mea," says the speaker of Maximianus's poem, and it is this penance that the old man now suffers. Like the sterile quaestor whom he faithfully expresses, he is condemned to a life-in-death of Cain-like wandering, and in his fruitless penitential yearnings he has descended into the hell of despair.

It is not difficult to see how the condition that is expressed symbolically in the old man should function literally in the Pardoner himself, for the mechanism that Chaucer provides is astonishingly precise. In detailing the Pardoner's eunuchry Chaucer renders it, as we know, meaningful in the medieval languages of both science and religious symbol. But the Pardoner egoistically misreads himself, and, like the rioters of his tale, takes letter for spirit, fleshly understanding for spiritual. As we have seen, contrition includes a powerful, at times overwhelming negative movement, its separate aspects traditionally termed *pudor, detestatio, dolor, and timor.*

In obvious ways, each of these feelings is known to the Pardoner, but he misuses and misapplies them: his obsessive self-regard is directed not to his sinful acts but to his physically-maimed body. Ashamed of his literal eunuchry, he hides behind a far more shameful spiritual sterility; fearing exposure to his companions, he mocks the judgment of God; his sorrow is not *de amissione patriae celestis, et multiplici offensa Creatoris* but simply *de ipso*; and his hatred is not *vilitatis peccati* but for the vileness of his body. In the "Parson's Tale" Chaucer quotes St. Paul's famous lament, "Allas, I caytyf man! who shall delivere me fro the prisoun of my caytyf body?" In a sense that exceeds his comprehension, this is the meaning of the Pardoner's words, and it is only in the symbolic displacement of the "restelees kaityf" that he finally reveals himself to us.

Change, of course, remains possible, even for the Pardoner, although his vain and self-indulgent literalism, his "ariditas litterae," seems to forestall any real conversion. As we remember, the fatality of despair is its ability to destroy its own cure. At once defiant and self-hating, wretched in his licentiousness and yet hardened in sin, the Pardoner yearns towards the release of confession but is unable to bring himself to it. The distortions and displacements of his speaking, then, are not superficial awkwardnesses or vestiges of irrelevant conventions but the essence of his paradoxical meaning. The "Prologue" presents inflated self-advertisements and fugitive glimpses of a more genuine self; the "Tale" displaces into fiction the Pardoner's deepest self-understanding, while hiding its meaning from the man who speaks.

Finally, the offer of the relics comes as the fitting conclusion to this sequence, an elliptical and compact gesture that is as contradictory as the Pardoner's previous utterances. On the one hand, he asks for inclusion, either in the fellow-feeling of a jest or the earnest respect due a "suffisant pardoneer"; on the other hand, he invites exclusion, even punishment. The punishment that is, in fact, inflicted is exquisitely apt; it clarifies what had previously been garbled and makes explicit the fruitlessness that only true confession can finally cure. In its full dimensions, then, as an invitation to be hurt and forgiven, the epilogue exactly fulfills the post-confessional part of pennncc: it provides a satisfaction that fits the sin and a gesture of absolution: "Anon they kiste, and ryden forth hir weye." Penitential theology has provided Chaucer not only with one of his subtlest pilgrims, but also with one of his finest structural achievements: a "Prologue" and "Tale" that are related at the deepest levels of language and doctrine, and for an epilogue a dramatic gesture which, while participating in these levels of meaning, provides emotional release from the problems raised.

Q.8. Comment on Chaucer's Pardoner Sexuality

Or

Q. Discuss Pardoner as a Flamboyant

The outrageous Pardoner has often seemed among the most real of Chaucer's pilgrims in the Canterbury Tales. Although only a few have thought him an actual portrait from life, the majority of modern critics has believed in the essential truth of the characterization. Paul Ruggiers speaks for many when he asserts that the Pardoner's performance provides "the ultimate example of Chaucer's subtle handling of human psychology.'Perhaps the most famous reading of the Pardoner as though he were a fully developed character from a realistic novel is by G. L. Kittredge, who at the beginning of the century demonstrated so brilliantly how much could be made by critical inventiveness from almost nothing. Kittredge's dramatic interpretation culminates in his finding the Pardoner's unremarkable three-line statement that Christ's pardon is best an expression of extraordinary emotional crisis in which the pilgrim "suffers a very paroxysm of agonized sincerity." More recently, in one of the most elaborate contemporary attempts by a critic to make the Pardoner new, Donald Howard puts forth a sinister yet compelling figure who is said to resemble the French thief and writer Jean Genêt.As these two interpretations suggest, the widespread assumption that the Pardoner is a psychologically whole and consistent personality is not supported by any deep agreement about the nature of that personality, and there is debate even over such basic matters as what it is he really wants — whether it is money, revenge, fun, approval, or love.

The various critical re-creations of the Pardoner tend to be ingenious, and most are interesting, but they are also overly subjective because they rest on little actual evidence in the text. Perhaps even more dangerous is the often unexamined assumption that since the Pardoner is a vivid, truly flamboyant presence in the *Canterbury Tales*, he can therefore be analysed as though he were a real person instead of a fictional, even allegorical character. In recent years, most Chaucerians seeking to reveal the "real" Pardoner have focused on the supposed irregularity of his sex life, and it is the assumption that the Pardoner's sexuality can be exactly known that I wish to call into question here. Of course it is impossible finally to prove a negative, but I will suggest that the various precise diagnoses of the Pardoner's sexual condition offered by so many critics are much less reliable than most Chaucerians have come to believe.

My purpose is not to offer a new explanation of the Pardoner's sexuality but to show the weakness of this entire approach, which is given a specious authority from its claim to be based on hard scientific evidence. The poet undoubtedly hints at sexual disorder of some sort as one part of the

Pardoner's general corruption, but the excessive modern preoccupation with the pilgrim's sexuality distorts Chaucer's method of characterization by demanding certainty where none exists.

The sexual interpretation of the Pardoner is quite new and first begins with Walter Clyde Curry's claim in 1919 to have discovered the Pardoner's "secret." Citing medieval manuals on physiognomy, Curry asserted that the description in the General Prologue of the Pardoner's staring eyes, small voice, beardless cheek, and long, soft hair would have been recognized by a contemporary audience as the marks of a *eunuchus ex nativitate.*In his survey of Pardoner criticism, John Halverson notes the wide acceptance of Curry's view, which has been further strengthened by its adoption in an allegorical and scriptural sense by exegetical critics. Only a few have seriously questioned the eunuch theory, and some of these, along with others, have then offered alternate sexual explanations — that the Pardoner is a homosexual or even a hermaphrodite. Indeed, although most critics today seem to agree that the Pardoner's odd sexuality is crucial to his performance, the exact form of that sexuality is as much an open question as other aspects of his character.

Some critics are rather cavalier about his condition. Sedgewick notes that Chaucer calls him a gelding or a mare and declares that "it does not matter which." Lumiansky calls him a eunuch and then, in a kind of sexual mixed metaphor, compares him to Shakespeare's Edmund. Others are breathtakingly precise. Eric Stockton labels the Pardoner "a manic depressive with traces of anal eroticism, and a pervert with a tendency toward alcoholism"; and Beryl Rowland, with enviable assurance, asserts that he is a "testicular pseudohermaphrodite of the feminine type."

Like most other attempts to treat the Pardoner as a real person, the sexual approach is based on a very few lines. All of the evidence comes from the first section of the brief portrait of the pilgrim in the General Prologue .Yet, even here, the supposed revelation of the Pardoner's sexual secret is not as clear or consistent as many have assumed. Although there are some other complementary details, the modern critical fascination with the Pardoner's sexual condition would probably not have been quite so popular except for a single notorious line: "I trowe he were a geldyng or a mare" .Certainly this line is important and suggests abnormality of some sort; but it cannot sustain the enormous critical weight it has been asked to bear, for it is not nearly as precise as it first seems. Chaucer undermines our confidence at the outset with the phrase, "I trowe."

This word most commonly indicates speculation, but even if we take it in its less usual meaning of certainty, is this the assertion of the same narrator who agrees with the Monk's idea of cloistered duty and finds the murderous Shipman a good fellow? Certainly the phrase "I trowe" qualifies what is to follow to some degree, as do the animal metaphors — "a geldyng or a mare." We may assume a eunuch or a homosexual is meant, but the figurative language adds a measure of doubt; a geldyng is not a *eunuchus ex nativitate*, and a mare does not necessarily mean a male homosexual but may simply indicate that the Pardoner is effeminate in some way. As often in the General Prologue, Chaucer raises questions but provides no definite answers. To increase our uncertainty even further, Chaucer deliberately confuses the issue by offering us two possibilities — a geldyng *or* a mare — by no means the same thing in any interpretation, though many critics write as if all eunuchs were homosexual and all homosexuals eunuchs. The two very different sexual explanations of the Pardoner offered so tentatively by the narrator do not reinforce one another but instead mock any attempt at precise identification.

The most serious flaw with the sexual interpretation of the Pardoner, however, is that the contemporary "scientific" evidence on which it claims to be based is not nearly as strong as its proponents assert. Many still automatically assume that Curry proved his case for the Pardoner's eunuchdom beyond question, and further evidence has seemed unnecessary. Michael Hoy reflects this consensus when he writes of the description in the General Prologue:

Those features clearly show that Chaucer's Pardoner is a eunuch, and we owe to Professor W. C. Curry the realization that Chaucer must have been very familiar with medieval physiognomy literature (which contained elaborate character judgments in accordance with a man's features and bodily form), for the Pardoner's physical characteristics are those of the medieval type of *eunuchus ex nativitate.*

Medieval physiognomy is not quite the exact science Curry and his followers suggest because its categories are so loose and overlapping, and if we re-examine the evidence Curry himself supplies, we shall see that it fails to prove all that he says he does.

To begin with, the specific condition Curry identified in the Pardoner (*eunuchus ex nativitate*) is difficult to accept. As Muriel Bowden has pointed out, the *eunuchus ex nativitate* is very much a *rara avis* and not the type Curry claimed, for even he can offer only a single example. Except for this one case described by Polemon, most of his evidence refers instead to geldyngs, unfortunates who presumably were made and not born. Realizing this problem, some critics have been satisfied to regard the Pardoner as a simple eunuch (ignoring Curry's specific diagnosis of *ex nativitate*), but even this interpretation is not justified by contemporary evidence.

Many of the quotations Curry provides from ancient physiognomists do not, in fact, identify the Pardoner's characteristics specifically with eunuchism of any kind, but instead with the more general states of drunkenness, impudency, and shamelessness, qualities that are no secret to any student of the Pardoner but have nothing to do with sexual efficiency. The lack of a beard does seem often to have been associated with geldings in the Middle Ages (though the condition was also thought to result from leprosy), but the other physical details Chaucer gives the Pardoner do not point to a specific sexual condition.

The Pardoner's apparently thinning hair, small voice, and glaring eyes say nothing definitive about his sexuality on the evidence Curry provides. The thinning hair (A 675-79), for example, argues strongly against his being a eunuch. Curry quotes Bartholomaeus Anglicus stating that gelded men, like women, do not become bald, and the single *eunuchus ex nativitate* cited had "abundant hair," not the "ounces" which ay "thynne," by "colpons oon and oon" of the Pardoner. The Pardoner's voice is said to be "as smal as hath a goot" (A 688), which both medieval physiognomy and modern common opinion associate with a lack of full virility. But even such a voice does not automatically indicate castration, for like the "gentil Pardoner,' the presumably functional, though effeminate, Absolon woos Alisoun in the Miller's Tale by singing in a voice that is similarly "gentil and smal" . Curry supports his case by citing a Middle English version of the *Secreta Secretorum* to the effect that those who have a voice "hei, smale and swete and plesaunt, bene neshe, and haue lytill of manhode" and are like women.

Even if this is accepted as a description of the Pardoner's voice, it does not necessarily mean he is a eunuch (or a homosexual) any more than Nicholas in the Miller's Tale is one because he is described as being meek as a maiden . Moreover, the passage from the *Secreta Secretorum* continues, although this part is omitted by Curry, to say that a related kind of voice, a "smale hey stronge voice," indicates a person who is easily made angry.This second quotation seems just as good a description of the Pardoner's voice as the first one and suggests nothing about the pilgrim's sexuality. The Pardoner's third unusual physical attribute, his eyes ("Swiche glarynge eyen hadde he as an hare" [A 684]), also does not prove he is a eunuch. Curry refers to the *Secreta Secretorum* again to the effect that "ryst opyn eighyn and glysinynge" indicate shamelessness. We should note that as before no anatomical secret is revealed by Curry's evidence (shamelessness is not the same as being a eunuch) and that elsewhere in the same work "ouer-oppyn eyen, lyke as they were y-thryste owte," are said to indicate a fool, which the Pardoner is not. Another Middle English version of the *Secreta Secretorum* declares that "eyen glysteryng as yse, and shynyng, sheweth a gilefull man, bolde, playn, a waker, a gatter of þynges by malice." This seems to describe both the Pardoner's strange glance and his general character as well or better than Curry's passage, but it suggests no specific sexual condition.

The animals associated with the Pardoner's physiognomy - and not discussed by Curry - also do not indicate a eunuch. As we have seen, his voice is compared to that of a goat and his eyes to those of a hare. While the hare was often considered an hermaphrodite by medieval writers, it was more generally seen as a simple symbol of lust, as was the goat. The latter, far from being associated with eunuchs, is an ancient symbol for the male phallus. D. W. Roberston, Jr., may suggest why these animals were linked with the Pardoner when he notes that "one common medieval device for illustrating lechery is to depict a man riding a goat and either carrying or pursuing a rabbit." Rather than identifying him with the specific states of eunuchism or homosexuality, Chaucer seems to want to present the Pardoner as a more general example of unspecified lust, a condition which the pilgrim himself freely admits and the 'gentils" seem to suspect when they demand that he "telle us of no ribaudye".

The second sexual argument, that Chaucer means us to see the Pardoner as a homosexual, is even more impressionistic than the eunuch theory and is based on much less medieval evidence. The homosexual thesis is quite a recent idea, first suggested tentatively by Bowden and Gerould, but is currently a dominant strain in analyses of the Pardoner, perhaps in response to the prominence of the subject in contemporary society. As with the eunuch theory, the homosexual interpretation also starts from that one line in the General Prologue: "I trowe he were a geldyng or a mare". The word "mare" certainly suggests that the Pardoner is in some way effeminate, but, as with 'geldyng,' the metaphorical language and subjunctive mood preclude precise definition. Although Jill Mann asserts that the "image of the mare" is used by Walter of Châitillon to refer to male homosexuals, the actual phrase she quotes, "equa fit equus," is a play on Latin grammatical gender and not really parallel to Chaucer's term. No one has found other examples of such a use of "mare" in either Latin or English.

Indeed, the discussion of this question in Mann's excellent book on estate satire shows that attempts to define the sexuality of the Pardoner can confuse even the best scholars. Mann states that "Curry has done useful work in documenting the medieval picture of the homosexual," even though Curry's actual claim was that the Pardoner is a eunuch. Moreover, Mann's own argument for the Pardoner's homosexuality relies less on medieval sources than on the questionable assertion that "the modern stereotype of the homosexual is identical [to him] in every respect." More usefully, Mann also notes that many of the details Chaucer uses to describe the Pardoner in the General Prologue come from "the satiric tradition on foppery" previously used in connection with the Squire (a dedicated heterosexual),thus suggesting that Chaucer may have had no specific, sexual condition in mind and reminding us that effeminacy in the Middle Ages, of which the Pardoner is definitely guilty, does not necessarily mean homosexuality but also the reverse — too great a concern with women.

Some who support the idea of the Pardoner as homosexual make much of the supposed pun on "stif burdoun," which the Summoner is said to hold to the Pardoner's rendition of "Com hider, love, to me". Paull Baum first suggested that in addition to the literal musical meaning of bass accompaniment, Chaucer is playing with other words, including *bourdon*, "staff," to suggest a homosexual relation between Summoner and Pardoner. Two other critics have supported the argument that *bourdon* as staff could be used as a reference to the male phallus, although the evidence they cite is either later (from Gascoigne and, less relevantly, Dylan Thomas) or from medieval French literature. Even such weak evidence for the pun should not be dismissed absolutely, but sexual metaphors are notoriously various and must be treated carefully. Donald Howard notes that the next line in the General Prologue ("Was nevere trompe of half so greet a soun" [A 674]) supports the literal meaning and that it is far too easy to imagine that any elongated object is a symbol of the phallus. The one other use of *burdon* in Chaucer, which describes the wife's snoring in the Reeve's Tale refers to sound only without the slightest phallic hint. Likewise the adjective *stif,* which I believe is the word that strikes modern ears as most sexually loaded, has no such association in its only other certain use by Chaucer and in the alliterative tradition commonly refers to military prowess.

The Pardoner and Summoner are undoubtedly two of the most grotesque and repellent figures in medieval literature, but Chaucer offers no definite evidence that their association is mutually amorous. The Summoner is a thoroughgoing lecher, and even if we do not accept Morton Bloomfield's suggestion that the "yonge girles" the pilgrim is said to associate with refer only to females, there is no hint among the many accusations in his portrait that his lust is homosexual. If anything like this were meant, one would expect to find it among the other crimes attributed to the Summoner in the Friar's Tale. If the Pardoner and Summoner did share an erotic relationship, it is hardly possible that they would sing of their love so publicly. Their musical offering, "Com hider, love, to me," if not meant as parody of the *Canticum Canticorum,* probably indicates that these two admittedly very strange characters want to present themselves as two wild and crazy guys ready for a little fun. A more likely, and more important, explanation than homosexuality is that the friendship of the Summoner and Pardoner points to serious ecclesiastical corruption, since the former was supposed to regulate the latter.

In the most interesting recent brief for the Pardoner's homosexuality, Monica McAlpine wisely rejects the claimed pun on "stif burdoun," but her own argument adds little in the way of solid, new evidence (nor is that the primary ambition of her speculative essay). McAlpine relies largely on the claim, borrowed from Mann, that "mare" might mean male homosexual without offering any additional proof ("even if the primary meaning of 'mare' was 'an effeminate male,' a second meaning may have been 'a *possibly* homosexual male'" [emphasis added]) and on the doubtful notion that since medieval people had confused and fluid ideas about homosexuality, it alone can account for all of the Pardoner's peculiar characteristics. Although McAlpine says she is only exploring the consequences that would follow from the assumption that the Pardoner might be homosexual, her article demonstrates some of the dangers of the sexual interpretation. In spite of careful qualifications early in her essay, what begins as hypothesis eventually seems to become accepted as fact. Although she first talks about the Pardoner's "possible" status as homosexual, McAlpine later discusses the Pardoner's performance as Chaucer's "study" of homosexuality.

The most serious problem with this approach, in my opinion, is that it produces interpretations of the Pardoner's Tale as a whole that are too unhistorical and fashionably modern. Although her earlier argument had rested on the claim that Chaucer, like most of his contemporaries, had confused ideas about homosexuality, McAlpine now insists that Chaucer intends to "challenge the sexual phobias of his readers." Finally, she arrives at the surprising conclusion that the poet asserts "the dignity of the Pardoner" and that the reader is reminded that "through his sexual sufferings the Pardoner participates in the crucifixion." For all its ingenuity, McApline's article provides no new evidence from medieval sources to prove that Chaucer means us to see the Pardoner specifically as a homosexual. What she has done is to produce a spectacular new re-creation of the Pardoner in the tradition of the critic as Chaucer's collaborator that descends from Kittredge and that is still very much alive today. We may well be impressed with the power of such complex psychological interpretations of the Pardoner, while finally concluding that they are based on little real evidence in Chaucer's text.

I do not mean to deny there is definitely something odd about the Pardoner as described in the General Prologue, but I would suggest that his sexuality remains too imprecise to serve as a reliable guide to his entire performance and Tale. Chaucer throws out several hints, but he does not define. He may have aroused our suspicions, but he does not indicate any exact condition that can be used as a sure foundation on which to build an interpretation. The physiognomists quoted by Curry may be more correct than he acknowledges in associating the Pardoner's features only with the general states of shamelessness, impudence, and lust. Despite suggestions of sexual abnormality in his portrait, other information in the rest of the Canterbury Tales — such as the Pardoner's announcement to the Wife of Bath that he is thinking of marriage his claim to have a wench in every town, and even the Host's threat to cut off his "coillons" — suggest a more ordinary sexual life, forcing those who insist that the Pardoner does have a sexual secret to read these passages ironically. The apparent contradiction between portrait and tale raises an important theoretical question that applies to other pilgrims as well. Does Chaucer really mean for the reader to take a delicate hint in the General Prologue and apply it thousands of lines later in the Pardoner's Prologue and Tale?

Near the end of his essay, Curry cites without analysis the pseudo-Chaucerian *Tale of Beryn* as proof of his interpretation of the Pardoner. But *Beryn*, with its long prologue chronicling the adventures of the pilgrims at Canterbury, suggests a very different and more innocent sexual figure from the one created by modern critics. Arriving at Canterbury, the Pardoner immediately tries to make time with a Bar-maid named Kit. He arranges to spend the night with her, "þat was his hole entencioun", but when he arrives that evening "as glad as eny goldfynch", he finds the door locked and Kit in bed with her paramour. The Pardoner becomes furious because of his dashed expectations:

For who hath love longing, & is of corage Hote,
He hath ful many a myry þou3t to-fore his delyte;
And ry3t so had the Pardoner, and was in evil pli3te. (494-96)

In this early "interpretation" of Chaucer's Pardoner, he is seen as neither eunuch nor homosexual, but a randy, if silly, heterosexual whose quest for a "joly wenche in every toun" causes him to be thoroughly duped. He is reminiscent of Absolon in the Miller's Tale (whom we have compared to the Pardoner before), another effeminate cleric who also is not so much incapable of heterosexual love-making as incompetent at it.

The most telling objection to the sexual interpretation of the Pardoner is that, like many other attempts to describe the "real" Pardoner, it trivializes Chaucer's accomplishment. Baum long ago protested that the Pardoner was a fictional character with no existence off the printed page; thus claims that he is a "testicular pseudo-hermaphrodite" or medieval Jean Gênet seem somewhat irrelevant. The modern demand in biography for the sexual secrets of real people (however doubtfully ascertained) is suspect enough, but a similar curiosity about fictional characters easily becomes ridiculous. The figure of Gluttony in *Piers Plowman* or Shakespeare's Falstaff has, like the Pardoner, a strong dramatic impact on the reader, but they also derive from the medieval allegorical tradition and are not individuals in the modern sense at all. The Pardoner is a fascinating literary character; he is not a genuine human personality. We should not take the vague and contradictory hints of sexual peculiarity in one part of the Pardoner's portrait as the key to his character, for such hints merely prepare us for the more serious ecclesiastical corruptions to follow. The real perversion of this pilgrim is not sexual but moral, as we see in the rest of his portrait and Tale. If we give up the futile and ultimately trivial attempt to define the psyche and exact anatomy of the Pardoner, we shall gain something of infinitely greater value: a clearer view of one of the most challenging of the Canterbury Tales.

Q.9. Analyse The Death of a Salesman in Pardoner's tale

Or

Q. Discuss the character's of Chaucer as physiognomies

Of all the *Canterbury Tales*, the *Pardoner's Tale* is the most fully articulated within its dramatic context. The description of the Pardoner in the *General Prologue* is entirely and in detail consistent with the Pardoner's account of himself in his *Prologue,* where he gives a more extended description of his ways of "affiling" his tongue to win silver, and the tricks by which he gets money out of his simple-minded audiences, particularly his use of false relics. The tale that he tells grows directly out of his autobiographical *Prologue,* being in its entirety a specimen of the kind of moral tale that be is wont to use in his preaching. At the conclusion, the dramatic framework is completed with an extended end- piece where the Pardoner explicitly signals the termination of his recital and turns again to the pilgrims, his primary audience. The exchange that follows, between Pardoner, Host, and Knight, is one of the very few occasions where Chaucer allows the pilgrimage frame to admit a conversation between more than two persons (the *Introduction* to the *Tale*, with the expostulation of "thise gentils,' is another).

For good measure, there is the intrusion of the Pardoner into the *Wife of Bath's Prologue*, which is the only occasion in the Canterbury Tales where a pilgrim is interrupted in full spate and then resumes. Kittredge, though acknowledging that the Pardoner is a lost soul," clearly wishes to find in him some traits of disfigured humanity, and reads the explicit of the Tale as a paroxysm of agonized sincerity, a moment of moral convulsion, "an ejaculation profoundly affecting in its reminiscence of the Pardoner's better nature, which he had himself thought dead long ago." Sympathy for the tortured soul of the Pardoner was forthcoming from a different quarter some years later, when Walter Clyde Curry, basing his argument on the physical features attributed to the Pardoner in the General Prologue — his long fair hair, his glaring eyes, his thin, high-pitched voice, his beardlessness - and the hint in line 691, "I trowe he were a geldyng or a mare," revealed "the Pardoner's secret" and pronounced him to be a congenital eunuch, or *eunuchus ex nativitate.*Curry detects a wistful sadness in the Pardoner's talk of his plans to get married (in the *Wife of Bath's Prologue*), and declares that he is more to be pitied than censured:

> Born a eunuch and in consequence provided by nature with a warped mind and soul, he is compelled to follow the urge of his unholy impulses into debauchery, vice and crime. Being an outcast from human society, isolated both physically and morally, he satisfies his depraved instincts by preying upon it. His character is consistent throughout both with itself and with nature as described in the physiognomies .

This has proved a very influential reading of the Pardoner's nature, and provides the basis for the standard iconographic interpretation of the Pardoner, as expounded by R. P. Miller. According to this interpretation, which derives from patristic distinctions between good and bad eunuchs, the Pardoner is the type of the perverse cleric who is sterile in good works, impotent to multiply the number of the faithful, lacking in the organs of spiritual generation and increase.

But the outspokenness of our age has allowed attention to dwell also on the neglected second term of equine comparison applied to the Pardoner, and to identify him as a practitioner of "thilke abhoinynable synne, of which that no man unnethe oghte speke ne write." The association of effeminacy (the mare) with homosexuality is age-old, and several of the physical features attributed to the Pardoner concur in suggesting that he is a homosexual. The powerful association between homosexuality and inveterate wickedness and heresy fits well here, of course, as does every other circumstance once the secret is out: the Summoner's "stif burdoun" becomes an obscene double entendre, the Pardoner's claim to have "a joly wenche in every toun" becomes a pathetic and ludicrous attempt to cover up his sexual deviancy, and the Host's threat to seize his coillons" and have them enshrined in "a hogges toord" (instead of in a reliquary) comes to have a singular pointedness.

Likewise, psychologically, we can recognise that his boasting of "normal depravity, especially avarice, is a kind of screen for his tortured sense of abnormal depravity, and a hidden plea for acceptance. Everyone, it seems, wants to rescue the Pardoner: perhaps some obscure sense of reassurance is to be obtained from asserting his essential humanity.

These are the main lines on which the Pardoner has been "psychologized," though there have been many other incidental lines of speculation. To the question, why does he speak so frankly about his wicked life? various answers have been proffered: he is on holiday and does not expect to meet these people in the future course of business; be is offended by the unwillingness of the "gentils" to let him tell a tale of "myrthe" and therefore deliberately gives an exaggeratedly diabolical view of himself so that they will realise how foolish they have been; he is drunk and does not know what he is doing. Equally prolific have been the explanations of the Pardoner's inconsequential behaviour in attempting to sell pardons to the pilgrims after having told them of all his knavish tricks: he is joking wildly because he is ashamed of having given way to a momentary spasm of sincerity; he is carried away by his own tale; he is in earnest; he sees the pilgrims carried away by his tale and seizes the chance to make the most spectacular coup.

It must be clear that there is no basis in the text for the verification of any of these interpretations. Psychologizing, that is, fantasizing about motives to be attributed to characters who appear to have none, is a sport that has no rules and is, therefore, in the end, not very satisfying. On the other band, what is equally clear, it will not do to push the Pardoner back into the conventional frame of the confession of sin made by an allegorical personification, such as that of Fals-Semblant in the *Romance of the Rose,'* where Chaucer found his primary model.

The sense of menace, of some stirring of unspeakable evil, the sense of death, is too strong and too universally apprehended to allow any easy fitting of the Pardoner to a literary scheme. Furthermore, it is not easy to accept the "historical' argument that the Middle Ages were not interested in the inner workings of the individual consciousness, or in character. it would be difficult to know how we could read their writing with any understanding if we did not believe that we shared some assumptions about the way people behave and the intentions on which they act. But we must understand through the clues we are given, and through the literary conventions within which writers work, and not use their writings as a stimulus for speculations that feed our own fads and sensibilities.

Perhaps a comparison will lead the way to some more specific of the author understanding. The Wife of Bath, not to move outside the *Canterbury Tales,* is a prime example of Chaucer's interest in the workings of the individual consciousness. She speaks constantly of her thoughts and feelings, her hopes and regrets: she does not always speak consistently or honestly, but it is in that region of inner being that she moves. Her discourse embodies the movement of her mind, and her mind often moves counter to the plan of her performance. She reacts to what she herself says, and is aware of the larger moral world in which she has her being, even though she does not much like it.

She has a present, in which she lives, pd a past and a future within which that present exists coherently. The Pardoner, by contrast, has no thoughts or feelings (except for the anger aroused by the Host's violent speech, which makes him speechless), no hopes or regrets. He never talks about his motives, except to reiterate monotonously that his purpose is ever one. He never once says "I think" or "I feel," but only describes what he has done or what he will do. Without soul, feeling, or inner being, he is a creature of naked will, unaware of its existence but in the act of will. In transferring the kind of expository matter he found in the *Romance of the Rose* into the context of a discourse by a realised individual, Chaucer is not so much writing unpsychologically as creating zeropsychology. There is one flicker of awareness of a world which is not an extension of the Pardoner's will —

Yet kan I maken oother folk to twynne
From avarice, and soore to repente. (430-31)

This gives him a momentary unease, but he does not seem to understand why it should do so, and it fades into mere words. To say that he "relishes the irony" is to misinterpret this hollow juxtaposition.

The Pardoner thus creates in us a powerful response, and yet as a character he has no capacity for change or self-awareness, and no insight into himself. There is no inner consciousness, because there is no "within." He puts on a brilliant performance, but it is like that of a marionette, or a clockwork toy, which once wound up goes through its motions mechanically. This image of automatism is explicitly evoked by the existence of the Tale as a performance within a performance: the Pardoner does not actually tell a tale, but merely reproduces verbatim his habitual performance, even to the extent of including the homily and peroration, which are out of place here. It is as if he exists only in the act of performance.

The horror, therefore, is the horror of vacuity. The Pardoner is not a rotten apple, but rather like one of those apples that grow near the Dead Sea, that look like true apples but turn to 'wynnowande askes" when touched. His moral being has undergone a total atrophy, and in this state he exists, speaking but not understanding. The association of this atrophied state with his profession by no means accidental. The reduction of the system of indulgences, conceived of first as a solace to man in his sinful state — providing he looks inward to his sinful state — into a form of mercantile exchange, not only encourages but actually requires an atrophy of the moral sensibility on the part of its professional practitioners. In this respect it is like all forms of human activity which substitute monetary values for human values: it leads to an unawareness of and an inability to distinguish between good and bad, true and false, real and illusory. Even the Pardoner's cynicism is only skin-deep, since it exists only as a demonstration of the triumph of his will. He is, both theologically and in ordinary human terms that need no gloss, dead.

The mention of death brings us at last to his tale of the three rioters, which is about death. It is a brilliantly told tale, and there would be little point in trying to find flaws in it, or features of expression which would reveal the character of the Pardoner. In essence it is that type of tale, favourite in folklore, which depends on a trick, in this case a double meaning of *death* which we understand but the rioters do not. They go in search of death in order to kill him, and they find death and die: "No lenger thanne after Deeth they sougbte" . The tale bears a strange affinity, as narrative, to Langland's dream of the search for Dowel: just as they find death in dying, so Langland's dreamer finds Dowel in doing well. The mixture of planes of reality, the way in which real people behave as if they were characters in an allegory, creates the same surreal effect as in Langland.

But the trickery of the narrative is only the simplest level on which it works. The context provided for it by the Pardoner's prologue and homily, and by his very profession, makes it resonate with a much deeper note. For the death that the rioters find is no more than the physical correlative, an allegorical enactment, of the death that they have already undergone: "For if you live according to the flesh you will die, but if by the spirit you put to death the needs of the body you will live". This has already been alluded to in the homily . The rioters' attempt to go out in search of death in order to slay him is not the act of public-spirited vigilantes, but a sign of moral deadness, as well as a grotesque parody of Christ's struggle to overcome Death, which brought about, of course, not the elimination of physical death, but the release of man from the certainty of eternal damnation. Physical death is by no means to be regarded as an enemy: in Piers Plowman Conscience calls Kynde to send Death to help man in his battle against the Seven Deadly Sins led by Antichrist, since Death, as a reminder of necessary mortality, is a stimulus to the life of the spirit.

Likewise, in Lydgate's *Dance of Death,* the Carthusian and the monk both welcome death as a friend who has been a long time coming. Death in this sense is thus the physical enactment of the death to the world which is the life of the spirit: "You must consider yourselves dead to sin and alive to God in Christ Jesus" . Death is the only means to life,,whether considered as the dying into life which is the act of abnegation of sin, or the dying into immortal life which is physical extinction.

Some of these underlying meanings are focussed in the figure of the Old Man, to whom Chaucer has given some of his most unforgettable lines, and a part in the story quite different from that of the corresponding figure in the analogues, and quite gratuitous if we consider only the needs of the narrative. The Old Man seeks death, and is prepared for death: he is dressed already in his grave-clothes, it seems. He does not seek it in any spirit of presumption, and he recognizes that he must live out his days, "As longe tyme as it is Goddes wille" (726), but his weariness of the world makes him see life as an exile, an imprisonment in which his soul is restless: "Thus walke I, lyk a restelees kaityf" (728). Here he is echoing Paul, as translated by Chaucer in the *Parson's Tale*: "Allas! I caytyf man! who shall delivere me from the prisoun of my caytyf body?" (I 344).

On the other hand, the Old Man, though he may derive from the hermit of the analogues, is not a truly contemplative figure: there is some ambiguity about him, and his regret at his inability to find any young man to exchange his youth for his age suggests some unappeased yearning after life, or maybe after spiritual life, since it is by putting off the old man — crucified with Christ on the cross — that he may be reunited in life with the new man .

I dismissed earlier the possibility that the *Pardoner's Tale* might be thought of as "the Pardoner's Tale," that is, a tale thought out and conceived and written by Chaucer as an expression of the Pardoner's character. But it is still the tale told by the Pardoner, and it is impossible to forget the context in which it is told, and the person who tells it. The effect of this continued awareness is to strike a chill in us at the gulf that exists between his words and his understanding. The smoothness of his performance, though it may compel a reluctant admiration of the power of his will, is all the more shocking in relation to his reptilian deadness to all that he says. And though he may have seemed an unusual portrait in his day and perhaps the suggestions of physical deviancy are intended to explain or rationalize his unusualness — he is only unusual in being rarely portrayed, for his kind is ubiquitous, and his inheritors are all around us, in our own day, in salesmen and politicians and all other public traffickers in words for profit.

Finally, if we believe that Kittredge's instinct was right, and that neither we nor Chaucer could bear a vision' of a totally depraved human being without redeeming features, there is the glimpse of the stirring of spiritual life in the Pardoner which is given in the portrait and words of the Old Man. It seems appropriate that this obscure and ambiguous movement of inner life should be made apparent, not in his own words about himself – since these after all are part of the carapace of oblivion that be has allowed to grow around himself – but in the self-revelation prompted by the imaginative act of telling a story.Only thus can the Pardoner uncover his consciousness of his outcast state.

Q.10. Discuss the element of Queer Performativity and the Natural in Chaucer's Physician's and Pardoner's Tales

or

Q. Analyse the gender identities discussed in Chaucer

Some ways that queer theory offers a methodology less likely, at least at the moment, to colonize and erase the differences of the pre-modern body. While not averse to a certain "strategic essentialism" (to use Spivak's turn of phrase), queer theory seeks to historicize and deconstruct the activities of identity politics. In contrast to the latter's stabilizing categories, the term "queer" would resist nominalization, functioning as an adjective, adverb, even verb, stressing epistemology rather than ontology. Emphasizing the performativity of gendered and sexualized identities, and stressing the impossibility of "proving" sex, sexuality, and gender by recourse to a prior, foundational biological body, queer theory thus attempts to map a more dynamic, less assured account of the body in motion within prevailing discourses of power. Moreover, it is precisely in seeking such destabilizing dis- identifications that the queer project should find points of intersection with feminist and post-colonial inquiry.

As Butler suggests, it ought "to be possible to assert a set of non-causal and non-reductive relations between gender and sexuality, not only to link feminism and queer theory, as one might link two separate enterprises, but to establish their constitutive inter- relationship." For "no one term can serve as foundational, and the success of any given analysis that centers on any one term may well be the marking of its own limitations as an exclusive point of departure."

But how exactly might the gay male / queer / feminist medievalist go about this? In the title chapter of his recent book, Lee Edelman proposes a project of "homographesis" to critique the current cultural conceptualizations of gay identity. For Edelman the term homographesis maps simultaneous processes of oppression and resistance inherent in modern reading strategies. In the first instance, homographesis signifies the process by which dominant ideological strategies assign to gay bodies a visible "difference." Thus as Edelman describes it, "the construction of homosexuality as a subject of discourse, as a cultural category about which one can think or speak or write, coincides . . . with the process whereby the homosexual subject is represented as being, even more than inhabiting, a body that always demands to be read, a body on which his `sexuality' is always inscribed." . But Edelman also outlines another, resistant homographesis, a reading and writing practice that counters the labour of disciplinary inscription by resisting categorization, that is "intent on de-scribing the identities that [a conserva- tive social] order has so oppressively inscribed" .

Edelman's analysis thus helps me, as a product of that modern regime, variously constructed as homosexual/gay man/queer, to dis-identify and destabilize current oppressive modes of representation, to think otherwise my own place within the present. But if I want to adjust Edelman's discussion of difference to suit a late medieval context, I need both to substitute gender for sexuality categories—that is, "the feminine" for "the homosexual"—and to retheorize the relations between gender, sex, and sexuality. Thus: "the construction of the feminine as a sub- ject of medieval discourse, as a cultural category about which one can think or speak or write, coincides . . . with the process whereby the feminine/feminized subject is represented as being, even more than inhabiting, a body that always demands to be read, a body on which his/her gender/sexuality is always inscribed."

For there may be analogies between medieval sodomite and modern homosexual as subject categories negatively interpellated by dominant culture; it may even be possible to discern the occasional utopic resistance to such representations, anticipating modern "gay" liberation, as James Miller has recently argued for the newcomers who have no name for themselves in Dante's *Purgatorio* 26 . But in the end neither the homosexual nor his more optimistic gay younger brother will be found in medieval representational practices because they are produced along modern not pre-modern axes of difference. What this indicates is not that it's impossible or irrelevant to talk about sexuality (in the sense of an identity organized around a bodily reading of sex, gender, sexual practice difference), only that it shouldn't be the modern hetero/homo axis of sexuality we are presuming or seeking.

So too, with sex difference. The work of Laqueur, Cadden, and others is making us increasingly aware of the instabilities and slippages inherent in medieval somatic models of sexual difference. Whether a one-sex model that views the female body as an inferior male body turned in on itself or a humoural model organized around differences in vital heat, medieval views of biological sex and the difference they inscribe on the body seem far less stable and absolutist than the modern two-sex model, and less likely foundations for cultural meaning in the Middle Ages.

Thus the process of identification that happens in modern dis- cursive regimes along parallel essentializing axes of sex (male/female), sexuality (homo/hetero), and race (white/black), in medieval practice might more likely take place along the axis of gender (masculine/feminine). Essentialized gender difference provides the stabilizing foundation by which medieval dominant culture regulates "the natural." In doing so, the suppressed/oppressed category of the feminine inscribes and identifies a greater variety of othered bodies—

women's, heretics', Jews', Saracens', effeminates', sodomites'—than is the case in modern Western regimes of representation.

Moreover, I would argue that the connection made throughout the Middle Ages between an essentialist gender system and a coer- cive narrative frame provides one of the controlling fantasies by which medieval dominant culture constitutes and maintains its identity. Such a model of "the natural" presupposes for the male or female body, or by analogy the sexualized textual body, a structuring gendered frame that either authorizes its inherent truthfulness as "the natural" or condemns its lack as perversity. Just as an unstable sexual body needs to be framed by a hierarchized and essentialist account of gender difference, so too with the analogous sexualized textual body. Rather than text or author providing the foundational moment for cultural production, the instabilities occasioned by their dependence upon material, and thus ephemeral and contingent, media demand the stabilizing frame of a "higher" authority in order to make manifest an essen- tial truthfulness and "masculine" will. Virginity (and its lesser cousin, chaste procreation) delineate the true nature of the "masculine" will for the sexes; just as citation of authorities, allegorical explication, or sententious kernel of wisdom, do for the text. The frame of gender and narrative authority then becomes the controlling presence that warrants the body's con- tinued existence and usefulness as signifier.

In this model the feminine can signify only as a ventriloquized voice and a dummy's body, everything which the masculine is not. As such, the feminine must be fantasized as Other in order to be absolutely transformed into speaking pictures of the truly masculine: as with female saints like St. Cecilia, or Saracen and Jewish converts, who all surmount their natural bodily weakness by manifesting a higher, "masculine" will. Or the feminine must be absolutely expunged (as with heretics and disobedient Jews or the effeminate Appius in the Physician's tale), or exiled beyond the margins (as in Saracen kingdoms of the East), or hermetically sealed (as in the Jewish ghettos of European Christendom).

However, if this essentializing connection between gender and narrative frame constitutes the coercive fantasmatic ideal of medieval dominant culture, the performativity inherent in its actual cultural instantiation guarantees that both masculine will and narrative authority remain far more anxious and unstable sites of meaning than their "nature" would appear to allow. In the remainder of this paper I want to focus on one such moment in the performativity of medieval gender difference: Fragment VI of the Canterbury Tales (in particular on the Physician's tale, but with brief reference to the Pardoner and his tale).

Throughout, the Physician's tale focuses on the care of masculinity necessary to secure the proper procreation/ reproduction of masculine identity and authority. To do this, his tale enacts a series of transcendental metaphoric substitutions: Virginia stands in for Virginius, Virginius for Nature, Nature for "my lord" God, copy for original. Stabilizing and securing Virginius' name thus secures not only his individual authority as potent patriarch but the originary status of all patriarchal authority and control. Curiously, then, the sex of Virginia's body is at once central and irrelevant to a tale concerned less with the inscription of sex difference than with "proving" the natural ability of an active and essential "masculine" will to frame and control the perversity of a passive and accidental "femininine" carnality. What gives biological "women" like Nature and Virginia instrumentality in The Physician's Tale, then, is their ability to stand in for and give voice to the will of the Father. And in order to do that and be properly mas- culine, their bodies must signal away from irrelevant material accidents of sexed and sexualized bodies ("the feminine"), back to some always already present originary ("the masculine"). The "a" of Virginia's name thus indicates carefully gendered grammatical control; for as subject it should point only to a vir- ginal rootedness in the antecedent will of the Father. In this way, conformity of the (wo)man's body to the inherent, "masculine" will of Nature brings about the rule of the universal transcendent will of God.

Thus, when the perverse gaze of Appius threatens to sully first the body of purity (Virginia) and then its essence (Virginius' reputation), the "natural" order must be inscribed on the physical and social body in ever more extreme ways. Because the distinction Virginius/Virginia should signal only accidental, not essential, difference, when Appius desires Virginia's female body rather than her signification as emblem of Virginius' power, he sexualizes and feminizes both Virginia's and Virginius' body, disrupting the normal homosocial exchanges within proper mas- culinity. Appius thereby feminizes his own signifying power as a proper man, foreclosing on his own agency as his actions objec- tify and bring into view his own excessive materiality. Moreover, such gender slippage threatens the hierarchized binaries of accident/ essence, lying/truth, perverse/natural, that gender essentialism maintains, and exposes as proximate a feminizing, cupidinous perversity proper masculinity insists must always be out- side itself.

To deny such perversity, it seems, the tale must excise the accidental altogether—whether in cutting off Virginia's head, in hanging Appius, or in denying its own embodied state as fable— all in order to maintain the active subject position defined as proper masculinity. In particular, the tale asserts its status as authoritative text by emphasizing the absence of narrative play: "this is no fable, . . . The sentence of it sooth is, out of doute." (VI.155-7). At every level materiality is rendered unproblemmatic by a series of metaphoric substitutions that occlude the various sexual/textual bodies encountered in the tale. In this world, it would seem, there is no time to "complain," no allowance for individual desire, for accidents of time and place. The truth will out no matter what. The textual body, like Virginia's, is a dispensable and unproblematic vehicle; what's crucial for this foundational myth of purity is the con- tinued vitality of an essential masculine presence.

But there remains a residue of the personal and rhetorical, even in such a simplifying, pared down account. And in that sense the "body" of the Physician inheres in his tale, and in doing so, exposes a "me" (objectifiable and appropriable) to view. Only by extreme, coercive activity on the part of Virginius, the Physician, and the other successful men who follow their example in framing and controlling what the tale means, can the individual and the ideological be aligned as one and the same activity. For the supposedly "natural" boundaries separating Virginius from Appius, masculine from feminine, essential truth from perverting falsity, are themselves constructions requiring the continuing "work" that (1) Virginius does to maintain intact what Virginia means, notably by cutting off her head; that (2) the Physician does to the materia of his text, by attempting to excise its materiality as fable; and that (3) the tale's audience (Host and gentils) do, by announcing their "proper" reception of the tale in their rejection of the Pardoner.

The Host's subsequent efforts to appropriate the Physician's "sothe" more actively and renumeratively for his own ends in the present Canterbury "game" foregrounds this residue of the personal even more explicitly. For what the Host so clearly admires is not simply how the Physician as tale-teller was subsumed within a "higher" masculinity and will—as the tale would demand—but rather how, in doing so, the Physician also expressed his own agency and power in shaping and regulating feminine lack and perversity.

The Host responds as one man to another, acknowledging the presence of the Physician as body in his tale constructing a "nature" that demands constant vigilant surveillance of that body in order to avert perversity and loss of con- trol. The Host's comments thus recognize and seek to reproduce the homosocial "packaging" of identity taking place in the Physician's tale, providing an insightful account of how the Physician secures agency as a true man within the masculinist economy of language and power outlined by his tale.

Moreover, the Host's stress on the Physician's potent "tools of the trade," his emphasis on his own potency by denying a proper "tool" to the Pardoner, and even his more general allu- sions to the medical benefits of recreative play (including storytelling), underscore the material bodies so perfunctorily "killed off" in the Physician's tale. The "sentence" of the Physician's tale would have us focus on Virginia's inner beauty and nobility, that is, on that "original" nobility in her father, and ultimately, in God. The Host's assessment that "too dear she bought beauty" and "her beauty was her death" stresses a material, gendered body; the feminine supplement of the tale— story as story; fable's affect rather than effect. And the Host concludes: "This is a pitous tale for to heere/ But nathelees, passe over; is no fors" (VI.302-3), even though the Physician has been absolutely explicit that his "historial thing" is "fors" and cannot be passed over. But in bringing the materia excised by the Physician's tale back into play in this way, the Host comes dangerously close to destabilizing the Physician's absolutist account of the natural on which dominant culture relies for its hegemonic power.

And these gaps in the seamless garment of masculinity which the Host's appriation of the Physician's tale make visible are precisely what the Pardoner draws attention to at the opening of his tale:

> *First I pronounce whennes that I come,*
> *And thanne my bulles shewe I, alle and some.*
> *Our lige lordes seel on my patente*
> *That shewe I first, my body to warente.* (VI.335-38)

That is, the Pardoner too begins with the assumption that the sign of an originary authority (here papal) will naturally subsume any potentially perverse materiality by overwriting its mas- culine will on that body. The Physician's tale proclaimed itself as a "historial thing" that would necessarily impose its unifying will on all who listened to it; body would "naturally" give way to "sentence.". Yet ironically, it is just this absolutist claim, to produce the same effect no matter what context, that makes the tale such a useful commodity for the Physician and Host, that allows them to use the story of Virginia to gain agency within the existing configurations of ideology. And an awkwardly similar absolutism and commodification of desire characterizes the commerce between the Pardoner and his "lewed" audience. Isn't it just such a "perverse dynamic" that the Par- doner underscores with his reminder that he uses Latin merely to "saffron" his preaching and stir lewed folk to devotion?

In this way the Pardoner makes explicit what the Physician and Host dare not acknowledge: the activity of the objectifying desire of his audience being written on him and the body of his text even as he stands in for "the father" and existing ideological configurations. Whereas the Physician purported to tell one "true" storial thing that repeats the originary name over and over without alteration, even at the risk of killing off the body itself; the Pardoner regularly tells a hundred or more "false japes" in his preaching, chooses "olde stories" not because they will transmit an anterior, primal will, but because they're what his audience wants to hear. And he does the same thing now by situating the exemplary tale demanded by his current audience within a dizzying series of frames that emphasize duplication and dissemination without a controlling, originary subject, the copy- ing of copies, rather than "masculine" procreative reproduction.

Thus when we reach the Pardoner's tale "proper" the kinds of foundational binaries emphasized in the Physician's tale have collapsed. Is it "false jape" or some honest thing, made up or historial, ephemeral or essential, the Pardoner's or our own? The Pardoner's excessive reproduction of the constructions of masculinity and "the natural" taking place within medieval identity politics thus "spoils identity" to the extent that it de-scribes the identities that a conservative social order has so oppressively in-scribed via gender difference.

If the question of "How we work upon the world and constitute it as a social entity" emerges as a crucial one in this Fragment, equally pressing by the end of the Pardoner's tale is our recog- nition of the socially constructed "bodies that matter" that enable this representational "work" to take place, and that are themselves always already subjects and objects of desire. The Pardoner's queer re-presentation of the feminine, to adapt Sedgwick, "far from being capable of being detached from the originary scene of shame, cleaves to that scene as a near- inexhaustible source of transformational energy." As such it constitutes that queer performativity Butler has described as:

> this relation of being implicated in that which one opposes, this turning of power against itself to produce alternative modalities of power, to establish a kind of political contestation that is not a "pure" opposition, a "transcendance" of contemporary relations of power, but a difficult labour of forging a future from resources inevitably impure.

Thus, rather than marking a hermeneutical dead-end of feminine non-identity which can only write true identity as someone else's and elsewhere, the Pardoner's troubling body—ceaselessly per- forming gender and sexuality but never getting it "right"— provides an important way back into the perversities of a medieval politics of representation that the Physician's tale of Virginia and its fictional frame both enact and attempt to disguise.

Q.11. Discuss the elements of Schismatic Heresy in the Performances of the Physician, Pardoner, and Shipman.

Or

Q. Analyse Chaucer's use of source material

When Chaucer has his Physician refer to the story of Virginia as an "historial thyng notable" (VI.156), just after he introduces by name the false and corrupt "juge" Apius, some sense of temporal dislocation may well strike the modern audience's perception of value as that concept resonates through the Doctor's discourse. One ought to ask immediately why such a story is historically notable. The question matters because so many of Chaucer's readers and editors over the years have found the Tale notable only in its failure to exhibit any redeeming artistic value whatsoever. Nevill Coghill, for instance, notes that it is the "faultiest" story in the collection—"in spite of much line-to-line brilliance in the writing"—and "even when it is considered in isolation, simply as a story, it has crushing demerits". The reasons Coghill gives for this assessment are suggestive. He says that "a story that extols the protective murder of a young girl by her father, to save her from violation, is a horrifying piece of sentimental savagery; had the murder been done in the heat of the moment, it might be endurable". Coghill's comments here are suggestive because Chaucer's alterations to his source material deliberately creates its "sentimental savagery," since the murder of Virginia in the original version was committed in the "heat of the moment," whereas Chaucer makes it the result of a contemplative act on the part of her father. We can, of course, simply assume a lapse in Chaucer's artistic ability here and never look for a motive underlying the changes he made to the source. That approach, however, does suggest that contemporary critics are more sensitive to what constitutes horror in human society than fourteenth century poets were.

In order to reach a full appreciation of Chaucer's work in the Physician's Tale, it is necessary to note that he appropriates an idea from the Man of Law's Tale and brings it forward as a supplement to the Physician's speech performance, using it to define the philosophical parameters of his story of Virginia. When Custance responds to her father's decision to send her to Syria to marry the Sowdan, she says that "Wommen are born to thraldom and penance,/ And to been under mannes governance" (II.286-287). The Sowdanesse plucks that same concept out of Custance's mouth and uses it as the foundation of her argument against Christian law, expanding its application to include both men and women as long as they are infidels, when she says to her council that they must resist the spread of Christianity:

What sholde us tyden of this newe lawe
But thraldom to oure bodies and penance,
And afterward in helle to be drawe? (II.337-339)

What is so remarkably striking about the transformation of that statement is its obvious connection to Bakhtin's concept of how the word of the other is transformed by its reinscription from Custance's relatively innocent Christian perception into the Sowdenesse's menacingly destructive Islamic version of the same thing. Custance does not mention the concept of physical slavery ("thraldom to oure bodies") that becomes so important to the Islamic version of the sentiment as the Sowdenesse rejects the possibility of the spread of the "newe lawe."

Chaucer's use of source material often follows a similar pattern of subtle alteration and we need to take note of the fact that these two statements are not exactly identical. In fact, the profound difference between one and the other begs an equally profound question: what precisely is it about Christianity's distinction from Islam that makes the Sowdanesse claim that Christian law will bind Islamic people to a thralldom to their bodies (and penance) which they do not already have and suffer from? One can understand how betraying Mohammed will condemn Islamic people to hell if they convert to Christianity, from their perspective at least. What is considerably less clear is why the Sowdanesse argues that Christian law will convert them to a slavery to their bodies if they accept Christianity.

Christ's law, after all, is supposed to be just as otherworldly in its orientation as Islamic belief claims to be. Both are concerned primarily with the beatific afterlife and how one must behave to have any hope of achieving it. The Sowdanesse's addition of only three words ("to oure bodies") curiously amplifies and transforms Custance's earlier complaint to her father, where she is responding to being sent away to the land of the infidels, into a statement that seems "nowadays" to be slightly off the mark of how Christianity is generally perceived.

Even a cursory reading of the Parson's Tale, however, greatly clarifies the issue. The Parson argues that Adam's sin was essentially one of concupiscence brought about by Eve's "delit of the flessh," when she saw the forbidden fruit. He says:

> The feend tempted Eve—that is to seyn, the flessh—and the flessh hadde delit in the beautee of the fruyt defended, yet certes, til that resoun—that is to seyn, Adam—consented to the etynge of the fruyt, yet stood he in th'estaat of innocence.

Of thilke Adam tooke we thilke synne original, for of hym flesshly descended be we alle, and engendred of vile and corrupt mateere. (X.331-332)

He goes on to suggest that as soon as the soul enters the body it comes into contact with the flesh and is corrupted by original sin (X.333). There is a rather inevitable tendency in this view to equate sex with sin, since human beings are conceived sexually and that act brings the soul into contact with the body in every newly "engendred" person. In a rather lengthy passage outlining venial sin (X.371-380), the Parson lists the following offenses:

Every tyme that a man eteth or drynketh moore than suffiseth to the sustenaunce of his body. . . . whan he is in heele of body and wol nat faste whan other folk faste. . . whan he slepeth moore than nedeth, or whan he cometh by thilke enchesoun to late to chirche, or to othere werks of charitee . . . whan he useth his wyf withouten soveregn desir of engendrure to the honour of God or for the entente to yelde to his wyf the dette of his body . . . [then] thise thynges, and mo withoute nombre, been synnes, as seith Seint Augustyn. (X.372-380)

Since most of the sins he lists are concerned either directly or indirectly with overt physical activity, the fact that Christians are enslaved by their bodies by faith is indisputable. He even suggests that to be ill is better than to be well when he notes that "the flessh is a ful greet enemy to the soule, and therfore, the moore that the body is hool, the moore we be in peril to falle" (X.457). The cure for every sin, of course, is penance.

The fact that Chaucer pulls the notion that Christianity creates a physical slavery among its adherents forward into the world of the Physician's Tale is precisely the proper artistic thing to do for any number of compelling reasons. Both stories sport a veneer of setting in ancient Rome. Both, however, can be shown to possess as much concern for Chaucer's contemporary milieu as they do for the foreign and alien past. The first section of the Man of Law's Tale, as already noted, points toward the disaster of the Nicopolis crusade which was raised as a joint venture of militant Christianity against the spread of Islam into the Balkan peninsula in the later half of the fourteenth century, a joint venture because it involved knights loyal to both the Avignon and Roman obediences of the Great Schism, which did not end until nearly twenty years after the crusade in 1417. One can say, then, that the crusade was sent "from Rome" just as Custance was. The result in both cases was the nearly total annihilation of Christians by the infidels. Both stories also concern Christian virgins who are oppressed by "mannes governance": Custance by her father; Virginia by Apius first, and then by her father, Virginius, afterwards. It is also true, of course, that both women suffer in their bodies as much as they do in any other way. Custance is condemned twice to floating aimlessly on the ocean and Virginia losses her head. In short, there are significant parallels between the two stories.

That Chaucer assigns the story of Virginia to a fourteenth century Physician can perhaps only be understood and fully appreciated in light of the idea that Christianity converts, or condemns, women to a thralldom to their bodies and penance. The Physician, as his portrait in the General Prologue makes clear, is primarily concerned with material reality ("he lovede gold in special"—I.444) and because of his profession is given to the treatment of a person's physical ailments in a context (pilgrimage) that may more properly demand attention to the spiritual needs of his community. If one perceives his audience of fellow pilgrims as patients, a reading of the story suggested afterward by Harry Bailly's response to the speech performance, it is clear that the Physician's words have failed to cure anyone of a spiritual "disese." The Parson's notion that a healthy body is a danger to the life of the soul (X.457) may also implicate the Physician in a kind of inescapable sin by virtue of his profession.

The notion that Christians are forced by their faith to become slaves to their bodies, where spiritual concerns are a predominant aspect of the official discourse of the church, entailing an obvious contradiction, if not outright hypocrisy, which has always coloured the concerns of the official doctrine of the ecclesiastical estate, comes clearly into focus in the Physician's performance because he is a materialist who has been given, or foolishly takes upon himself, the impossible task of addressing the spiritual needs of Harry Bailly's flock. Chaucer plays him off against the unspoken existence in everyone's mind of the ideal of absolute perfection in that role which the church has always attributed to Christ as the Great Physician.

The Savior, whose exalted role as "man-God" saves the world of sinners by his sacrifice on the Cross, is both man's best and only hope for the cure of souls. Giving that function over to the Physician of the General Prologue constitutes an inescapably obvious parody which the speech performance actualizes in a complex series of alterations to the source. The changes Chaucer makes in Livy, Jean de Meun, and Gower, if he actually knew all three versions, determine the development of characterization and event along the lines of his conscious purpose to create a parody of "mannes governance" of every woman's "thraldom to [their] bodies and penance" that both Custance and the Sowdanesse mention in the Man of Law's Tale.

Some critics of the Physician's Tale have objected to Chaucer's addition of the long digression on "governance" to his sources (VI.72-102), claiming in general that it detracts from the swift execution of the moral sentence required by an exemplum. Careful analysis of the passage, however, in light of what has already been said about the relationship between "mannes governance" and Christianity's enforcement of a law that makes women thralls to their bodies and penance, reveals that those objections run largely against the intentions of Chaucer's design in pairing the Physician and the Pardoner together in Fragment VI of the Ellesmere sequence. The Physician says:

And ye maistresses, in youre olde lyf,
That lordes doghtres han in governaunce,
Ne taketh of my wordes no displesaunce.
Thenketh that ye been set in governynges

Of lordes doghtres oonly for two thynges:
Outher for ye han kept youre honestee,
Or elles ye han falle in freletee,
And knowen well ynough the olde daunce,
And han forsaken fully swich meschaunce
For everemo; therfore, for Cristes sake,
To teche hem vertu looke that ye ne slake. (VI.72-82)

The first three lines here need to be read as mockery unless one can believe that a man who tells the story of a father who cuts off his daughter's head to preserve her virginity actually cares if he offends an apostrophized governess or two. The Physician surely does not believe he will offend anyone by saying they have kept their honesty. He must, therefore, mean to imply that the other reason is the one that has brought them to the occupation of being governesses and explains why they are so well-equipped to perform that service to the lords. They know the "olde daunce" (sexual intercourse) and may, or may not, have managed to forsake it for "everemo," as he implies they must do if they are going to be able effectively to "teche hem vertu." And finally, what precisely is it they must "ne slake?" Does he mean teaching "vertu"; or avoiding the "olde daunce?"

Chaucer probably clarifies that point in his depiction of the Physician's character when he has him speak directly to fathers and mothers in closing the digression. He says that if they exhibit "necligence in chastisynge" to the extent that their children perish ("perisse"), the parents themselves "shul it deere abeye" (VI.98-100). The one thing Virginius can never be faulted for is showing any reluctance to chastise Virginia, since he cuts off her head simply because she has inspired a corrupt judge to lust after her excessive physical beauty, if Harry Bailly is to be taken seriously, or because of her excessive virtue, if the Physician has read his own sentence correctly. One can argue that both qualities are the de facto causes of her murder. The point to be taken here, whatever the cause might be for Virginia's death, is that the Physician's Tale severely undercuts and calls into question the validity of the idea that Christian law should be read in such a way as to force women especially, and everyone else in general, to become thralls to their bodies and penance "under mannes governance." That is what happens to Virginia and no one has ever argued that she deserves the fate she receives.

One obvious intention of approaching Chaucer's Physician in this way is to suggest that he plays the deliberate role of the fool in telling the story of Virginia's murder. That reading may seem contradictory in one sense because there is nothing parodically humourous about a father who cuts off his daughter's head in order to present it to the corrupt judge who threatens to rob her of her virginity. In comments M. M. Bakhtin makes about the role of the rogue, the clown, and the fool in medieval literature, he suggests that, while the characterization of the three forms may differ slightly in actual application, the author's objective in having them in place never varies. That purpose is to unmask the hypocrisy or duplicity of the official word of a society's dominant discourse. While it might also be true that the Physician does not play a traditional role as a fool, Harry Bailly's ridicule of his speech performance, especially in the Host's deliberate use and misuse of medical jargon (VI.304-307), referring to his self-diagnosed heart-attack ("cardynacle"—VI.311-312), for instance, and in his jest about having "oure lady Seinte Marie" (VI.308) bless the Physician's "urynals," the Doctor is exposed as a man too foolish to be trusted in his attempt to create or project the proper curative or moral atmosphere necessary to sustain the telling of a serious tale of moralitas.

The connection this has to Chaucer's motivation in placing the Physician's Tale at the beginning of part two of the Canterbury pilgrimage, as the first story in the final twelve tales yet to be told, is purely a structural decision on the one hand but is a decision that speaks directly to the development of his theme in the tale-structure of the work as a whole on the other. Implying that the Physician ought to be read as a type of the "Great Physician," but one who is clearly inept and medically suspect, since he fails to provide any sense of cure to his patients, constitutes a vital ground upon which Chaucer builds a parodic interplay against the dominant discourse of the church in spiritual matters where they intersect with the notion that Christian believers are traditionally seen and described as becoming thralls to their bodies and penance. This plays out against "mannes governance," of course, since the church's ruling hierarchy is essentially masculine.

Another way to approach this same issue is through Chaucer's use of pagan myth to suggest the Physician's connection to the Great Healer of Christian faith. He does this initially by referring to Esculapius in his portrait of the Physician in the General Prologue (I.429) as being one of the Doctor's medical authorities. Balancing Esculapius against Christ simply juxtaposes the great healer of the ancient and pagan world against the Great Physician of the contemporary Christian milieu of Chaucer's era. Chaucer approaches the subject of Esculapius's birth in the Manciple's Tale but does not include every detail about the affair in his redaction of Ovid's story. In the Metamorphoses, Ovid relates the fact of Coronis's infidelity, which is communicated to Phebus by the white raven, as the Manciple says.

In the Manciple's Tale, however, mention of the unnatural birth of Esculapius is not included in the story. Esculapius was torn from his dead mother's womb by Phebus after the god killed her and was given into the care of the Centaur Chiron, who taught him the arts of medicine. Being a demi-god, Esculapius is immortal and hence cannot die. As the fates would have it, however, Esculapius gains the power to raise the dead from the realm of Hades, an act which angers the god of the underworld, and Esculapius is killed by a lightening bolt from Jove. Later, Esculapius is restored to life; that is, he is resurrected from the dead.

The most obvious connection this material from Ovid's story has to Fragment VI and Chaucer's concern there with physical and spiritual healing concerns the identity of the old man who leads the three revelers to "Deeth" in the Pardoner's Tale. One can say, in fact, that Esculapius acts as a bridge between the two narrators in the Fragment. A close reading of the old man's characterization and interaction with the three revelers reveals a series of parallels with the mythic figure of Esculapius that makes Chaucer's intention to identify him as such apparent. The Greek form of the name (Asclepius) itself means "unceasingly gentle" and Chaucer marks that aspect of his character immediately upon his appearance in the Tale when the Pardoner describes how he greets the revelers: "This olde man ful mekely hem grette" (VI.719). The rioters respond to his greeting by calling him a "carl, with sory grace" and ask impertinent questions, completely ignoring throughout the encounter even the most minimal demands of courtesy and gentillesse. The old man refuses to be provoked by their unrelenting rudeness and threats of physical violence, taking his leave of them 53 lines later by commending them to the safety of God's grace: "God save yow, that boght agayn mankynde,/ And yow amende!" (VI.766-767). One aspect of a sense of schismatic heresy that can be gotten from the scene concerns the fact that the old man's blessing and God's grace do not save the three revelers. The blessing of a "Great Physician," pagan though he may be, and their refusal to "amende," mark them for the same kind of spiritual death everyone else in the century faced because of the Schism.

The Latin form of the name, which seems more likely to contain a knowledge Chaucer would have known, means "that which hangs from the esculent oak", where Chaucer's spelling of the name ("Esculapius") is wholly consistent with the "edible" signature of the tree. This reading of the Latin plays well into the subject of the Pardoner's concerns with gluttony. The reference, of course, is to mistletoe, which, if consumed in too great a quantity, can be poisonously fatal. Robert Graves notes that the parasitic plant was regarded as the oak-tree's genitals, and when the Druids ritually lopped it with a golden-sickle, they were performing a symbolic emasculation. The viscous juice of its berries passed for oak-sperm, a liquid of great regenerative virtue. Sir James Frazer has pointed out in his Golden Bough that Aeneas visited the Underworld with mistletoe in his hand, and thus held the power of returning at will to the upper air.

The fact that the old man points the revelers specifically to an oak tree ("Se ye that ook?"—VI.765), telling them that he has recently left death there himself ("For in that grove I lafte him"—VI.761), where they find instead "Wel ny an eighte busshels" (VI.771) of gold florins and suspend their search for "Deeth" (VI.772), suggests strongly enough that Chaucer may well be drawing here on his own natural knowledge of native English myth and legend as a way of supplementing his Latin source to identify the character of the old man as Esculapius. That the Pardoner does not "wynne" the pilgrims' gold at the end of the Tale also suggests he is cut off, even emasculated, in his desire to enrich himself. The fact that Harry Bailly threatens to castrate him functions as a further sign of his failure to win the pilgrims' gold and also points compellingly to this reading of the Pardoner's story. It does not overburden one's sense of logic to equate the gold florins with the golden bough of the mistletoe in light of the Pardoner's avaricious interest in money, as he "quytes" the Physician, who shares the same overblown concern for gold, when that is conjoined with all the other parallels this interpretation suggests. Once again it seems imperative to note the significance of the reference to the "Great Physician" that both stories draw to our attention. The failure to cure body or soul in Fragment VI stems from the condition of schismatic heresy in the church.

The Pardoner's sexual deformity, if it actually exists, can be read quite comfortably in the context of the "symbolic emasculation" associated with Druidic legend. The "stile" (VI.712), where the revelers encounter the old man, suggests the existence of a barrier between one world and another—or the next—that must be crossed in order to reach the killing ground in the sacred grove of trees where the murders actually take place. Graves also notes that in sacred rituals "the blood of the sacrificed oak-king, or of his child surrogate, is likely to have been dispensed, as well as mistletoe juice" . The fact that the youngest rioter, chosen through the drawing of lots, is killed by his knife-wielding companions when he returns from the town, while they both die from ingesting the poison he left for them in the wine, is consistent with the terms of the ritual sacrifice associated with the oak-hero. Gluttons, in this case, overindulging in the sacred juice of the mistletoe/wine, die. That Chaucer's Pardoner draws this element of his story from pagan myth and legend, the very ones that Christianity struggled so long to overcome and supplant in native England, can come as no surprise to anyone, since that is perfectly consistent with his very nature. He does promise, with his bulls of indulgence, a way out of the underworld (purgatory) to anyone foolish enough to invest in his style of "grace." The fact that he exchanges that passage for gold also binds his actions, in another comic-ironic twist, to the golden bough of classical myth. The fact that Chaucer does not mention the birth of Esculapius in the Manciple's version of the story serves to double the sense of how lost and forlorn ordinary Christians were during the Schism, since the "Great Physician" was never born at all in the story that concludes the fabula told before the Parson begins his sermon.

To return to the question of whether the Physician is deliberately cast in a parodic role and takes on the character of the rogue or the fool consciously in his speech performance, or whether he is merely inept as a story-teller and makes a fool of himself because he does not know better than to take on a theme beyond his own verbal and intellectual expertise, is one that cannot be answered on the basis of Harry Bailly's response to Virginia's fate. As we have already seen, Harry's perception of Chaucer's intent, and it is Chaucer who determines the Physician's role in the context, cannot be trusted to tell us anything about the motivations of his creator. Chaucer's intent, whether the Physician is consciously engaged in achieving it with his maker or not, is to expose the hypocrisy and falsehood that underlies the dominant discourse of the church, especially with respect to the fact or impression that Christians must become thralls to their bodies in the practice of their faith. Bakhtin argues that the rogue and the fool have the right "to be 'other' in this world" because the normal categories of life are ill-suited to them . The Physician has read numerous medical authorities, according to the General Prologue (I.429-435), most of which were probably as obscure to Chaucer's audience as they are to us, whereas "His studie was but litel on the Bible" (I.438), a line that has attracted considerable critical attention in proving one thing or another about the Physician's character. What seems obvious about the juxtaposition is that, in an age dominated by scriptural reality, as the Parson's Tale makes clear, the Physician has chosen for himself another path, one that denies the "normal" categories of biblical study in favour of more arcane and mysterious pursuits that most people do not comprehend. Bakhtin also argues that rogues and fools "see the underside and falseness of every situation" and act in response to that duplicity .

In the case of the Physician, of course, he exposes the falseness and duplicity of Apius's court but, at the same time, because Chaucer manipulates the source material made available to his narrator, the Doctor also calls into question the response of Virginius to the court's corruption by having him carefully and deliberately contemplate, and then perform, a brutal and savage murder against his own innocent daughter. That act cannot be more perfectly described than as one which demonstrates how Christian law, pursuant to virginity especially, makes women thralls to their bodies and penance under "mannes governance."

Coming to terms with this issue in Chaucer's work carries us forward again, without any noticeable discontinuity, to the Pardoner's Tale in Fragment VI. Early critical opinion occasionally refers to Chaucer's Pardoner as a rogue, but without ever developing or pursuing that idea in terms that might bring us to a clearer understanding of Chaucer's intent in his depiction of the man. As already noted, M. M. Bakhtin has provided a useful assessment of the figure of the rogue in his relationship to parodic forms that speaks well and consistently to the issues raised by Chaucer's Pardoner. A significant advantage in Bakhtin's assessment is the fact that he relates it specifically to medieval contexts.

Before turning directly to that assessment, however, it is necessary to take note of the fact that Chaucer's depiction of the Pardoner cannot be characterized as a straightforward presentation of a unidimensional figure. One can argue that Chaucer starts him out as a rogue but changes him into a fool, which is not at all the same thing, when he gives him up at the end of the Tale to trying to sell his indulgences to the pilgrims. In short, "the simpleminded incomprehension of the fool," as Bakhtin puts it, asserts itself in the Pardoner's attempt to sell the power of his relics and indulgences to people who have already heard him admit their authenticity might be questionable. He simply misjudges his audience and his own power to persuade them to his point of view. He must believe at the end of his performance that he has gulled his audience into accepting his promise of pardon in the afterlife. He does not anticipate the possibility that anyone, especially his primary target—Harry Bailly—will stand up with principle between him and the gratification of his desire. His failure to recognize himself as others see him does tend to stamp him clearly as a fool.

Bakhtin characterizes the figure of the rogue under three broad and general categories of place, identity, and behaviour. He notes, for instance, that rogues "carry with them into literature first a vital connection with the theatrical trappings of the public square, with the mask of the public spectacle; they are connected with that highly specific, extremely important area of the square where the common people congregate". This statement reflects several obvious facts about the Pardoner. He makes it clear that his usual audience is composed of "lewed peple." He goes where he finds them; in church preferably because the pulpit from which he preaches acts as the "mask of the public spectacle" behind which the duplicity of his own performance is concealed. Since his performance is sanctioned by the church, his duplicity becomes the duplicity of the official word.

The pulpit reinforces the validity of the seals and signs affixed to his bulls of indulgence. The act we are allowed to witness takes place as a theatrical performance of the road. It is carnivalesque to say the least. His insistence on stopping at the "alestake" so he can "drynke and eten of a cake" (VI.321-

322) draws the ultimate theatrical performance of the medieval church into his parodic play because it reflects the Passion of Christ in the mass.

In discussing the identity of the rogue, Bakhtin notes that "[t]heir very appearance, everything they do and say, cannot be understood in a direct and unmediated way but must be grasped metaphorically . . . one cannot take them literally, because they are not what they seem". With respect to the Pardoner, of course, this evaluation is virtually self-evident. In the General Prologue, Chaucer uses three different metaphorical figures to present various aspects of his character: "Swiche glarynge eyen hadde he as an hare" (I.684); "A voys he hadde as smal as hath a goot" (I.688); and, "I trowe he were a geldyng or a mare" (I.691). Each of these figures has received its share of critical attention and are put forward here only to emphasize the metaphorical aspects of Chaucer's depiction.

The most significant point might be that the Pardoner is metaphorically presented from the inside out, since the glaring eyes are visible to anyone, the voice reflects an interior quality perceived externally, while the reference to the horse, if it has anything to do with his sexual being, is external but concealed beneath his clothes. In the Prologue, the Pardoner identifies himself metaphorically as a bird, "As dooth a dowve sittynge on a berne" (VI.397), when he preaches in church, and later as a serpent, "Thus spitte I out my venym under hewe/ Of hoolynesse" (VI.421-422). The figure of the "dowve" is used by Chaucer to cast a shadow of piety across his speech performance, since the biblical dove metaphorically suggests the Holy Spirit descending from Heaven during Christ's baptism. The fact that it ends up on the roof of a barn in Chaucer's redaction points more than just a subtle finger at his parodic intent.

Given so many metaphorical dodges, it becomes nearly impossible to say who or what the Pardoner actually is; or perhaps more properly in the spirit of Bakhtin's analysis of the rogue, one must recognize the fact that under the various masks of hare, goat, horse, bird, serpent, and savior, there is little or no identity under the Pardoner's metaphorical masks at all. He is so covered over with metaphorical skin that he ceases to exist as anything recognizable as human. Bakhtin states that the rogues' existence "is a reflection of some other's mode of being—and then, not a direct reflection. They are life's maskers; their being coincides with their role, and outside this role they simply do not exist" . In elaborating this final point, Bakhtin argues that "they can exploit any position they choose, but only as a mask" . The rogue's entire purpose "consists in externalizing things" but he is never able to bring out his own character, since he has nothing of his own but is only able to produce "a reflected, alien being" .

Bakhtin also argues that the origin of the rogue and the fool is tied directly to medieval life and literature. He suggests that during the Middle Ages the "feudal structure" of society pervaded all areas of human life with a "vulgar conventionality" that prevented the expression of natural human needs and desires. An example of what Bakhtin is referring to here might be the fact that the Pardoner preaches against gluttony, where eating and drinking, and sexual expression too if lechery is included under the heading of gluttony, are not only natural human instincts impossible to repress but are also, in the case of the first two, absolutely necessary to sustaining life. While excessive eating and drinking may be the actual object of condemning gluttony, where any pleasure at all derived from sex is prohibited, the fact remains that attempts to repress what every person experiences as necessary to life, and hearing those things routinely condemned from the pulpit, can only result in a sense that hypocrisy and falsehood must lie somewhere under the surface of every official speech act pronounced by a representative of the clergy.

The Parson's sermon makes this point perfectly obvious, since everything he condemns, and everything the Sowdanesse objects to, comes back to rest on the condemnation of the physical body. This again is precisely the concept that the notion of Christians becoming slaves to their bodies represents in Chaucer's examination of both physical acts of curing and spiritual acts of absolving sins through penance.

The Pardoner clearly focuses on physical activity considered by the church to be sinful and Bakhtin argues that hypocrisy and falsehood did indeed "saturate all human relationships" during the Middle Ages and that, as a result,

> healthy 'natural' functions of human nature are fulfilled, so to speak, only in ways that are contraband and savage, because the reigning ideology will not sanction them. This introduces falsehood and duplicity into all human life. All ideological forms, that is, institutions, become hypocritical and false, while real life, denied any ideological directives, becomes crude and bestial.

In response to the hypocrisy of the official, direct word, and in forms that are meant to mock and undermine its authority, Bakhtin sees both the rogue and the fool as emergent forces in society directed against the official position of the dominant discourse: "[o]pposed to convention and functioning as a force for exposing it, we have the level-headed, cheery and clever wit of the rogue (in the form of a villain . . . a young itinerant cleric, a tramp belonging to no class), . . . and the simpleminded incomprehension of the fool". The Pardoner's performance exposes, through his failure to collect alms from the pilgrims, the fact that the church, at Becket's shrine, will certainly not fail to "fleece" the pilgrims when they arrive at their destination but will collect as much money from them as it possibly can. Chaucer's parody is meant to place one act beside the other where one cannot help but look beneath the exposed skin of the official, direct word which lives its full and glorious life "under hewe/ Of hoolynesse" at Canterbury. This is not to say that Chaucer necessarily condemns such practices out of hand but, in the age of Schism, where the issue of simony and ecclesiastical avarice have become so public in debate, as Kaminsky suggests, and are seen as causes in themselves for the profound disunity of the church, one must credit Chaucer with bringing those issues to the attention of his audience in the full force of his articulation of them. The fact that Chaucer depicts the Pardoner as a schismatic heretic in the General Prologue suggests his target for parody is the state of the church itself and not some general and non-specific concern for abuse in ecclesiastical circles. That Canterbury itself might be a target of Chaucer's parody is a possibility that cannot be overlooked.

The argument, then, that brings both Tales of Fragment VI together in a single purpose can be found in the fact that the story of Virginia, in its capacity as an "hisrorial thynge notable," is a fictional account of the circumstances that led to the election of Urban VI on April 8, 1378, where the Pardoner's performance is meant to demonstrate the social, political, and ecclesiastical consequences of schismatic heresy in society at large. Reading the Physician's Tale in this context demands recognition of several relatively apparent facts. Chaucer's alteration of his source material, as several critics have noticed, foregrounds the character and fate of Virginia as a central focus of attention, where previous versions of the story concentrated on the political implications of corrupt civil justice in Roman courts of law.

That could also be a concern of Chaucer's, since both civil and ecclesiastical justice in England at the end of the fourteenth century were not paragons of virtuous activity. Chaucer's redaction of the story, however, tends to de-emphasize that aspect of the Tale in favour of a more predominant concern for the state and nature of Virginia's virginal and virtuous character. Going outside Canterbury, as R. Howard Block has attempted to do, for an explanation of Chaucer's possible motives in foregrounding virginity oppressed by "mannes governance," which in this case is more properly called lechery, is actually unnecessary, since the Parson, in two separate passages, provides us with a reasonable cause for Chaucer's decision.

In his discussion of remedies to lechery, the Parson argues that "chastitee" is one available recourse to the avoidance of sin:

The thridde manere of chastitee is virginitee, and it bihoveth that she be hooly in herte and clene of body. Thanne is she spouse of Jhesu Crist, and she is the lyf of angeles. She is the preisynge of this world, and she is as thise martirs in egalitee; she hath in hire that tonge may nat telle ne herte thynke. (X.948-949)

The Physician characterizes Virginia in terms that seem perfectly consistent with the Parson's description of the "spouse to Jhesu Crist". when he says

For in hir lyvyng maydens myghten rede,
As in a book, every good word or dede
That longeth to a mayden virtuous,
She was so prudent and so bountevous.
For which the fame out sprong on every syde,
Bothe of hir beautee and hir bountee wyde,
That thurgh that land they preised hire echone
That loved vertu, save Envye allone, (VI.105-114)

One hesitates to belabor the obvious here but Virginia does seem to be very much the same thing that the Parson's description of the perfect virgin embodies. She is herself best read like a book by other people because in her is everything that "tonge may nat telle ne herte thynke." With the impulse to occupatio aside, the Physician here implies that Virginia's virtue is so complete and absolute that words cannot do justice to her nature—just seeing her is like reading it in a book. The Parson's virgin is the glory ("preisynge") of this world and everyone in Virginia's land, except "Envye allone," who loves virtue, praises her. And, clearly, lechery literally raises her "in egalitee" to the level of the other martyrs when her father cuts off her head to preserve her virginity from being despoiled by Apius's lust. Virginia does not just embody the Parson's word; she enacts it.

That Virginia is also the "spouse of Jhesu Crist" cannot be overlooked or ignored in the wider context of fourteenth century ideological history. In describing his first remedy against lechery, the Parson explains the church's official position with regard to "chastitee in mariage" (X.915). He says:

This is verray mariage, that was establissed by God, er that synne bigan, whan natureel lawe was in his right poynt in paradys; and it was ordeyned that o man sholde have but o womman, and o womman have but o man as seith Seint Augustyn, by many resouns.

First, for mariage is figured betwixe Crist and hooly chirche. And that oother is for a man is heved of a womman; algate, by ordenaunce it sholde be so. For if a womman hadde mo men than oon, thanne sholde she have moo hevedes than oon, and that were an horrible thyng biforn God; and eek a womman ne myghte nat plese to many folk at oones. And also ther ne sholde nevere be pees ne feste amonges hem, for everich wolde axen his owene thyng. (X.920-922)

The true bride of Christ, as the Parson points out, is "hooly chirche" and that inescapable union between the savior and the virgin is the model that underlies all human marriage relationships. A pertinent question here is why Chaucer elected to suppress the existence of Virginia's fiancee, Icilius, from the other versions of the story he may have known. As the bride of Christ, as a symbol of "hooly chirche," Virginia cannot be betrothed to any human being. She must be completely unattached, free of involvement with the human world, so that there will be no impediment to her elevation as the bride of the "Great Physician," who hovers over the story, as its de facto "narrator," until the sword of the Father relieves her of her head ("heved"). This happens because the Roman mob in 1378 threatened to kill the college of cardinals if they failed to elect an Italian (Bartolomeo Prignano) to replace Gregory XI.

In September of that same year, after deposing Urban VI on August 9th, they replaced him with Robert of Geneva (Clement VII) and thereby rendered "hooly chirche" headless because no woman can have "moo hevedes than oon" and no church can survive with more than one pope.

After the church is "beheaded" in the Physician's Tale, Chaucer gives us a "gentil Pardoner/ Of Rouncivale . . . That streight was comen fro the court of Rome" (I.669-671) and we are allowed to witness in every way possible precisely what the schismatic heresy of the fourteenth century gave to each and everyone of its varied citizens—all of whom accompany Chaucer on his pilgrimage.

That Chaucer means for us to read the Pardoner in that way is inescapable because his form of abuse, converting alms collections to his own avaricious use, is precisely the one that Boniface IX condemned in 1390, just before or just after he gave the Pardoner his indulgence. He springs into view like a tree—complete down to his very root—"Radix malorum est Cupiditas!"—and he grows out of the ground of the Schism.

What remains to be seen in this context is how Chaucer linked his Physician and Pardoner to the Shipman's Tale and the rest of Fragment VII in the Ellesmere sequence. That connection rests on the end of Fragment VI, specifically Harry Bailly's threat to castrate the Pardoner, and the first line of the Shipman's speech performance: "A marchant whilom dwelled at Seint-Denys" (VII.1). Some of the questions that can be answered by recognizing Chaucer's intention to link Fragments VI and VII definitively in a straightforward and unequivocal sequence speak to concerns about the state of his work when he died and whether or not Canterbury is whole or fragmentary, revised or unfinished. Was the Shipman's Tale, at some point in the development of the literary production, assigned to the Wife of Bath? Are the apparent feminine references in lines 11-19 of the Shipman's story an indication that, after Chaucer switched narrators for the Tale, he failed to revise his work?

Answering these two questions with ideas that differ from conventional critical wisdom necessitates a reasonable response based on evidence gathered from Chaucer's text in a best case scenario but, failing that, one must offer a reasonable explanation based on the fourteenth century sociohistorical milieu that affected Chaucer's work as he developed the Canterbury Tales as a whole. Qualifying a projection of evidence in this way does not mean that there is none to support the position but does suggest that both approaches are necessary to make the argument convincing.

C. David Benson, in his recent assessment of Chaucer's use of a "dramatic principle" in the Canterbury Tales, cites discussion of the Shipman's Tale as an example of a connection between a narrator and a tale where "the two have nothing in common" . He goes on to assert that the observation of inappropriateness between the two is a "flagrant example" because of "the obvious disjunction between the rough, murderous Shipman of the General Prologue and the cool, sophisticated art of the Shipman's Tale". This issue can be blunted by simply observing that the pilgrims are not credited with creating the stories they tell as literary artists in their own right but are simply repeating stories they happen to know and remember.

In referring to critical traditions relating to the Tale, Benson notes that one group of "dramatic interpreters" sees harmony between narrator and tale because the Shipman might harbor hostility toward merchants . Others argue that it was originally intended for the Wife of Bath because she is the only female member of the company likely to tell such a story. This assumption, as already noted, is based on the apparent references to a feminine identity for the narrator at the beginning of the Tale and, according to Benson, the argument supporting that view is "inherently weak". Frederick Tupper is one critic opposed to the notion that the story was ever intended for the Wife of Bath or for any other female narrator. That same assumption will be stressed here.

The idea that Harry Bailly's threat to castrate the Pardoner both determines and anticipates Chaucer's decision to forego a compositional link between Fragments VI and VII in the Ellesmere sequence is based on the assumption that virtually any member of Chaucer's original audience would have recognized the connection between that threat and the reference to "Seint-Denys" that follows it in the first line of the Shipman's Tale. The fact that a central figure in the plot of the fabliau is a monk "at Seint-Denys," if not one also attached by holy vow to the abbey there as well (though that assertion is made somewhat ambiguous by the evidence of the text itself), does make it clear that Chaucer means for us to associate the exploits of daun John with the well-known and widely disseminated events in the life of another monk connected to that abbey.

The man in question, of course, even if he is never directly named by Chaucer, is Peter Abelard. Since Abelard took his vows at "Seint-Denys," after he was castrated by assailants hired by Heloise's uncle, it requires only a simple and straightforward leap to connect the threat of castration at the end of Fragment VI to the first line of the Shipman's Tale to begin Fragment VII. The connection is so obvious and immediately recognizable, at least to a member of Chaucer's original audience, that no one needed to be told who and precisely what Chaucer meant by the juxtaposition.

That the Shipman might be the proper kind of man to epitomize an assailant capable of committing an actual castration comes complete with the fact that he carries a concealed knife under his arm (I.392-393) and his verbal taunting of the Pardoner in his use of feminine, even wifely, references (VII.11-19) can be read as a kind of verbal castration directed toward his lack of manliness and toward his obvious homosexual association with the Summoner. Reading those lines in this context is made inevitable by virtue of the fact that the Pardoner, when he interrupts the Wife of Bath's Prologue to compliment her ability as a preacher, also claims he had been contemplating marriage (III.165-168). The Shipman takes the opportunity to embarrass him further by suggesting how unclear it is whether, in such a marriage, he would be the husband or the wife. Harry's threat to castrate him prompts the Shipman to respond in kind, an act perfectly consistent within the limits of Chaucer's depiction of the seaman.

The metaphor of the "tonne" (III.170ff), which the Wife fabricates in her response to the Pardoner's comment about his fictitious marriage, that he will "drynken of another tonne,/ Er that I go," and shall "savoure wors than ale" (III.170-171) from her story, also points to the Shipman because of his habit

"Ful many a draughte of wyn . . . ydrawe/ Fro Burdeux-ward, whil that the chapman sleep" (I.396-397). The narrator comments that this sign of his behaviour demonstrates "Of nyce conscience took he no keep" (I.398). One fact these comments establish is that a definitive connection exists between the Wife of Bath and the Pardoner-Shipman transition between Fragment VI and VII, a fact which has drawn many critics to assume the Shipman's Tale once belonged to the Wife of Bath, when in fact it may be more reasonable to assume that Chaucer is simply linking one thing to the other in the normal course of his poetic practice.

Clearly, however, other explanations about the nature of those connections exist naturally in Chaucer's text. The idea that the Shipman is taunting the Pardoner about his claim to be considering marriage, in the context of Harry Bailly's threat to castrate him, which points to Peter Abelard as a monk of the abbey at "Seint-Denys," is a more reasonable, and much more fruitful, line of inquiry than arguing how Chaucer changed his mind and switched narrators without bothering to revise the feminine references out of the Shipman's Tale. All the latter argument demonstrates about Chaucer's poetic vision is that he was incompetent. It not only tells us nothing about his perceptions of fourteenth century social reality; it also obscures our ability to comprehend the heart of his Canterbury project by deflecting our attention away from the actual matters at hand at a point in the unfolding narrative where he has invested a considerable effort to constitute his thematic meaning.

Connecting Chaucer's Shipman's Tale to the life and times of Peter Abelard, who died in 1142, requires the simple recognition that his artistic intent in the use of the fabliau tradition is predominantly parodic. In other words, the love between Abelard and Heloise formulates the ideal against which the affair between the latter-day monk of "Seint-Denys," daun John, and the merchant's wife is played out. Donald R. Howard, in his discussion of Chaucer's fictional techniques, has laid a groundwork for making this essential observation.

He notes, for instance, that many of Chaucer's religious pilgrims "exemplify obsolescent styles of life based on obsolescent ideas and practices" . He also argues that all "reveal what was throughout the Middle Ages the fundamental flaw in the practice of the religious life, that its values and ideals were contaminated by secular—and chiefly aristocratic" styles of life.

This fact is nowhere more obvious than in the issues raised by the Great Schism. Howard asserts that "The Canterbury Tales gives us a picture of a disordered Christian society in a state of obsolescence, decline, and uncertainty; we do not know where it is headed" . One can argue that pilgrimage, as a way of solving the issues of the disunity in the church, is wholly inadequate in its form as Chaucer creates it to address those problems. As a consequence, the pilgrims, and Chaucer himself as a poet, never reach the desired goal of Canterbury and the holy city of Jerusalem. Specifically about the Shipman's Tale, Howard claims it "is downright immoral; in it the most sacred relationships of medieval society (the monk's vows, marriage, brotherhood) are purposefully violated, and the one character who is not a scoundrel, the merchant, is himself venal, stuffy, and credulous—a gull" .

If one accepts Howard's view of Chaucer's work in general, and his perception of the Shipman's Tale specifically, it becomes a relatively simple matter to understand how Chaucer's oblique reference to Abelard, who died two hundred years before Chaucer's birth, becomes a fertile ground upon which to build a definitive expression of the decline of religious principles at the end of the fourteenth century, especially so in the context of the Great Schism.

One must also recognize, of course, that Abelard may not have been the most compellingly saintlike man Chaucer could have chosen as a model upon which to construct his pair of parodic mimes. Abelard was under threat of examination for heresy when he died. He also seduced Heloise while functioning as her tutor and was thought, by her uncle, to have abandoned her in a convent when he grew tired of her affections. That belief prompted the assault which resulted in his castration.

Peter Dronke, in his assessment of the authenticity of the Abelard-Heloise correspondence, a copy of which belonged to Petrarch, notes that the story of the "two lovers had become a romantic legend" as early as the beginning of the thirteenth century (23). He also discusses the fact that Jean de Meun began a translation of the letters and mentions Heloise several times in the Roman de la Rose, all of which indicates that Chaucer probably knew the details of the story by the time he began working on the Canterbury Tales. Chaucer's use of the "romantic legend," which can be called, with certain qualifications, an ideal form of Christian marriage, plays parodically against the total absence of any ideal sentiments in the tale of daun John and the merchant's wife, whose relationship in the Shipman's Tale, apart from its adulterous, and even incestuous, character, is little more than simple prostitution. Chaucer's interest in the marriage of Abelard and Heloise, which was clandestine, turns out to be a complex structural element in the development of his theme in the tale-structure of Canterbury as a whole.

As already noted, for instance, in the Clerk's Prologue, Chaucer refers to John of Legnano who was best known in Europe and in England for his strident defense of Urban VI as the legitimate pope of the Roman church. Urban so appreciated Legnano's support that he offered to elevate the lawyer to his college of cardinals. Tradition has it that Legnano refused the offer because his wife would not agree to enter holy orders herself, which was required by the church of any layman's spouse when he (or she) took the vows of holy office. With regard to Heloise, who was secretly married to Abelard before he became a monk, there is considerable evidence in her letters that she did not want to take holy orders and only married him reluctantly because she believed he was destined to enter the service of God. Dronke notes that "Heloise obeyed Abelard spontaneously, however unwilling she was to become a nun".

The point here, of course, is that the Clerk's Tale, one source of which may be Petrarch, has as its primary theme the subject of a wife's obedience to her husband's will and, in the case of Walter and Grisilda, obedience to that will no matter how unreasonable it may become.

This concept does not disappear from Chaucer's work after the Clerk tells his story, since the poet returns to it parodically in his depiction of the sexual union between daun John and the merchant's wife in the Shipman's Tale. Her disobedience to her husband's will, in the form of her adultery with the monk "at Seint-Denys," reverses the balance of power in fourteenth century male-female relationships where the issue of sovereignty is concerned. William F. Woods argues that "the wife assumes the governance of the merchant's house, and of herself, insofar as she is considered part of his domain" and she "does this by admitting the monk as a substitute master of the house" . Woods also notes that the wife retains her sovereignty over her husband after he returns and the monk departs.

From a structural point of view, the transition from a state of thralldom to her husband at the beginning of the story, which is perfectly consistent with Grisilda's state of being in the Clerk's Tale, to one of mastery over him at the end, where the issue is essentially carnal in the Shipman's version of things, we find an additional transformation back to a purely spiritual state of affairs in the Second Nun's Tale to begin Fragment VIII. In other words, the Shipman's Tale functions as a bridge in the issue of whether a husband or a wife has mastery in marriage: we see Walter dominant over Grisilda in the Clerk's vision of marriage; find a transformation of that formula as the wife takes control of her husband in the Shipman's Tale; and finally, come to see St. Cecile dominant over Valerian in the Second Nun's Tale. St. Cecile, after all, with the assistance of her angel of death, completely dominates Valerian precisely at the point of living asexually with her husband in a chaste marriage. As the dominant partner shifts, we move from sex for the sake of procreation to the glory of

God, to sex for delight in a state that falls to adultery, incest, and prostitution, and, finally, to no sex at all. The transformation of the concepts expressed by the Clerk, of a husband's right to demand total obedience from his wife, begins to shift in the Shipman's Tale, as exemplified in the merchant's wife, and reaches its full realization in Cecile's assertion that an angel of death will slay Valerian "with the dede" if he so much as touches her in "vileynye."

The point of Chaucer's parody, which clearly revolves around the concept of a Christian's thralldom to his or her body and penance, first encountered in the Man of Law's Tale, depends upon the concept of "chastitee in mariage," which is described by the Parson. Where Abelard and Heloise are concerned, who did produce a child named Astrolabe as a sexually active couple, before Abelard entered holy orders and before Heloise became a reluctant nun, the issue was taken out of their hands, so to speak, by the fact that Abelard was castrated by Heloise's uncle.

With respect to Cecile and Valerian, the same issue was removed from their direct control by virtue of the existence of Cecile's angel of death. One can argue here, and probably should, that Chaucer's deepest perception of the issues swirling around Abelard-Heloise, monk-merchant's wife, and Cecile-Valerian are essentially parodic and preeminently meant to be taken as a joke. In terms of the way parody works to undermine and question the official word of the dominant discourse, Chaucer's design in having Harry Bailly threaten to castrate the Pardoner initiates this complex of comparison, contrast, and mockery of the all too serious concerns he expresses in the Parson's sermon. This seems to be the best, most productive way to read Chaucer's purpose.

Another important direction Chaucer's discourse takes here concerns the fact that two instances of moral condemnation directed at Abelard over his affair with, and marriage to, Heloise survive from the time after news of his castration reached the public square. Peter Dronke compares those responses to the kind of discourse common in fabliaux.

One of Abelard's enemies, his former teacher Roscelin, who some credit with the invention of nominalism, wrote a letter to Abelard soon after his castration in which he makes out that Heloise is actually a prostitute supported by the money Abelard makes through his "false and unauthorized teaching". Roscelin, according to Dronke, says:

> You don't even send the money to your whore, to pay for your debauchery, you still take it to her yourself. While you could enjoy her, you paid in advance; now you sin even more, rewarding her for the past debauches rather than buying future pleasures.

Dronke characterizes this passage from Roscelin's letter as being in a vein of "viciousness that is hardly matched even in fabliaux". The point here is that Chaucer may have drawn some of the inspiration for his parody of Abelard and Heloise from the invective directed at the two lovers by Abelard's enemies. There is no evidence, however, that Roscelin's letter to Abelard ever came to Chaucer's attention but one can assume, perhaps, that such vicious attacks circulated as part of the legend itself during Chaucer's lifetime. The fact that prostitution becomes an issue in the Shipman's Tale came to Chaucer from some source or another and reaches back to the Cook's Tale for its structural integrity in the work as a whole. The aptness of Dronke's observation about the fabliau characteristics of the attacks against Abelard's reputation is also worth noting, since Chaucer may have transformed the perception of prostitution in the relationship into an actual example of the genre. If nothing else, the connections to the legend of Abelard and Heloise that seem such an integral part of Chaucer's Shipman's Tale provide it with a wider frame of reference than most scholars have so far found for it.

Placing the Tale in a wider frame of reference, Richard K. Emmerson and Ronald B. Herzman argue that the scene in the garden where the monk and the wife swear oaths to each other is a parodic inversion of the Easter-morning encounter between Mary Magdalen and Christ in which He warns her not to touch Him ("Noli me tagere") because He has not ascended yet to his Father. Chaucer's monk instead "caughte hire by the flankes/ And hire embraceth hard, and kisse hire ofte" (VII.202-203). Emmerson and Herzman argue that the Shipman's discourse shows us how "the love of money has replaced the love of God and the 'privetee' of adultery has replaced the joyous proclamation of charity" that followed the Easter-morning encounter in the biblical garden (167). The scene of oath swearing in the garden, which was meant to conceal rather than reveal the truth, plays into the heart of the problem of abuses in the fourteenth century church, especially where money is exchanged for benefits that are freely given through the church's mediation of God's grace.

The abuse and sin of simony, as always, comes to the surface in Chaucer's parodies of biblical messages. One cannot overlook the fact too that the reference anticipates the real saint's legend in the Second Nun's Tale which has other thematic connections to the Shipman's story. How much more terrible is it that we all see so clearly the decline of the fourteenth century church reflected in the behaviour of the very people who were attempting to reform it and, in the process, see them use money so freely to purchase adultery and incest along the way?

The fact that no one is punished in true fabliau fashion in the Shipman's Tale, even the husband is unaware of his wife's infidelity, suggests that Chaucer sees through the hypocrisy of the notion that every Christian must be made a thrall to his or her body and suffer the consequent penance associated with the sin of physical life. A major part of the problem exemplified by the Great Schism, and here expressed so completely by Geoffrey Chaucer, is that too much of the penance paid for bodily sin becomes an object of greed and avarice in the benefice because it is reduced, not to a spiritual correction, but to financial gain, to money in exchange for salvation (Pardoner's Tale). The formula Chaucer expounds in the Shipman's Tale is that money for sex equals more money for being absolved of the sin of having it in the first place. His motivation for putting it where he does, at the beginning of

Fragment VII, immediately after the Physician and Pardoner clarify the issue, is to anticipate the peace negotiations between England and France (Tale of Melibee) and the solution to the Great Schism which is to follow after the peace is achieved (Second Nun's Tale and the Canon's Yeoman's Tale).

Q.12. Critically analyse the Pardoner's prologue and tale

Or

Q. Do you think Chaucer's characters express any kind of character?

The Wife of Bath and the Pardoner are both given particularly ample space to expose their own way of living before telling their Tales, in developed Prologues which have certain qualities in common. In both cases, the speaker seems unaware that the hearers (the readers) might not be so full of admiration as they seem to be about themselves. Both speak in a rather boasting mode about lives and actions which others might find less than appealing. The Pardoner's Prologue is less lengthy than the Wife of Bath's but serves to provide a powerfully ironic frame to the sermon that forms the body of his Tale. The Prologue serves to make us aware of the difference that can exist between a Tale and its Teller.

Critics often call the form used in these two Prologues 'literary confession' but neither of Chaucer's characters expresses any sign of regret. Rather, the two prologues are rooted in satirical traditions in which a figure embodying some vice speaks a 'confession,' almost entirely without shame, illustrating the way it lives. Chaucer found examples of this in the Romance of the Rose, the Pardoner's Prologue has some vague similarities with the figure Faux-Semblant (False Seeming) found there.

As seen in the General Prologue, a pardoner is a layman who sells pardons or indulgences, certificates from the pope by which people hoped to gain a share in the merits of the saints and escape more lightly from the pains of Purgatory after they died. This particular Pardoner works for a religious house notorious for fraud in this trade. Just as the indulgence bought with money seems to make confession, absolution and repentance unnecessary, so the fact that pardoners had permission to preach in the churches led to a confusion between them and ordained priests (who alone had power to absolve sinners from guilt).

There was widespread dissatisfaction with pardoners (as also with money-loving Friars) in Chaucer's time, and both were popular subjects of satire and joking. This can be found especially in parts of Piers Plowman, which Chaucer may have known. There was a fully developed satire of the avarice and corruption manifested by so many people associated with the Church, an awareness of the failure of many to practice the teachings of Christ. In Chaucer's age that gave birth to the challenge expressed by Wyclif and the Lollards, which in turn later found full expression in Luther's protest and the Reformation.

In the General Prologue, the Pardoner was portrayed as a very strange creature indeed, with physical features suggesting that he is some kind of eunuch and with a faint suggestion of sexual deviancy. None of that plays any role in the Pardoner's Prologue and Tale, which are entirely centered on the Pardoner's professional activities.

At the start of his self-presentation in the Prologue, the Pardoner tells us that he preaches in churches and that he always preaches the same sermon, which he knows by heart, on the text "Greed is the root of evils". He begins by establishing his legal rights, for Pardoners were unpopular with parish priests, as Friars were, since they took money which otherwise might have gone to them.

He begins by advertising a private sideline having nothing to do with his work as Pardoner. He has a collection of 'sacred relics,' bones and rags for which he claims supernatural powers, able to cure sick animals, increase wealth, and make husbands trust unfaithful wives. These desirable effects are all available for a small fee, and he uses a familiar trick to encourage the unwilling to come forward by insisting that those guilty of sin, especially unfaithful wives, must stay in their places and not offer him money. As a result, he expects, no one will dare to hold back. He boasts that this relic-business brings him a hundred marks a year in private income.

Then turning to his preaching, he begins by stressing that his only goal is to get people's money; he expresses total indifference to the fate of their souls in a mocking reference to eternal damnation as 'goon a blackeberyed'. The only other reason he has for preaching is hatred: to attack and defame someone who has dared insult pardoners.

The strongest irony comes in lines 427-31 when he explains that avarice (greed) is his own vice and at the same time the vice he preaches against with such powerful effect that he brings people to repent of their avarice sincerely (but not himself, he is glad to note). His only concern is that, realizing their sinfulness, they give him money to benefit from his pardons. All the money he gets he seems to regard as his own and he explains that he does not intend to be like Christ's apostles who worked hard with their hands; he does not care if he takes from very poor people, so that their children starve, so long as he can enjoy himself. He ends by stressing the irony: he himself is 'a full vicious man; yet he can tell a moral tale.

As the sermon (the Tale) begins, we become aware that there is an additional layer of irony. The sermon he preaches is not only against love of money as such, it first attacks all the 'tavern sins' of lechery, gluttony, drunkenness, which are allied with gambling (a way of getting money without work) and blasphemous swearing, which leads finally to anger, lying, and murder. Before the Prologue began, in the link passage providing the transition from the Physician's Tale to the Pardoner's Prologue, the Host asks the Pardoner to tell 'some mirth or japes' ('solas'). His response is to insist that he must have a drink in an alehouse first. The pilgrims reject the Host's suggestion and demand 'some moral thing' from which they may learn ('sentence'). The Pardoner accepts their request, but he prepares for it by having a drink. He is not only guilty of avarice, but also of frequenting taverns.

The Pardoner's opening denunciation of the tavern sins gains its force by two main strategies. First, he evokes the ugliness associated with each of the sins, provoking physical disgust; in addition he uses exclamations (apostrophe) to denounce the sins. Second, he lards his sermon with biblical and classical references, giving examples of the sin and its punishment or quotations attacking it.

In line 660 he finally intervenes to indicate the start of what he considers to be his 'Tale' although his sermon has begun long before. The Tale is the central, developed exemplum forming the central 'punch' of his attack on avarice. It is the well-known tale of the three 'riotours' who end up killing each other for greed.

This exemplum is widely admired (like the Miller's Tale) for the sheer artistry of its composition. It develops far beyond the strict demands of its sermon-frame, as can be seen from the entire opening section, in which the riotours are confronted by the personification of Death and set out with drunken bravado, like knights on a fantastic adventure, to kill Death. This serves to bring them face to face with the Old Man at the stile who longs to die (because his life is over and his conscience is at peace), who chides them for their violent language and insulting attitude, then prays that God will bring them to repentance as he directs them toward the grove where, he says, Death awaits them.

None of this is strictly necessary, all that is required is: "One day three friends discovered a pile of treasure hidden in a forest." The accumulation of detail, particularly the much-discussed Old Man, serves to bring increased irony (even poetic and religious depth) to the exemplum that then follows its familiar course to the disaster. The story is an exemplum illustrating not so much the text "Greed is the root of all evil" as the (unquoted) text "the wages of sin is death".

The Pardoner continues his memorized sermon to its standard conclusion which includes an invitation to come up and make offerings to receive the pardons. When this is done he turns triumphantly to the Pilgrims: "And lo, sires, thus I preach." This ought to be the end, only he cannot stop there. He may be thought to see that his Tale has had its usual effect, that the Pilgrims too are pondering deeply on their own forms of greed. He sees an occasion to make some extra money and (being greedy) cannot resist it. He becomes the eager salesman and forgets that he has begun by treating the Pilgrims as sharers in his secrets (which includes his contempt of the gullible people who believe his descriptions of his 'relics').

He pinpoints the Host (who keeps a tavern) as most likely to be feeling guilty of tavern sins and tries to pressure him. The result is a dispute that the Knight has to resolve, by forcing the Host and the Pardoner to kiss so that an atmosphere of harmony and mirth can be restored.

The main interest of the Pardoner's Prologue and Tale, taken as a whole, is the complexity of the irony. In the overall exploration of the functions of sentence and solas in the Canterbury Tales, we see here how a Tale can contain deep sentence and yet be told by a teller who is completely untouched by it, so firmly committed he is to the opposite values. The Pardoner has composed this wonderfully powerful Tale (sermon) in such a way as to move his hearers to the utmost. Only his motivation in doing this is not love (a desire to save them from their sins) but vice (a desire to make them anxious so that they give him much money).

This recalls the classical debate about whether a deed can be termed a 'good action' if it is done for bad reasons, with evil intentions. The Pardoner's Prologue and Tale confronts us with the question (already posed in other ways by the Miller's Tale) as to what makes a 'good' story. Can a 'good tale' (a potentially prize-winning one) be termed 'good' when it is told by such a shameless scoundrel for entirely selfish and indeed sinful reasons? Is this nonetheless a 'moral tale'?

Such questions make it clear that Chaucer was sensitive to the role of the reader / hearer in the interpretation and evaluation of texts. The complexities of response to the Pardoner's tale-telling may be compared to the equally complex responses provoked by the Clerk's Tale, be it within the text, or among its readers. The Pardoner is a prime example of one who refuses to listen, whose folly or disbelief is such that he firmly opts for this world's petty happiness ('Nay, I wol drynke licour of the vyne / And have a joly wench in every toun.' And to hell with hell!

Q.13. Discuss The Canterbury Tales as Framed Narratives.

Or

Q. Explanations of the function of the Prologue and frame of the Canterbury Tales which fall back on the Gothic nature of the late medieval period may to some extent are right. Do you agree? Discuss

Or

Q. We can, if we wish, look upon two narrative levels—the level of the world of fact and the level of imaginative creation—as an imitation of life itself as it is lived. Elucidate

Robert Jordan in his interesting book has made the point that "the Canterbury Tales... invites piecemeal criticism; it also invites the total view. In the equality of these two claims on our attention lies much of the critical problem." Jordan tends to see the historical explanation of this paradox in the Gothic nature of Chaucer's art, the dominant aesthetic mood of the period, wherein "the total form is determined by the accumulation of individually complete elements." The whole can be regarded as a collection of complete parts which involve varying perspectives and unusual juxtapositions, the very opposite of modern "organic" art wherein the parts are at least theoretically subordinate to the whole.

Although I think that the notion of modern art as organic must be qualified and questioned, there is a certain force and validity to Jordan's distinction between medieval and modern art. Modern art expects the parts to be somewhat subordinate to the whole. The dominant stress of New Criticism was on the organic nature of art. This principle applies mainly to certain poets and novelists of the Renaissance and later periods but certainly not to all. The Victorian novelists did not write organically. Many of the eighteenth-century poets did not. On the other hand, some medieval literature is organic— Gawain and the Green Knight, for instance, and some of Chaucer.We do not, therefore, have to relate the individual Canterbury tales to the frame in any psychological, symbolic, or dramatic manner, but we can treat them as separate units. We can look at the frame separately as at another part of the poem, as well as a unifying device. We need not be concerned with the dramatic unity of the Canterbury Tales.

I do not, however, deny that some relation even if not an organic one, exists between the frame and the tales. The former is at least causative and authenticating. As we shall see, it provides the narrative cause for the other narratives, and it attempts to authenticate the stories, that is, to help make the reader or audience suspend their disbelief. This is the usual procedure in most collections of tales. We shall here examine the rather complex background of the frame and its numerous aesthetic functions to see what light this knowledge may throw on Chaucer's general intention. It may help us to learn how Chaucer himself regarded his great masterpiece.

There is a sense, it must, however, be acknowledged, in which the tales—or most of them—are also reflections of their tellers, and this relationship adds another dimension to their complexity of perspective and meaning. This aspect has, however, been much overstressed by early twentieth-century criticism, an emphasizing which has blurred the structure of the units in their own right. Chaucer is a great psychologist, but he was not the exclusive psychologist-realist and prober of the human heart that modern critics and scholars prodded by early twentieth-century interests have made him out to be. Modern criticism, with its strong mimetic bias, has tended to emphasize character and dramatic incident at the expense of structure and sequence, and it is time to redress somewhat the balance. Chaucer was influenced by the literary and rhetorical tradition as much as by life.

There were many possible precedents for a collection of tales more or less unified in some way, and before we proceed further we should glance briefly at some of these collections.

As Nevill Coghill has pointed out, Chaucer's idea of a collection was novel and original, but he could also have been indebted to predecessors. He certainly would have relied in some way, no matter how original his idea was, on the tradition of a collection of tales to interest readers. We must then look at several possible exemplars.

Before we go into some detail, it is important to note the religious and moral suggestions which a collection of tales would connote to readers in fourteenth-century England. Not all of Chaucer's models are religious, but the really popular collections of tales had a didactic purpose. Collections of saints' lives, of fables, of miracles of the virgin, and of exempla for sermons certainly provided the fundamental exemplars for Chaucer and even Boccaccio.These collections had a practical purpose and came into existence for the convenience of religious teachers.

I do not wish to deny that early secular collections like The Seven Sages and other Oriental collections may have influenced Chaucer in some way. I think, however, the English audience, even a court audience, would have normally expected a didactic and religious purpose in any collection of tales presented to them inasmuch as these didactic assemblages were the most common type of narrative collections in the period.

The twelfth century for the first time in the West saw the development of collections of tales, tales primarily for the convenience of preaching and devotional purposes. The earlier collections such as the Vitae patrum and some hagiographic collections were essentially for monks, making provision for communal and spiritual readings in the monastery. The Moslem world, though these were mainly secular and entertaining, did have collected and framed tales dating from before the twelfth century—notably the Arabian Nights (in some of its forms) and The Seven Sages. Among Oriental fable collections the Arabic Kalilah and Dimnah or Fables ofBidpai are also of early date. Nevertheless The Seven Sages and Kalilah were not translated into Western languages before the twelfth century.Aesopic collections made in classical times and Ovid's Metamorphoses were, however, known. The latter at the beginning of book 4 even has three daughters of King Minyas carry on discussions between their tales.

The great upsurge in collections dating from the twelfth and thirteenth centuries is due, as might be expected, to a demand for moralizing stories as literate and religious audiences increased in size. Collections of tales were useful for preaching friars who turned increasingly to sermons to win over urban audiences. Stories and anecdotes have always been used in teaching but the notion of an organized collection of such, if not new in the West, at least received a new attention. The later Middle Ages is a great period of collected stories—the legends of the Virgin began to appear in the twelfth century, and proliferated until the Reformation; exempla books are very numerous indeed in the same period; great legendaries, especially Jacob of Voragine's Golden Legend, flourish; even works on other subjects, like Peraldus 's Summa virtutum et vitiorum, are infiltrated by exempla; older collections like those of Valerius Maximus and the Vitae patrum take on, as their MSS show, a new life in this period. We also find collections of a De casibus type wherein tragedies or strictly speaking falls are told, or of a De illustribus type wherein brief biographical lists of great people are provided.

It is possible that the Gothic spirit was responsible in part for the efflorescence of an older genre, but there is probably a more prosaic reason at the bottom—sheer convenience. These collections were useful for preachers. The authorities on preaching emphasize the importance of illustrating homiletic points by concrete stories. There is perhaps no "clear-cut treatment of the exemplum" in the Artes predicandi, those rhetoric books for preachers, but that its use was strongly urged there can be no doubt.

This passion for collecting also extended to anthologies of poetry and dictionaries of various sorts. Traditionally, in the medieval period, we find classical poetry introduced by the accessus ad auctores in which the circumstances of the composition of the work presented are often given, sometimes in terms of four Aristotelian causes. St. Jerome applied what the Rhetorica ad Herennium and Cicero's De inventione has recommended, an introduction to the beginning of each of his commentaries on the books of the Bible he translated. His example was very influential. We sometimes find brief biographies embedded in accessus. Medieval literary history was conceived of as introductions to particular literary works.

This passion extended to the Provencal razos, discussions of the external circumstances of composition of poems preceding them in a number of Provencal manuscripts. These are also accessus of a sort. Biographies of these poets, usually separate from the razos, abound. The Prologue to Canterbury Tales, if not all parts of the frame, can be regarded in part as an accessus. It exists in part to describe the fictitious authors and the "causes" of the tales themselves.

A distinction should be made between collections of tales with a prologue from the author as a real person and framed tales with a prologue which is also a fiction and which may have, as the Decameron and Canterbury Tales do, framing interludes. The accessus is from the author as a real person. The Prologue to the Canterbury Tales is an artistic, made-up accessus, not a real one.

A frame, besides justifying the tales or collected stories, also exists for authenticating purposes. Most stories pretend to be real, to be "historical" in some sense. Part of the pleasure of a story for a reader or hearer lies in the suspension of disbelief engendered by the claim, open or implied, that the story is true. If the magic of art is to work, it must be true. This feeling that what is told really happened is a very old tradition, almost certainly going back to early oral societies. The host when he describes the Canterbury scheme says that each pilgrim will tell four tales "of aventures that whilom han bifalle" (1. 795; F. N. Robinson, 2d ed.), each tale to be about things and matters which really happened. One of the major purposes of the frame, then, is to authenticate the tales—to play the game that the stories are real. Here, as I have elsewhere written, "Chaucer has moved from dream and past history [in his earlier poetry] to a report on the contemporary world and present history.... We are given a social world in the frame, not an individual's problems or attitudes." The "realism" of the Canterbury Tales which lies in great measure in the frame rather than the tales themselves, however, does not arise out of a desire to give us a "true" picture of fourteenth-century life as a medieval Zola might wish to do but to an important degree out of a well-known literary purpose—authentication. The attempt to show the truth of a tale; "it really happened," is its indirect theme. Besides this aim, the genre of collected tales—not only the Gothic spirit—demanded a prologue and sometimes a total frame.

Then, further, the frame is in the form of a supposititious pilgrimage to St. Thomas's shrine in Canterbury.This imagery suggests, on a literary level, the pilgrim's report, which is told in the first person, presumably of a personal experience. The pilgrimage notion, besides its obvious religious symbolism, serves as a literary authenticating device for the Chaucer persona. We are all pilgrims on the way to our different Canterburys.Life is a journey to our final homes; and besides, this governing image helps us to suspend our disbelief and listen to a pilgrim's tale, of one who has just made a voyage. A good more or less contemporary report in English is that of Margery Kempe who, in her Autobiography, tells inter alia of her journey to Palestine in Chaucer's period. Most pilgrim's tales are in Latin, but by Chaucer's time, vernacular reports were beginning to appear.

It is also significant for the understanding of the framed tales of the period that the single-centered narrative of early Arthurian romance began to give way in the thirteenth century and even more in the fourteenth to the Arthurian prose cycle type of narrative which is formed by rambling disgressions having a common Arthurian background but introducing a vast number of what seem to and may actually be irrelevant stories. The story within the story goes wild and multiplies in a bewildering way. The collections as well as the Canterbury

Tales are held together by a recognizable purpose or plan, the prose cycles are not. Yet the urge to proliferate tales is there and may also be explained by this later medieval drive to create collections. It is so urgent that Chaucer makes one of his tales, the Monk's Tale, a smaller collection of tales—"little tragedies"—within a larger collection.

All this may be seen in some great late medieval collections. In the fourteenth century, three remarkable men, Juan Ruiz in Spain, Boccaccio in Italy, and Chaucer in England, took the religious or moralizing genre of collected tales and infused it with new life and vitality in a way that few early secular collections were able to be animated. This is not the place to go into a detailed comparison, but each author had a complex artistic vision, and however different in aims and form produced masterpieces. They diversified their narratives by "retrospection and anticipation," and by subtle shifts in perspective they gave us several worlds held together in a most subtle articulation.

None of Chaucer's predecessors, however, use exactly his device. Nor does any combine the religious and secular attitudes and subjects to the degree he does. Chaucer gives us a spiritual vision both directly and indirectly.

The Decameron has no interludes except at the beginning of the whole work and between days. As Robert Pratt and Karl Young point out, "it is clear that the frame of the Decameron could not be regarded as Chaucer's model in any precise or thorough-going sense." (See Sources and Analogues of Chaucer's Canterbury Tales, ed. W. F. Bryan and Germaine Dempster.) The Ameto and Filocolo, both by Boccaccio, especially the Ameto, are somewhat closer to the Canterbury Tales but even they differ from the latter in significant ways. Sercambi, whose collection of tales used to be considered the closest Italian source of or analogue to the Canterbury Tales, now seems out of the running because of a correction in his assumed dates. The Libro del buen amor is even less like the Canterbury Tales than the Italian examples I have named. We must not forget, of course, Ovid's great collection of tales, especially because Ovid was so popular in the later Middle Ages, but the Metamorphoses is fundamentally different in structure from the Canterbury Tales.

Art traditionally teaches and amuses. These three masterpieces, the Libro del buen amor, the Decameron, and the Canterbury Tales, stress these two aims differently. Chaucer teaches most of all. They all make some use of circumstantial realism for literary ends, but they are all pictures of life only in the most profound sense. They are also partly true to life because the religious tradition out of which they come is true of life. The sermons and penitential books of the Christian tradition are realistic.

Chaucer's notions of dialogue and the elaboration of the role of the persona are too varied in origin to trace here, but they no doubt are part of the complex sense of the world which Chaucer delighted in. Wyclif, Chaucer's great contemporary, said that "pulcra alternacio delectat animam" and that "multi delectantur in loquela dialogi." Chaucer knew too that debate and dialogue delighted and soul. Many of the religious collections of tales had prefaces, but they were written by the author as author, commenting on his collection, praising God and possibly offering reasons and uses for the tales that follow. What Ruiz, Boccaccio, and Chaucer did was to make the prologues and frames linking the tales part of the artistic creation (a very rare device indeed in religious collections, and usually confined to titles). The tales themselves were pushed to a secondary level so to speak. The prologue and framing links became the setting out of which the tales came. Neither Ruiz nor Boccaccio used the links in as complete a way as nor to the same extent that Chaucer did. An imitation of reality, not an opinion of the author or presumed author speaking in his own person, provided, however, the rationale of the collection for all three.

Chaucer and his Mediterranean colleagues used circumstantial detail of time, place and description in their prologues and frames, and following an old tradition, descriptions of characters and lively dialogue. The circumstantial detail of the frame we have already discussed elsewhere. It is especially presented for its purpose in authenticating. The portrait goes back to the classical world as a literary genre and was recommended by medieval writers on rhetoric and poetics. Dialogue was considered, as we have seen, a proper form for medieval writers to use to increase the delectation of their audiences.

In making something of this genre, these writers then used dialogue, debate, and circumstantial realism to make a complex perspectivism and a rich, ironical, self-aware sense of life. Each was a maker of a world or worlds. Each "thickened the mixture" and made their audience see the bitter-sweetness of existence.

The frame of the Canterbury Tales serves many functions and is not there, as some think, only to serve as an introduction to some attractive tales. It sets the tone for the richness and complexity of human experience presented to us. It authenticates, prepares us for morality and entertainment in various subtle ways. It offers another level of experience, another world out of which the ideal, that is the unreal, world of the tales come. It introduces us to characters of extraordinary range; it universalizes, in a religious sense, the stories; it satisfies the Gothic urge for wholes within wholes; it gives a sense of completeness and plenitude such as suggests on a very small scale God's activity within the world. The practical purposes of an introduction to stories are there, of course, but above all a real act of creation is suggested in which a new world appears made out of the stuff of the old.

The spring setting of the Prologue continues the notion of creation, for God was supposed to have created the world in this season. Chaucer, following the medieval rhetoricians, is less concerned with describing spring than with emphasizing its powers (vires). The beginning of the poem then suggests creation just as the end suggests the ultimate end of man the pilgrim, and finally of the world. The world of Canterbury Tales moves from its own genesis to its final revelation in the Parson's Tale and Chaucer's palinode.

The great character of the frame is the host. He is both the speaker for Chaucer and Chaucer's great critic. He is the supposed creator of the scheme of the tales and is the sole judge of it. He is therefore a Chaucer surrogate and at a great remove a surrogate for God. Yet he lacks complete freedom to impose his will as he quickly learns. God also in a mysterious way is limitied by his creation, but it is a voluntary limitation for man's good.

When Dryden wrote of the Canterbury Tales in his Preface to the Fables, "Here is God's plenty," he no doubt had the notion of divine plenitude in the back of his mind as an enlightening metaphor, but he builded better than he knew, for the creation (both natura naturans and natura naturata) of the Canterbury Tales with its encompassing and richly variegated frame is really an artistic parallel to God's creation. Traditionally the variety of the world (its plenitude) has always been taken as evidence of God's goodness which overflows into his creation in a variety of ways and manifests itself in as many forms as possible.

Just as secondary causes operate in the world below, all ultimately dependent on God, the primary cause of all, so secondary causes in the forms of Chaucer's many characters create their own stories. But we who observe the whole scene, who read the tales and frame are aware of a mind behind it all, the controlling guide and spirit, to whose goodness we are indebted— Chaucer the man.

As Charles Owen writes, "the embracing fiction [of the pilgrimage] not only gives a value to most of the narratives more important than any they inherently possess, but it manifests itself frequently within the stories influencing their form, their ideology, their style, their language." The Prologue and frame is Chaucer's tribute to and imitation of God's creative activity. Because it is set, unlike Chaucer's other works, in the "real" world, it suggests that we too are characters in a pilgrimage and that we have our little flurries of creation, our narratives as we pass by the way. As Owen has said above, the frame penetrates the stories by creating their form and their rationale. We are both free and determined, masters and slaves, and our lives are the parameters of innumerable variables in a multidimensional continuum.

A further parallel between Chaucer and the Divine is the retrospective stance, the telling of events after they have occurred. As R. Baldwin pointed out a number of years ago, the scheme of the Canterbury Tales demands a Chaucer who has already made the journey to Canterbury and is telling it in retrospect. The pilgrim Chaucer as he tells us of the first meeting of his fellow pilgrims describes them fully, something which could only have been done after he had got to know them. The tale of Canterbury Tales is being told after the events, even if not in tranquillity. It is cast in the shape of an autobiographical reminiscence. In this, Chaucer is following a very common tradition in art which uses a retrospective teller—perhaps the best known example to him was the Divine Comedy. Dante has already completed or pretended to have completed his whole journey as he sits down to relate it to his audience. Paradise has already been reached before Dante the author sits down to write of hell. Chaucer too must have pretended to have reached Canterbury and even to have returned to London before he turned to write

Whan that Aprill with his shoures soote
The droghte of March hath perced to the roote.

In at least this sense then the end is the beginning and the beginning is the end in a tale in which the teller is an active character. The motto "En mon commencement est ma fin" and its converse are the truth which Christianity and life give us. This kind of reminiscence then in which the whole work is cast into retrospect is a paradigm again of God's creation and the divine attitude to existence. As in life, the end hovers over every act and all is cast in a perspective of double time. The potential pastness of the present continually being forced upon us by the conditions of this act is what gives the present its edge and its tragedy. We can forget this great truth most of the time, just as we do when we read the tales in the

Canterbury Tales or as the pilgrims do as they tell their tales, but at times the warning bell clangs as the voice of the narrator, of this elvish man Chaucer, is heard above the clamour in measured tones giving us his report of this journey to Canterbury.

The Prologue and frame then of the Canterbury Tales interpenetrate the tales in many and varied ways and set the conditions for the complex worlds which are revealed. The tales are in another time than the time of the pilgrimage for the pilgrimage is given to us in the persona's retrospective time, in illo tempore. In a sense the tales then are lyric interludes or perhaps lyrico-narrative interludes, especially because we are strongly aware of most of the tellers. We are held down by the forces which control us, and yet these forces allow each one of us to tell his tale, to open up for a little while the sequence of something that has happened.

Explanations of the function of the Prologue and frame of the Canterbury Tales which fall back on the Gothic nature of the late medieval period may to some extent be right. Obviously in some sense the spirit of the later medieval period with its preference for framed painting and framed doorway has some relation to the popularity of the framed collection of tales in the same period and with what Jordan calls "nonorganicist sensibility" so characteristic of Gothic art. Jordan himself is well aware of the difficulties in making precise such parallels. The dispute over whether we can use the term "baroque" or how to use it in discussing seventeenth-century literature is instructive in this matter. Jordan writes, "I do not press the analogy very far."

It is perhaps more helpful in our goal of understanding the function of the frame and Prologue in the Canterbury Tales to stress what Chaucer was doing in his concept of the tales; how he conceived his own masterpiece. I think the analogy of creation and God was before him deliberately and often. If we like, we may also interpret Gothic cathedrals thus—remembering though that romanesque and baroque cathedrals also aimed at creating God's house on earth and a replica of the creation and its results in salvation history. It is better to think of Chaucer as a divine surrogate in his task than only as a Gothic artist, though certainly no one can object to these analogies if they are helpful.

The poetic world created by the poet is not really ex nihilo, as Chaucer would surely not wish to put himself on a level with the real God. He is, however, analogously creating a world or several worlds, even if using already existing materials. He is creating, to use an expression of M. H. Abrams, a heterocosm, and is suggesting a parallel to the divine activity. The notion of artist as God is implicit in his greatest poems. The idea of the poet as creator only became explicit in the Renaissance. Yet the poet as vates, as prophet who is divinely inspired, is very old, older than Homer. But the notion of the prophet-poet as a god probably had to wait on Christianity and the development of Western thought, especially in the Romantic period.

The idea that the poet is a kind of god is implied in the very subject matter of The Divine Comedy. The fact that such a journey should be granted to him as it was to St Paul who visited the third heaven was a sufficient guarantee that Dante was specially favoured and was by precept and example made a special imitation of God, who in the form of Jesus made a journey similar in some respects to what his was to be.

With Chaucer the evidence is less clear but none the less impressive. His characters carry their heavens and hells about with them. They are on their way to the heavenly Jerusalem and are fortuitously joined by Chaucer just as we fortuitously join our own contemporaries at our birth. Chaucer is withdrawn and different. He is called upon by the Host twice, is poked fun at by the Man of Law, tells a dull story. All this gives us a sense of his reality and helps to guarantee his artistic truth. He gives us a world which reflects a real world and in which we find new worlds. It presents its own truth. Its epistemological guarantee is Chaucer's own retrospective report.

We can, if we wish, look upon these two narrative levels—the level of the world of fact and the level of imaginative creation—as an imitation of life itself as it is lived. We live in time punctuated by events which take us out of time, our dreams, some of our contacts with others, our hearing stories, our introspective and imaginative moments. The Canterbury Tales reflects these two basic levels of life. It lets us enjoy and lament over our scattered introspective and neighbourly moments as well as keep us aware of the pilgrimage, the via we are all bound on. We are the pilgrims, the viatores, but just as the Canterbury Pilgrims could get away from their journey carried by the wings of narrative, so we can temporarily forget the serious and fundamental passage to Canterbury we are all engaged upon. The relation between the two levels, then, need not be purely psychological, as Professor Kittredge, Lumiansky, and many others have thought, but religious and humanist.

Thus, the Canterbury Tales with its elaborate frame and its Prologue is a prologue to a prologue—our earthly life in its plenitude, variety and multitudinousness. We recognize our world in Chaucer's world and cross in reading it another bridge in "thilke parfit glorious pilgrymage/That highte Jerusalem celestial" (. -).

We must remember that the pilgrims do not reach Canterbury.It is possible that this failure is due to the accident of Chaucer's death or it may be deliberate. I tend to the latter explanation. Chaucer may very well have decided before he reached the Parson's or Manciple's Tale not to finish his work as he had originally planned and reduced it to fewer tales, perhaps even as few as one-quarter of the number. Perhaps not. But the cessation of the work before Canterbury is reached is certainly a happy circumstance or notion in terms of the spiritual function of the Prologue and frame, and the necessity of the return to London.The heavenly Jerusalem is certainly not yet reached by the pilgrims, nor indeed us.

The heavenly Jerusalem is the ultimate goal of earthly man and until the end of time will be for all human beings still in via. Even more important, only because more immediate, is the emphasis in the Canterbury Tales on the journey of life which all who read it must still be on, with its double aspect of the travelling and the experiences within that journey which seem to take us, even if only momentarily, out of time.

Q.14. What is The Role of Women in The Canterbery Tales?

Or

Q. Chaucer, in his female pilgrimage thought of women as having an evil-like quality that they always tempt and take from men. Discuss

They were depicted as untrustworthy, selfish and vain and often like caricatures not like real people at all. Through the faults of both men and women, Chaucer showed what is right and wrong and how one should live. Under the surface, however, lies a jaded look of women in the form that in his writings he seems to crate them as caricatures and show how they cause the downfall of men by sometimes appealing to their desires and other times their fears. Chaucer obviously had very opinionated views of the manners and behaviours of women and expressed it strongly in The Canterbury Tales. In his collection of tales, he portrayed two extremes in his prospect of women.

The Wife of Bath represented the extravagant and lusty woman where as the Prioress represented the admirable and devoted followers of church. Chaucer delineated the two characters contrastingly in their appearances, general manners, education and most evidently in their behaviour towards men. Yet, in the midst of disparities, both tales left its readers with an unsolved enigma.

The Wife of Bath represents the "liberal" extreme in regards to female stereotypes of the Middle Ages. Unlike most women being anonymous during the Middle Ages, she has a mind of her own and voices herself. Furthermore, she thinks extremely highly of herself and enjoys showing off her Sunday clothes whenever the opportunity arises. She intimidates men and women alike due to the power she possesses. Because of her obnoxious attitude Chaucer makes her toothless, fat and large. Doubtlessly, she is very ugly, almost to the point of "not-presentable. This to me shows how Chaucer depicts what men don't want. The Prioress, on the other hand, serves as a foil to the Wife of Bath. Chaucer describes her as "tender-hearted" who cannot bear the sight of pain or physical suffering. She will cry at the thought of a dog dying.

It could represent that she has a frail soul with low tolerance for pain and suffering. The latter description carries over into the modern stereotypes about women as skittish and afraid members of society who need to be cared for. Chaucer paints a very delicate and elegant picture of the Prioress. Her manners of eating are far from the brutish festivals of the time. Chaucer describes her table manners as very graceful, not a drop of anything would fall from her mouth, and she was very polite when taking thing at the table. (Lines 131-4). Chaucer's last description of Prioress - the letter "A" around her neck that stood for "Amor vincit omnia" meaning "Love conquers all." The brooch symbolizes love with which her rosaries are adorned is a common accessory for religious devotion, which carries the courtly love anthem: love conquers all. The symbol that she wears shows that she is perfect and obviously a representation of what most men of the time want but of course they can't have her. Accordingly, the Wife of Bath is daunting, ostentatious and ultimately ugly. She is nothing in comparison to the Prioress who is elegant, well mannered and above all loving.

The Prioress's superiority over the Wife of Bath is shown again in the presence of education. The Wife of Bath has travelled a great deal and seems knowledgeable about things of the world. She brings up many a valid point throughout the prologue but Chaucer voids her opinion because of her social class and looks when in truth she is actually wise. The Wife of Bath has understanding for the world and knows very well what's going on. However, during the Middle Ages, only scholarly or academic knowledge is recognized. What the Wife of Bath understands and pursues may not be commendable. On the contrary, the Prioress is considered "scholastic" and high class due to her good manners. Her ability to speak the noble language of French puts her character in a higher class as well. Thus, once again the Prioress is considered intelligent. Basically, the Wife of Bath is kind of a foil to the women during the Middle Ages. Her actions and thinking not only differ from the Prioress but almost from everyone else!!!

The Wife of Bath is radical especially when it comes to relationship with men. She is characterized as knowing much about love, which is illustrated by her physical defect-being gap-toothed symbolizing "sexual accomplishment." The Wife of Bath cannot resist telling her companions about all of her sexual experiences. She also had five husbands and countless affairs, thus breaking innocent men's hearts. Her husbands fell into two categories. The first categories of husbands were rich but also old and unable to fulfil her "sexual" demands. The other husbands were sexually vigourous, but harder to control. None of her five marriages were successful because the Wife of Bath was constantly seeking to have power and control over them, Chaucer I think characterises the Wife of Bath in this way to show men's fears. For instance, her fifth but not the last (it was said that she is on her way of marrying the sixth before she told her tale) marriage was unhappy because her husband who is half of her age beats her. To anger him, she tore three pages from his book. After this he beats her again. She pretended to be dead and he felt so guilty that he threw his whole book in the fire.

This gave her the upper hand for the rest of her life. This contrast between the Wife of Bath and the Prioress describes fully the difference between what men do and do not want in a woman. First, the violent and deceitful act of tearing books then the deceitful act of lying to her husband will never be done by the Prioress as the Prioress is well mannered, educated, "powerful" and above all, is loving. Second, is the issue of marriage and "sexual demand" which will never have its roots in the Prioress's life as she has taken the vow of chastity. This being the case appeals to both fear and desire, as all men would desire the Prioress, but fear they could not have her. The Prioress is pure in heart and thinks of men and women alike. It's interesting how the Wife of Bath was always striving to have sovereignty and the Prioress was granted sovereignty even though she didn't seek for it intentionally.

The Wife of Bath and the Prioress alike have power over men once again this characterisation would scare men. It is rare that women are given such high stature during the medieval period. The Prioress as her name suggests is "a superior being in a monastic community for women" is so important that three priests were in her company; as this shows her status as the boss, this dominance would be very fearful for men of the time. The hag, whom the Wife of Bath identifies with, initially was granted sovereignty and power over man. This is proven when the hag offers her husband the choice: he can have her old and ugly and faithful or young, beautiful, and possible unchaste. He tells her to choose; he grants her the sovereignty.

As mentioned above, the Wife of Bath desires what most women want and that is power over men, her being described as being ugly and wanting power to probably exploit that power as she did with husband number five definitely shows a representation of what men don't want. Early in the tale, there is a quotation said by the Wife of Bath supporting this idea. "I don't deny that I will have my husbands both my debtor and my slave, and as long as I am his wife he shall suffer in the flesh. I will have command over his body during all his life, not he." In other words, she is saying that she will have total control over herself, her husband, and their household and very specifically, not just the husband. However, there are also situations where she seems to submit to her husband. "Nevertheless, since I know your pleasure I will satisfy your physical pleasure."

This was said by the Wife of Bath and supports the non-feministic view. It is considered non-feministic because the woman is giving in to the man's desire, which goes against feministic beliefs. The Wife of Bath has a choice of not giving in to the man, but she decides to let the man have pleasure for his desire not hers, because from her past experience she knew how much men enjoy it when women are submissive. This quotation obviously goes against feministic beliefs, leaving an unanswered contradiction about the Wife of Bath. However, Chaucer does show through this characterisation that the Wife of Bath is desirable in one way to men because she is willing to be submissive to their desires. This raises an unseen question of desire for her as I think most men of the time would desire a woman who would grant this. The character of the Prioress in the same light, certainly keeps one guessing. Is her tale the product of the simple mind, or of one poisoned by anti-Semitism? The Prioress is, well mannered, educated, powerful, and loving. Ironically, her prologue and tale contain strong elements of anti-Semitism.

This is shown through her use of the Jew as the villain of her tale. However, there is no historical evidence of ritual murder of Christian children by Jews, but that would not have mattered to the pilgrims. Anti-Semitism, directed at a people thought to have both rejected and murdered Christ, was distressingly deep-seated. This bigotry unfortunately was rampant at the time, and both the sentiments and their being expressed in the context of a religious story would not have seemed strange to Chaucer's pilgrimage. Nevertheless, on a less depressing note, her tale can tell us something of the medieval attitude towards simple piety and miracles, which also was quite prevalent. I don't think it is about the Jews because; they were expelled from England in 1290. Yet, whether this tale is the product of the simple mind or anti-Semitism still remains an enigma. This story also reinforces her devotion to the church and this characterisation can be seen as a fear to some men as they are unable to obtain her. It is here we see the only time when the Wife of Bath and the Prioress relate to each other. In this we can see that Chaucer is telling us that the Prioress is not as perfect as she might of first seemed, and in this way we can see that both women have both got parts that men desire and men fear.

The Wife of Bath seems to be feministic yet there are also some situations in which she does as the men wish. The Prioress on the other hand keeps you wondering and seems to be a perfect lady however she is unobtainable and probably to well educated and out of reach for most men. Chaucer portrays the tale of Wife of Bath as hypocritical but between the lines there is some helpful advice for many women in the world today. In this way Chaucer is trying to educate women through her tale, and say that there are times one should be a feminist and times one should not. This characterisation of her strong head would have scared the men of the time. In his contrast with the two he shows in both women what men fear. In the Wife of Bath it's that men don't want to be controlled and in the Prioress it's the fact that she is unobtainable and maybe too clever for everyday man. These representations however when put together, create a women that seems to be perfect for what most men want and desire.

Women and Spring in The Canterbury Tales

In Geoffrey Chaucer's collection of stories; The Canterbury Tales, there is a recurring theme of love being the most important aspect of a person's life. The author enforces this theme through the usage of springtime imagery, especially an emphasis on the month of May. Not only May, but the importance of it and the flowers that bloom in it. May is when spring begins to turn into summer and flowers really bloom. This fact makes May a very pivotal month in the calendar and effects the weather and nature from there on out. If flowers bloom late then it will be different weather in June than if the flowers bloom early. In The Canterbury Tales, women are often compared to flowers and to May making them seem very powerful yet beautiful. Most of the women in this collection of tales are very beautiful, and very influential and authoritative towards men in their lives.

In the "Knight's Tale" the two prisoners see the beautiful woman in the garden and fall in love with her. When Emily is described, it is said that she was "fresher than May with its flowers." (Chaucer, pg 51) The two prisoners haven't even seen this woman yet and she is already being described like this. She is compared to flowers in May, which is a very good image to be compared to. May is known for flowers, like in the saying

`April showers bring May flowers', some of the most beautiful flowers bloom then. Flowers such as daisies, poppies, lavender, baby's breath, and tulips all bloom in May, just to name a few. When a flower just blooms it is fresh, just like in spring when the snow melts and everything seems fresh and clean. To say that Emily is like this makes a very beautiful image come to mind. The theme then comes in with this when the two prisoners fall in love with her. She is compared to spring constantly, and two men fall in love with her simultaneously, to the point where they would kill each other for her. Their lives become consumed with her, and she is identical to spring. Emily is the springtime of these two men's lives and their love for it is the most important thing to them. She is influential on men when she begins to weep at the thought of them dying. She uses her beauty to make the Duke not sentence the two prisoners to death. He feels bad and decides to not make the order.

In "The Miller," the leading lady of the story is also very beautiful. She is well dressed, talented and good looking. "She [is] a morning glory, she [is] a daisy," (Chaucer, pg 153) both of which are May flowers. Morning glories and daisies are well known for their beauty and they both are happy flowers. They remind people of happy things, such as springtime and May. Again, comparing a woman to a flower is a very positive thing to say, and the fact that she is later on helps bring out the reoccurring theme. Many men in this woman's village are infatuated with her; including her husband, the parish clerk and Nicholas. They all try to win her by confessing their undying love for her. The parish clerk sings to her under her window at night "like a nightingale." (Chaucer, pg 159) A bird like a nightingale is usually associated with summer or spring, in fact any bird usually is. But the making him a bird, and her a flower that he is singing to is an ultimate springtime image. May is all about flowers and birds. The men again are devoting their lives to her, and she is once again springtime. The spring makes them want to love and her beauty makes them want to love her. She has power over all of these men because she decides which one she will love.

These images occur over and over again through out the stories. Not only is love the most important thing in life, but also women are in charge when it comes to love. The women in the stories are fair and beautiful like spring, and can control when love occurs. The lusty feeling that spring causes only happens because it is spring, when women are beautiful they control men. Pretty women can with hold sexual pleasure like in the "Wife of Bath" or they can limit sex to certain men like the woman in "The Miller" does. The first sign of spring is flowers, they control when spring begins; a beautiful woman who is compared to a springtime flower can control when the lust and the love begins.

Q.15. Analyse the Characters of The Canterbury Tales

Or

Q. An interesting aspect of the famous literary work, "The Canterbury Tales," is the contrast of realistic and exaggerated qualities that Chaucer entitles to each of his characters. Discuss

When viewed more closely, one can determine whether each of the characters is convincing or questionable based on their personalities. This essay will analyse the characteristics and personalities of the Knight, Squire, Monk, Plowman, Miller, and Parson of Chaucer's tale.

One of Geoffrey's less believable main characters is the Knight, for reasons of chivalry. The knight displays many traits which make him seem almost too good to be true, and a true gentleman that rarely exists in reality. The narrator sums up the knights character by stating that "Though he were worthy, he was wys,/And of his port as meeke as is a mayde." (pg. 5, The Canterbury Tales) The knight holds four main admirable traits, making him the most liked traveler in "The Canterbury Tales," and also amplying the doubt of his realism. The reader is prepared to learn of each of his noble accomplishments and importance when the narrator remarks that" A knight ther was, and that a worthy man,/That fro the tyme that he first bigan/To ryden out, he loved chivalrye,/Trouthe and honour, fredom and curteisye." (pg. 4, The Canterbury Tales) From the characters impressive introduction, it is clear that this man is the most valued and honourable traveler among the group. This perfect gentleman holds a love of ideals that are often not displayed by people. First and foremost, he believes in the ideals of chivalry, and always stays true to its principles. He also feels that one should be honest, truthful and faithful, which many people are not all of these ideals. The knight thinks one should only do what is right, and what will gain him honour and reputation.

This character also believes in freedom and generosity towards all, and displays this ideal repeatedly throughout the novel. And lastly, the knight also strongly feels that any proper person should display courtesy and elegance at all times. Another aspect of this character's life which makes him seem too prestigious to be truthful is his impressive military career. He fought in the holy war, known as the Crusades and was involved in 15 "mortal battles." In the prologue, the narrator informs the reader that "Ful worthy was he in his lordes werre,/And therto hadde he riden, no man ferre,/As wel in Cristendom as hethenesse,/And ever honoured for his worthinesse." (pg. 4, The Canterbury Tales) The knight obviously held a very respectable reputation, and was treated with much honour and respect. He was a perfect gentleman, showing kindness and understanding to everyone he came in contact with.

The knight was extremely well-mannered, always being on his best behaviour. His appearance was the "finishing touch," adding honour and integrity to his courageous and gentle spirit. This main character was clothed still in his armor, wearing a tunic of harsh cloth and his coat of mail is rust-stained, clearly showing remaining signs of past battles. "Of fustian he wered a gipoun/Al bismotered with his habergeoun;/For he was late y-come from his viage." (pg. 4, The Canterbury Tales) The qualities of the knight resemble those of very few people in modern society, giving a quality of exaggeration to the perfectness found in the knight. He represents the embodiment of the ideal man as seen by Chaucer.

The knight's son however, the Squire. does not display the degree of falseness the knight does. The vivacious personality of this young man closely resembles that of a modern man. He is a "lusty bachelor" of twenty, who is ultimately concerned with his appearance. He places more importance on fighting for his lady's honour, unlike his father who fought for abstract ideals or God. He also wore stylish, but very "daring" garments. The squire was dressed in a very short gown, equal in extremity to today's modern mini-skirt, which was looked down upon by the Church. The vain squire made every effort to ensure that he had perfectly curled hair. "With lokkes crulle as they were leyd in presse." (pg. 6, The Canterbury Tales) It seems as though it appeared that this young man purposely curled his hair, just as a woman would do. He is described as being as fresh as the month of May, showing his cleaniless and delightful appearance to which he took so much pride. "He was as fresh as is the month of May." (pg. 6, The Canterbury Tales) This young man is slowly but surely aspiring to knighthood just as his father did, therefore he's courteous, humble, and respects his father because he is an apprentice to his father. The young man did however, hold many social talents, which were important to have when becoming a knight. He has the abilities to sing, dance, write songs and poems, and joust, which were all important social accomplishments.

The vain attitude of the Squire, and his selfish outlook, relate closely to the shallow demeanor of people today. However, due to the acuteness of the squire's perfection in the sense of manlihood, he can also be viewed as a sort of a fairytale "Prince Charming." Fairytale heros relate very well to the squire, because both are willing to do whatever they can for the love of a lady. The squire seems to possess all that a lady might dream of: agility, strength, courtesy, a nice family, manners, and good looks. Prince Charming would also possess these ideal traits and follow these lines almost exactly. Both the squire and Prince Charming are meant to be "good guys," and they both are in many aspects. They are well bred and chivalrous, fight well for honour, and have the flaw of falling in love for beauty and passion. This comparison and likeness to the fairytale prince also gives this young squire his own degree of falseness and exaggeration. In certain aspects, the Monk also displays the impression of realism through his personality and actions.

The Monk is not an ordinary holy man, but yet a worldly man who holds dear his means of personal enjoyment. He holds a very cocky, sarcastic attitude, not normally found in men of the church, which is the biggest sign of his realistic vitality. Monks usually stay apart from the outside world, not go out for "venery," a word that carries sexual connotations, or in other words hunts for pleasure, which definately sets this Monk apart from his other church officials. The narrator states that "This ilke Monk leet olde thinges pace,/And held after the newe world the space." (pg. 10, The Canterbury Tales) This statement indicates to the reader that this Monk finds joy and happiness in modern priviladges, differing him from conventional church officials. He is introduced as "An outrydere, that lovede venerye;/A manly man, to been an abbot able." (pg. 8, The Canterbury Tales) The author describes him as being a "manly man," providing the reader with the assumption that the monk took his hunting and other "manly" activites very seriously.

The author also makes it a point however, to state that he was a "fat and personable priest." So in essence, this particular monk has an unusual appearance, such explained by the Host, that he appears as though he's in charge of food and drink, or like a rooster with plenty of hens. This description confirms the impression that this Monk appears quite different from other religious figures, but yet is realistic due to his actions and appreciation of worldly pleasures.

In order to explain his love of the hunt, the narrator states: "Of prikyng and of huntyng for the hare/Was al his lust, for no cost wolde he spare." (pg. 34, The Canterbury Tales, A Literary Pilgrimage) He differs greatly from other church officials in that he appears to believe its pointless to follow his monastic duties. His rejection of the life of one's mind is explicit, and the narrator agrees: "And I seyde his opinion was good./What sholde he studie and make hymselven wood." (Pg. 35, The Canterbury Tales, A Literary Pilgrimage) This Monk particularary enjoys hunting, a pastime of the nobility, which proves that the Monk cares about enjoyment rather than concerning himself with his religious duties all the time. The monk often "hunted a hare" or any other type of game that suited him. His values and attitude resemble the selfish corrupt ideals of people, who partake in actions without considering the consequences or benefit of others. This character seems to have a mix of both realistic aspects and exaggerated ones. The Monk's selfishness and desire for recreation gives him the realistic feature. However, the author's stress of his sarcassim and selfishness also applies an angle of exaggeration to his character. An emphasis of a certain trait can also be examined in the Plowman.

The Plowman is stressed as the example of an ideal middle class citizen. "A trewe swinker and a good was he,/Livinge in pees and parfit charite;" (pg. 26, The Canterbury Tales) This character is a very chivalrous workman, just as the knight was. By looking closely at this character's actions and dialogue, it can be inferred that he is the type of individual who would gladly work for a person without pay. He pays all his Church taxes on time, and is a devoted churchgoer. This citizen treats his neighbor as he would want to be treated, making him well-liked, much as the knight was. Also, he is certainly not as rowdy as the other characters. He is a decent human being, and portrays a hard-working, devoted citizen, giving him much in common with the chivalrious knight. The plowman's personality can be related to the common working class citizen of today, with the exception of a slight exaggerated flawlessness. Another character portraying an actual individual would be in the case of the Miller.

The Miller is an obnoxious character who represents the modern day bully in a sense. He is a large man with imposing figure, making him seem more powerful than the other characters. This intimidation is developed by the physical description of the miller. The workman is brawny, big-boned and muscular, and is also a good wrestler. This character is said to have a red beard and hair. He also has a rude and corrupt attitude treating his fellow travelers with contempt. His character matches the medieval conception that millers were the most important but dishonest tenants on a manor farm. He is shameless and selfish, and has a bad temper and is easily angered.

In one instance, this character stole corn and proceded to charge three times the price, thinking nothing of the person he stole from. This man shows his vulgar and rude temperment when he becomes irritated upon hearing the Knight's tale of kings and queens and knights and ladies. He drunkly shouts, "I wol now quyte the Knyghtes tale." (pg. 146, The Canterbury Tales) The Host interupts the drunken man and pleads with him to wait to tell his tale, but he refuses and the Host critisizes him for his stubborness. "Thou art a fool; thy wit is overcome." (pg. 146, The Canterbury Tales) He continues to entertain his fellow travelers by telling a tale about a devious student who plans to have an affair with the wife of a dimwitted carpenter, showing his immaturity and delight in other people's misery. He also is said to have developed a "Hell mouth," or speaks "in Pilates voys." (pg. 146, The Canterbury Tales) The miller's character can be viewed as realistic, because his personality matches that of a modern day bully, in that he is very intimidating, rude and uncaring. However, his characteristic anger is slightly overstressed.

The Parson on the other hand, was a very religious, devoted, decent man. He is described as being very principled and intelligent. The parson is very noble and sets a good example towards his fellow parishioners. It is stated by the author that he is "also a lerned man, a clerk, / That Cristes gospel trewely wolde preche" (pg. 480, The Canterbury Tales) He even hates collecting income taxes from his citizens. He is known to practice what he preaches, and his values and hard work sets a good example for the common people. He worked very hard to better the lives of others around him, and therefore worked in the absence of the comforts that tend to come along with fame and glory.

The Parson is in many ways the ideal traveler on the journey to Canterbury. He is learned, but unlike the other men, possess much virtue. He realises that if the priest that the people put their trust and faith in is machiavellian, then no one can ever expect the people to be virtuous. "For if a preest be foul, on whom we truste,/No wonder is a lewed man to ruste;/" (pg. 24, The Canterbury Tales) This Parson is favourable over many other church officials, because unline them he does not run off to bigger and better places and rent his parish to someone else. These ideal qualities make him more approved than many of the other travelers, especially spiritually. He worked hard to spread goodness, act charitably, and was never hypocritical. These commendable qualities makes him a suitable parellel to what the world might view now as a model human being. Such virtue and qualities seem too good to be true, and in a way represent what every person should be like instead of how they really are.

In essence, the plot development is also based on the development of the characters and the contrast of reality and exaggeration. Chaucer purposely chose to give his characters certain aspects of reality and exaggerated traits to help develop each of the characters' tales. It is noticeable in the novel that each character's tale matches his or her personality in one way or another. For example, the knight's heroic tale of chivalry and kings and queens obviously coinsides with his traits and lifestyle. The Miller's tale of dishonesty and cheating also matches his personality of anger and rudeness. Chaucer's use of characterization helps to establish the plot and motives of the tale. Of course, the tales told by each of Chaucer's characters reciprocates the personality traits displayed by them.

The knight spoke a tale of chivalry and virtue and of ladies in waiting, while the Squire spoke of love and intrigue in his story. The differences in their personalities leads to the conflicts and balance of reality and exaggeration. The knight for example, shows a great degree of embellishment because he is so well mannered and holds such virtuous ideals, which are not commonly displayed by normal beings, because of the selfish nature of humans. The knight seems to represent what Chaucer believes everyone should be like, and holds the values that people seem to overlook. The Squire, on the other hand, shows a more realistic display of characteristics, and adds variety to the story line. He displays a sense of reality in that he isn't as concerned with honour and values as his father, but rather with his own enjoyment and vanity. Chaucer's novel would be incomplete without the continuing budding of his characters.

Chapter 16

Critical Essays

"Love" in the Courtly Tradition

by Anonymous

May 03, 2000

In the "Franklin's Tale," Geoffrey Chaucer satirically paints a picture of a marriage steeped in the tradition of courtly love. As Dorigen and Arveragus' relationship reveals, a couple's preoccupation with fulfilling the ritualistic practices appropriate to courtly love renders the possibility of genuine love impossible. Marriage becomes a pretense to maintain courtly position because love provides the opportunity to demonstrate virtue. Like true members of the gentility, they practice the distinct linguistic and behavioural patterns which accompany the strange doctrine of courtly love. The characters' true devotion to the relationship becomes secondary to the appearance of practicing the virtues of truth, honour, and generosity. After establishing the inverted hierarchy of values, Chaucer paints a bleak picture of the potential for love and relationships in a world in which a distinction needs to be made between secular and private roles. Dorigen differentiates between "hir housbonde" and "hir love" and Arveragus distinguishes between "his lady" and "his wyf".

Immediately, Chaucer signals the practice of chivalric courtship as the knight who is of noted "heigh kinrede" ceremoniously completes the "many a labor" of a courtly lover. The description of the duties that must be undertaken by a classic courtly lover seeking a wife for social fulfillment corruptss the image of courtship being motivated by the existence of true love. The emphasis on the inconvenience with which Arveragus, "dide his payne" suggests he performs "many a greet empryse" out of obligation and convention rather than as a part of a genuine amorous pursuit. The weakly disguised presence of the "ye" in each of these words announces Arveragus' awareness of the eyes of the courtly audience observing his performance. The concern with the outward appearance of the relationship extends to Dorigen as she dutifully accepts his proposal as a means of repaying the "distresse" undergone by her lover. The brief description of the couple's courtship covers only 13 lines, suggesting that the relationship's foundation has little time to progress beyond the preliminary stages of lusty, physical attraction before the marriage is instated.

Framing the already bleak portrayal of this "accord," a word typically used to refer to business agreements or compromises, is the contractual terminology of their agreement which further downplays the emotional foundation of the relationship. Instead, the negotiated terms that "frendes everich other moot obeye" indicate that the lovers are settling for amicable companionship. The agreement itself is ridden with contradictory terms trying to reconcile the tensions between the inner sphere where passionate love resides and the outer sphere which operates under the codes of courtly love. The two agree that Arveragus will be her "Servant in love, and lord in merrage", but the in reality these two social positions are mutually exclusive, indicating the impossibility of the success of this relationship. One of the two will have to be the dominating figure for it to survive, but then this will eliminate the possibility of love which "wol nat ben constreyned by maistrye".

The "lawe of love" in the medieval period mandates that a husband is the lord of his wife, and Arveragus grants her sovereignty only within the scope of their private life because he must uphold the tradition of male domination in the outside world. Arveragus' promise to becomes a way to demonstrate that " [p]acience is a heigh vertu" . Always aware of the connection between his actions and his rank he states, "Save that the name of soveraynetee, / That wolde he have for shame of his degree.". If the two truly were in love, these sorts of issues would not need to be settled or would even arise because a couple would assume that a wife would be true to her husband and that he would treat her with respect and honour. Instead, marriage is being used to further one's opportunity to perform noble and virtuous roles, explaining the struggle between a lover's commitment to his personal or public life. Chaucer foreshadows the improbable success of this duality with the Dorigen's proclamation, "Ne wolde never God bitwixe us tweyne". Not only does this contain a double negative, suggesting that a force will indeed disrupt this arrangement, but the phraseology also indicates that their relationship will be without God who should be a uniting force in any marriage.

Chaucer takes pains to mention that "[t]he joye, the ese, and prosperity" of their relationship last only a "yeer and more" . Chivalric love's preoccupation with appearances impels behaviour that stymies the success of love. In addition to the previously noted irony of a lover undergoing a painful courtship to win his desired object, Arveragus undertakes additional burdens under the charade of being a good lover. Chaucer criticizes the requirements of courtly love by placing such pursuits directly at odds with their objects. Arveragus self-imposes a two-year separation from Dorigen is an effort "to seke in armes worshipe and honour.".

Why must a husband leave his wife to prove he is worthy of her love? His decision to leave his bride after only a year of marriage suggests the value he places upon success in the public eye overrides the need to be attentive to his private affairs. In fact, Arveragus pursues this task with more enthusiasm than he shows in any of his interactions with this wife. "Perhaps the "lust he sette in swich labour" indicates Arveragus' preference to be a warrior lover in the public sphere instead of a servant in his private sphere. On the battlefield, he can through virile performance release some of the sexual frustrations which develop from the constraints in his marriage. Assuming this is true, his departure represents a revolt against his powerless position in his marriage.

Dorigen strengthens the possibility of marital bliss existing only as a pretense when she pines away for her husband not as one would secure in the belief that he will return to her, but as if she is apprehensive about his desire to voluntarily leave the battlefield. He sends her "lettres hoom of his welfare," establishing that her worries extend beyond mere concern with his health. Although Dorigen's reaction to the separation from her husband is marked by her profound sense of grief, there seems to be a melodramatic insincerity in her response. She weeps "as doon these noble wyves whan hem lyketh," suggesting her mourning is a ploy to win her friends sympathies and their attentions to "every confort possible in this cas". Perhaps she is behaving in concert with the belief that true lovers suffer from a physical and emotional malady, amor hereos. Her belief that "with good hope lete hir sorwe slyde" further establishes the facade of grief is easily replaced with a face of good cheer when it befits her interests.

The already weak links in this marriage culminate in Aurelius' pursuit of Dorigen. The very fact that Aurelius undertakes the methods of a courtly lover in an attempt to covet another man's wife implies that in this courtly environment the sacred vows of truth in marriage are commonly corrupted by adultery. Although Dorigen rejects his advances and pledges to grant him her love only if he performs a task she deems impossible, it shows the fault of a society operating under a system where relationships exists only when they fulfill predetermined conditions. If Dorigen faithfully enters her promise of truth to her husband, she would not respond to Aurelius as she does- "Than wol I love yow best of any man / Have heer my trouthe in al that evere I can". The last few words imply that truth in marriage is all but impossible for its promisors to uphold. Dorigen's conflicting words "Ne shal I nevere been untrewe wfy" reveal the inevitable failure of her pledge of faithfulness.

Once Arveragus discovers Dorigen's promise to Aurelius, his humble reaction reflects the state of imbalance in the marriage. The ridiculous length with which Arveragus goes to maintain his adherence to the idea that "[t]routhe is the hyest thing that man may kepe" is incompatible with the behaviour of a man deeply in love. Although their marital vows provide grounds for Dorigen to avoid fulfillment of her promise, he releases her to commit adultery "with glade chere in freendly wyse'. His response seem highly inappropriate, perhaps there is a pun on the word fiendish, considering that he values the pledge of truth to an outsider who plots to sabotage the preexisting truth in the relationship with his wife. He values the societal maintenance of truth to such an extreme degree that he would rather "dye in sorwe and in distresse" than allow his wife to tarnish her commitment to truth less it be a reflection upon him.

Concurrently, he treats truth hypocritically by forbidding Dorigen upon the "peyne of deeth" of telling anyone of this affair. There lies a contradiction in his pledge to kill her if she threatens his honour while he concurrently allows himself to be cuckolded which is also a peril to his honour. Explaining this discrepancy could be the possibility that he dispatches her as a demonstration of his "maistre"over her actions- the one condition that eliminates the possibility of love. The tears could be either a melodramatic attempt to feign his concern for her well being or a realization that he sacrifices a bit of honour in gaining dominance in the relationship.

Marriage becomes a conduit for men to display their "grete gentillesse" instead of a union of lovers. After Dorigen's careless promise to Aurelius, she becomes a pawn in the high stake display of chivalric behaviour. The concerns with rank emerges as a challenge of gallantry and honour which forces the knight, squire, and the philosopher to release each other from their truths. The fact that they are so willing to part with their pledges demonstrates the value placed upon words is directly tied to how it reflects upon social standing. The virtue of generosity becomes so entangled with the self-interests that no one commits acts of good will without ulterior motives of personal gain, framing this irony is the Franklin's question "Which was the moste free, as thnketh yowe?" . If a world places a higher position on truth in external interaction than it grants to private relationships, true love in the courtly tradition of behaviour targeted to further self interest can never survive. In the tale's conclusion, Dorigen and Arveragus place the masks they wear when facing the outside world and reunite in a farce of mutually contentment. Perhaps "never eft ne was there angre hem bitwene" although the wording suggests likewise, but even assuming that there is no discord, there appears to be no passionate love either.

The Pardoner and the Word of Death

This book concludes with an analysis of *The Pardoner's Prologue and Tale,* for several reasons, some more obvious than others. Most obvious is that the Pardoner of all Chaucer's posers is the most skillful, theatrical, and elusive. Only slightly less obvious is the connection in the Pardoner and his discourse between language and money. He is obsessed with both and uses the one as a magnet for the other: "`Of avarice and of swich cursednesse / Is al my *prechyng,* for to make hem free / To yeven hir *pens*'" (*PardP* C 400-402; emphasis added). Then there is the emphasis on "entente," this word so insistent in Chaucer's vocabulary: not only does it occur three times (lines 403, 423, 432), but the problem which revolves around it is vivid in the Pardoner's claim that "`though myself be a ful vicious man / A moral tale yet I yow telle kan'" (lines 459-60). Here is an open breach between intent and content, and the emergent crisis of reference demands attention and scrutiny. Next, less obvious but no less important than these other reasons, is the insistence on buying and especially on the buying of the Redemption.

On three occasions the Pardoner recurs to the "buying again" which Christ's sacrifice effected, and twice he uses the exact phrase "boght agayn," as if the etymology of "redemptio" held some sort of magical power for his own personal redemption (*PardTC* 501, 766, 902). Answering to this insistence on the Redemption is Harry Bailly's pointed remark, just before he calls on the Pardoner, about Virginia of the *Physician's Tale*: "'Allas, to deere *boughte* she beautee!'" (*PhyPardL* C 293; emphasis added). In addition, there is the large and almost oppressive fact, if also usually implicit, that the Pardoner's audiences as a rule "buy" his words— his, so to speak, "pitch"—when he wins pence from them (see *PardP* C 403-404). The Pardoner's desire for personal redemption, I think we can suggest, is, in fact, displaced and materialized in the purchase of him which his audiences make when they buy his words.

The manner of this displacement is crucial to understanding the Pardoner and the crisis of reference; in fact, it relates to the final and perhaps most important reason for concluding this book with the Pardoner, or the agon in his prologue and tale between the literal and the allegorical. Commentary on this and related matters is by now very extensive.Here I make no pretense to the last word and certainly no attempt at a summary of all the previous words. I do propose, however, to open the question of the letter and the spirit from the position which this book has so far mapped out. In particular, I will argue that, if the Merchant's allegory is counterfeit, the Pardoner's is, on the contrary, true; and the truth in which he deals, I will go on to argue, is what makes him so dark and ominous a figure. He is a liar, a consummate liar, who nonetheless deals in the truth, and deals in it even to the point of truly confessing that he lies.

This mixture of truth and lies resembles the mixture of life and death in the Pardoner. For a lie is the word of death. Recall that the Father of lies brought death into the world; and "when the Devil speaks a lie, he speaks from his own", and just so the Pardoner "from his own speaks" (from his own "proper") when he lies. But when he lies, his word of death is a very live word, having its own strange efficacy. Hence the word of death (a lie) is the death of the word—but while it still lives. And is this not the Pardoner? A living death?

The Pardoner recurs to the Redemption twice in his own voice, once in that of the Old Man. The first time he is castigating gluttony (*PardT* 500-504):

O original of oure dampnacioun,
Til Crist hadde boght us with his blood agayn!
Lo, how deere, shortly for to sayn,
Aboght was thilke cursed vileynye!
Corrupt was al this world for glotonye.

The second time, at the end of the tale, he is attacking the "cursed synne of alle cursednesse" (lines 900-903):

Allas! mankynde, how may it bitide
That to thy creatour, which that the wroghte
And with his precious herte-blood thee boghte,
Thou art so fals and so unkynde, allas?

Finally, the Old Man, as he directs the revelers to Death, says (lines 765-67):

"Se ye that ook? Right there ye shal hym fynde.
God save yow, that boghte agayn mankynde,
And yow amende."

Note in passing that in the first example the Pardoner uses "bought" twice ("Aboght was thilke cursed vileynye"); and I suspect that the point he is suggesting is that, as Adam dearly bought damnation, so Christ in turn bought us back from damnation, just as dearly. In good homiletic fashion he is alluding to the doctrine of first and second Adam, so emphasized by Saint Paul. But whether or not he is, in fact, flourishing his preacher's skill in this way, certainly the notion of buying holds some special importance for him. And we can trace this importance to its source in his longing for personal redemption, a longing which is part of a personality at once desperately incomplete and unbearably brilliant.

That the Pardoner's personality is incomplete should need no arguing: he is a "geldyng" or a "mare" (*GP* A 691). But the amount of ink spilled in arguing anyway over these words and their implications cannot go unnoticed. Some say that the Pardoner is a *eunuchus ex nativitate;* some say that he is a homosexual; some say that he is a hermaphrodite; some say that the question is open; and Donaldson says that "the fact seems to be that there is good evidence that the Pardoner is and is not homosexual, and you may read him either way you please, with perfect confidence that you are probably wrong."

I say that all this is beside the point, the point being that the Pardoner's identity is a question to others, such as Chaucer the pilgrim, and therefore almost certainly a question to himself. To this extent, then, he is incomplete.

That the Pardoner is also an unusually brilliant man would seem evident from his skill with words: he delivers a sermon which is a model of rhetorical finesse. An incomplete but brilliant man is likely to suffer wrenching emotions and as a consequence to be abnormally sensitive. Chaucer has a number of ways of suggesting this abnormal sensitivity. At this point I want to call attention to the one which I consider most important, the Pardoner's position in *The General Prologue.*

He comes last among the portraits. To be sure, Harry is described after the Pardoner (at lines 751-57), but in introducing the last five of his "compaignye," the last of whom is the Pardoner, Chaucer goes out of his way to remark, "there were namo" (line 544). Hence, obviously, Chaucer must have consciously placed the Pardoner last. Now in itself the Pardoner's position might indicate some special emphasis but no more. In opposition to the first position, however, and the figure who holds it, the Knight, it does considerably more than that. The Knight and the Pardoner form a polarity of far-reaching significance, especially since it is the Knight who attempts to reconcile Harry and the Pardoner at the end of the latter's sermon. The Knight, in contrast to the Pardoner, enjoys the highest social status of the pilgrims; moreover, as a crusader, he is a valuable servant of the church, though he has taken no orders as far as we know and obeys no direct mandate from Rome; his great piety seems obvious from his haste to go on the pilgrimage; and he is presumably masculine since he has fathered a son. All these characteristics, and doubtless others one could name, suggest a positive to which the Pardoner is a negative. And yet Chaucer never leaves anything so simple as that. From the tale which the Knight tells—where order is so stifling it is a kind of disorder, where a soldierly Stoicism fills out an ostensibly Christian mold, where an old man's weary wisdom disconcertingly recommends a bloodless and a dubiously Christian resignation, where the highest human achievement is the pagan and heroic, hardly Christian, ideal of good fame after death (*KnT* A 3047-49), and where passion is cynically laughed at (*KnT* A 1785-1814)—from all this it is possible to conclude that the Knight is one of the least passionate and most rigid men whom Chaucer ever imagined.

To this negative the Pardoner is a certain though highly problematic positive, and this is principally why Chaucer positions his portrait last. With his vivid imagination, powers of projection, and ability to identify with roles, the Pardoner could never, for example, take such a mechanical and coldly matter-of-fact position on Arcite's death as does the Knight when he describes the dissolution of the latter's body (*KnT* A 2743-60, especially 2759-60: "And certeinly, ther Nature wol nat wirche, / Fare wel phisik! go ber the man to chirche!"). The Pardoner would give as vivid a description, if not one more vivid; but he would entertain none of the Knight's clinical pedantry or any of his soldierly brusqueness—he would feel more of what he was saying and communicate more of that feeling. Thus he and his position counterpoise the Knight and his in order to suggest the significant difference between them, or the Pardoner's capacity for feeling.

The Pardoner's capacity for feeling, I perhaps should note, is hardly the same thing as sympathy; it is, quite the contrary, more like abnormal sensitivity. And in this condition the Pardoner suffers his mutilated personality morbidly. He is not whole, and he knows it; moreover, the community in which he must live can include him only by ostracizing him.And yet, brilliant as he is, he must have an abstract appreciation of what it would be like to be whole and to belong— he can imagine it, for imagination is supremely if also pervertedly his gift. And in his imagination would be borne the longing for personal redemption, such as Christ holds out to man, and thence would arise the obsession with buying. He keeps coming back to that possibility which he knows he can never enjoy .

It is important to this argument that Christianity, both before and during Chaucer's day, emphasized the element of "purchase" in the Redemption.Saint Augustine may be considered representative: "Behold, Christ has suffered; behold, the Merchant shows us the payment; behold the price which he paid: his blood is poured out."

This example could be supplemented by many others from the patristic and later medieval periods. More important for the moment, however, is to set the emphasis on purchase and debt in its wider scriptural context. It goes back to Paul (1 Cor. 6.20, for example) and ultimately to Christ himself (Matt. 13.44-46, for example). Christ and Paul are also responsible, in different ways, for the fundamental notion supporting the Pardoner's vocation, or the selling of pardons. For these pardons derive ultimately from the treasury of merit which Christ's sacrifice and that of his saints established in and for the church. Strictly speaking, the church dispenses to the Pardoner merit from its superabundant store, and he, in turn, sells this merit in the form of pardons for a profit which is indisputably illicit in his case. Buying and selling, credit and debit, merchandising, are structured into everything the Pardoner says and does; and they are as much a part of the legitimate church as they are a part of his illegitimate desires and deeds.

A ravaged personality, mutilated; a brilliant mind, unbalanced; abnormal sensitivity; a probable desire to be saved, to be redeemed, precisely for these reasons; a profession which involves merchandising out of the store of the Redemption and the treasury of Christ. The pattern of the obsession should be clear by now.

According to Saint Augustine, men "were able to sell themselves, but they were not able to redeem themselves." The Pardoner, I am suggesting, is well aware of this. He sells himself, his act, every day in his profession; but, to judge from the pattern of his obsession, he knows because he regrets that he cannot buy himself back. Only the Other can redeem. Hence his unmistakable but also nervous delight in duping his audiences: by means of his poses and impostures he wins their pence. In a very "literal" or "carnal" or material sense, they purchase him, and this purchase is a surrogate for the Redemption he can never otherwise have. Although I have used the word "literal" here, its precise application is problematical; and we will need to return again and again to the problematic of the "literal." Already we can see one element in it. If the Merchant is a "proprioloquist," always seeking his own meaning of meaninglessness, the Pardoner, on the contrary, is an "alieniloquist" because he needs and he craves the Other and others:

> What results is the "vertige du même," the fear or the blank awareness that comes when you realise that you are only one, that you do not have the colourful interest of variety about you, that there was only yourself to deal with all the time. With this recognition, with the lack of a genuine "other," you collapse into nothingness. Hence the myth of the suicide of Narcissus, the meeting in sameness that extinguishes the tautological consciousness (Massey 1976:116).

In order to escape his "tautological consciousness," the Pardoner desperately seeks the Other: hence the coruscation, the torrent, of meanings he releases in his prologue and tale—he never stops talking until Harry shuts him up.

But at the same time, all the meanings, we suspect, do somehow serve the letter; somehow they are carnal and material. Instead of the blood with which Christ redeemed man, the Pardoner desires the coin of his audiences. Instead of the sacrament which "effects what it signifies" because the blood of Christ instituted it, the Pardoner desires "real" money whose tangibility and materiality solace him and whose efficacy is visible and present. For the efficacy that is invisible and intangible, the Pardoner substitutes the materiality of purchasing power. Where the pardon he preaches is sacramental, immaterial, and invisible, but efficacious for the faithful, the Pardoner himself is relentlessly carnal and material. And this because his faith, like his body, is sterile: it exists, but it bears no fruit.

My concern here is the connection between the Pardoner's sexual and spiritual conditions. Whatever the former is said to be, there seems to be little doubt that the Pardoner is physically sterile. Now from this condition, some have reasoned that he is also spiritually sterile. And I agree that he is, even as I also doubt such reasoning. I doubt it because the Pardoner does in fact produce (*PardP* C 429-34; emphasis added):

> *"But though myself be gilty in that synne,*
> *Yet kan I maken oother folk to twynne*
> *From avarice, and soore to repente.*
> *But that is nat my principal entente;*
> *I preche nothyng but for coveitise."*

The Pardoner saves souls, or at least he claims that he does. He is doubtless boasting, but boasting is usually an exaggeration of fact, and given the Pardoner's powers at preaching, it is not difficult to concede the probable fact that he has saved *some* people from avarice. The Pardoner does, then, probably produce fruit, or good works, through the seminal power of his verbal art. But he is himself, as has rightly been said, sterile because he does not believe in this fruit; he has no faith in its efficacy—he has, as he says, a different intent. The Pardoner has no faith, though he certainly knows in the abstract what faith is, because his intent is "nothyng but for coveitise." Be- tween him and the efficacy of the word, blocking that efficacy for him, is a covetous intent, like a dead body across the way.

The Pardoner *does* good works; he *is* sterile and faithless. So much is in keeping with his role of actor or poser or impostor: nothing in himself, he can play anyone or anything. Between his act and his "self" falls his "yvel entencioun" (line 408) to "wynne gold and silver" (line 440). Hence, of any simplistic theory of the instrumentality of words the Pardoner will make a mockery. His words are almost always duplicitous. And in the "yvel entencioun" where this duplicity arises is the failed reference of the Pardoner's "dead" or sterile body.

The Pardoner lives in a body that has no referent. He is not really a man, not really a woman, and if he is both, he is neither- -in fact, as we say of animals, he is *neutrum,* or neuter. And this I take to be the importance of Chaucer the pilgrim's doubt, "geldyng *or* a mare" —the Pardoner is *neither* this *nor* that. *In* his body, consequently, the Pardoner can refer to all sorts of things; *with* his body, however, he can refer to nothing (not even to pleasure, I suspect, since a man who could enjoy pleasure would not dirty it the way the Pardoner does). Sterile and thus without reference with his body, the Pardoner must rely on the surrogate seed of language, in something like the same way an actor relies on the costumes and props attending a role. This surrogate seed is obviously as much a fishwife's or a sailor's or Harry Bailly's as it is the Pardoner's; and this must gall him, wound his pride. Nevertheless, it is fertile; it does produce.

It produces, however, not the Pardoner's property but the converted souls of others. And the Pardoner is dependent on this creativity. Without it, he could not fulfill his "yvel entencioun." With it, he works roughly as follows. He lets the seed of language (or the seed of the signs which are his relics) inseminate others with conversion, but he charges them for it so that, as language converts them, they convert language or seed into money which then "inseminates" and "fertilizes" as it "redeems" the Pardoner and his "dead" body. Words become seeds, seeds become money, and money becomes seeds to fill the Pardoner with the sexuality and fertility which he otherwise lacks. Hence the "yvel entencioun" and duplicitous reference can accurately be said to originate in the Pardoner's "dead" body. The desire to "quicken" that body gives rise to them both.

Because of his sexual anomalousness, the Pardoner indulges an "yvel entencioun" which eventuates in a "literal" or "carnal" acceptation of signs. Instead of spiritual redemption, he desires the "literal" purchase which audiences make when they pay him for preaching. But this "literalism," we can see, is peculiar: it depends, in fact, on metaphoricity.

We must never forget the Pardoner's manifest intelligence. He knows that he cannot be spiritually redeemed because he is in a state of sin. He also knows (he is too self-conscious a poser not to know) that he is playing a game with his audiences and their pence. Hence he probably also knows that he wants and accepts their hard cash because metaphorically as well as literally it is redemptive. The Pardoner knows his metaphors—every poser must.

And if he takes Christ's redemption "literally," reducing it to "real" coins, he covets "real" coins in part because of their metaphoricity in the theology of Redemption: their lure for him in part is that metaphoricity. Because Christ's saving work is understood in terms of purchase, merit, treasury, wealth, and so on, these and related concepts and objects hold a special appeal for the Pardoner, who desires even as he resents and resists Christ's saving work. The Pardoner is a "literalist," yes, but to be a "literalist" in his case is to take metaphors very seriously. The word of death, to repeat, is a very live word.

Hence, one can argue that the Pardoner has a sort of faith—he takes metaphors seriously, and he believes that words are creative- -and one can argue that he produces good works. But, and this is at the center of the tragedy he suffers and the terror he inspires, the works are not the product of the faith—they are the product rather of his "yvel entencioun" to "wynne gold and silver."

Hence the Pardoner's faith is without works, and "even as the body without the spirit is dead, so also faith without works is dead". The Pardoner's faith is like his body, his body like his faith—there but sterile, alive but dead, neuter and ready for any position. Neuter and ready for any position, the Pardoner obviously has no position of his own. Rather, he takes his position from the available cue. And in the present case, Harry Bailly provides the cue. He not only anticipates the Pardoner's obsession with buying but also suggests to him the two fundamental themes of his sermon, or Fortune and Nature. In "the wordes of the Hoost to the Phisicien and the Pardoner," Harry exclaims of Virginia, "`Allas, to deere boughte she beautee!'" and then proceeds immediately to pontificate (*PhyPardL* C 293-96; emphasis added):

> *"Wherfore I seye al day that men may see*
> *That yiftes of Fortune and of Nature*
> *Been cause of deeth to many a creature."*

Just so, the Pardoner proceeds to deliver a sermon whose central exemplum is a story very much involving the "yiftes of Fortune and of Nature." Moreover, and this is as important though perhaps less noticeable, these "wordes of the Hoost" begin with the statement that "Oure Hooste gan to swere as he were wood" (line 287), and, of course, the Pardoner goes on to attack the sin of {218/219} swearing in his sermon. Then, too, Harry introduces the "`draughte of moyste and corny ale'" (line 315), which spurs the Pardoner to abominate drunkenness. Finally, and of fundamental importance, Harry jargonizes with the Physician's profession (lines 304-306):

> *"I pray to God so save thy gentil cors,*
> *And eek thyne urynals and thy jurdones,*
> *Thyn ypocras, and eek thy galiones."*

As Harry himself says, only too truly, he "`kan nat speke in terme'" (line 311). But by the attempt he inspires the Pardoner to pull out all the stops in his own jargon engine of preaching. Hence, when the "gentils" (line 323) protest: "`Nay, lat hym telle us of no ribaudye! / Telle us som moral thyng'" (lines 324-25), the Pardoner obliges them by drawing, like the parasite he is, on their Host.

A parasite, with no position of his own, an actor and an impostor ready for any role, a neuter who is sterile, the Pardoner is both alive and dead. In fact, this is the way in which the very theology he exploits would characterize and analyse him. He himself shows us the way (lines 542-43, 547-48; emphasis added):

> *For they /cooks/ caste noght awey*
> *That may go thurgh the golet softe and swoote.*
> *But, certes, he that haunteth swiche delices*
> *Is deed, whil that he lyveth in tho vices.*

Every sinner, like the glutton, is dead while he lives in his vices. Of the Pardoner this is especially true since his body is "literally" dead as far as fertility is concerned. Hence theological analysis of the sinner and his condition realises itself "literally" in the Pardoner: the metaphor, no less actual for that, of the sinner's living death is literal in the Pardoner. The Pardoner is literally a metaphor, the living death of sin—he is himself the word of death. At the same time, because the letter is not only dead but also "killeth", the Pardoner is metaphorically a letter: he figures in his body and in the use of his body the literalism which kills—he is also the death of the word. He is (once again the text draws us back to this formula) neuter: he is neither a metaphor nor a letter but a positionless mixture of both. He can pose as either and poses either as he will.

In fact, this—posing either indiscriminately—is the way in which he generates his sermon exemplum. It is a way much like the way in which cooks provide for a glutton's "wombe" (*PardT* C 534). He says (lines 538-39): {219/220}

> Thise cookes, how they stampe, and streyne, and grynde,
> And turnen substaunce into accident.

The Pardoner is himself a kind of cook: he boasts to the pilgrims that "'in Latyn I speke a wordes fewe, / To saffron with my predicacioun'" .His preaching is indeed a kind of stew of rhetorical sleights-of-hand. And he, like his culinary "scholastics," turns substance into accident: he reduces the substance of meaning into the accident of the letter or its carnal, material manifestation. The best brief example is his conversion of the Eucharist into its literal and material elements: "'But first...heere at this alestake / I wol bothe *drynke*, and eten of a cake'". Although ale is not wine, eating and drinking just before preaching are obviously gestures reminiscent of the Eucharist. And the Pardoner doubtless intends to pose the materials of the sacrament (anything to eat and drink) as the meaning of the sacrament which most interests him.

So also with his exemplum. Here the best illustration is the revelers' boast that "this false traytour Deeth / . . . shal be slayn, he that so manye sleeth" (*PardT* C 699-700). While the text hardly needs scriptural exegesis to be interpreted, once interpreted, it profits from the context which exegesis provides. The revelers' words allude, of course, to Hosea 13.14, to which Saint Paul himself alludes in 1 Corinthians 15.55: "I will deliver them out of the hand of death. I will redeem them from death. O death, I will be thy death; O hell, I will be thy bite." The cry of the prophet, "O death, I will be thy death," exegesis consistently understands as the triumphant claim of Christ the Redeemer. It is He who will conquer Death or Hell or the Devil (ultimately one from the theological perspective) during his "descensus ad inferos" when He will liberate all those whom Death or Hell or the Devil think to hold in their power.

The revelers, who number three probably in deliberate mockery of the Holy Trinity, are a drastically carnal version of the Triune Lord, and they are hardly likely to equal His victory in the struggle with Death. Indeed, they become the victims of Death instead of the victors precisely because they are so carnal. Scripture and its exegesis predict as much. In Hosea, after the outcry against death, the voice goes on: "Because he shall make a separation between brothers. The Lord will bring a burning wind that shall rise from the desert, and it shall dry up his springs, and shall make his fountain desolate; and he shall carry off the treasure of every desirable vessel."

According to the commentaries, the one who "makes division among brothers" is the Devil or Hell or Death. Just so, when the three revelers were four, Death divided them by taking their "old felawe" (*PardT* C {220/221} 672), whereupon the remaining three swore an oath of brotherhood together (as though each were the other's "owene ybore brother"; line 704). But this brotherhood is destroyed in just the way in which Scripture and its commentaries suggest that it would be. When the youngest reveler decides to betray the other two, "*the feend*, oure enemy, / Putte in his thought that he sholde poyson beye" (lines 844-45; emphasis added), and the result is precisely "division among brothers." The text consistently accords with what a contemporary would have expected from exegesis of this famous verse in Hosea. The Pardoner's allegory—almost, we might say, his allegorical method—is very neat and prim.

But he continues to serve the word of death. If his allegory reveals the fate of carnal men—of gluttons, gamblers, and oathtakers—it is, just so, an allegory about the carnal, about all those acts and features of carnality which so obsess the carnally frustrated Pardoner. Moreover, if his allegory is creative and fruitful, it nonetheless allows him once again to literalize the Redemption—if Christ's Redemptive work is the death of Death, the Pardoner's version of this work is the story of three youths who would literally kill Death. Once again the Pardoner has posed the metaphor of Redemption as literal: all the materials of the Redemption are here—a trinity, a tree, money (gold), death—to serve as the meaning of Redemption. And this pose is explicable, once again, in terms of his obsession. Himself "dead" and spiritually an "old man", he longs precisely for the death of Death, but for the literal death of Death. If Death literally died, then the "death" (of sterility) in his body might also die.

He knows full well, I hasten to add, that this cannot be, but once again he takes the metaphor seriously. And he mixes metaphor and letter indiscriminately in a story about the death of death. The death of Death *is* the promise to spiritual man: if a man dies to sin and the flesh, then he shall live —the life of the spirit. But the Pardoner does not want this life: he does not want to die—he is already dead. He wants rather the life of a virile, fertile body, and he wants the renewal of youth. Hence, necessarily, he longs for the literal death of Death. Just as his desire carnalizes or materializes the benefits of the Redemption, so it must also carnalize or materialize, literalize, the work of the Redemption, or the death of Death.

One other illustration of the Pardoner's "stew" of metaphor and letter will perhaps be of help. The Old Man directs the three revelers up a "croked wey" (*PardT* C 761) to a grove where he left Death "under a tree" (line 763). Now it was under a tree that sin entered the world—the Tree of Knowledge of Good and Evil. It was *on* a tree—typologically and according to legend, the same tree —that Christ by His sacrifice conquered sin and destroyed Death. The metaphoricity of the tree where the three revelers, carnal parody of the Lord, will struggle with Death is manifest, even ostentatious. But this ostentatious metaphoricity only servcs the greater triumph of the letter. For when this unholy trinity dies under/on the tree, Death—which is to be equated with the letter— consumes the metaphoricity itself as well as three foolish mortals. Death and its letter not only win the unholy trinity, they also win the *holy* Trinity.

Death and its letter do not merely kill three men; they subvert the Crucifixion and the Redemption, "turning" their spiritual "substance" into the "accident" of three ordinary greedy men killing each other over "eighte busshels" (line 771) of gold florins. Even as the event sets up the meanings, the very banality of the event undermines the meanings, and this is the way the Pardoner *intends* it: for him, the closest men get to redemption is a brief glorying over gold, then daggers and poison.

And this because he has himself failed of redemption. It is probably obvious by now that in the debate over the Pardoner's sudden *volte face* at the end of his sermon, I will incline to the old—and, I suppose, most would say, sentimentalized—view of Kittredge that he suffers a "paroxysm of agonized sincerity." While I disavow the late-nineteenth-century characterology implicit in this evaluation, and while I am sympathetic with the more modern position that the Pardoner is not a character at all but an instance of the illusoriness of self, I still maintain that the text asks us to hear a sudden reversal of positions. The crux is the word "leche" (*PardT* C 915-18; emphasis added):

—And lo, sires, thus I preche.
And Jhesu Crist, that is oure soules leche,
So graunte yow his pardoun to receyve,
For that is best; I wol yow nat deceyve.

Of course, the first problem is the "I wol yow nat deceyve": given his "yvel entencioun" to "wynne gold and silver" and his confession of hypocrisy —"'Thus spitte I out my venym under hewe / Of hoolynesse, to semen hooly and trewe'" (PardP C 421-22)—it is difficult to believe that the Pardoner would ever will not to "deceyve"; it is difficult to believe that he would ever take a position—would ever expose himself as "himself" rather than as some imposture. But the same evidence—evidence of the lack of a self— can suggest, quite humanly and understandably so, the opposite conclusion. For a man of "yvel entencioun" and gross hypocrisy who "'wol noon of the apostles countrefete'" (line 447) is necessarily a man of acute self-consciousness. A poser always knows he is in a pose—that is the definition of a poser. And because of such knowledge, because of such self-consciousness, the Pardoner cannot but realise that he is sick, that he is moribund.

His very obsession with Death and the Redemption also argues the same conclusion. Hence it only makes sense that he would at some point take that position, of all the positions in his neutrality he might take, which is the least possible, most tenuous, and yet desperately attractive to him—the position of "I want to be whole." So, for a moment, he admits, he poses (and takes the position) that Christ is the "leche" who makes whole, by means of his "pardoun." My point is not to sympathize with him but to understand him. He has enough intelligence to know the truth of what he has said. The actor or impostor can shift into truth just as easily as he can shift into a lie. Moreover, a neuter and a parasite who so desperately wants and needs healing would predictably refer to *the* Healer at some point, especially since he lives his life in carnal parody and imposture of the Healer—selling the latter's pardons to persons who are in fact from time to time healed. But the tragedy of such a poser is that he cannot hold this position for long; he knows his sickness too well—it has become almost comfortable for him. And so the Pardoner abandons "oure soules leche" and "his pardoun" so as to lapse back into the by now much more familiar role.

Hawking his pardons once again, the Pardoner confronts and affronts Harry Bailly (*PardT* C 941-45):

> *"I rede that oure Hoost heere shal bigynne,*
> *For he is moost envoluped in synne.*
> *Com forth, sire Hoost, and offre first anon,*
> *And thou shalt kisse the relikes everychon,*
> *Ye, for a grote! Unbokele anon thy purs."*

Much attention has been paid recently to the Pardoner's sexual affront of the Host. While I recognize the validity of this position, I am also intrigued by the *truth* of the Pardoner's accusation. Whether Harry is the *most* "envoluped in synne" we might want to debate, but *that* he is "envoluped in synne" we can hardly deny: he swears outrageously, drinks, indulges games of chance (the meal at his inn for which the pilgrims are contending), backbites his wife (*MerT E 2427-29),* and gives in to rage. The Pardoner has read Harry very closely and read him very well.

His intelligence continues awesome. The measure of how well he has read Harry is Harry's very rage. Harry reacts not only or most importantly to sexual effrontery but also and crucially to the bitter, sharp sting of truth. The Pardoner has penetrated the "envelope" ("envoluped in synne") of Harry's position or role or act—interpreted the *in- volucrum* of his position (and pose) —and this penetration *does* threaten Harry, not only sexually but also spiritually. Before the consummate actor his act is transparent. His envelope or covering or mask is like a set of easily decipherable codes for the master manipulator of codes.

Hence Harry's violence and attempt not only to penetrate the Pardoner's role but also to reduce him, to drag him down, to his positionless position, his sexless neutrality (*PardT C 951-55):*

> *"But by the croys which that Seint Eleyne fond,*
> *I wolde I hadde thy coillons in myn hond*
> *In stide of relikes or of seintuarie.*
> *Lat kutte hem of, I wol thee helpe hem carie;*
> *They shul be shryned in an hogges toord!"*

Whatever the Pardoner's sexuality, Harry's threat to his "coillons" questions that sexuality and hence the Pardoner's identity. And the question is enough, enough to expose the pose of the consummate poser: "this Pardoner answerde nat a word; / So wrooth he was, no word ne wolde he seye" (lines 956-57). At this moment the Pardoner is fixed in wrath, and it is the only position in which he can be fixed. "No word ne wolde he seye": of course not—words are the stuff of poses, and all poses have just been disposed of.

As the Knight of all the pilgrims occupies the most fixed position, so the Pardoner occupies the least. Indeed, it might be said that the opposition between the two in *The General Prologue* is that between fixed position (knight, soldier, noble, etc.) and no position at all. Therefore, when the Knight reconciles Harry and the Pardoner, a massive discrepancy opens up which in itself defines the Pardoner's tragedy. The very security of the Knight's and Harry's positions must oppress the Pardoner, who can only submit to the Knight's will because he has no position of his own. Exposed, the Pardoner disappears in a kiss.

The importance of the Pardoner to *The Canterbury Tales,* if they are understood as a collection of the possible positions of poets and poetry, is that, consummate impostor, he occupies the extreme of "irreference." The Pardoner's very "self" is "counterfeit." If he "`wol noon of the apostles countrefete,'" that is because they are apostles and not because he does not or is not "countrefete." If the Wife of Bath would substitute herself for the allegorical plenitude of Scripture and exegesis, like a heretic, if the Merchant would annihilate that plenitude because it accuses and condemns his own poverty, the Pardoner, on the contrary, revels in it because it is an inexhaustible supply of masks, feints, sleights-of-hand, and gimmicks—an inexhaustible supply of counterfeit selves. Unlike the Wife, who has a self (and such a self) to sell, or the Merchant, who has no self, only his craft, the Pardoner has a multiplicity of selves whenever he wants them—he is a broken mirror whose fragments reflect a brilliant but forever incomplete identity. And everything the Pardoner says or does is a frantic effort to collect the fragments in the ultimately vain attempt to say, "I am."

Hence the insistent and finally pathetic "self"-referentiality, itself only imposture: "'for myn entente is nat but for to winne'" (*PardP* C 403). This declaration of his intent only proves the poverty of the Pardoner's content. In fact, it might plausibly be argued that the "character" of the Pardoner (understanding by the word "character" here the literary construct) is to be a character who has *only* a character. Chaucer, it may be, explores through the Pardoner the illusoriness of the boundary between inside and outside in phenomena so linguistic as "character." Any attempt to discover what makes the Pardoner tick, to get "inside" him, invariably meets with only more words, with only more "outside." The Pardoner seems continuously to transform content into intent, turning himself "inside out," through torrents of speech. Hence his "inside" is his "outside"; his "outside," his "inside." He is a "character" (itself only words) whose character is to be only words: we might subtitle his *Prologue* "'Character' and Its Dis/Contents."

Where the boundary between inside and outside is pure illusion, where there are only words on words, where there is only "character," the character (and we as well) are discontented. Where there is no content, there is no meaning to content. Where there are only words on words, there is only endless reference, never meaning. If reference is the "gold" of signs,then the Pardoner's gold is never minted. He never tells us what he means; or, if he does, as perhaps he does through the reference to Christ, "oure soules leche," he immediately takes it back—he is precisely *avaricious*. And just as the Old Man, probably a figure of avarice,is never understood, so is the Pardoner, "hoarding" his "meaning" or "content," never understood. And this because he only talks—it seems as if he could talk endlessly—and only talks so as to appropriate the coin of others to be his meaning, his content. His only content is his intent: coin, the coin of others—"'nobles or pens, whiche that be goode and trewe'" (*PardT* C 930). Hence his poverty (and the poverty of the avaricious). Just enough of the moral sense of "goode and trewe" lingers in the monetary and commercial sense that it is possible to hear the pathetic irony: "goode and trewe" coin is as close as the Pardoner comes to the good and the true. Meaning for the Pardoner is coin, and coin is meaning: this is both extreme literalism and extreme metaphoricity, a "stew" of language. More important, it is an appropriation of meaning to the self and its desires which exploits community. The conversion of the substance of language into the accident of coin is a materialization of desire which exploits the community's need for media of exchange. It is a radical assertion of the priority of the private precisely there where the private should cooperate with the public if community is to exist and flourish. But the community, the household, of Christendom, unable to allow for the peculiar privation of the Pardoner, will win no mercy from his relentless desire to practice his privacy upon it.

And yet the poet, for whom the private is also prior, does not thrive without a community. It is merely a vanity of Romanticism that the poet writes only for himself. The poet writes to be heard- -and thus *for* a community. At the same time, however, it is true that the poem begins in the mind, "a fine and private place," and that "the mind, / In the act of finding what will suffice, destroys / Romantic tenements of rose and ice". The tremendous anxiety inscribed in the Pardoner is the anxiety that from the mind to the community there is no translation—that the priority of the private in the world of art is absolute, so that no reconstruction follows the destruction of the tenements. And this is the anxiety that motivates even as it frustrates the Pardoner's problematic confession. He goes out of his way to betray his act and his pose to the pilgrims because he wants to involve them in his act and his pose—he wants to establish with them a sort of community of imposters, on his own terms. The Wife of Bath wants to be an "auctoritee" in whatever community she happens to live in; the Merchant does not give a damn about community; the Pardoner wants a community of his own—

and tries for it with the pilgrims. For if they participate with him in his act and his pose, they thus bestow upon him the self he otherwise lacks and cannot possess. They make it possible for him to say "I am your pardoner" (*PardT* C 931-34):

> *"It is an honour to everich that is heer*
> *That ye mowe have a suffisant pardoneer*
> *T'assoille yow, in contree as ye ryde,*
> *For aventures whiche that may bityde."*

I am not so naive as to think that the Pardoner's motives here are pure; they obviously are not. But I do believe that his impure motive is the desire for an identity as their pardoner. In this regard, consider the extraordinary word "suffisant": it suggests something more than just "legitimate" or "authorized"; it suggests something like "I really am adequate, you know," a sentiment in which conviction and self-doubt keep uneasy company. The response which the Pardoner is seeking is not only nor perhaps most importantly "nobles or pens" but also something like "Yes, yes, well, tell us another—you really are quite good at it." What he gets instead, though, is violence— violence because words do refer and refer, moreover, to the truth. In the agonized privacy of his unredeemed (and just possibly unredeemable) self, the Pardoner, consummate impostor and artificer of roles and master of words though he be, has forgotten that words always refer. Harry Bailly's reaction is sufficient evidence of that. The word, even the word of death, refers. But words do not always or necessarily translate unless and until the community understands their intentionality and thus also their instrumentality.

If all instrumentality is narcissistic, then the Pardoner's is a narcissism so drastic as to be incapable of even an echo.He would have the pilgrims so completely suppose his pose that they can only oppose him. He would have them identify so far with him that they would end being he: he exposes his gimmick, works his gimmick, then asks them to buy his gimmick—all of which assumes that they are one with him, do not differ from him. But they are not one with him, and they do most certainly differ from him. The Pardoner, in short, has made no effort to translate. Rather he supposes that by exposing his pose he can impose upon the pilgrims a will to repose in him their trust. I recognize that this play of words is too much; I intend it so. It helps me to demonstrate the Pardoner's excess. To turn on the pilgrims, as he does, expecting them to buy his gimmick, the Pardoner must suppose not that they are his but that they are he. The Merchant, by contrast, supposes that the pilgrims will become his, his property—his creatures seeing the world as he sees it— and Harry Bailly almost obliges him. The Pardoner, however, supposes that the pilgrims are so completely one with him that they will obey him even as he obeys himself. Such a supposition, of course, is psychotic. It precludes any effort of translation—of taking the positions of others so as to see how they see the world. It is the supposition of one so accustomed to posing and imposture that he has forgotten that people are more than their poses.

Something Chaucer never forgot. We revere Chaucer precisely because he was a master of taking the positions of others so as to see how they see the world. The Pardoner, in contrast, is exclusively about himself. The exemplum he tells is about the old man he meets everyday in his own body. The Pardoner does not translate. When he chooses Harry to begin his pardoning, it is not only the fact that his words refer to the truth that so distresses Harry but also the fact that he supposes that there is no difference between Harry and him. Truth and lie are horribly mixed. And the Pardoner is only talking to himself. Harry, of course, will have none of it—hence he fixes precisely on the most glaring difference between them when he talks back.

The Sexual Normality of Chaucer's Pardoner

Anyone who contemplates "a new explanation of the Pardoner's sexuality" so hard on the heels of C. David Benson's admirable demonstration of "the weakness of this entire approach" might justly be charged with temerity.I share

Benson's suspicion of what L. C. Knights long ago referred to as the critic's "readiness to abstract a character and treat him (because he is more manageable that way) as a human being,"and I applaud the skill with which he exposes the specious and factitious character of earlier attempts to prove the Pardoner a eunuch, hermaphrodite, or homosexual. If I find myself still inquisitive about the Pardoner's 'pryvetee" it is because I am not wholly convinced that he is an example of "unspecified" lust or that his sexuality remains quite as "imprecise" as Benson suggests; I am in fact emboldened to take the question a little further because I believe that the general character of what I take to be the nature of the Pardoner's sexuality is already implicit in Benson's own argument, and because I believe that neither of us strays as far from the "actual evidence in the text" as those critics from whom we both dissent.

Let me begin with the Pardoner's friend, the Summoner. I entirely agree with Benson that although the Summoner is portrayed as a "thorough-going lecher," Chaucer gives us "no hint among the many accusations in his portrait that his lust is homosexual." I agree, too, that the primary reason why the Summoner and the Pardoner have been linked together is that Chaucer wishes to make a point about "serious ecclesiastical corruption" (presumably the pair should be read as a grotesque perversion of the twinned virtues, justice and Mercy), not because he is interested in their sexuality *per se*. Nevertheless, their sexuality is a vivid symptom of their deeper corruption, and in the case of the Summoner at least, its precise nature seems quite clearly articulated. The Summoner is a "good felawe"; in fact, one could hardly fine a "bettre felawe' . He consorts with other good fellows, accepts bribes from them, and keeps them out of the archdeacon's hands; moreover, when his double, the hero of the Friar's Tak, runs across the devil, he too is recognized as a good fellow . That this phrase "oftenthat she could never withhold her "chambre of Venus from a good felawe", but in fact we have excellent external evidence for the general currency of this term among Chaucer's contemporaries from Sir John Clanvowe:

But now swiche as been synful men and wacches of þe feend been cleped of þe world 'goode felawes'. ffor þei þat woln waste þe goodis þat God hath sent hem, in pruyde of the world, and in lustes of here flessh, and goon to the tauerne and to þe bordel, and pleyen at þe dees, waaken loonge any3tes, and sweren faste, and drynken, and ianglen to muche, scoornen, bakbiten, iaapen, gloosen, boosten, lyen, fi3ten, and been baudes for here felawes, and lyuen al in synne, and in vanitee, þei been hoolde goode felawes'.

Chaucer's description of the Summoner as a quintessentiauy "good felawe" thus reinforces other details in his portrait to suggest that he is an habitué of taverns and brothels, the companion of pimps and prostitutes, and a quite open debauchee.

The Pardoner is his "compeer", that is, literally, his `equal.' The only other compeers to be found in Chaucer are the jolly prentice the Cook's Tale and:

A compeer of his owene sort
That lovede dys, and revel, and disport,
And hadde a wyf that heeld for contenance
A shoppe, and swyved for hir sustenance.
(A 4419-22)

These two, it seems to me, are cast in much the same mold as the Summoner and the Pardoner (the Pardoner, after all, gravitates naturally to a tavern at the beginning of his tale, and later boasts of having "a joly wenche in every toun" [C 453]), and all four have much in common with the three rioters of the Pardoner's own tale, who "haunteden folye, / As riot, hasard, stywes, and tavernes" (C 464-65). In other words, Chaucer seems to intend the Summoner and the Pardoner to be taken as a pair of rakes, fellow patrons of the brothel and the alehouse, and companions in crime. Like Benson, I find no hint that their relationship is in any way homosexual, still less that the Pardoner is impotent or in some way sexually incapacitated.

The *Tale of Beryn* provides striking confirmation of this view of the Pardoner's "more ordinary sexual life." As Benson implies, Curry's use of this tale to support his view of the Pardoner as a eunuch is an example of transparent special pleading.In fact, I would go further than Benson to claim that the author of the Tale of Beryn, an early and far from inattentive reader of the *Canterbury Tales*, portrays a Pardoner who is neither homosexual nor sexually incompetent. The bedroom farce which occupies much of the prologue to the *Tale of Beryn* becomes far funnier if its butt is less a maladroit bungler than a thoroughly experienced womanizer who has finally met his match. Prom the very outset the Pardoner flirts with Kitty, "as a man I-lernyd of such kynd[e]nes"; he worms his way into her confidence, sings her a love-song — not "Com hider love to me," but "Now, loue, þou do me ri3te" —, offers her money, and hints at the possibility of marriage . The lines in which he appears finally to win her over (which contain the truly inspired come-on, "Shall I help you keep the cat off the bed?") reveal a thoroughly practised seducer at work:

Thou the Pardoner, 'this goith wele', & made hir better chere,

> *And axid of hir sofft[e]lly: 'lord, who shall ligge[n] here*
> *This ny3te þat is to comyng? I prey 3ewe telle me!'*
> *"Iwis it is grete nede to telle 3ew," quod she:*
> *"Make it nat ovir queynt, þou3e yee be a clerk!*
> *Ye know wele I-nou3 I-wis, by loke, by word, by work!"*
> *"Shall I com þen, Cristian, & fese a-wey þe Cat?"*
> *"Shul yee com, sir? benedicite! what question is that?*
> *Where-for I prey yew hertly, do be my counsaille;*
> *Comyth somwhat late...." (345-54)*

This Pardoner seems quite at home flirting with barmaids, and when his plans ultimately go awry it is just punishment for his glibness. I see no difficulty with finding the original for such a Pardoner in Chaucer's own work.

Those who are unsympathetic to the view shared by Benson and myself that the Pardoner is portrayed as neither homosexual nor physiologically abnormal will wish to lay the greatest possible emphasis upon the effeminate characteristics he unquestionably exhibits: the fine hair, the high voice, and the beardless chin. Howard's point that "many limp-wristed and reedy-voiced men are heterosexual," is well taken, but we must still explain what Chaucer intends by making his Pardoner effeminate. The final cause, which clearly has to do with the Pardoner as a type of ecclesiastical corruption, is not really part of my brief, but I suspect that from this perspective he is made to appear effeminate because the Christian virtue of mercy, of which he is a walking parody, is a feminine virtue; probably, too, the doubleness of his physical nature is intended to reflect his spiritual duplicity — his hypocrisy and treacherousness. The material cause, however, seems to me to be hinted at in Benson's passing comment that effeminacy in the Middle Ages might imply quite the reverse of homosexuality — "too great a concern with women" — and it is this insight that I should like to take further.

When Lancelot expresses a manly horror of sensual self-indulgence — "for knyghtes that ben auouturous or lecherous shal not be happy ne fortunate vnto the werrys" — he is echoing a long-established tradition that equates sexual intemperance with physical debilitation. In the Middle Ages, Samson, a strong man weakened by a woman's wiles, is frequently cited as an example of this effect, but others — Mars ensnared with Venus, or Paris bewitched by Helen — are also adduced. In this context, it is hardly surprising that one of the verbs most commonly chosen to describe the deleterious effects of licentiousness is *effeminare*: "O extrema libidinis turpitudo," writes Innocent III, 'que non solum *effeminat*, sed corpus enervate"a phrase which Chaucer renders, "Nat oonly that thou feyntest mannes mynde, / But verraily thou wolt his body shende" (B 925-26). Nor is it surprising that such effects might be seen to go beyond a simple loss of manly fortitude: by a piece of etymological logic well within the power of even the humblest successor of Isidore of Seville, if a lecherous man was *effeminatus* then he became womanly. As Sydney writes in the *Arcadia*, "this effeminate love of a woman, doth so womanish a man...."The *Secretum Secretorum*, discussing the consequences of lechery, seems to understand effeminacy in this extended sense; James Yonge's version reads, "the foly company of women destrueth the body . . . And doghty men and hardy hit makyth lyke women, neshe and feynte, dedis of armys to don."Other versions render this: it "makith a man oft femynyne," "it engendrys women maners," or "gendryth womannys condycionys."

In the Middle Ages, the prime example of the effeminizing effects of lust, a man who, as Surrey puts it, "scace the name of manhode dyd retayne, / Drenched in slouthe and womanishe delight," was the Assyrian king, Sardanapalus. In the *Speculum Morale,* Vincent of Beauvais writes, "qualiter autem luxuria emolliat, & resoluat animum virilem & regimen, patet per Sardanapalum.... Hic inter mulieres conuersabatur omni muliere mollior, in operibus muliebribus gestu & habitu."

His story, in a form which seems to go back to Cicero's *Tusculan Disputations,* appears in the *Gesta Romanorum* and in Robert Holcot's *Moralitates.* John Gower uses it in the *Confessio Amantis* to show how a man might become "muliebri oblectamento effeminatus":

. . . thilke fyri rage
Of love, which the men assoteth,
Wherof himself he so rioteth,
And wax so ferforth womannyssh,
That ayein kinde, as if a fissh
Abide wolde upon the lond,
In wommen such a lust he fond,
That he duelte evere in chambre stille,
And only wroghte after the wille
Of wommen.
The story is repeated in Lydgate's Fall of Princes:
To vicious lust his liff he dede enclyne;
Mong Assiriens, whan he his regne gan,
Off fals vsage he was so femynyne,
That among women vppon the rokke he span,
In ther habite disguised from a man.

Lydgate, however, omits the detail which appears in his source, Laurence Premierfait, that Sardanapalus encouraged "flateurs & iangleurs et ruffiens sentans la flaireur des bordeaulx qui sont fiente et reffus de toutes gens," men whom the Summoner would no doubt have regarded as "good felawes."

In this pre-Krafft-Ebbing world, sexual over-indulgence might have even graver consequences than effeminacy or transvestitism: it might turn one into a hermaphrodite. That at least is the implication of the description of a well in the Garden of Cupid which appears in Lydgate's *Reson and Sensuallyte*:

In this Erber of Deduit
Ther ys a welle wonderful,
That, who drynketh hys bely ful
And ys bathed therin oonys,
Among the colde cristal stonys
The nature shal him enclyne
To be-come Femynyne,
And ouer, yif I shal not feyne,
Departed in-to kyndes tweyne,
Double of nature and yet al oon.
....
But prudent folkys that be sage
Eschewe of wisdam the passage,
Wher Cupide hath most hys haunte
And is of custom conuersaunte.
The place yt is so perilouse,
So dredful and contagiouse,
Ful of treson and of gyle.

Even if we do not take too literally this curious metamorphosis of Ovid's Fountain of Salmacis (which Lydgate takes from *Les Echecs Arnoureux*), it illustrates dramatically the medieval belief in the effeminizng effects of sensuality. Indeed, this is one of the morals which the Ovide *Moralisé* draws from the original story of Hermaphrodite:

Il n'a au monde home si sage,
Tant soit de ferme volenté,
Plains de vertu, plains de bonté,
S'il se soulle en son fontenil
Dont la jonchiere est de penil,
Que molz et fleches ne deviegne.

The relevance of all this to Chaucer's effeminate Pardoner scarcely needs elaboration. It suggests that there is no need to take the line which compares him to a gelding or a mare in any literal sense (as Benson rightly argues), and makes clear that the marks of effeminacy which he bears are (like the finch-pulling Summoner's poxy complexion) emblems of his carnality. Like Benson, I believe that the time has come to reject the arguments of those who wish to claim that the Pardoner is a eunuch, a hermaphrodite, or a homosexual, and to replace them with an account of his "more ordinary sexual life" — ordinary in everything, perhaps, but its debilitating excesses.

University of Western Ontario

Bibliography

Aers, David. *Chaucer*. Atlantic Highlands, NJ : Humanities Press International, 1986.

Alford, John. "The Wife of Bath Versus the Clerk of Oxford: What Their Rivalry Means." *Chaucer Review* 21 (1986): 108-132.

Anderson, David. *Before the Knight's Tale: Imitation of Classical Epic in Boccaccio's Teseida.*Philadelphia: U. of Penn. Press, 1988.

Andrew, Malcolm. "Context and Judgment in the *General Prologue*." *The Chaucer Review*. 23 (1989): 316-337.

Baird, Joseph L. "The Devil in Green." *Neuphilologische Mitteilungen* 69 (1968): 575-578.

Beichner, Fr. Paul E. "Absolon's Hair." *Medieval Studies*12 (1950): 222-33.

Bennett, J. A. W. *Chaucer at Oxford and at Cambridge*. Oxford: Oxford UP, 1974.

Benson, C. David. *Chaucer's Drama of Style: Poetic Variety and Contrast in the Canterbury Tales*. Chapel Hill: University of North Carolina Press, 1986.

Besserman, Lawrence. *Chaucer's Biblical Poetics*. Norman, OK: Oklahoma UP, 1998.

Bethurum, Dorothy, ed. *Critical Approaches to Medieval Literature*. New York: Columbia U. Press, 1960.

Birney, Earle. *Essays on Chaucerian Irony*. Beryl Rowland, ed. Toronto: U. of Toronto Press, 1985.

Boenig, Robert. *Chaucer and the Mystics*. Lewisburg: Bucknell UP, 1995.

Boitani, Piero and Jill Mann. *The Cambridge Chaucer Companion*. New York: Cambridge U. Press, 1986.

Bowden, Betsy. *Chaucer Aloud: The Varieties of Textual Interpretation*. Philadelphia: U. of PA Press, 1987.

Brewer, Derek S. *An Introduction to Chaucer*. London: Longman, 1985.

Brown, Peter. "The Prison of Theseus and the Castle of Jalousie." *Chaucer Review* 26, #2 (1991): 147-152.

Burger, Glenn. "Kissing the Pardoner." *PMLA* 107 (1992): 1143-56.

Burlin, Robert B. *Chaucerian Fiction*. Princeton: Princeton University Press, 1977.

Calabrese, Michael. "Make a Mark that Shows: Orphic Song, Orphic Sexuality, and the Exile of Chaucer's Pardoner," *Viator* (1993): 269-86.

Casey, Charles. "Adversus Jerome: Liberation Theology in the *Wife of Bath's Prologue.*" *Assays* 6 (1991): 55-71.

Chickering, Howell. "Unpunctuating Chaucer." *Chaucer Review* Vol. 25, #2, 1990: 96-109.

Cooper, Helen. *Oxford Guides to Chaucer: The Canterbury Tales*. 2nd Edition. Oxford: OUP, 1996.

Copeland, Rita. "The Pardoner's Body and the Disciplining of Rhetoric," in *Framing Medieval Bodies*, Sarah Kay and Miri Rubin, eds. Manchester UP, 1994: 138-59.

Crane, Susan. *Gender and Romance in Chaucer's Canterbury Tales*. Princeton: Princeton University Press

Crow, Martin M., and Clair C. Olson, eds. *Chaucer Life-Records*. Oxford: Clarendon Press, 1966.

Curry, Walter Clyde. *Chaucer and the Medieval Sciences*. New York: Barnes and Noble, 1960.

French, Robert Dudley. *A Chaucer Handbook*. New York: Crofts, 1927.

Hallissy, Margaret. *A Companion to Chaucer's Canterbury Tales*. Westport, Conn.: Greenwood Press, 1995.

Jeffrey, David Lyle, ed. *A Dictionary of Biblical Tradition in English Literature*. Grand Rapids: Eerdmans, 1992.

Lounsbury, Thomas R. *Studies in Chaucer: His Life and Writings*. 3 Vols. New York: Harper & Brothers, 1892; rptd. London: Russell & Russell, 1962.

Miller, Robert P. *Chaucer: Sources and Backgrounds*. Oxford: OUP, 1977.

Robertson, D.W. *A Preface to Chaucer: Studies in Medieval Perspectives*. Princeton: Princeton University Press, 1962.

Rossignol, Rosalyn. *Chaucer A to Z: The Essential Reference to His Life and Works* . New York : Facts On File, 1999.

Rowland, Beryl, ed. *Companion to Chaucer Studies*. New York: Oxford U. Press, 1979.

Skeat, Walter, and Hiram Corson. *Index of Proper Names and Subjects to Chaucer's Canterbury Tales, Together with Comparisons and Similes, Metaphors and Proverbs, Maxims, etc., in the Same*. New York: Johnson reprint Corp., 1967.

Weever, Jacqueline de. *A Chaucer Name Dictionary: A Dictionary of Astrological, Biblical, Historical, Literary, and Mythological Names*. New York: Garland, 1986.